Babylon of Egypt

American Research Center in Egypt
Conservation Series 4

Babylon of Egypt

The Archaeology of Old Cairo and the Origins of the City

Peter Sheehan

An American Research Center in Egypt Edition

The American University in Cairo Press

Cairo New York

Sources of Illustrations:
Travelers in the Middle East Archive: fig. 5; The British Library: figs. 6, 17; Michael Mallinson: fig. 8, pls. 38, 39; Jose Santos: figs. 9, 51, pl. 34; Rare Books and Special Collections Library, American University in Cairo: figs. 13, 35, 39, 49, 50, 58, 59, 61, pl. 35; Lehnert and Landrock: fig. 14; Fotocea Unione, American Academy in Rome: fig. 22; Comité and SCA archives: figs. 28, 29, 46, 54, 62, 64, 65, 66, 67, 68, 69, 71, 72, 73, 74, 75; Mohammed Fahmy: figs. 38, 47; Nicholas Warner: fig. 45; Canadian Centre for Architecture: fig. 55; Institut français d'archéologie orientale (IFAO); fig. 60, pl. 27; Peter Sheehan: figs. 70, 76; K Lutley and J Bunbury: pl. 18; Imaging Papyri Project, University of Oxford and Egypt Exploration Society: pl. 25.

This revised edition published in 2015 by
The American University in Cairo Press
113 Sharia Kasr el Aini, Cairo, Egypt
420 Fifth Avenue, New York, NY 10018
www.aucpress.com

Copyright © 2010, 2015 Peter Sheehan

This publication was made possible by the generous support of the American people through the United States Agency for International Development (USAID). The contents are the responsibility of the author and do not necessarily reflect the views of USAID or the United States Government.

All rights reserved. No part of this publication may be reproduced, stored in a retrieval system, or transmitted in any form or by any means, electronic, mechanical, photocopying, recording, or otherwise, without the prior written permission of the publisher.

Exclusive distribution outside Egypt and North America by I.B. Tauris & Co Ltd., 6 Salem Road, London, W4 2BU

Dar el Kutub No. 26283/14
ISBN 978 977 416 731 7

Dar el Kutub Cataloging-in-Publication Data

Sheehan, Peter
    Babylon of Egypt: The Archaeology of Old Cairo and the Origins of the City / Peter Sheehan.—Cairo: The American University in Cairo Press, 2014.
        p.   cm.
        ISBN 978 977 416 731 7
        1. Archaeology
        Egypt

        930.1

1 2 3 4 5 6   19 18 17 16 15

Designed by Sally Boylan
Printed in Egypt

Contents

List of Illustrations	vii
Foreword *Gerry D. Scott, III and Michael Jones*	xi
Acknowledgments	xiii
Timeline of Significant Events	xvii

Introduction 1
   Old Cairo: Topography and Archaeology 8
   Toward an Archaeological Model of Old Cairo 18

Part 1
The Making of Babylon 21

1 The Ancient Landscape of Cairo 23
   Introduction 23
   Geological Background 24
   The Nile at Cairo 25
   The Earliest Settlements on the East Bank at Cairo 29
   The Archaeology of the Ancient Landscape at Old Cairo 32

2 The River of Trajan 35
   Introduction 35
   Connecting the Nile with the Red Sea 35
   Trajan's Canal and the Harbor of Old Cairo 40
   Archaeological Evidence from Old Cairo for the Canal
      and the Harbor of Trajan 42
   Archaeological Evidence for the Wider Roman Landscape of Cairo 51
   The Heritage of the Canal and Its Importance
      to the Later Topography and Development of the City of Cairo 51

3 Diocletian and the Roman Fortress of Babylon   55
   The Building Campaign of Diocletian in Context   55
   The Building Campaign of Diocletian:
      The Topography of the Roman Fortress of Babylon   59
   The Archaeology of Diocletian's Fortress   67
   Postscript: Babylon between Diocletian and the Arab Conquest   74

Part 2
The Making of Old Cairo   77

4 Al-Fustat and the Making of Old Cairo   79
   From Fortress to City: Babylon as the Nucleus
      of al-Fustat and Its Role in the Development of Medieval Cairo   79
   Archaeological Evidence for the Making of Old Cairo   82
   Al-Fustat and the Early Medieval Making of Old Cairo   85
   Topographical Influences on the Foundation of al-Fustat:
      The River and the Canal, Ancient and New Roads   85
   The Reuse of the Roman Fortress   86
   The Archaeological Evidence for the Foundation of
      the First Churches in Cairo   88
   The Rebuilding of Old Cairo from the End of the Tenth Century   92

**5 Cycles of Decline and Revival: Ayyubid, Mamluk,
   and Ottoman Old Cairo**   97
   Introduction   97
   The Changing Medieval Topography
      of Cairo and the Position of Old Cairo within the Metropolis   99
   The Churches and the Medieval Archaeology of Old Cairo   105
   Early Ottoman Decline and the Eighteenth-Century
      Revival under the "Sultan of the Copts"   115

6 The Re-Making of Old Cairo in the Image of Its Past   121
   The Rediscovery of Old Cairo at the End of the Nineteenth Century   121
   The Work of the Comité in Old Cairo   128
   The Activities of the Jewish Community around the
      Ben Ezra Synagogue from 1892 to 1948   136
   Old Cairo: The Present and the Future   137

Notes   143
References   157
Glossary   167
Index   171

Illustrations

Figures

1. Egypt and the Near East c. AD 110.
2. Babylon in context: Topographic and urban features of the East Bank of the Nile at Cairo.
3. Plan showing the monuments of Old Cairo.
4. Axonometric view of the monuments of Old Cairo.
5. Greek Church of St. George viewed from the railway in a postcard of c. 1930.
6. Mid-nineteenth-century view of the Greek Church of St. George and the entrance to Old Cairo.
7. Modern view of the entrance to Old Cairo from Shari' Mari Girgis.
8. Approach to the arched entrance of Haret Abu Serga from the north, taken in 1984.
9. Early nineteenth-century plan of Old Cairo.
10. Plan of Contract 102 shaft locations in the core area of the project.
11. Concrete blocks loaded onto one of the shafts to make it sink.
12. A bronze processional cross from Abu Serga.
13. Alfred Butler's 1884 plan of Old Cairo.
14. Nineteenth-century view of the Pyramids taken during the Nile inundation.
15. Part of a stele of Tuthmosis III found 10 m below modern ground level in Shaft HC 1.
16. Amphora handle stamped with the flaming torch motif of the potter Sokrates II.
17. Bourdon's 1925 plan of the ancient and modern canals linking the Nile with the Red Sea.
18. Poséner's sketchplan showing the find locations of the Persian stelae.
19. Plan showing the areas of the Trajanic harbor.
20. The stepped Trajanic quayside below the eastern tower of the South Gate at Babylon.
21. Slots for the swallow-tailed bronze cramps.
22. Relief showing the unloading of amphorae from boat to quayside.
23. The stone block from the Trajanic harbor wall recovered from Shaft HC3.
24. Axonometric of the southwest corner of the Trajanic harbor and the later fortress.
25. Plan of Old Cairo showing the areas of the Roman fortress standing above ground.
26. Reconstructed plan of the Roman fortress.
27. Axonometric reconstruction of the Roman fortress and the entrance to the Amnis Traianus c. AD 300.
28. The surviving southern side of the East Gate.
29. Excavations in the southern round tower in the late 1940s.
30. Decorated blocks reused in the foundations of the western flanking tower of the South Gate.
31. Plan of the round towers.
32. Section through the round towers.
33. Axonometric view of the round towers.
34. The original stonework of the entrance to the southern round tower.
35. Pococke's 1734 plan of the Roman fortress.
36. Axonometric reconstruction of the Roman barracks in the area of the Ben Ezra Synagogue.
37. An early Islamic aqueduct at Istabl 'Antar.
38. Plan showing al-Fustat, al-'Askar, and al-Qatai taken from Bahgat Bey's 1921 *Fouilles d'al-Foustat*.
39. Pococke's 1734 'Chorograph of Grand Cairo.'
40. Plan of Abu Serga Church showing the phases of its development.

41. Axonometric view of Abu Serga Church showing the new archaeological information.
42. Abu Serga proto-church: Part of the colonnade of the early church.
43. Remains of the vaulted tombs in the nave of Abu Serga church.
44. The early medieval building revealed beneath the floor of the Convent of St. George.
45. Cairo around 1800. From the *Description de l'Egypte*.
46. Comité plan of the Convent of St. George.
47. Plan from Bahgat Bey's 1921 *Fouilles d'al-Foustat*.
48. The 1918 Survey of Egypt plan.
49. Frederik Norden's plan of the island of Roda from 1757.
50. Niebuhr plan of Cairo, 1774.
51. Engraving of the Battle of the Pyramids, 1798.
52. The Church of Abu Serga. Remains of the tall medieval niche in the central sanctuary.
53. Axonometric view of the qa'a or medieval hall of the Convent of St George.
54. Comité plan of the Wedding Hall.
55. The Ben Ezra Synagogue: The medieval mastaba.
56. Abu Serga: Marble cross from the medieval floor of the crypt.
57. Abu Serga: Terra Santa cross on the main façade of the church.
58. Abu Serga crypt: A detail of one of the patches of limestone medieval floor.
59. Alfred Butler's plan of Abu Serga.
60. Jullien's view of Old Cairo.
61. Caetani's 1911 panoramic photograph of Old Cairo.
62. Panoramic photograph of Old Cairo after the disastrous fire of 1904.
63. The Ottoman façade of 'Atfat Abu Serga.
64. Somers Clarke view of the South Gate of Babylon.
65. Somers Clarke view of the Hanging Church.
66. Comité detail of the interior of the Hanging Church.
67. Comité section through the northern round tower.
68. A 1897 view of the southern round tower.
69. Unpublished proof of a cross section through the South Gate and the Hanging Church.
70. A view of the southern round tower probably taken in the 1930s.
71. An early photograph taken by the Comité of Abu Serga around 1897.
72. A photograph taken in the crypt of Abu Serga around 1919.
73. The façade of the Church of St. Barbara before the Comité restoration.
74. The façade of the Church of St. Barbara after the Comité restoration.
75. A photograph taken around 1950 showing the façade of the Convent of St. George.
76. Architectural drawings from 1909 showing a proposed design for the Greek Church of St. George.
77. Vaulted tombs of the former Catholic cemetery in the Muqauqas area.
78. The arch leading to the *hara* of Abu Serga as rebuilt in 2008.

Plates

1. Aerial view of Old Cairo looking north.
2. Aerial view of Old Cairo looking southeast.
3. Aerial view of the Mosque of 'Amr looking east.
4. Aerial view of the Mosque of 'Amr, Old Cairo, and the Nile looking southwest.
5. Façade of the Ottoman-period *sabil* at the east end of the Harat Dayr Mari Girgis.
6. A general view of the church of Qasriyat al-Rihan taken in 2000.
7. Ceramics workroom at the SCA inspectorate in al-Fustat.
8. The groundwater level under Mari Girgis Church before the project began.
9. Groundwater level in the crypt of Abu Serga Church before works began.
10. Part of the complex medieval drainage system below the Convent of St. George.
11. Mari Girgis: The northern round tower and the 1940s arcade, looking east.
12. Mari Girgis: The northern round tower and the 1940s arcade, looking west.
13. Material excavated during a night shift at Shaft 7.
14. A Roman stone wall 2.5 meters below the modern ground surface in Shaft 5.
15. The massive stone wall forming the eastern side of the Amnis Traianus.
16. Medieval wall paintings in the southern apsidal sanctuary of Abu Serga Church.
17. Detail of the Abu Serga wall paintings during the conservation work.
18. Shifts in the course of the main channel of the ancient Nile in the Cairo area from 5000 to 500 BP.
19. The lion-headed mooring post from the Trajanic harbor wall coming to the surface.
20. The north end of the earlier Trajanic quay wall revealed in the westernmost room of the southern round tower.
21. The curving outer face of the quayside wall beneath Mari Girgis Church.
22. The huge stone column base within the niche of the northern tower.

23. The massive stone wall built between the round towers to block the entrance to the canal.
24. The central arcade of the southern round tower of the Roman fortress.
25. Fragment of an Oxyrhyncus papyrus of 208 mentioning the Canal of Trajan.
26. The South Gate of the Roman Fortress of Babylon.
27. A comparison of the plans of the Roman fortresses at Babylon and Luxor Temple.
28. Detail of one of the columns in the central arcade of the northern round tower.
29. The entrance to the northern round tower.
30. First floor arcade in the northern round tower.
31. The north wall of Abu Serga showing how the ground level rises to the east.
32. The entrance to the crypt of Abu Serga from the north sanctuary.
33. The entrance to the crypt of Abu Serga from the south sanctuary.
34. Pagano map variant 1549 showing the urban layout of Cairo.
35. Claude Sicard's view of Old Cairo from 1715.
36. The Convent of St. George: Medieval foundations below the great wooden doors.
37. Eighteenth-century painted wooden ciborium from Abu Serga.
38. A 1984 view of the Ottoman house façade in 'Atfat Mari Girgis.
39. A 1984 view of the Ottoman house to the north of Abu Serga church, demolished in 1989.
40. Mari Girgis. The central area of the northern round tower.
41. Medieval vaulted cistern to the east of the northern round tower.
42. Abu Serga: The columns of the crypt separating the 'nave' and the northern aisle.
43. Two blocked doorways to the southern sanctuary of Abu Serga.
44. A view of the exterior of the central apse of Abu Serga.
45. Painted figures of saints on the columns of the nave in Abu Serga.
46. The ornate interior of the Greek Orthodox Church of St. George.

Foreword

The American Research Center in Egypt (ARCE) first supported a project in Old Cairo in 1999 that was conducted by Mallinson Architects under the auspices of ARCE's Egyptian Antiquities Project (EAP), generously funded with a grant from the United States Agency for International Development (USAID). This project identified some ways in which the rich cultural heritage of Old Cairo could be conserved for the benefit of current visitors and future generations.

When USAID decided to fund a project to lower the groundwater in Old Cairo in 1999, ARCE/EAP also decided to fund an archaeological monitoring component to accompany it. The project remained active until 2005, and it is gratifying to see the results of this pioneering effort now presented in this handsome volume in the ARCE Conservation Series published through the American University in Cairo Press.

It is important to understand why we are drawn to such a difficult and complex area as Old Cairo and why the archaeological work and its results presented in this book matter. First, there is the cultural and intellectual significance of the origins of Cairo, one of the world's great cities. Second, the impressive remains of Roman architecture belonging to the fortifications of Diocletian still inspire admiration despite the adaptations that have taken place over the centuries. Third, the numerous churches and the synagogue have played a major role in the multi-cultural and diverse heritages, which have been a vital aspect of Egypt from ancient to modern times. Fourth, the remarkable survival of so much tangible and intangible heritage in such a small and defined area presents a challenge. Both act as powerful influences on identity and reinforce social, political, and religious affiliations. Numerous interest groups represent a range of frequently conflicting agendas and opinions, yet their presence and their weight result directly from, and have a direct bearing on the survival of the rich cultural inheritance preserved here. Life goes on for the local residents in an area where the main focus is historical monuments and where the numerous claims made on them often overshadow other more pressing needs. For the archaeologist these issues are complicated by the physical constraints of working in confined public and private spaces.

At Old Cairo, the American Research Center in Egypt had the opportunity to work in this challenging environment and thereby recover archaeological information that has transformed present scholarship on the history and development of Old Cairo. After over a century of theorizing based on sporadic excavations, reading of historical literature often in isolation and the religious traditions of the area it is now possible to construct a plausible model for the founding, development, and history of settlement here based on actual archaeological data gathered from a wide area and using a variety of different methods and approaches.

The archaeological work and its results presented in this book accompanied the implementation of the Old Cairo Groundwater Lowering Project. This project was funded by the United States Agency for International Development and was carried out under the supervision of the designing engineers, the U.S. firm C.C. Johnson & Malhotra (CCJM), in collaboration with the Supreme Council of Antiquities and the Cairo Wastewater Organisation. Numerous individuals contributed to the success of the project. Nevertheless it was due largely to the encouragement and support of Shree Gokhale and Rajan Patel of CCJM and the determination and persistence of Peter Sheehan, Muhammed Khalifa, and their teams on site that information was recorded and is now published.

The project began in 2000 and was developed by Robert 'Chip' Vincent and Michael Jones at ARCE in consultation with Ann Paterson, project officer at the United States Agency for International Development (USAID) for the Egyptian Antiquities Project of ARCE, and Gokhale and Patel at CCJM. Sheehan was contracted to manage the archaeological work on site. His job, together with his site assistants', was not limited to conventional archaeological excavation. Waterlogged conditions required specialized approaches and equipment, including fishermen's waders and assessing archaeological deposits from the reports of divers feeling their way blind in the muddy water at the bottom of test trenches and manhole excavations. The project presented a one-time opportunity to investigate buried archaeology that may never be repeated, and it developed beyond its initial conception of monitoring the construction work into a team of professionals collaborating in the field and on post-excavation research.

Peter Sheehan's work in Old Cairo and his assessment of the discoveries made during the course of the groundwater lowering project present two major successes and an important challenge. They show how archaeological work carried out in accordance with modern standards and procedures, often under very difficult circumstances, can augment and even enhance the results of a major construction and engineering project. They have also successfully amplified knowledge about Old Cairo on an unprecedented scale, thereby providing extensive new raw material for historians and other professionals in related disciplines. This project establishes a model that can be repeated elsewhere, and there is now a pressing need for similar successful partnerships to be applied wherever major construction works designed to protect and preserve cultural resources impact archaeological sites.

As ever, we at ARCE are grateful to all of those who contributed to the success of this project, and especially to our colleagues at Egypt's Supreme Council of Antiquities under the leadership of Vice-Minister of Culture and Secretary General Dr. Zahi Hawass, to the generous and thoughtful support of the United States Agency for International Development, and to our friends at the American University in Cairo Press.

Gerry D. Scott, III
Director
ARCE

Michael Jones
Associate Director for the Egyptian
Antiquities Conservation Project
ARCE

Acknowledgments

Writing in June 2010 it seems a little ironic to recall that it was following discussions with the late Robert (Chip) Vincent of the American Research Center in Egypt's Egyptian Antiquities Project (EAP/ARCE) at the beginning of 2003 that I agreed to submit the draft text for a book, instead of a final report, on the archaeological monitoring of the groundwater lowering project in Old Cairo, in order to speed up the process of publication.

A lot of groundwater has passed under the bridge since then, and a number of drafts have been written, partly because the project advanced in a number of distinct extensions and partly as a result of the realization that the longer our team stayed in Old Cairo the more we would learn simply by being on hand to observe and record the activities of a whole host of other individuals and agencies, most of them with very little interest in archaeology. Of course this particular spectator sport, like the making of Old Cairo itself, could continue indefinitely, and, consequently, much credit is due to Kathleen Scott, publications director of ARCE, and her predecessor Kelly Zaug, for helping to draw a line in the sand after 2007. I would like to offer particular thanks to Debbie Blome, Senior Project Editor at the American University in Cairo (AUC) Press, and to designer Sally Boylan, for taking the latest of these drafts and establishing and then maintaining a schedule to take it through to publication. Thanks are also due to Debbie's predecessor, Noha Mohammed, and also to Randi Danforth, Nadia Naqib, and Neil Hewison at the AUC Press.

The contribution of others to this book actually goes back to 1989, when the first stimulus to what has been our more or less continuous archaeological presence in Old Cairo over the past twenty years was provided by the work of the Ben Ezra Synagogue Restoration project from 1989 to 1992. The archaeological component of that project came into being through the direct intervention of Phyllis Lambert, director of the Canadian Centre for Architecture, and Johan Bellaert, the architect of the restoration project, so we owe a great debt of gratitude to them and everybody else involved in those far-off days. The archaeological work carried out at that time by Charles Le Quesne, Kate Spence, and myself, much of it photographed by Tim Loveless, has formed the basis of many observations in this book.

From 2000 to 2006, our small core team, funded by EAP/ARCE, through a generous grant from the United States Agency for International Development (USAID), carried out a continuous program of archaeological monitoring during construction work and other activities relating to the Cairo Wastewater Organization/USAID Old Cairo Groundwater Control Project, commonly known as Contract 102. Archaeological investigations and recording were carried out by myself and the indefatigable Mohammed Khalifa, Sami El Masri, and Charles Le Quesne, with the ongoing assistance of a great many people from the Arab Contractors (AC), and their various sub-contractors, who adapted themselves to our peculiar requirements and consistently demonstrated that truly admirable Egyptian capacity for combining hard work with good humor.

The nature of the excavations, and the broad aims of the project in terms of understanding the processes of site formation, made ceramic analysis and recording a fundamental part of the project. This pioneering work carried out by Alison Gascoigne, Gillian Pyke, Sami El Masri, and Mohammed Khalifa in the congenial surroundings of the Fustat inspectorate of the Supreme Council for Antiquities (SCA) has provided a ceramic corpus for Old Cairo dating from the mid-first millennium BC to the present day that will be of inestimable value to future archaeologists working both in the city and beyond. Although other types of small finds were fairly infrequent in the shaft excavations, they were encountered in much greater numbers during manual excavations at sites such as Abu Serga church, and were diligently recorded by Gillian Pyke and Mohammed Khalifa. Analysis of the human remains found during the course of the project was undertaken by Ambika Flavel in 2007. Our thanks also go to Alan Clapham for his initial assessment of soil samples from a number of shafts and boreholes.

From the beginning of the project we realized the importance of producing illustrations for this book that would present the new archaeological findings to the reader and at the same time convey some of the context, and, indeed, the excitement of this work in what often seemed like another world deep below the ground. The extent to which this aim was achieved can be gauged from Nicholas Warner's magnificent axonometric drawings of the various project locations, executed in collaboration with George Dawes for Mari Girgis and the Hanging Church, and thereafter alone. Recording the survey data for these drawings was always a challenging and labor-intensive exercise, carried out largely by myself and Mohammed Khalifa, but also by Nicholas Warner, Charles Le Quesne, and Sami El Masri, as well as the AC survey team. Complementing these drawings as a unique primary record of the work are Tim Loveless's textural and atmospheric black-and-white large-format photographs of the ancient structures below Mari Girgis and the modern crypt floor of Abu Serga, all taken under extremely difficult lighting conditions.

Liaison between the contractor (AC) and the archaeological team was carried out by the consulting engineers, C.C. Johnson and Malhotra (CCJM) of Washington, D.C., in the persons of Shree Gokhale and Rajan Patel, with engineers Houssam Ouf, William Aziz, Ahmed Ibrahim, Mohammed Sadek, Boulos Lamei, Wassim Abdel Aziz, and Hatem Nour. The aerial photographs used in the book were taken by Rajan Patel of CCJM in January 2005 on behalf of the Cairo Wastewater Organization. The funding for Contract 102 was provided by USAID, and the agency's officers Wafaa Faltaous, Gary Cohen, and latterly Gene Lin were involved in the planning and coordination of the entire project. USAID's Egyptian counterpart in this project was the Cairo Wastewater Organization, represented by Samia Banaoub and Engineer Nadi Heshmet.

All archaeological work was conducted under the constant supervision of the SCA. In Old Cairo and al-Fustat we would like to record our sincere thanks firstly to Ibrahim Abd al-Rahman, director of al-Fustat Inspectorate, who has been a true friend to this project from its inception in 1999, and all his staff in al-Fustat including Mamdouh al-Said, Muawad Hassan Hussein, Mustafa Abdel Halim, Abeer Nabiil, and Zeinab al-Tayya. We also acknowledge with gratitude the constant involvement of the director of the Old Cairo Inspectorate, Mohammed Mahgoub, and of our inspectors, principally Ahmed 'Abd al-'Ati, but also Soheir Qonsuh, Osama Abd al-Shakuur, Baha Sobhi, Sharif Hamed Hassanein, and Sheima Salah.

The support of ARCE and the EAP was steadfast throughout the fieldwork in Old Cairo, and has continued as we have entered the analysis and publication stage. In particular we record our thanks to Gerry Scott and previous directors of ARCE, Robert Springborg, Jere Bacharach, Irene Bierman, and Mark Easton, as well as the late Chip Vincent, director of the EAP from 1994 to 2005, EAP technical director Jarek Dobrowolski, and Michael Jones, project manager and frequently 'ideas man,' not just for ARCE but also for the archaeological monitoring project. We would also like to record our thanks to EAP grant administrator Janie Abd el-Aziz and her predecessor Cynthia Shartzer, Lara Shawki, Ibrahim Ali Ibrahim, Marwa Shehata, Mariam Sami, Ghada El Batouty, and all the rest of the staff at EAP and ARCE. On the ARCE side we must also offer special thanks to ARCE deputy director Amira Khattab for conducting the administrative liaison between our project and the SCA with such consummate good grace.

In Old Cairo, we are grateful to Carmen Weinstein, the late representative of the Jewish community in Cairo, for her kindness and interest in the project. Likewise Mother Keria and the nuns of the Convent of St. George, whose hospitality and warmth made working at the convent a real pleasure. We were also warmly and hospitably welcomed by successive incumbents at the Greek Monastery of St. George. In Abu Serga, we note the constant involvement in the project of the late Father Gabriel Bestavros, and we would like to thank the church's consultants, who were particularly concerned with structural repairs to the crypt carried out during the project, notably Mounir Tawfiq and Adel Fareed of the Egy-Tech group. In Abu Serga we also had the pleasure of collaborating with the Spanish conservation team (ONG Cooperación Internacional) that worked in the church from 1998 to 2004 under the direction of José Sancho Roda and Antonio Sánchez Barriga, and in particular with Jesus Arena, the team archaeologist.

Our knowledge of the buildings of Old Cairo was enhanced by the engineers of Camp, Dresser & McKee (CDM), Conor Power, Craig Wilson, and Helmut Hass, who carried out a structural assessment and a review of the potential impact of Contract 102 at the request of USAID in 2002. My understanding of the history and workings of the canal of Trajan was greatly assisted by discussions with John Cooper of Exeter University, who generously made available his then-unpublished survey of the sources pertaining to the Nile–Red Sea Canal in its various incarnations. More recently, my understanding of a whole range of related issues in the Red Sea and beyond has benefited considerably from ongoing conversations with Tim Power.

During and subsequent to work at the various project locations I have also benefited from the observations and advice of Jarek Dobrowolski, Adeline Jeudy, Bernard Maury, Seif El Rashidi, Michael Mallinson, Betsy Bolman, William Lyster, the late Luigi de Cesaris, Alberto Sucato, Father Maximous al-Antony, Silvia Armando, Angela Millward-Jones, Roland-Pierre Gayraud, Cedric Meurice, Peter Grossmann, Dietrich Raue, George Scanlon, and Alaa al-Habashi. At various times the text has been read and commented on, either in part or—by the more long-suffering—in its entirety, by Sara Montgomery, Tim Loveless, Alison Gascoigne, Jere Bacharach, David Jeffreys, Judith Bunbury, and Michael Jones. I have also recently benefited from discussions with Petra Sijpesteijn, Arietta Papaconstantinou, and Tarek Swelim at the IFAO conference "Fustat et le contrôle des territoires" organized by Sylvie Denoix, and Sobhi Bouderbala. I am grateful to Dimitry Karelin and Radu Urloiu for recent correspondence on various issues related to the Roman military in Egypt. To all these individuals, and the many others not named here who have helped and cooperated with the project, I wish to express the team's sincere thanks.

I trust that the above shows how the work in Old Cairo and the production of this book have been, above all, a team effort based on the contribution and expertise of a large number of people. Like most attempts at summarizing an imperfect understanding of a complex situation based on partial information, there are bound to be some parts that are weaker than others, and I am confident that these will turn out to be all my own work.

Finally, I would like to thank the captives brought to Babylon who never revolted—my wife Sara and my children Gabriel, Hester, and Theodore—for their continued love and forbearance.

Timeline of Significant Events

Conjectural dates in *italics*; events directly relating to Babylon/Old Cairo in **bold**. All quotes in the timeline are cited in full in the main body of the text.

664–525 BC   Pharaohs of the Twenty-sixth Dynasty ruling from Sais in the Western Nile Delta. Pharaoh Necho II (610–595 BC) makes unsuccessful first attempt at canal linking the Nile to the Red Sea, probably as an alternative to the southern land route to Punt (Somalia), which had been cut by war and political changes in the lands south of Egypt during the 660s. The fifth-century BC writer Herodotus reports that 120,000 workers perished in this attempt.

525 BC   First Persian occupation of Egypt (Twenty-seventh Dynasty) continues to 404 BC. Darius I (521–486) successfully cuts canal. He marks the event with a series of commemorative stelae set along the canal route linking the Nile and the Red Sea, "which is in communication with Persia."

515 BC   Scylax of Caria sails down Indus River and navigates westward through Indian Ocean and Red Sea to Suez.

323–30 BC   Ptolemaic rule of Egypt. Ptolemy II Philadelphus (284–46) re-cuts Red Sea Canal and founds new port city at Clysma (Suez), at the head of the Gulf of Suez. His activities in this area include campaigns against "pirates" of Nabataea (modern Sinai, Jordan, the Negev, and parts of Arabia).

62 BC   First Roman campaign in Nabataea under Aemilius Scaurus (deputy of Pompey). Nabataea becomes a Roman client-state.

50 BC   **The earliest historical reference to Babylon of Egypt. The Roman writer Diodorus Siculus describes its foundation by "captives brought from Babylonia," who first "seized a strong position on the banks of the river" and after being granted an amnesty "established a colony on the spot which they also named Babylon, from their native land."**

31 BC   Octavian's victory over Cleopatra and Mark Antony at Actium ushers in more than six hundred years of Roman rule in Egypt. The new Roman province of Egypt becomes one of the major sources of wheat for the city of Rome. Its economic importance and strategic significance give Egypt a special status, ruled by a prefect appointed directly by the emperor. **Around 26 BC the Greek geographer Strabo, traveling with the first prefect Aelius Gallus, describes how Babylon, "a strong fortress, built by some Babylonians who had taken**

refuge there," is the location of one of the three legions stationed in Egypt at that time. By AD 25, however, only one legion remains, probably stationed at Alexandria. Aelius Gallus also tries but fails to take direct control of the important trade routes passing through Nabataea.

AD 50 — Arrival of Saint Mark the Evangelist in Alexandria and the foundation of the Egyptian Church, the early history of which remains clouded in uncertainty.

AD 107 — Trajan annexes Nabataea into the Roman Empire as the new province of Arabia. Around this time the emperor re-cuts the Red Sea Canal (renamed the *Amnis Traianus*) that now links Egypt via the new province with his new *Via Nova Traiana*, the trans-Levantine "King's Highway." Milestones along this new road celebrate the fact that it ran "from the border of Syria to the Red Sea." **Where the Red Sea Canal now joins the Nile at Babylon, Trajan underlines the economic and strategic motives behind the new organization of the eastern provinces and their importance to the supply of Rome by building a great stone harbor.**

AD 208 — Papyrus from Oxyrhynchus refers to work on Trajan's Canal, showing it was still in use until at least the beginning of the third century.

AD 250–51 — First major official persecution of Christians in Egypt and throughout the empire during the reign of the emperor Decius. Egyptian Christianity and the character of its leadership begin to be shaped by its identity as "the Church of the Martyrs."

AD 298–302 — Visits of the emperor Diocletian to put down revolt of L. Domitius Domitianus and to pacify Egypt. **During this period Diocletian builds the massive fortress of Babylon dominating the entrance to the still-functioning canal of Trajan.** The fortress forms part of a comprehensive military and administrative reorganization of Egypt (and the rest of the empire) to provide manpower and money for the armies of Rome against the threat of invasion along the Danube and from Parthia.

AD 303–11 — Renewed persecution of the Christians in Egypt under Diocletian, Galerius, and Maximian, including the martyrdom of the Patriarch Peter I. Persecution of the Christians is part of an attempt to enforce solidarity and a return to "traditional" Roman values. The Egyptian Church marks the severity of these persecutions by beginning its present era with Diocletian's accession in 284, "the Year of the Martyrs."

AD 312 — Constantine becomes emperor and ends persecution of the Christians. His patronage of the Church begins the process of uniting Empire and Church—in 378 the emperor Theodosius makes Christianity the official religion of the empire, although pagan worship continues into the seventh century despite increasing persecution from the Egyptian Church. Freed from outside persecution, the Church embarks on the long road of internal schism and controversy over what constitutes "orthodoxy," arguments which continue for the next three hundred years.

AD 325 — Council of Nicaea condemns Arian "heresy" of Christ's subordinate status to God. Arianism, however, continues to have many adherents and even imperial support, dominating the Councils of Tyre in 335 and Milan in 355. However, in 381 the Council of Constantinople reaffirms the theological position adopted at Nicaea.

AD 431 — Egyptian-dominated First Council of Ephesus **(attended by a bishop of Babylon)** condemns Nestorius (bishop of Constantinople) for his opposition to the term *Theotokos* (Mother of God) in relation to the Virgin Mary. Issues of protocol and theology cause a rift between the bishop of Alexandria and the sees of Rome and Antioch. This rift deepens further with the tactics of the Egyptian

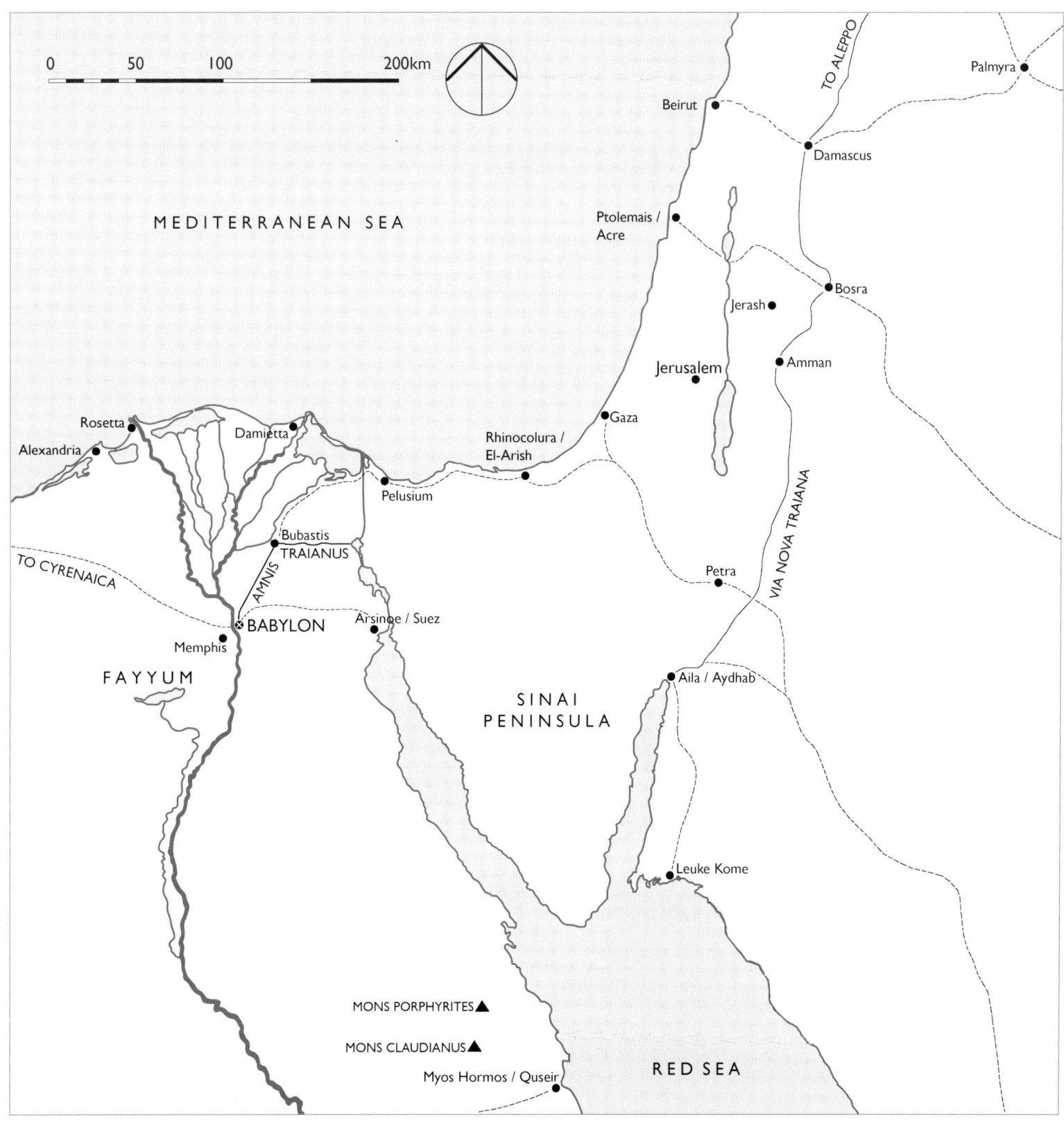

Fig. 1. Egypt and the Near East c. AD 110. (Nicholas Warner)

	Church at the Second Council of Ephesus in 449, called to resolve the christological dispute created by the teachings of the Egyptian monk Eutyches on the "one nature" of Christ.
AD 451	Council of Chalcedon marks formal and irrevocable schism between the church in Egypt and those of Rome and Constantinople by invalidating the Second Council of Ephesus, deposing the bishop of Alexandria, and replacing him with a Chalcedonian appointee linked to the Byzantine state. The conflict in Egypt between pro-Chalcedonian and anti-Chalcedonian factions for the see of Alexandria continues until the coming of Islam nearly two hundred years later.
AD 538	Justinian's re-establishment of the Chalcedonian bishop of Alexandria as a "soldier-patriarch" forming an integral part of the imperial administration at Alexandria in 538 ushers in a period characterized by increasingly bitter resistance of the native Egyptian Church to the Melkite (imperial) church.
AD 582–602	Disturbances and local uprisings in Egypt during the reign of the emperor Maurice. In 602 Maurice is deposed and murdered by the usurper Phocas, who is in turn defeated by the last Byzantine ruler of Egypt, the emperor Heraclius (610–41).
AD 619	Egypt occupied by the Sassanian Persian empire, which had been bought off with regular payments of tribute throughout the sixth century. The province is reconquered for Byzantium by Heraclius in 629.
AD 622/AH 1	Flight *(hijra)* of the Prophet Muhammad from Mecca to Madina inaugurates Islamic era.
AD 631	Appointment of Cyrus as new "soldier-patriarch" of Alexandria with orders to achieve doctrinal uniformity and thus solidarity in the face of external threats to the empire, by force if necessary.
AD 632	Death of the Prophet Muhammad.
AD 635/6	Arab defeat of Persian army at al-Qadisiya. Success against the Persians is followed by victories over the Byzantine armies and the capture of Damascus and Jerusalem.
AD 640–41	Arab Conquest of Egypt under 'Amr ibn al-'As. **Babylon is surrendered after a seven-month siege, following news of the death of Heraclius in April 641. The 'camp-city' of al-Fustat is founded around the nucleus of the former fortress, with the congregational (Friday) Mosque of 'Amr built immediately to the north of the fortress. The location of the new city reflects the focus of Egypt's new rulers eastward and away from the Mediterranean. This strategic shift of the center of government is encouraged by the short-lived recapture of Alexandria by the Byzantine emperor Manuel in 645. Fueled by an influx of settlers from Arabia, al-Fustat grows spectacularly for the first hundred years. The Red Sea Canal is now used to transport grain supplies diverted from Alexandria to Syria/Palestine and Arabia. By this time, however, Trajan's harbor has silted up and a new entrance to the canal is cut to the north of Old Cairo. With the end of Chalcedonian influence in Egypt and a stable relationship with the new rulers, the Egyptian Church experiences a strong revival from 644 to 668. Much church building is carried out in these years, probably including the foundation of many of the churches of Old Cairo.**
AD 656	Election of 'Ali as caliph leads to great rift in Islam between *shi'a* ('the Party of' ['Ali]) and *sunni* (orthodox), culminating in the death of the son of 'Ali, al-Husayn, at the battle of Karbala.
AD 658–750	Egypt ruled by governors appointed by Umayyad caliphs in Damascus.
AD 750	Egypt is conquered by the army of the Abbasid caliphs ruling from Baghdad.

	Much of the southern and eastern parts of al-Fustat may have been destroyed during the fighting or deliberately burned by the last Umayyad ruler Marwan II; at any rate, these parts were afterward abandoned. The Red Sea Canal appears to have gone out of use around this time, either as a deliberate measure or through lack of maintenance. Foundation of separate military/administrative enclosure al-'Askar immediately to north of al-Fustat, but this is soon subsumed as the city continues to expand to the north.
AD 859	**Election of the Coptic Patriarch takes place in the Church of SS. Sergius and Bacchus (Abu Serga) in Old Cairo, a tradition that continues until the mid-eleventh century.**
AD 860	Governor of Egypt appointed by Abbasids, Ahmad ibn Tulun, breaks away to form separate Tulunid dynasty. Founds spectacular new royal enclosure of *al-Qata'i'* on the northeastern edge of al-Fustat, including new congregational mosque of Ibn Tulun.
AD 885	**Massive earthquake with epicenter 14 km from Old Cairo causes destruction of many brick and masonry buildings. Mosque of 'Amr rebuilt following this**.
AD 905	Egypt reconquered by Abbasid empire. From 935–69 it is ruled by Ikhshids as a client dynasty of the Abbasids.
AD 969	Egypt conquered by Shi'ite Fatimid dynasty from North Africa, and its capital becomes the center of the Shi'a caliphate. New royal enclosure of al-Qahira (Cairo) founded to the northeast of al-Fustat on the east bank of the former Red Sea Canal, straddling the line of the great road to the north. Large influx of settlers from North Africa.
AD 1047	**Coptic Patriarchate moves from Alexandria to Old Cairo, reflecting the shift in the political and economic importance of the two cities that has taken place since the Arab Conquest.**
AD 1060–90	**The "Great Disaster"** (*al-shidda al-'uzma*) **of the latter part of the reign of the Fatimid caliph al-Mustansir. These disasters include a series of low Nile floods and resultant famines, plague, and an earthquake in 1070 that probably causes extensive damage to structures and necessitates a major rebuilding program. These natural disasters are accompanied by political instability and near anarchy. The abandonment of much of al-Fustat at this time is attested to by a 1072 edict of the vizier Badr al-Gamali allowing the residents of Cairo to remove building material from the houses of al-Fustat.**
AD 1099	Capture of Jerusalem by First Crusade.
AD 1138	Cairo and al-Fustat hit by major earthquake.
AD 1168	**Crusaders invade Egypt and advance on Egyptian capital before being driven back. Much of al-Fustat allegedly burnt at this time to prevent it falling into their hands.** Salah al-Din (Saladin) becomes vizier in 1169 and in 1171, on the death of the last Fatimid caliph, has the Friday sermon read in the name of the Abbasid caliph, thus returning Egypt from Shi'a to Sunni (orthodox) rule. Salah al-Din founds Ayyubid dynasty that until 1250 rules Egypt from the great citadel built overlooking the city. He and his successors achieve notable victories against the Crusaders, including the recapture of Jerusalem in 1187. Mindful of the recent attacks on Cairo, he begins a project to enclose the whole city within great defensive walls that is completed by his successors.
AD 1240	**Construction of a new citadel by the Ayyubid sultan al-Salih Najm al-Din Ayyub for his army of Turkish slaves (Mamluks) at the southern end of the island of Roda facing Old Cairo.**

AD 1249	Sixth Crusade invades Egypt but is defeated at Mansura. Ayyubid dynasty ends and is succeeded until 1382 by rulers chosen from among the Bahri Mamluks (from *bahr*, river) based in the Roda citadel.
AD 1258	Mongols capture and destroy Baghdad, and Egypt receives a great influx of refugees from the East, including an Abbasid prince who is pronounced caliph (1261), putting Cairo at the center of the Sunni sphere. An Egyptian Mamluk army under the sultan Baybars defeats the Mongols at 'Ayn Jalut in Palestine in 1260, gaining control of large areas of Syria/Palestine. Another Mamluk faction is installed in the citadel from 1280 and these Burgi Mamluks (from *burg*, tower) eventually prevail over the Bahri faction. **Between 1250 and 1320 the churches of Old Cairo suffer official persecution and frequent attacks by mobs as by now the majority of the population of the city is Muslim.** Anti-Christian sentiments are fueled by the wars against the Crusader states, who are finally expelled from the Holy Land in 1291. **The Mamluk defeat of the Crusaders brings European (especially Italian) merchants to Cairo in search of a new base for the spice and luxury trade with the East. It also increasingly becomes a more accessible pilgrimage destination than Jerusalem. Old Cairo begins to be much visited, venerated, and described by these merchants and pilgrims.**
AD 1353	**Black Death reduces Cairo's population by about a third.**
AD 1382	Barquq seizes power and Egypt is now ruled by a succession of Burgi Mamluk sultans until 1517. Notwithstanding revivals under several outstanding individual sultans, Egypt's wealth and power within the changing economic and political climate of the region gradually decline. **The Geniza archive found in the Ben Ezra Synagogue in Old Cairo (known as the Cairo Geniza) documents the area's declining fortunes and the contrast with its high point in the early years of Fatimid rule.**
AD 1453	The tiny remnant of the Byzantine Empire expires with the fall of Constantinople to the Ottomans.
AD 1497	Vasco da Gama circumnavigates Africa and opens up new trade route to India and the East.
AD 1517	Egypt is conquered by the Ottomans and Khayrbak is made its first governor or *pasha*. It returns to its Ptolemaic and Roman role, supplying the needs of a great empire to the north. Control and administration are carried out by corps of Caucasian slave-soldiers commanded by *bey*s who by the mid-seventeenth century are only nominally under the control of the pasha. Factional fighting among the *bey*s and an increasingly weak Ottoman hold on the province characterize the period until the end of the eighteenth century. **However, these conditions facilitate the making of great individual fortunes and at Old Cairo the eighteenth century sees a great revival under the influence of a wealthy Coptic notable, Ibrahim al-Gohari.**
AD 1798	The French force invading Egypt under Bonaparte is accompanied by professors and scholars who make exhaustive studies between 1798 and 1801 of Egypt's natural and cultural riches (including detailed plans of Cairo), published between 1809 and 1828 as *Description de l'Égypte*.
AD 1805	Muhammad 'Ali becomes pasha and disposes of the last Mamluks. He introduces a wide range of modernizing measures throughout Cairo and Egypt.
AD 1869	Suez Canal opened to navigation after ten-year construction program costing thousands of lives.
AD 1882	British and French bombard Alexandria to protect their financial interests threatened by political developments in Egypt. From 1883 the Egyptian administration is controlled by a British Consul-General.

AD 1896   A large section of Trajan's Canal (the medieval al-Khalig al-Misri) is filled in during a cholera outbreak and becomes Shari' Port Said.

AD 1897   **The "rediscovery" of the architectural and archaeological importance of Old Cairo by antiquarians is recognized by the decision of the Comité de Conservation des Monuments de l'Art Arabe to initiate a detailed program of survey and restoration. In the same year, the Cairo–Helwan Light Railway simultaneously reconnects Old Cairo to the modern city and severs its relationship to the River Nile.**

AD 1908   **The Coptic Museum is opened on land in Old Cairo belonging to the Church, and is further extended in 1931.**

AD 1952   Coup d'état deposes King Farouk. Egypt becomes a republic in 1953; nationalization of the Suez Canal in 1956 leads to the Suez Crisis.

AD 1971   Completion of Aswan High Dam ends annual inundation of the Nile. **This and other changes to the groundwater regime of Old Cairo brought about by the huge expansion of informal settlements over the former ruin heaps of al-Fustat leads to an increase in groundwater levels of around 2 meters and flooding of the monuments of Old Cairo.**

AD 2000   **A USAID-funded project to lower groundwater levels in Old Cairo begins, with archaeological monitoring of the works provided by the American Research Center in Egypt.**

1. Fortress of Babylon
2. Mosque of 'Amr ibn al-'As
3. Monastery of St. Mercurius (Abu Sayfayn)
4. Mosque of Abu Su'ud
5. Mosque of Ibn Tulun
6. Mosque of Sayyida Zaynab
7. Monastery of St. Menas (Mar Mina)
8. Mosque of Zayn al-'Abidin
9. Mosque of Sayyida Nafisa
10. Fatimid tomb of Muhammad al-Ga'fari, tomb of Sayyida 'Atiqa, and mashhad of Sayyida Ruqayya
11. Nilometer
12. Fumm al Khalig intake tower
13. Churches of Babilun al-Darag
14. Dayr al-Malak (Church of the Archangel Michael)
15. Birkat al-Fil
16. Birkat Baghala
17. Azbakiya
18. Rumayla and hippodrome
19. Mosque of al-Hakim
20. Churches of the Harat Zuwayla
21. Mosque of Baybars I, al-Zahir

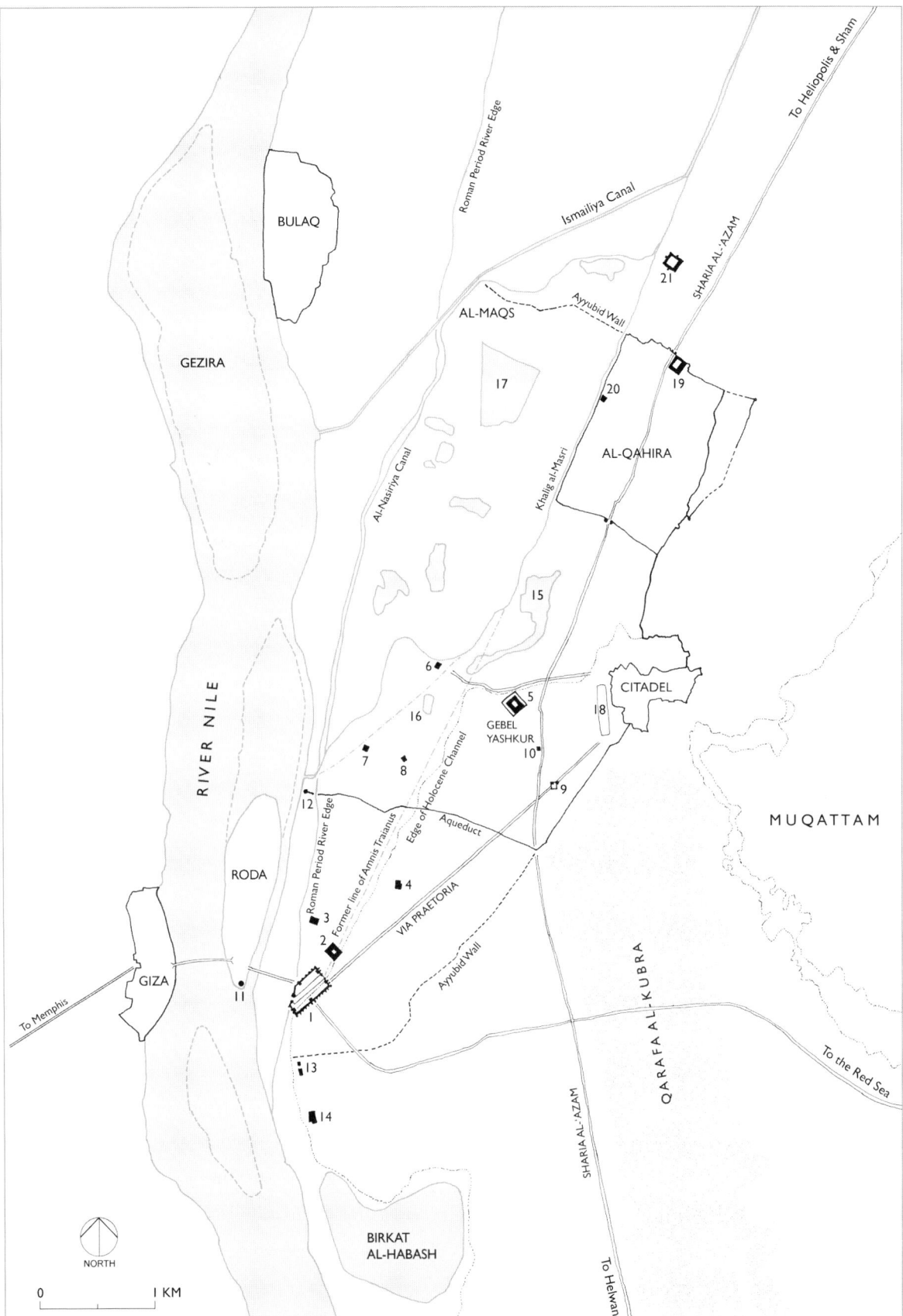

Fig. 2. Babylon in context: Topographic and urban features of the East Bank of the Nile at Cairo. (Nicholas Warner/Peter Sheehan)

Introduction

This book presents a history of Old Cairo based on new archaeological evidence gathered over a six-year period between 2000 and 2006. During this period, a small archaeological team representing the American Research Center in Egypt (ARCE) continually monitored the construction activities of a major USAID-funded project to lower the groundwater level affecting the churches and other monuments of Old Cairo. The wealth of diverse data and the information this work has produced on the origins and development of Old Cairo make it among the most important archaeological projects ever undertaken in the city. Boreholes, tunnels, and excavations deep below modern ground level have produced evidence for the formation of the natural landscape of Old Cairo and the first settlement here during the middle of the first millennium BC. For the archaeologist the importance of Old Cairo lies in a preserved sequence of continuous occupation extending from the sixth century BC to the present day. Material and structural remains of this historical layering abound. The massive stone walls of the canal linking the Nile to the Red Sea and the harbor constructed by the emperor Trajan at its entrance in c. AD 110 have now been exposed and recorded below two of the most ancient churches of Old Cairo. Around AD 300 the emperor Diocletian built the Fortress of Babylon around the harbor and the canal, and a great deal of new information has come to light concerning the construction and the internal layout of the fortress, which continues to enclose and define the enclave of Old Cairo. Important material and structural evidence for the early medieval transformation of the area into the nucleus of the Arab city of al-Fustat and its later medieval development has also been recorded.

This work has contributed to two separate yet related histories. The first of these is that of ancient Babylon of Egypt, from its foundation in the middle of the first millennium BC through to the end of Byzantine rule in Egypt that was signaled by the Arab Conquest and the coming of Islam in 641. The victory of the Arab armies marks the historical divide between the end of Babylon and the beginning of the history of Old Cairo, as well as of the churches and synagogue within the walls of the former fortress, which became the nucleus of a great medieval city and ultimately the modern metropolis of Cairo. For the archaeologist this historical distinction between ancient Babylon and medieval Old Cairo is problematic, for archaeology reveals continuity as well as change: how the topography of ancient Babylon, for example, governed the development of medieval Old Cairo, and the way in which its ancient structures were adapted to medieval use. The derivation of much of the medieval city from elements and alignments of the ancient landscape of Cairo also provides a strong antidote to the prevalent view that "Cairo stands pre-eminently as a Muslim city, bearing only slight traces of the physical and cultural imprint of its pharaonic and Greco-roman precursors."[1]

The names 'Babylon' and 'Old Cairo' are part of the complexity of this story, for they do not simply represent ancient and medieval names for the same place. Ancient writers, starting with Diodorus Siculus in the middle of the first century BC, explained how there had come to be a Babylon in Egypt by linking its foundation to settlers from the great Mesopotamian city of the same name. Taken together, these sources have such a remarkable resonance with the archaeological record revealed by our recent work that they represent a more convincing view of the foundation than that previously proposed for an etymological derivation for Babylon linked to the ancient Egyptian city of On. This interpretation sees Babylon as a corruption of an ancient Egyptian toponym, *Pr H'p[y] m 'Iwnw* (The House of [the Nile-god] Hapi in On [Heliopolis]).[2] The name Babylon continued to be applied by Europeans to the area of the fortress and sometimes even the whole city of Cairo as late as the seventeenth century.[3]

'Old Cairo,' on the other hand, is clearly anachronistic, for the fortress was built more than six hundred years before the foundation of Cairo and the first settlement dates back to more than eight hundred years before that. Its use from the medieval period onward, however, reveals that European merchants, travelers, and pilgrims recognized that this area represented the origins of the medieval city. The Arabic term for Old Cairo, *Misr al-qadima*, is more accurate, explicitly confirming that this is the oldest area of the city. *Misr* (pl. *amsar*) is the Arabic word for 'garrison town' that was applied to the settlement that grew up where the Arab armies had besieged Babylon, but appears to derive from an earlier Semitic word for Egypt that refers to its natural boundaries. In any case it is a name that has been used for both the country of Egypt and its capital since at least the seventh century, while *qadima* is 'old' or 'ancient.'

Today Old Cairo contains a uniquely important group of early medieval religious buildings within and around the impressive remains of the Roman fortress of Babylon.[4] These visible antiquities of Old Cairo draw an added and vivid significance from their historical and mythological associations with such evocative themes as the Flight of the Holy Family into Egypt, the first footfall of Islam in Africa, and the lives and deaths of martyrs, saints, and prophets. The ancient churches of Old Cairo make it one of the foremost pilgrimage centers of Christian Egypt, and the continuing devotional importance of the site is signaled by the presence of the Coptic convent of St. George with more than sixty nuns. Along with the churches, the presence of the Mosque of 'Amr and the Ben Ezra Synagogue have recently made Old Cairo a potent political symbol of the way in which the religious communities of Egypt have coexisted since the seventh century of our era.

The recent excavations carried out far below the groundwater level have produced evidence for the formation of the natural landscape of Cairo and its transformation by man and nature over time. The earliest archaeological material points to the first settlement of Babylon in the Late Period (probably during the Twenty-sixth Dynasty, 664–525 BC). This period witnessed changes of great and lasting significance, during which Egypt became part of the wider political and cultural worlds of the Mediterranean and the Near East. Once started, this trend was never reversed, and throughout the periods of Ptolemaic and Roman rule the junction between the canal and the Nile at Babylon remained a vital node connecting Egypt and these worlds. The Romans first transformed Babylon under Trajan around AD 110 with the construction of a massive stone harbor around the entrance to the canal. Around two hundred years later, between AD 298–302, Diocletian underlined the strategic importance of this location by enclosing the harbor and the mouth of the canal within the powerful walls of the Fortress of Babylon.

Babylon was captured by the Arabs in AD 641 and became the nucleus around which the 'camp-city' of al-Fustat grew up at a tremendous rate over the next hundred years. The decision to create a new capital around ancient Babylon was dictated by its existing links with Arabia by land and via the Red Sea Canal, which allowed it to replace Mediterranean Alexandria as the administrative and economic capital of Egypt. At the same time, the foundation of a new city allowed the division of land into tribal allotments for the land-hungry tribes of the victorious army. Babylon/Old Cairo thus represents an important physical link between the end of Byzantine Egypt and the beginning of its medieval and modern identity within the Arabic-speaking Muslim East. In AD 750, and again in 870, separate new enclosures at the northern edge of al-Fustat were created to contain the administrative or 'royal' center and to distinguish it from the growing metropolis. A gradual shift to the northeast, necessitated by the recurring desire to separate royal and public functions, became a feature of the development of the medieval city. It was continued with the foundation of the royal enclosure of al-Qahira (Cairo) following the conquest of Egypt by the North African Fatimid dynasty in 969. Political and economic crises under Fatimid rule in the second half of the eleventh century AD caused much of al-Fustat and the southern part of the metropolis to be abandoned. These events also arrested the shifting progress of the center of the city toward the northeast; from the reign of the Ayyubid dynasty, founded by Salah al-Din in 1169, the separation of the center of government and royal residence from the metropolis was achieved instead by the creation of an impregnable citadel on a spur of the Muqattam hills detached from the city. Only in the nineteenth century, when the Mediterranean and the East were once again connected by sea, this time via the Suez Canal, did the city of Cairo resume its relentless expansion northward.

Protected by the walls of the Roman fortress, Old Cairo survived as an island within the ruin fields of al-Fustat, linked to the metropolis of Cairo by the narrow strip of the settlement that continued in use along the eastern bank of the river. In the thirteenth and fourteenth centuries the survival of Old Cairo was aided by its proximity to the port of Cairo and to the Ayyubid and then Mamluk citadel at the foot of the island of Roda. Its significance declined after the citadel was abandoned and the port facilities began to be shifted downstream to Bulaq. However, the historical associations of Old Cairo and its churches, synagogues, and mosques meant that it continued to be revered and visited by Egyptians and foreign travelers alike.

The urban landscape of Old Cairo has been formed by a vast series of individual acts of building, rebuilding, demolition, and dumping. Some of these can be assigned to historical periods or even particular events, but all are preserved in some way as archaeological layers or components of its buildings. What archaeologists see as complex layers of archaeology, however, others simply lump together as "fill" or "made ground," heterogeneous and resistant to a precise characterization of its properties. In building up a picture of the buried landscape we have made much use of engineering and geotechnical reports that simply listed the depth of "made ground" lying above the natural strata. This introduction discusses the processes by which this ground was "made," by considering the nature of the archaeological evidence and the various circumstances under which it has been possible to record this data in recent years. We can now add archaeological observations to the medieval historical sources largely used in previous studies of the historical topography of Cairo. Archaeology can also be combined with the evidence provided in relatively modern times by old photographs and historic maps.

Part 1 of the book, "The Making of Babylon," deals with the evidence for the ancient site, from its beginnings in the middle of the first millennium BC until the Arab Conquest of AD 641. Archaeological information obtained during recent large-scale engineering work around Old Cairo is used in Chapter 1 to reconstruct a picture of "the ancient landscape," now long buried, upon which later changes and developments were based. The geology and ecology of this landscape are presented through a wide range of observations drawn from various kinds of data. The fundamental role of the River Nile in the formation and rhythms of the landscape is explored and, as background to the later chapters, archaeological evidence for early settlement in the area of modern Cairo is considered. This chapter culminates with a discussion of the archaeological evidence for the first settlement at Old Cairo in the sixth century BC and its association with the canal linking the Nile and the Red Sea.

The Red Sea Canal was the defining influence on the topography of ancient and medieval Cairo and forms the subject of Chapter 2, "The River of Trajan." Between 2002 and 2004, work beneath two of the most ancient churches of Old Cairo revealed the massive stone walls constructed by the Emperor Trajan around AD 110 at either side of the entrance to his canal, the Amnis Traianus. The foundation of the canal is traced and its working is discussed, as well as its heritage and later transformation into the medieval canal known as al-Khalig al-Misri.

In AD 300 the emperor Diocletian enclosed the mouth of the canal and secured this important strategic location by constructing the Roman fortress of Babylon, the subject of Chapter 3. The reign of Diocletian represents a watershed in the history of Egypt and its major themes are briefly discussed. His twin concerns to reorganize and finance the defense of the frontiers of the empire led to wholesale reform of the tax system and the army. Taxation and conscription in Egypt contributed to a flight from the land and created the conditions for the establishment of the great rural estates, which continued into the modern period. The suspicion of conflicting loyalties for Christians in the army led to persecutions and the creation of the martyrs to whom many of the churches of Old Cairo are dedicated. Like the Canal of Trajan, the walls and streets of the fortress exerted a fundamental influence on the topography and thus the later development of the city. Its walls continue to define the Christian enclave of Old Cairo, and we present new archaeological information on the internal layout of the fortress from which many of the later medieval buildings derived.

Part 2 of the book concerns "The Making of Old Cairo." The archaeology of the individual medieval buildings for which we have detailed information—the Church of Abu Serga, the Convent of St. George, the Wedding Hall of the Church of St. George—forms the basis of this analysis and enables us to draw important conclusions regarding the development of the group and the area as a whole.

Chapter 4, "Fustat and the Making of Old Cairo," considers the early medieval changes that occurred from the time of the Arab Conquest until the abandonment of the southern part of the city at the end of the eleventh century AD. The chapter presents topographical and archaeological information relating to the foundation of al-Fustat and the reuse of the Roman fortress, as well as the archaeological evidence for the date of the foundation of the first churches in Old Cairo and subsequent cycles of restoration from the ninth to the eleventh century.

Chapter 5, "Cycles of Decline and Revival," discusses the changing medieval topography of Cairo and the position of

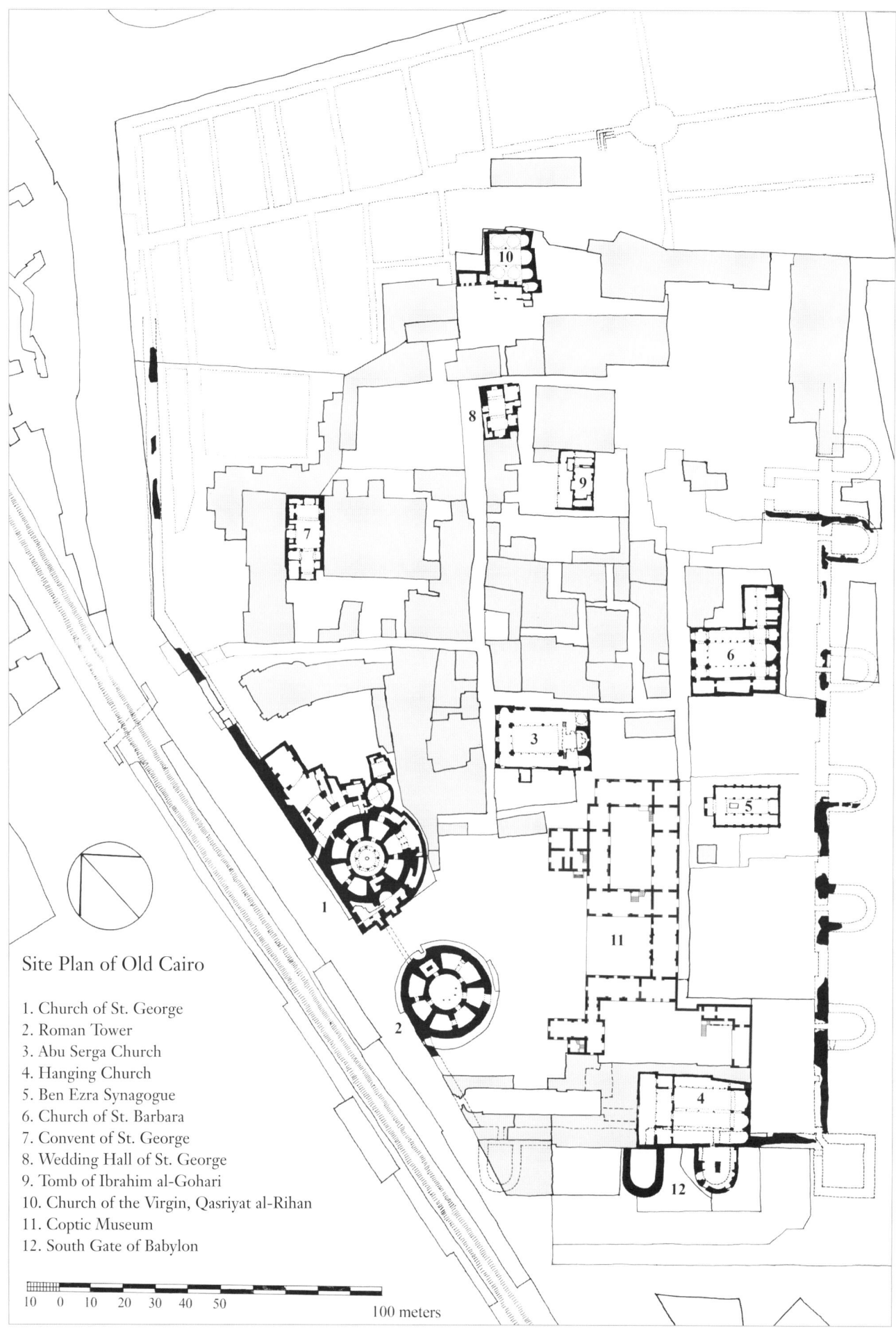

Fig. 3. Plan showing the monuments of Old Cairo. (Nicholas Warner)

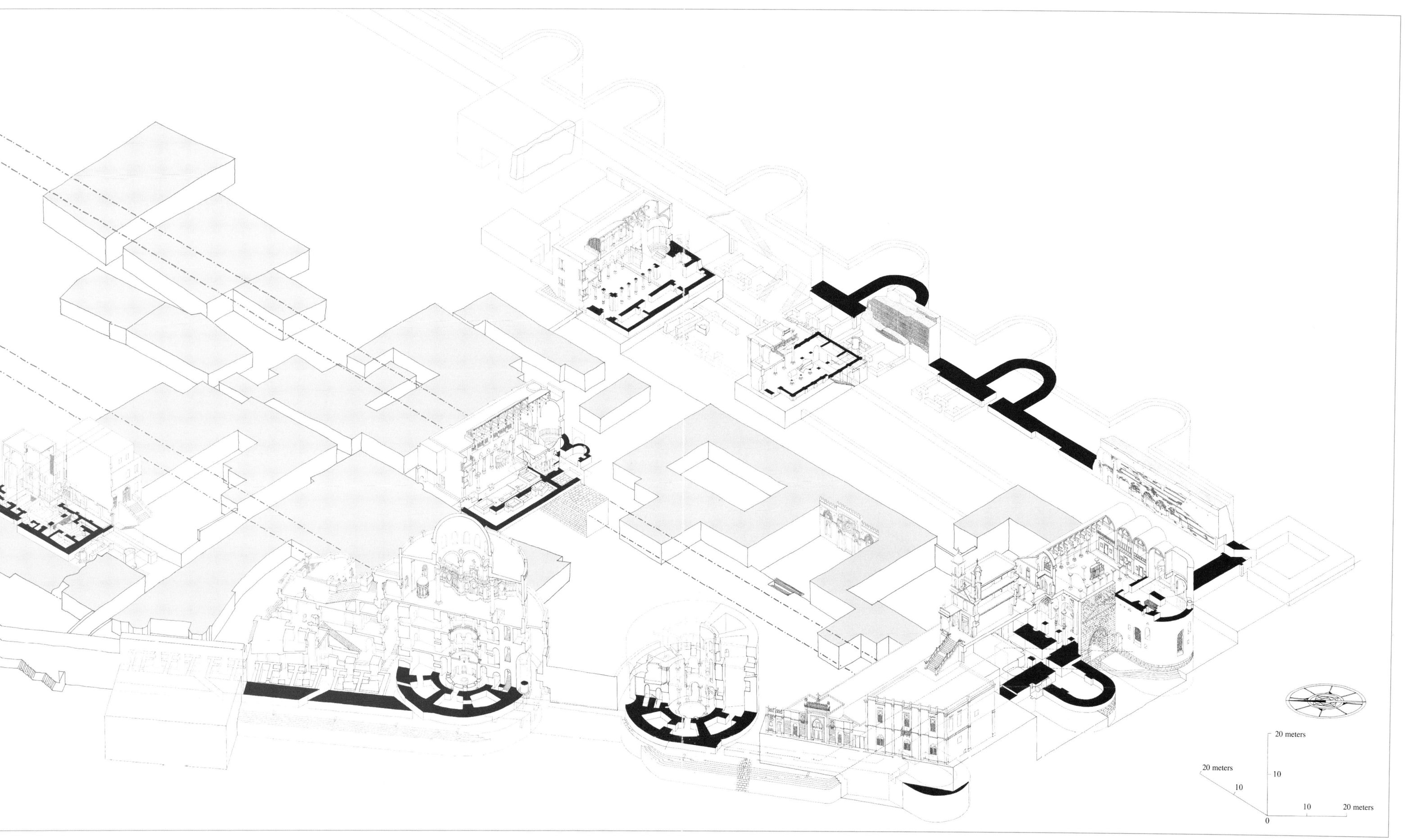

4. Axonometric view of the monuments of Old Cairo showing the new archaeological information ...ed during the groundwater lowering project. (Nicholas Warner)

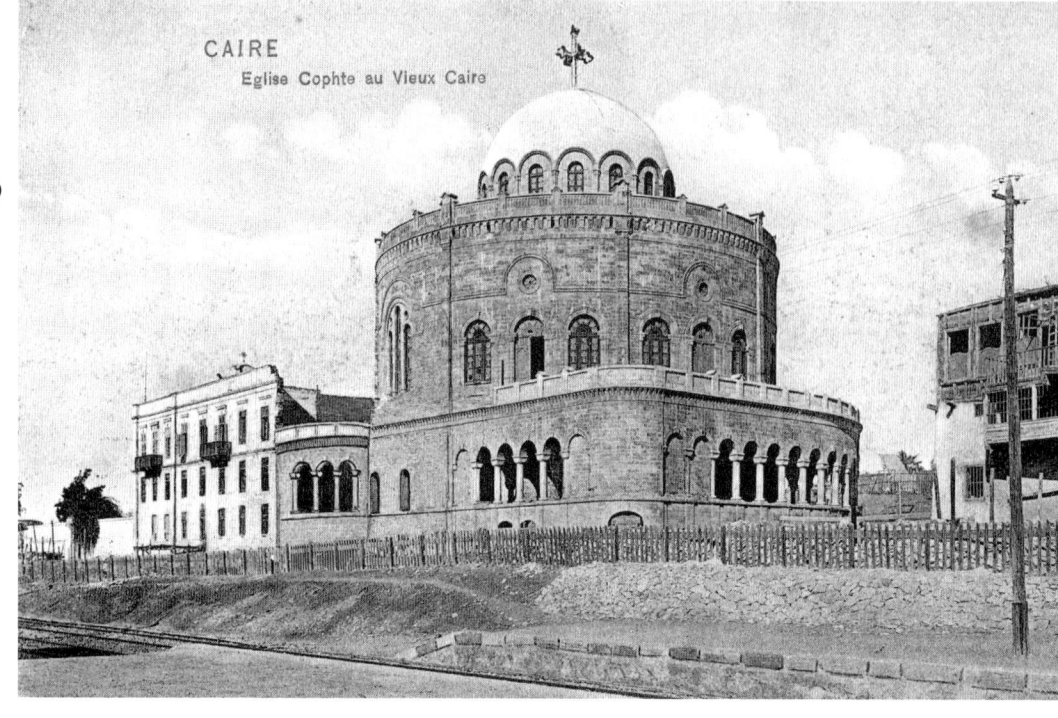

Fig. 5. Greek Church of St. George (Mari Girgis) viewed from the railway in a postcard of c. 1930. Note the incorrect identification as "Coptic Church." Travelers in the Middle East Archive (TIMEA) www.timea.rice.edu.

Old Cairo within the metropolis. It also presents the archaeological evidence for the medieval development of Old Cairo preserved within its churches and buildings, in particular a major phase of restoration and rebuilding in the middle of the thirteenth century and subsequent changes in the more troubled times under Mamluk rule from the fourteenth century onward. The growing attraction of Old Cairo to European pilgrims from around the same time is reflected in the increasing number of travelers' accounts with which we are able to supplement the archaeological evidence. In 1517 Egypt became part of the Ottoman empire, and after the decline in activity that appears to characterize the earlier period of Ottoman rule, we present the evidence for the widespread rebuilding of Old Cairo which took place during the "Coptic Revival" of the eighteenth century under the patronage of the "Sultan of the Copts," Ibrahim al-Gohari.

Chapter 6, "The Re-Making of Old Cairo in the Image of Its Past," begins with the antiquarian rediscovery of Old Cairo at the end of the nineteenth century. The extensive restoration work of the Comité de Conservation des Monuments de l'Art Arabe in Old Cairo from 1897 onward is described, as are the changes carried out by the Greek and Jewish communities of Old Cairo over the course of the first half of the twentieth century. After reviewing the course and effects of the efforts to restore and preserve its monuments over the past hundred years, the book concludes by examining the current condition and considering the future prospects for Old Cairo.

Old Cairo: Topography and Archaeology

Old Cairo is largely defined by the surviving wall Roman fortress of Babylon. This area forms a five-si ure enclosing about five hectares, and in plan approximate a rectangle but for the southwest wall runs at an angle of around thirty degrees to the re enclosure. The northern limits of Old Cairo are al irregular. Here, no part of the north wall of the fort vives above ground, so that the present northern Old Cairo is defined by a more organic arranger medieval and later walls (figs. 3 and 4).

Following the ancient alignment of the River N western wall of the fortress runs in a true north–sout tion, with two great round towers set at a tanger inner face in the southern half of its 190 m length. F southern end of the west wall, the enclosure runs southeast for a little over 100 m. Just under two-t the way along this distance is the imposing South the Roman fortress, flanked by U-shaped towers a mounted by the Coptic Church of the Virgin. This is commonly known as al-Mu'allaqa or the F Church, a name derived from its position suspend the Roman gateway. From the southeast corner fortress a further 190 m of its eastern wall is preserve ground, including traces of five more U-shaped tow northernmost of these is in fact the southern flankin of the former East Gate of the fortress.

The modern entrance to Old Cairo is at the bott flight of stairs about 3 m below the level of Shari' Mari

Fig. 6. Mid-nineteenth-century view by Fairholt of the Greek Church of St. George and the entrance to Old Cairo. © The British Library Board (Ac.2259.f.6).

the modern street running along the western edge of the fortress (figs. 6 and 7). From here Old Cairo is entered through a doorway cut through the wall of the fortress. This entrance was once closed by the massive iron-clad door that now stands permanently open. Behind this door the buildings of Old Cairo lie along several more or less straight lanes, the alignment of which is clearly derived from the larger Roman enclosure. The first of these streets is Harat Dayr Mari Girgis, and 40 m along this on the left is the entrance to the Convent of St. George, from which this lane takes its name.[5] After a further 50 m the lane turns to the right at the façade of an Ottoman *sabil* (public drinking fountain), restored by the Comité in the 1920s but now in a very poor condition and barely recognizable (pl. 5). To the left is the arched doorway to 'Atfat Mari Girgis, a lane that leads after 50 m to the Coptic Church of St. George, its medieval Wedding Hall (Qa'at al-Irsan), and the Tomb of the *mu'allim* Ibrahim al-Gohari, the wealthy Coptic official behind the major rehabilitation of Old Cairo that took place during the eighteenth century. Thirty meters further on is the entrance to the courtyard of the Church of the Holy Virgin (al-'Adra), popularly known as Qasriyat al-Rihan ('the Pot of Basil'). This is a modern copy of the medieval church partially destroyed by fire in 1979 and then demolished in 2000 (pl. 6).

Returning to the *sabil* and turning right, the Harat Dayr Mari Girgis is joined after 10 m on the left by the Harat Sitt Barbara. Harat Dayr Mari Girgis continues southward under

Fig. 7. Modern view of the entrance to Old Cairo from Shari' Mari Girgis. (Peter Sheehan)

another low arch past the façade of the Church of SS. Sergius and Bacchus (Abu Serga) to the point where the lane is blocked by the wall of the Coptic Museum (fig. 8). Another entrance to this church is located 10 m or so further east along Harat Sitt Barbara. The first part of Harat Sitt Barbara runs eastward for 55 m, rising quite sharply as it passes the eastern end of Abu Serga. It then joins a lane running north–south, which also rather confusingly remains part of the same Harat Sitt Barbara. This lane follows the line of a major Roman road, the via praetoria of the Roman

Old Cairo: Topography and Archaeology 9

Fig. 8. Approach to the arched entrance of Harat Abu Serga from the north, taken in 1984. (Michael Mallinson). Courtesy Michael Mallinson.

fortress, leading northward from the South Gate. To the north of the junction between the two parts of the Harat Sitt Barbara is the Church of St. Barbara from which this lane derives its name, while a little to the south and on the same eastern side of the lane is the Ben Ezra Synagogue.

Our recent work has shown that the western wall of the fortress was lapped by the waters of the River Nile, certainly until the construction of the fortress in AD 300 and probably as late as the tenth century.[6] In place of the waters of the Nile, the Roman fortress is now bordered to the west by Shari' Mari Girgis and the modern Metro line. In 1889 the construction of the precursor to the Metro, the Cairo-Helwan Light Railway, fundamentally altered the medieval topography of Old Cairo by isolating the fortress from the area along the Nile. Historic maps reveal that prior to this the two areas were closely connected. Indeed, the line of the main medieval spine road running east–west through the fortress still continues all the way to the river on the other side of the tracks. These maps and the surviving buildings show that this area formed an integral part of Old Cairo from at least the Mamluk period. Its growth and development therefore relate to the movement of the Nile westward from a position adjacent to the fortress wall in Late Roman times.

The late medieval enclosure of Old Cairo is now surrounded on the north and east by cemeteries that have grown around it in the course of the last century. To the north of the fortress is the great congregational, or Friday, mosque of 'Amr ibn al-'As, leader of the Arab army that conquered Egypt in AD 641. Its fame as the first mosque in Egypt and Africa and its importance throughout the history of Cairo make it one of the most significant sites of Muslim Egypt. North of the mosque is a Muslim cemetery, while to the northeast lies the modern slum of 'Izbat Abu Qarn which has grown up over the ruin fields of al-Fustat in recent years. Between the fortress and the mosque, the modern landscape is completed by a bus station, the newly built (2000) Souk al-Fustat, the 1980s USAID-sponsored medical center, and a huge empty area previously occupied by the *fawakhir* or potters of Old Cairo until they were bulldozed off the site in 1998 in preparation for a garden that finally began to be realized in 2005. Some 500 m from the western edge of the fortress is the River Nile, in the form of the smaller eastern channel separating the island of Roda from the east bank (figs. 3 and 4).

The most prominent markers of the ancient landscape of Old Cairo are the two massive round towers of the western wall of the Roman fortress of Babylon. The northern round tower is surmounted by the Orthodox Church of St. George, while the southern tower, cleared of later constructions, lies semi-submerged within the garden of the Coptic Museum. The difference in ground level between the threshold of this tower (17.4 m MSL) and the modern street at the entrance to the Museum (25.45 m) is just over eight meters.[7] However, inside the fortress the difference in levels is not so great, a fact that is already indicated by the steps leading down into the area from the modern street level. The level of the streets inside the western half of Old Cairo, bordered by buildings dating mainly from the eighteenth and nineteenth centuries, is around 21 m. To the east of a line running approximately through the middle of the fortress, the ground rises quite noticeably to the east, and the street level here is around 22.75 m. From these two different street levels, further steps lead down to the floor level of around 20 m within the churches of Abu Serga and St. Barbara. Inside the crypt of Abu Serga, the level of 17.34 m is very similar to that of the threshold of the Late Roman round tower.

These differences in level are the first indicators of an ancient landscape buried beneath Old Cairo. They have been created by archaeological processes that have gradually raised the ground level over time. New brick or stone floors were simply laid over the remains of earlier ones; domestic

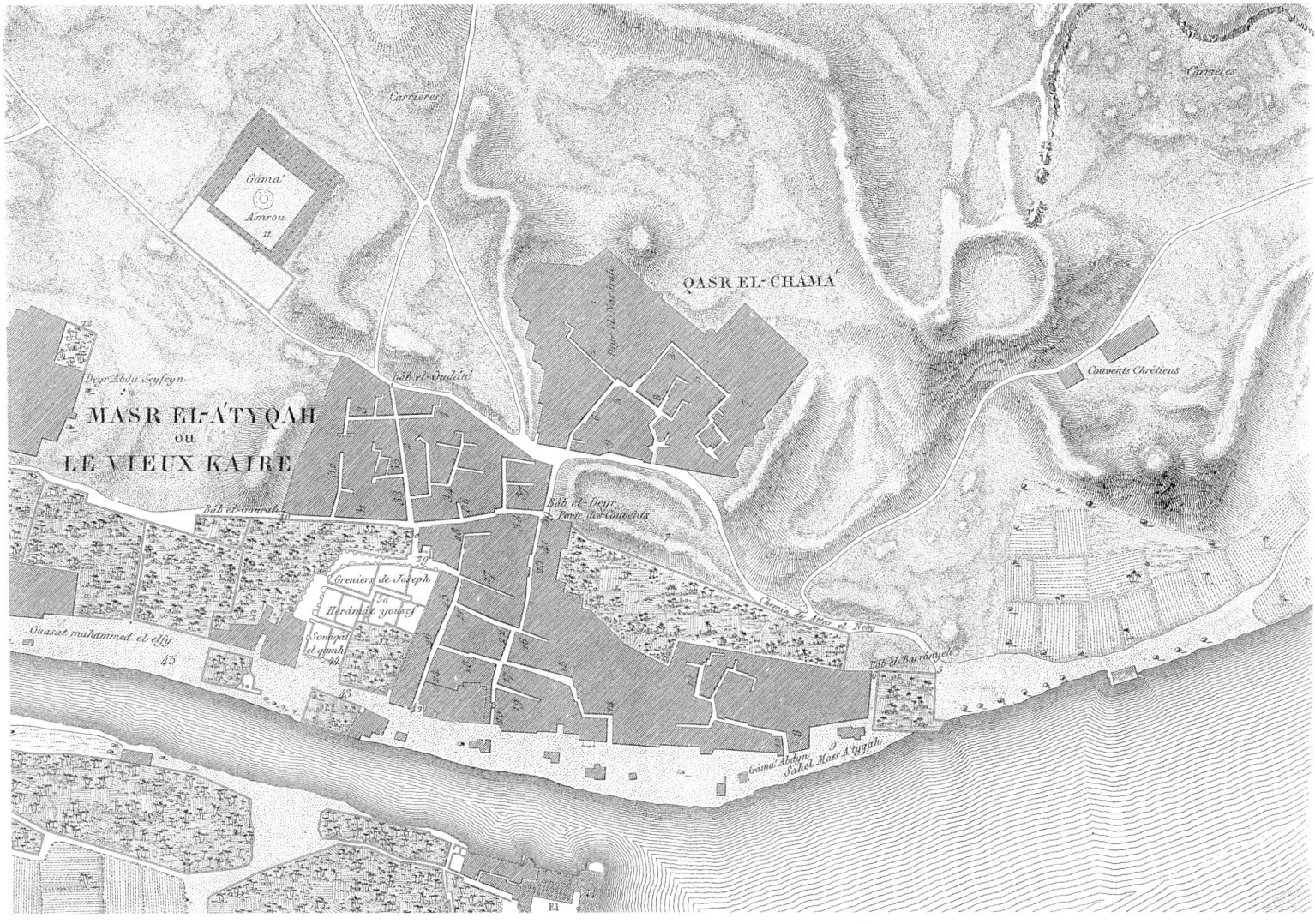

Fig. 9. Early nineteenth-century plan of Old Cairo produced by the surveyors of the *Description de l'Égypte*. Note a number of streets within the fortress that have now disappeared and the main thoroughfare leading west to the river. Courtesy Jose Santos.

rubbish was often not cleared away but flattened or trampled down to form external surfaces, sometimes covered by a *dakka* or layer of brick and stone rubble; buildings were rarely completely removed, often being simply razed to the current ground level and then filled with rubble to form a solid platform for new construction. The floor level inside some of the earlier Roman structures remained unchanged, turning them into basements as the ground level outside rose. These activities have created a series of distinct layers and the careful examination and recording of the sequence of these layers forms the basis of archaeological stratigraphy. In some cases the physical relationships produced by the stratigraphic process have been reversed, where later buildings have been cut down through the accumulated layers and are thus actually at a lower level than earlier structures. The same stratigraphic processes at work in the raising of ground levels can also be seen preserved within changes to the fabric of buildings above and below ground. Thus walls can be thickened or raised in height, and windows and doors cut through walls, only to be then blocked again as occasion demands. All these changes leave their mark in the archaeological record, and the recording and understanding of their sequence provides a relative chronology for the development of a site or a building. The presence of elements within these sequences which can be dated, such as coins, inscriptions, or more commonly pottery with an established chronological typology, then allows us to link certain points of the sequence to an absolute chronology.

Little archaeological work had been carried out in Old Cairo in modern times, and most of the observations discussed here were made during the ARCE/Egyptian Antiquities Project (ARCE/ERP) to monitor the engineering and construction activities of the USAID-funded groundwater lowering project (known as Contract 102) in Old Cairo between 2000 and 2005. These observations have supplemented those made in the area from 1989 onward.[8] The USAID project was designed to provide access to flooded basement levels in a number of historic monuments in Old Cairo affected by the 2 m rise in groundwater levels that has occurred since the late 1970s (pls. 8 and 9). Despite efforts to stem this rise, the crypt of Abu Serga and the lower levels of the Greek Orthodox church, for example, had remained effectively inaccessible for some twenty years. The reasons for the rise in this groundwater level are debated, but its component sources have been identified as the Nile, seepage from the Muqattam escarpment, irrigation, leaking water mains and waste pipes, and water extraction from wells.[9] In any case, since the higher average levels of the Nile following construction of the Aswan High Dam in the 1960s the river is no longer able to act as a drain for accumulated groundwater. The rationale of the ARCE/EAP archaeological monitoring project was to maximize the opportunities for archaeological recording presented by the activities of a large engineering project. It was also envisaged that this work would provide an archaeological evaluation of the site that could simultaneously become the framework for future research and a tool for site management.

Although ostensibly covering the period from the sixth century BC to the twenty-first century AD, the reader will notice a broad division in this book common to many archaeological publications: Old Cairo before the Romans, Old Cairo in the Roman period, and Old Cairo after the Romans. There is at least some practical justification for this, given our definition of Old Cairo as the area within the known limits of the Roman fortress of Babylon. Furthermore, in the cramped and waterlogged excavation conditions pertaining below ground, the distinctive nature and robust construction of the Roman buildings provide a degree of certainty in establishing stratigraphic sequences and relationships with other less clearly differentiated deposits. On the other hand, we have had to be wary of neglecting earlier or later structures that do not perhaps share the "dominating presence" of the large stone fortress buildings.[10]

At almost any time over the past fifteen years or so, the visitor to Old Cairo, wandering through what may often have seemed a succession of building sites, could well be forgiven for wondering why this place could attract visitors in numbers surpassed within Greater Cairo only by the Egyptian Museum and the Giza Plateau. The impressive remains of the Roman fortress discussed later in this book have been largely inaccessible due to high levels of standing water. Information about the fortress and the buildings within it is both scarce and largely inaccurate. The churches and the synagogue have all been at least partly inaccessible for long periods while major programs of restoration or rebuilding were carried out.[11] After restoration some of these buildings seem far removed from the antiquity ascribed to them by guides or guidebooks. In the narrow streets of Old Cairo, many of its Ottoman (and sometimes older) buildings and boundary walls, not defined as monuments and therefore not "protected," have been renovated or removed. During various restoration projects a number of large modern ancillary buildings have sprung up or been extended around the churches. Old Cairo's already somewhat idealized character as a pilgrimage center has been further eroded by the steady enlargement of its tourist bazaar and an increasingly heavy security presence. In 2000, the medieval Church of the Holy Virgin,[12] devastated by fire in 1979, was completely demolished. Work on a copy of the medieval church began shortly afterward, along with the construction of a new church alongside it and a range of new administrative buildings. To the north of the Roman fortress, at the Mosque of 'Amr ibn al-'As, the most recent major restoration involved the replacement of the reused ancient columns of the eastern *iwan* erected at the beginning of the nineteenth century (and therefore one of the parts of the current building with the greatest claim to authenticity). After 2000 the construction turmoil was notably augmented by the USAID-funded project aimed at lowering the groundwater level in a number of selected locations—the Orthodox Church of St. George (Mari Girgis), the Roman tower in the garden of the Coptic Museum, the crypt of Abu Serga Church, the Ben Ezra Synagogue, the Wedding Hall of the Coptic Church of St. George, and the Convent of St. George.

In short, we have seen the definitive end in Old Cairo of a particular historic look and 'feel' which was still both visible and palpable as late as the 1980s. Much of this feeling of antiquity had of course derived from neglect—many areas were still in the same *kharab* or "ruined" state noted on the only detailed cadastral survey of Old Cairo made in the early 1930s. On the other hand, some of the archaeology of the area, or at least the chronology of its walls and buildings relative to each other, was both visible and susceptible to interpretation.

In conservation terms, the explosion in restoration and construction activity since the 1980s has not been kind to Old Cairo. There has been a decline both in the understanding of traditional materials and of the building skills required to utilize them. In their place many of the restoration projects have introduced and institutionalized the application of modern construction technology and standards to the conservation of traditional buildings, and many tons of concrete have been poured and injected into the ground in a bid to overcome the perceived weakness of the "made ground" that has been accumulating as archaeological layers here over the past two thousand years and on which many of the monuments of Old Cairo are founded.

لولا الكسور ما كانت الفاخور

Without breakages there would be no potsherds.
(Egyptian proverb, recorded by J.L. Burckhardt in *Arabic Proverbs*, 1830)

Paradoxically, during a period when so much evidence for the making of Old Cairo has been destroyed or obscured, and the potential for its future conservation and presentation greatly diminished, an enormous volume of archaeological information has been produced and recorded. The geotechnical investigations associated with these restoration projects have provided much of interest for the archaeologist, as has the careful monitoring which was sometimes allowed or otherwise achieved during the demolition of historic structures. ARCE's project to provide archaeological monitoring of the groundwater lowering project recognized the inherent opportunity to record archaeological data on a large scale from locations that had previously been inaccessible to archaeologists (and would be so again after the project) due to the depth of deposits and a high groundwater level. The end of the USAID groundwater lowering project represents the closing of a window onto the archaeology of Old Cairo from which plentiful if more or less chance observations have been made. The scope and extent of this work is outlined below, as is the nature of the evidence upon which many of the themes and much of the chronology are based. The goal of this archaeological evaluation has been to trace the outlines of the sequences of activity on the site. To achieve this, the methodology of the archaeological recording used during the project aimed to break down human and natural activity over time into a series of actions—the archaeological "context." This is achieved by assigning unique numbers either to stratigraphically distinct units (layers, walls, the fills of pits, etc.) or to artificially designated assemblages of material, as for example, in the case of shaft excavation material, collected from various depths below the groundwater level. This definition of contexts as single 'events' or individual units of deposition or truncation is the basis of modern archaeological practice. Where stratigraphic excavation was feasible, the single context recording system widely used in British and European urban archaeology was employed.[13] In this system plans of individual contexts were drawn and a matrix showing the stratigraphic relationships of numbered individual contexts maintained. The locations of all plans (both of buildings and individual contexts) are recorded in terms of national grid coordinates. In this way their true

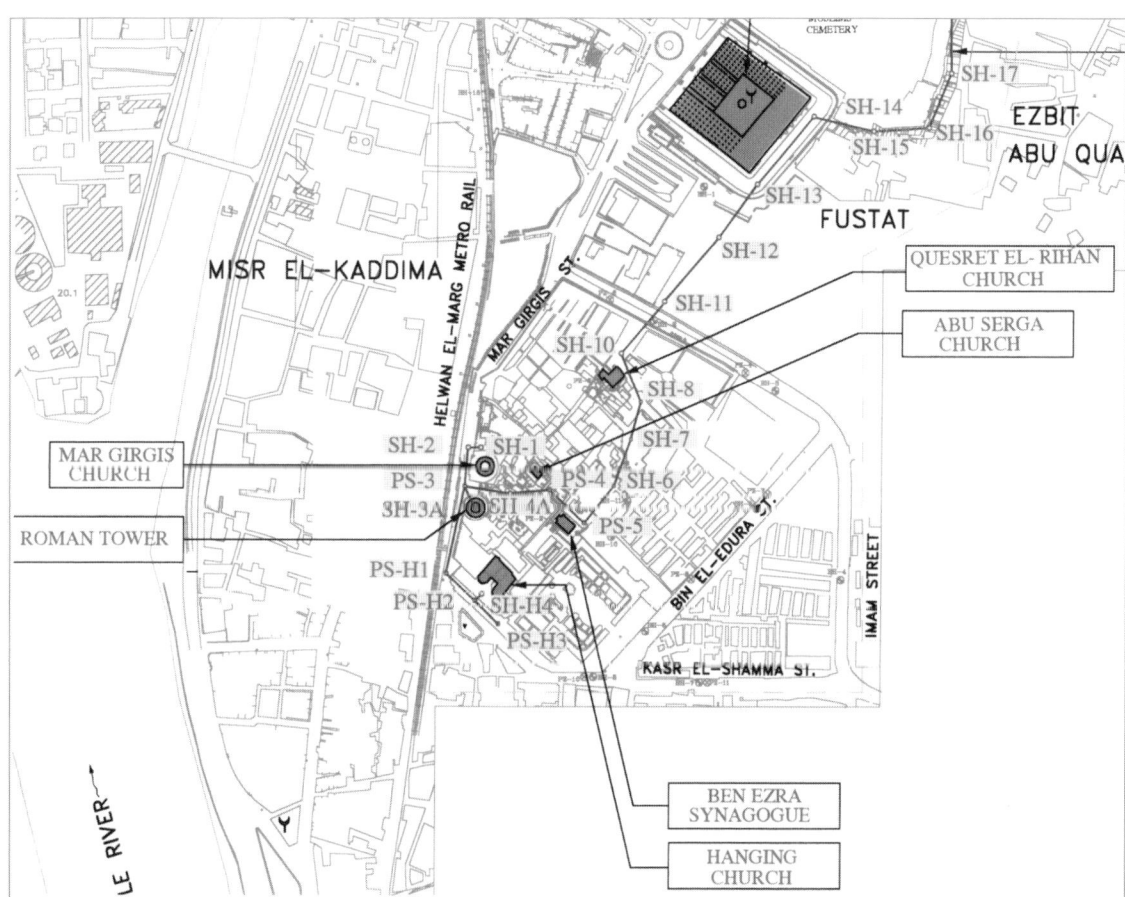

Fig. 10. Plan of the Contract 102 shaft locations by consultants C.C. Johnson & Malhotra (CCJM) in the core area of the project. Those prefixed PS are perforated shafts associated with localized dewatering methods.

Old Cairo: Topography and Archaeology

spatial relationship to known features (and to those discovered in the future) can be demonstrated. Making these links involved a substantial program of architectural survey to allow subsurface features to be linked to above-ground remains and extant buildings. Descriptions and locations of the individual contexts along with details of the various types of finds recovered (primarily ceramics, but also coins, building materials, and so on) are entered into databases to allow them to be linked to the drawn records and to form the digital archive of the project. The archaeological sequences recorded in this way allow us to interpret the way in which the site formation processes have taken place. Addressing the relative and absolute chronology of these processes has involved the creation of a comprehensive pottery type series for Old Cairo based on stratified groups of ceramics from locations throughout the area.

Geotechnical and archaeological evidence for the natural geology, topography, and hydrology of Old Cairo has emphasized how much the natural configuration of the landscape has dictated subsequent site formation. It is also worth noting the organic nature of changes to the built landscape over time and the influence exerted by earlier existing structures or topographical features on later building work. At the beginning of the nineteenth century, the layout of Old Cairo was recorded by surveyors working on the *Description de l'Égypte*, the great scientific project to record the geography and monuments of Egypt that accompanied Bonaparte's expedition between 1798 and 1801. The layout of the buildings inside the fortress has changed little to the present day, and the archaeological work has shown that many of the lines of these plots and properties were determined seventeen hundred years ago by the barracks and buildings laid out within the Roman fortress. In turn, the Late Roman layout responded to the existing topography of a place whose strategic location had already been recognized by the creation of the entrance to the Red Sea Canal and the harbor at its mouth.

The Scope of Works: Archaeological Opportunities and Limitations during Engineering Activities

During the groundwater lowering project in Old Cairo different types of groundworks provided varying levels of opportunity for recording archaeological deposits. All were monitored by the ARCE/EAP project and each produced significant new information on the nature and condition of archaeology on the site.

The initial phase of investigation carried out by the contractor and monitored by the archaeological project consisted of a series of boreholes aimed at assessing geotechnical conditions along the planned route of the groundwater lowering works. The first group comprised around forty eight-inch diameter boreholes sunk to depths of between 10 and 25 m but these were supplemented by others carried out during the project to address more specific local conditions and questions. The borehole records of this project and others carried out in Old Cairo over the past fifteen years total around 180 and represent an invaluable insight into the buried topography (both natural and manmade) of Old Cairo.[14]

The key nodes of the groundwater lowering system are a series of deep collector and conveyance shafts some 3 m in diameter into which the outflow from various drainage systems is directed (fig. 10).

These circular shafts are formed of pre-cast concrete segments forming superimposed rings mounted over a steel cutting edge. As the material is excavated from within the shaft, more rings are added, and the shaft then sinks under its accumulated weight to the desired level. At the base of the shafts a concrete plug is poured after excavation is complete (typically at 10–10.5 m MSL, between 10–15 m below modern ground level). Excavation of the shafts was carried out by machine and by hand. In view of the high groundwater level encountered in almost all the shafts, much of the manual excavation required to remove obstructions below the cutting edge of the shaft was carried out by divers feeling their

Fig. 11. Concrete blocks loaded onto one side of shaft 11 to make it sink straight. The mosque of 'Amr ibn al-'As is in the background. (Peter Sheehan)

way around in the almost total darkness of the muddy water filling the shaft. The shaft locations were dictated from the outset by the planned route of the conveyor micro-tunnels that link the shafts, the physical limits and constraints of the site, and the need to allow access from above to the micro-tunnel drilling head in the event of it becoming stuck. This occurred on several occasions, necessitating extra shafts to be sunk to recover the machine. Of course these extra shafts produced more archaeology, sometimes spectacularly so. Total destruction of archaeological deposits and structures within all the shafts was, however, predicated from the outset.[15] Archaeological excavation above groundwater level was carried out in advance at a number of these shafts, while the rest were monitored throughout the course of their excavation by machine. In all cases, archaeological material below groundwater level was recovered in artificially designated groups or "bands" differentiated by elevation above sea level.[16] Apart from ceramic material and other finds, almost all of these shafts encountered significant evidence of Roman or medieval structures or both. Pre-Roman finds largely consisted of ceramics, with the spectacular exception of part of an Eighteenth Dynasty royal stele of Thutmoses III discovered ten meters below ground level in a shaft at the southern end of Shari' Mari Girgis. Like all the excavated material from the shafts, the stele came to the surface covered in mud and was only recognized days later during the usual cleaning of more promising lumps of stone rubble set to one side during the actual excavation. Thirteen of the shafts are located either inside or in the immediate vicinity of the fortress, with a further sixteen conveyor shafts to the north (the Fawakhir, 'Izbat Abu Qarn, and Shari' Fustat areas) linking drainage from the core area of the dewatering project (the Roman fortress) to the existing main collector shaft north of the junction between Shari' Fustat and Shari' Salah Salim. The shafts are connected horizontally by 600 mm pipes laid in machine-dug microtunnels. These were generally excavated at elevations of between 12–13.5 m MSL, with the excavated material brought the intervening 10–12 m to the surface and made available for examination in powder form.[17] In a number of areas within the fortress, lowering of the groundwater was achieved by a system of pile-driven sand and gravel filter 'walls,' about 0.8 m wide and 10 m deep. Archaeological deposits on the line of these were destroyed, and material encountered during drilling for the piles came to the surface as slurry. Nevertheless, voids and obstructions encountered during this drilling provided additional topographical information on the location of cisterns or other buried structures filled only with loose material.

The most readily comprehensible archaeological information was recorded during manual excavation for the installation of about 350 linear meters of perforated drains. These perforated drains are enclosed in a gravel filter to ensure that the water flowing through is clean and free of material that could block the system. To allow for future cleaning, the perforated drains are accessible via manholes that also allow changes of direction in leading the water away from the affected monuments and into the collector shafts. Since the pipe trenches were usually less than one meter wide, the larger square areas (usually 2 x 2 m) excavated for the manholes often provided the widest archaeological context in which the excavated deposits could be better understood. Because these systems need to be installed under dry conditions, temporary dewatering using an array of shallow wells allowed archaeological recording to take place below the groundwater level. The opportunities for archaeological recording were significantly reduced when temporary dewatering was achieved merely by means of surface pumping, which allowed excavation albeit in a knee-deep mud bath. To avoid collapse, braced wooden planks supporting the trench sides were driven downward as the excavation proceeded. Apart from occasional vertical planks omitted to leave an archaeological 'window' or avoid an obstacle, there was therefore little opportunity to view the sequence of archaeological deposits in section. Consequently, the plan record of features and deposits encountered in the trenches and manholes remains of paramount importance, supplemented by frequent

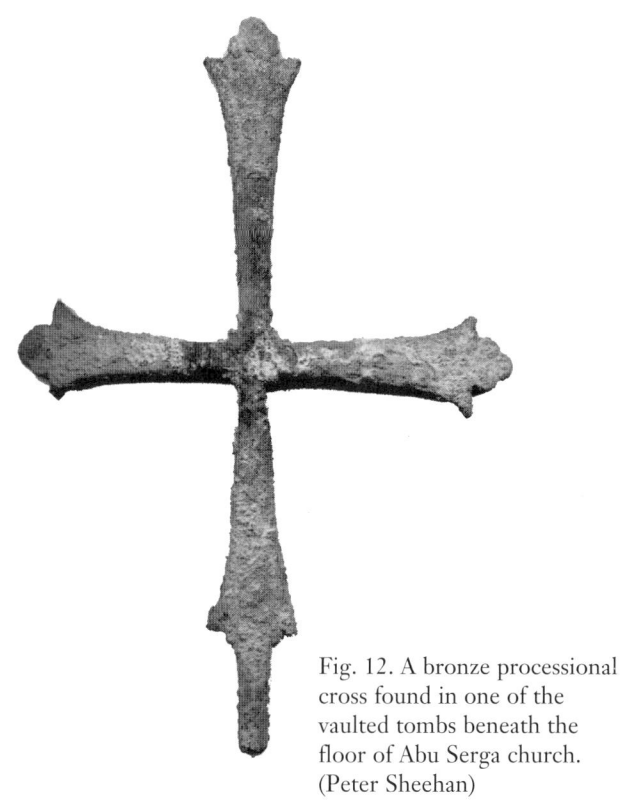

Fig. 12. A bronze processional cross found in one of the vaulted tombs beneath the floor of Abu Serga church. (Peter Sheehan)

recording of levels and digital photography of the maximum 50 cm exposed by each excavation stage before the planks were driven down once more.[18] Since the sequence of deposits in these trenches could be excavated archaeologically, a version of the single context recording system was employed, even if some of the contexts inevitably represented arbitrary amalgamations of complex deposits based more on depth than on an observable sequence. The identification and recording of individual contexts allows the stratigraphic succession of groups of deposits to be tabulated and the relationship of groups that are not stratigraphically linked to be inferred from their composition and contents.

Constraints on the quality of archaeological information obtained during monitoring work need to be borne in mind. On a practical level this was affected by everyday factors such as the presence and depth of ground water, safety and accessibility issues, and the technical considerations of the groundworks program. In examining the nature of the archaeological evidence we also had to consider broader issues such as which types of artifact and ecofact are preserved (and which are not) by the physical and chemical properties of the buried landscape of Old Cairo, as well as the difficulties of 'sampling' given the constraints on what material could be collected under the various conditions and types of operation associated with the project.

In general, however, a high level of cooperation between the archaeological monitoring project and all the elements of the construction team—from geotechnical consultants to the divers removing obstructions by hand from beneath the cutting edge of the caisson shafts—yielded a wide range of useful data.

The sequence of work during the project allowed for a gradual familiarization with the subsurface topography and the nature of the archaeological deposits on the site. In 2000 the geotechnical survey provided a brief introduction to the archaeological deposits through their entire sequence and over the whole project area. In the same year the excavation of shafts began and these first impressions began to be writ large. The divers' descriptions of massive stone walls below the water level in Shafts 2 and 3 in Shari' Mari Girgis revealed the nature of Roman structures along the contemporary bank of the Nile. A prime example of the impressive stone walls forming the internal layout of the Diocletianic fortress appeared early (2.5 m below ground level, around 20.7 m MSL) in Shaft 5 and had to be removed piecemeal as the shaft proceeded downward (pl. 14). Stratigraphic excavation of the first four meters of Shaft 4 confirmed our expectations that the medieval and post-medieval archaeology of Old Cairo would be complex and subject to repeated truncation by later activity. The same processes of medieval accretion and change, this time within a single building, were seen and briefly recorded during the demolition of the Church of Qasriyat al-Rihan at the end of the year.

Excavation of shafts continued into 2001, when these and the first perforated drains combined to focus attention clearly on the Roman fortress built by Diocletian. The drains installed to the east of the Ben Ezra Synagogue passed through a series of well-preserved barrack blocks built against the inner face of the fortress wall. The reuse and subsequent abandonment of these structures in the first centuries following the Arab Conquest was amply demonstrated, as was the truncation of later medieval deposits by the activities of the Jewish community in the early twentieth century. Most importantly, excavation was continued to a depth that showed that these barracks cut through extant occupational layers, the topmost of which were Early Roman and Hellenistic in date. These deposits and the ceramic material subsequently recovered from a number of deeper shaft excavations allowed us to propose an occupational sequence for the site of Babylon going back to the Late Period Twenty-sixth Dynasty, 664–525 BC. Later in 2001, attention shifted to the southern round tower in the garden of the Coptic Museum (pl. 24). Monitoring during installation of the perforated pipe network revealed the formidable engineering of the massive tower, thirty meters in diameter. Further stratigraphic evidence for its Late Roman date was recovered during sinking of a shaft in the center of the tower. This demonstrated that the tower was constructed on a rubble raft (containing redeposited Late Period material presumably taken from the existing settlement) in the river. Apart from recording details of the structure and its industrial reuse in the early medieval period, the archaeological team also supervised the careful dismantling and reinstatement of the concentric stone circles forming the tower to enable the pipes to pass through these walls and to enhance the future presentation of the tower.[19]

Having experienced at first hand the massive foundations of the southern tower, work in 2002 on its northern twin beneath the twentieth-century superstructure of the Orthodox Church of St. George might have been expected to provide more of the same. Instead a huge range of new archaeological information came to light. Firstly, dewatering and removal of garbage in the area north of the church revealed, in plan and over a wide area, a series of barrack structures excavated by the Greek community in the 1940s and identical to those previously reconstructed on paper from the small sections visible in the trenches and manholes east of the Ben Ezra Synagogue. Recording and surveying these structures and the Roman, medieval, and modern elements of the massive church complex was a major undertaking. Later in the year a key element in the ancient landscape of Old Cairo was discovered inside the tower. Unlike its southern counterpart, the northern tower is built over an earlier massive stone wall more than 6 m wide. The rounded southern end of what we named at the time "the river wall" followed the same curve as the later tower. However, as the tower curves round to the west to complete its circle, the earlier wall continues in a straight line toward the northeast. In the same year, perforated drain work in the north of the fortress around the Wedding Hall of the Coptic Church of St. George revealed a sequence of structures from the early medieval period through to the nineteenth century. The same work indicated well-preserved buildings of the Roman fortress around the eastern end of the Church of St. George, although Late Roman features around the Wedding Hall itself were notably absent.

The extension of the project into 2003 and 2004 enabled detailed recording to accompany the installation of the groundwater lowering system within the church and crypt of SS Sergius and Bacchus (Abu Serga), located approximately in the center of the existing part of the Roman fortress of Babylon. This is a building of great significance on account of both its great antiquity and its central importance in the history of the Coptic Church. It receives particular veneration as one of the locations at which the Holy Family is believed to have stayed during the Flight into Egypt. It is also a building of intense archaeological complexity and interest, and the recent work in the church has thrown a great deal of light on its history and architectural development. Work at Abu Serga Church also provided at least partial answers to the important questions concerning the development of the churches of Old Cairo and the topography of the area itself. The crypt and the eastern end of the church were seen to overlie a huge wall 6.5 m wide running north to south, composed of large limestone blocks (pl. 15). Only now could the full significance of the earlier discovery of the identical "river wall" beneath the Church of St. George be seen. These massive walls are the stone revetments on the east and west sides of the 40 m-wide entrance to the Amnis Traianus or Canal of Trajan, dug around AD 110 to link the Nile with the Red Sea.

Inside Abu Serga Church, excavation for perforated drains also indicated the existence of an earlier large colonnaded basilica in a slightly different position on the site. One of the most important archaeological conclusions of the recent work is that the crypt was built at the same time as the form of the present church took shape, probably in the first half of the eleventh century around AD 1050. Within the main church, a complex subterranean arrangement of vaulted tombs was also constructed as an integral part of the church at this time. The preparation of these tombs may be connected with the historically recorded shift of the patriarchate from Alexandria to Old Cairo in the mid-eleventh century.[20] At any rate, a number of finds of exceptional quality, including a bronze cross which would have been mounted on a staff, and a silver signet ring with an inset precious stone, pointed to an ecclesiastical identity (fig. 12).

Archaeological information and the evidence of remains of datable wall paintings recently revealed in the southern sanctuary have now indicated that much, if not all, of the church above ground was rebuilt in the early thirteenth century AD (pls. 16 and 17). From the early fourteenth century onward the church appears to have entered an extended period of decline, a picture reflected in historical descriptions from this period of anti-Christian riots and church closures. The fortunes of the churches of Old Cairo revived around the end of the seventeenth century and a large program of works, particularly at the eastern end of the church and in the southern aisle, can be dated to this period. Archaeological and historical evidence combine to show that the crypt was also extensively remodeled at this time.

At the end of 2004 and during the first half of 2005, work at the Convent of St. George uncovered a complex and well-preserved sequence of medieval buildings notable for the sophisticated systems of water supply and drainage still in place (pl. 10). This work provided the first indications of the nature and layout of the Roman buildings and streets in this area of the fortress. In the same period shafts and tunneling work designed to link the drainage of the South Gate and the Hanging Church into the wider Contract 102 system provided a vivid view of the Roman riverfront with a stepped quayside and lion-headed mooring posts. It also produced more detail of the reclamation, during the Diocletianic phase, of land that had previously been under water as well as the construction of high-quality buildings in front of the South Gate, which occurred during the first centuries after the Arab Conquest. In June 2005, investigations in advance of a proposed building for the Jewish community north of the Ben Ezra Synagogue provided a further example of the continuity and reuse of Roman buildings into the early medieval period.

Outside the core area of the project represented by the fortress walls, we also gained new information relating to the wider landscape of Old Cairo. In 2002, work to relieve groundwater and sewerage problems at Abu Sayfayn Monastery, located to the east of the Mosque of 'Amr, provided some close parallels and a somewhat wider context for the medieval and post-medieval church buildings in Old Cairo, as well as indicating the location of the early medieval cemetery of the monastery. In 2003 and 2004,

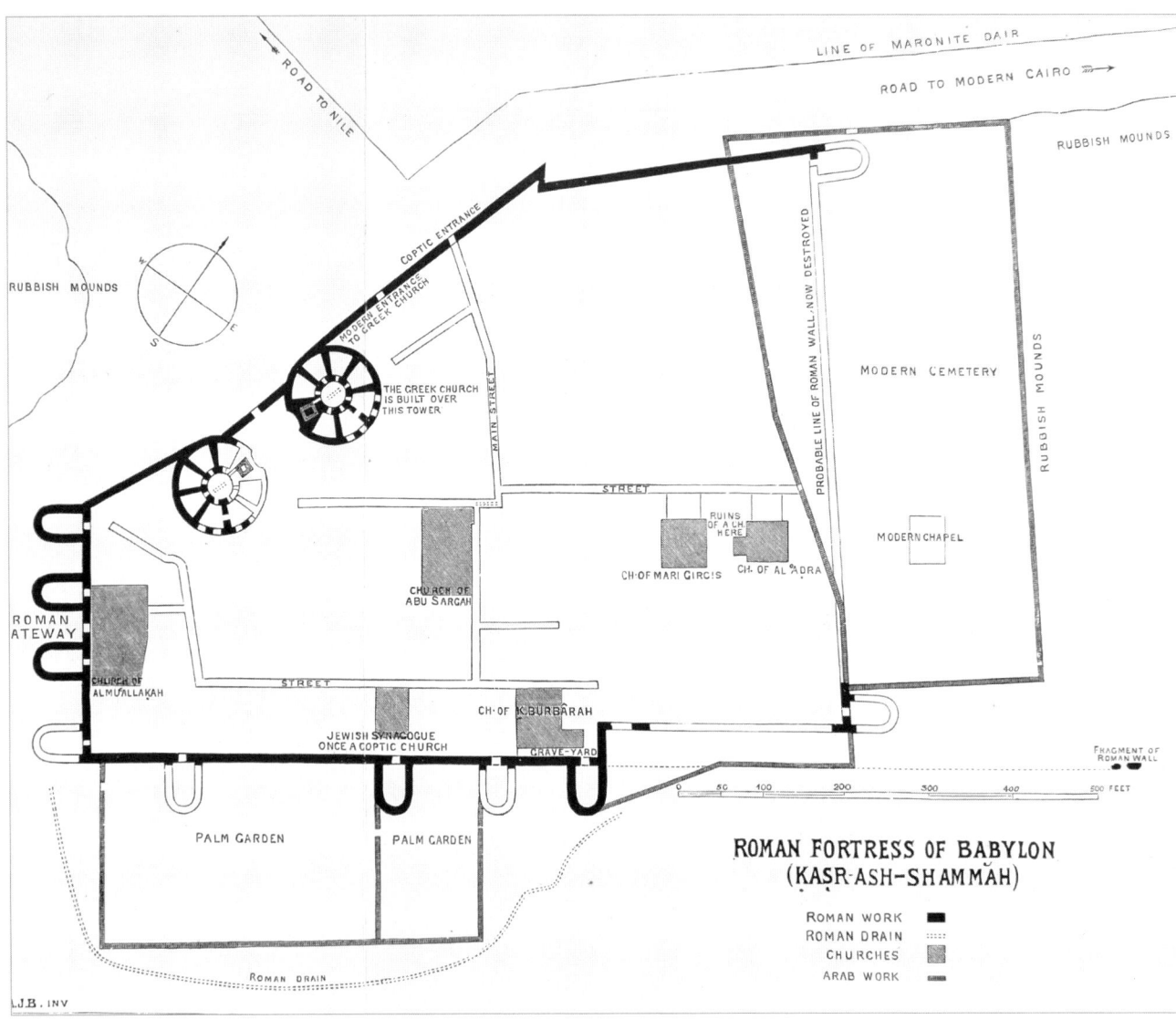

Fig. 13. Alfred Butler's 1884 plan of Old Cairo and the Roman fortress.

work on the Shari' Fustat shafts and microtunnels revealed deep-cut features related to the water supply of this central part of al-Fustat, buried beneath high mounds of medieval and modern debris.

Toward an Archaeological Model of Old Cairo

In modern archaeological work the process of evaluation seeks to define the nature and extent (both horizontally and vertically) of the archaeological resources on a site. Typically, this approach supplements historical and topographical material with limited investigative work (boreholes, trial trenches, etc). Since the aim is to assess the nature and extent of an unknown element (the archaeology), it follows that these initial investigations are by necessity somewhat random.[21] The diverse locations and types of data potentially available from monitoring a large-scale undertaking such as the groundwater lowering project in Old Cairo therefore essentially fitted the terms of just such an archaeological evaluation.[22]

The sum of archaeological knowledge available at the beginning of this project was small. Although maps showing Old Cairo and its environs began to appear from the seventeenth century onward, the first detailed and accurate plan of the area was made by the French surveyors of Napoleon's expedition at the beginning of the nineteenth century. Toward the end of the same century, when the medieval topography of the area and the architectural development of the unrestored churches was still relatively clear, independent antiquarian accounts like Alfred Butler's *Ancient Coptic Churches*, published in 1884, contained investigations of the extent of the fortress and detailed descriptions of the churches within it (fig. 13). From 1896, the growth of antiquarian interest in the area prompted the Comité to begin a long program of recording and restoring the monuments of Old Cairo. Important figures in this period were the Austrian Max Herz Bey and the Italian Ugo Monneret de Villard, both of whom were sadly prevented from completing their work by the outbreak of the First and Second World Wars respectively. Monneret de Villard in particular carried out extensive archaeological and historical investigations into various aspects of Old Cairo, and published the results of these in a number of scholarly books and articles.

Until very recently the fortress had been ascribed to the emperor Trajan largely on the basis of the description in the seventh-century chronicle of John, Bishop of Nikiu, translated from an Ethiopic version of the lost Coptic original for the first time in the early years of the twentieth century.[23] This identification was repeated by a number of articles in the 1930s, although it is worth noting that even by that time Monneret de Villard believed the fortress displayed a number of characteristic Late Roman features.[24] In the early 1990s we presented archaeological evidence and parallels to demonstrate that the fortress falls firmly within the canon of Late Roman military architecture and that its construction should be dated to the period around the end of the third century AD.[25] A similar confusion concerning foundation dates still pertains for the churches of Old Cairo. A mixture of historical information and art historical criteria has caused modern authors to differ widely in their suggested dates for these churches, in the process often underestimating the archaeological complexity of the buildings and the fact that they have undergone extensive change.[26]

The archaeological evaluation provides a broad model of the processes of site formation, which can be refined by more detailed observations, targeted excavation, and research in the future, perhaps unencumbered by the constraints of a particular construction project. The elements of an archaeological model of Old Cairo include the establishment of broad levels of activity (expressed in terms of elevation MSL). These levels may represent historical 'periods' or cultural 'horizons,' as well as episodes of either activity or disuse. Since our analysis indicates that the canal continued in use into the Late Roman period, for example, we should not expect to find structures from this period in the center of the fortress between the two great parallel walls of the canal. This theory is borne out by the archaeology, for early medieval deposits and structures (including the churches of Abu Serga and until recently Qasriyat al-Rihan) are the first *in situ* features found within the line of the filled-in canal. The deposits here are also notably more fluid and sludgy than elsewhere in the fortress. Below 17 m MSL, the composition of these deposits and the material found in them shows that they are the superimposed layers of silt and sand that eventually filled the canal. Late Roman and earlier archaeological material recovered from these deposits must have fallen or been dumped into the former watercourse. East of Abu Serga and the canal we have learned to expect the survival of up to two and a half meters of standing Roman walls above a ground level at 18.5 m MSL. Below this there is a Ptolemaic horizon at around 17 m, while the evidence of the ceramic material recovered from deep shafts indicates Persian period occupation layers starting at around 15.8 m MSL.

Other themes begin to appear when we consider the archaeological evidence from different parts of the site. Within the Roman buildings there is clear evidence of reuse and then abandonment in the period between the seventh and tenth centuries. The seventh and eighth century building boom which created al-Fustat appears in Old Cairo too, as does the abandonment of its buildings in the mid-eighth century and again at the end of the early medieval period around 1050. Unlike much of al-Fustat, however, the archaeology of Old Cairo shows activity in the time of the Bahri Mamluks and a major revival of the whole area in the eighteenth century, when the Ottoman ground level over most of the area within the fortress walls was uniformly around 21 m MSL.

How broad is this model and what are the criteria for the information that has been used in its formation? Obviously the significance of groups of material arbitrarily collected by depth becomes more significant when the number and spatial location of these samples allows us to infer patterns of deposition. Put more simply, one deep hole in the ground may not be either very revealing or conclusive, but twenty or thirty spread over an area will be. The same is true of reconstructing building layouts from fragments of structures, although in Old Cairo we have been assisted in this by the usual Roman penchant for straight lines. In pursuing the outline of this archaeological model, a wider spread of information allows us to extrapolate from particular areas to others not investigated in the same way or at the same level. Thus, for example, the detailed knowledge of the architecture of the Late Roman fortress gained during the installation of perforated drains in the two large Roman towers and the 'barracks' to the east of the Ben Ezra Synagogue can probably be applied to other areas so far indicated only from our increased knowledge of the plan of the fortress. Similarly, a consistent picture of post-Roman transformation at these locations, supplemented by information from work around the Wedding Hall and observations within a number of the shafts, provides a convincing model for the later processes of archaeological deposit formation at work over the site.

Enough data has been gathered to characterize the geology and topography of the natural landscape lying far below modern ground level. This is dominated by the outline and contours of the edge of the limestone terrace below Old Cairo, with bands of thick alluvial clay to the west intersected by long-buried water channels. This enables us to reconstruct a picture of the natural landscape upon which later changes and developments were played out. The data also gives new insights into the fundamental role of the River Nile in the formation and rhythms of the landscape and their relationship to human activities.

Related to this is another theme that can now be considered more seriously in the light of new data: the evidence for the existence and nature of the site of Babylon before the Roman period. Ceramics and other finds from deep shaft excavations have been supplemented by stratified deposits and structures recorded east of the Ben Ezra Synagogue, and previous isolated finds from the area of Old Cairo can now be considered in the wider context of landscape archaeology.

Some of the most important archaeological information provided by our recent work in Old Cairo relates to the evidence for the appearance of the Roman riverside. This work has gone a long way toward locating historically well-attested and substantial features, such as the ancient harbor of Babylon and the mouth and course of the Canal of Trajan, whose existence is not in question but whose actual location has remained obscure until now. The huge stone embankment walls recorded in the basement of the Greek Orthodox Church of St. George and in the crypt of the Church of Abu Serga allow the forty-meter-wide channel between them to be identified as the entrance to the Amnis Traianus, the canal dug by Trajan at the beginning of the second century AD to link Rome and the Mediterranean via the Nile to the Red Sea and the markets of the East. The location of the mouth of the canal here cemented the strategic and economic significance of Old Cairo from the second century AD onward and can perhaps be considered a defining moment in the history of Cairo. The existence of transport and trade links with the East contributed to the Arab conquerors' preference for this location for the new capital of al-Fustat over the Mediterranean-oriented Alexandria in 641. We can now begin to see more clearly the circumstances surrounding the foundation of the canal and how it functioned, as well as its heritage and later transformation in the early medieval period into al-Khalig al-Misri, one of the most significant topographical features of the later Arab city.

Around AD 300 emperor Diocletian enclosed the mouth of the canal within the powerful fortress that now largely defines the area of Old Cairo. The layout and character of this Late Roman fortress of Babylon is another field of study that has been greatly informed by recent work. Since the fortress of Diocletian essentially created the topography of Old Cairo from which much of the modern street plan and many of the later medieval buildings derived, information on the Roman layout clearly assists our understanding of its later transformation of the fortress into a Christian and Jewish enclave, and the processes by which the existing Roman buildings were adapted for re-use by these communities.

The groundwater lowering project for the monuments of Old Cairo has provided detailed information on both the origins and the development over time of several of its churches. It seems possible to extrapolate the development of individual churches to consider that of the group as a whole. In considering the continuity of Old Cairo as a sacred site and the longevity of significance associated with a particular location, it is worth noting that at least three of the churches (Abu Serga, the Hanging Church, and the Orthodox Church of St. George) display structural elements that go back at least as far as the Early Roman period. Detailed archaeological work in these buildings has made it possible to draw important conclusions regarding the development of the group and the area as a whole.

Other important themes have been clarified by the archaeological information obtained during recent work: the destruction caused during the Abbasid conquest of Egypt in 750; the abandonment of large parts of the wider area of al-Fustat and Old Cairo during the crises of the eleventh century; the declining economic fortunes of Old Cairo from the fourteenth century; the changes wrought by the "Coptic Revival" of the eighteenth century. Also very much present in the archaeological record is the subsequent decline of Old Cairo throughout the nineteenth century, its "rediscovery" at the end of the nineteenth century, and the subsequent history of restoration and then transformation into an object of cultural heritage. All of these themes are dealt with in the chapters relating to the chronological development of Old Cairo.

Archaeologically, this whole is greater than the sum of its individual parts, and evidence from the unbroken sequence preserved within the walls of the Roman fortress has enabled us to take a major step toward understanding the story of this ancient nucleus of the city of Cairo.

Part 1
The Making of Babylon

Chapter 1

The Ancient Landscape of Cairo

On one side is the Nile and on the other the mountain.
—al-Muqaddasi, writing in 985[1]

Introduction

This succinct medieval description of the east bank landscape of the city of Cairo indicates the elemental forces that have shaped the development of the city. In fact, the wider landscape of Cairo has been formed within the last ten thousand years by the movements of the Nile channel within far more ancient geological formations defining the edges of its valley. These natural formations and the shifting course and rhythms of the Nile have dictated the human relationship to the landscape and shaped the impact of this relationship.[2] The scale of these natural and human forces has meant that it is not a static landscape, but one constantly subject to subtle but relentless change. Indeed, parts of this landscape have been totally transformed several times over, and these changes or their effects can sometimes be detected in the archaeological record.

The strategic importance of modern Cairo and its ancient antecedents is derived from its position at the head of the Nile Valley, at the point where the river changes from the single stream which flows through Upper Egypt and the Nile Valley into the many channels and canals that make their way through the Delta to the sea. Although the exact location of the Delta head was not constant and moved north over time, the point at which this change occurs has always represented the fundamental division between Upper and Lower Egypt. The same natural formations of river and valley have also produced other conditions of strategic value—the confluence of important east–west land routes entering the valley through the wadis of the Muqattam hills and skirting the edges of the Delta—which in the summer months of the Nile flood would become practically impassable on foot.[3] The strategic and political advantages of this location have been recognized and made use of from the time of the foundation of Memphis as the first capital of a unified Upper and Lower Egypt in the Early Dynastic Period (fig. 1).[4]

Archaeological evidence for the human relationship to this landscape survives in a variety of forms. The changing location of settlements and cemeteries can be tracked to show the movements of the river over time. Geoarchaeological information from boreholes and other archaeological observations can characterize and identify the different layers and levels within this changing landscape. Certain limitations are, however, inherent in the data. For example, there is no evidence from those parts of archaeological sites that have been destroyed by changes in the alluvial landscape when the Nile has shifted its course to flow through formerly settled areas. Archaeological and geotechnical evidence aside, our understanding of how this landscape appeared at various times is also helped by the descriptions of ancient and medieval authors. Historical maps, satellite images, and the study of toponyms can also aid in reconstructing the extent of both change and continuity.

The alluvial environment of the Nile provided for both the subsistence and transportation of ancient societies living within its valley. It also influenced the nature of the physical and biological environment in which the archaeological evidence of these societies is buried and preserved.[5] In subtle ways the landscape itself can be seen as an artifact of human activity. The dumping of rubbish into the river, for example, appears both in historical accounts and in the archaeological record,[6] and the embankments and formations created by this dumping affected both the flow of the river and the pattern of its flooding. Control of the landscape for military and economic reasons (cultivation, trade, taxation) has left many prominent markers, while culturally the landscape has been integrated into the religious, mythological, and ceremonial aspects of the societies living within it.[7]

Geological Background

The growth of both planned and informal urban settlement in Old Cairo, particularly over the past twenty years, seems at first glance to have rendered the ancient landscape unrecognizable (pls. 1, 3, and 4).[8] Many of the elements of the ancient landscape have indeed been obscured or destroyed, but geoarchaeological information obtained through borehole surveys and deep shaft excavations allows us to trace its salient features. They also show how distinct the modern topography of Old Cairo is from the ancient landscape buried beneath.

Cairo lies at the end of the Nile Valley, formed five and a half million years ago by the uplifting of a far older limestone formation. Here the steep limestone cliffs fringing the eastern edge of the valley of the Nile in its course through Upper Egypt open out toward the northeast and the river divides into its Delta branches to flow to the sea through a vast alluvial fan 144 kilometers long and 193 kilometers wide. The archaeological 'making' of Old Cairo has occurred over the course of less than three thousand years, but on a geological timescale the great changes that this has involved are dwarfed by vast, largely unseen but literally world-changing stages in the geological formation of the landscape. These processes are now reduced to the natural features, the Muqattam hills and the River Nile, which form the physical backdrop to Cairo. The geology of Old Cairo, therefore, is the baseline from which the archaeological sequence begins.

The great mass of the rock formation forming the natural edge of the present Nile Valley, visible to the east of Cairo as the Muqattam range, was formed during the Eocene Epoch, 56–34 million years ago. These sedimentary rocks formed after a great subsidence of this area had caused the sea to move far to the south, where it remained for 25 million years. The Nile Valley results from the creation of a deep canyon extending for 2500 meters below the level of the present valley floor, which formed in the Late Miocene Epoch (11.6–5.3 million years ago) when tectonic movements caused the land to rise and the level of the Mediterranean to fall and almost empty through a major evaporation known as the Messinian Salinity Crisis following its isolation from the Atlantic.[9] The area of Cairo, located at the junction of this canyon and the sea, marks the northernmost point of this Late Miocene uplift, while the Nile Delta represents a huge area of this sea that gradually filled with alluvium brought down by the river.[10] The initial path of the deep channel forming the present Nile Valley was determined by tectonic movements. The valley was then eroded in the Eocene rock by a huge river, known as the Eonile, which flowed from 6 to 5.4 million years before the present (BP) and was fed by a number of large lateral channels. At the beginning of the ensuing Pliocene Epoch from 5.4–3.3 million BP the reflooding of the Mediterranean by the waters of the Atlantic turned this great chasm into a marine gulf (Cairo lies at the head of this gulf). Between 3.3–1.8 million BP this gulf or estuary filled with sands and gravels brought down from the eroding plateaus by lateral streams and by the Paleonile that flowed from the south. For a million years at the end of the Pliocene severe aridity in the region ended the flow of the Nile entirely. During the ensuing Pleistocene Epoch a vigorous flow known as the Prenile from 800–400,000 BP made the present course of the Nile channel in the Pliocene sediments, forming a series of gravel terraces (still visible in Upper Egypt) as it eroded its way downward. This was succeeded to the end of the Pleistocene by the intermittent flow of the Neonile from 400,000–12,500 BP. By the end of the geologically very recent Pleistocene, evidence exists for enormous differences in the levels of the river and the Mediterranean Sea from those of today. Sea level, for example, was some 43 meters lower and the coastline of Egypt extended a further 8–10 km to the north, while the Nile in the vicinity of Cairo was 33 m lower than its present level.[11] A large sea-level rise occurred in the early Holocene, and the modern Nile started to flow around the same time (around 12,500 BC), although it was only during the second half of the Holocene that it began to deposit the layer of fertile and cultivable Nile mud up to 9 m thick that prompted the Greek writer Herodotus to describe Egypt as the "gift of the Nile."[12]

Recent boreholes in Old Cairo provide a valuable indication of the geological processes at work in the formation of Old Cairo. The top of a 10m deep layer of sand beginning at around 10–12 m MSL indicates the edge of a Holocene Nile channel running over deep clay deposits against the steeply sloping limestone terrace edge eroded through the Eocene Muqattam formation by the Eonile from 6–5.4 million BP.

The survival of this Holocene channel within the clay beds provided a natural precursor that allowed the shifting of the entrance to the Red Sea Canal to Babylon in the Roman period, where the junction of the Nile and the canal could be combined with the strategic advantages of a location at a natural crossing point and the conflux of a number of land routes passing through the ravines of the Muqattam to Sinai and Palestine.

The Nile at Cairo

The days of the flood turn Egypt into a lake.
—al-Muqaddasi[13]

Given the depth of the geological formations outlined above, it is not surprising that geotechnical investigations associated with recent projects in Old Cairo have largely penetrated only the upper end of this vast process of landscape formation. They are useful, however, in providing further detail and new insights into the formation of this part of the Nile Valley. Along with evidence from the deep shaft excavations, the sum of the individual sequences recorded in these boreholes also allows a crucial link to be made between the archaeology and the 'natural' landscape of the site.

One of the most significant results obtained from these boreholes is that they have allowed us to identify and plot the contours of the Muqattam limestone formation as it descends in a series of shallow terraces from the east. One of these terrace edges lies between the 10–12 m MSL contour and runs more or less north–south through the center of the area now enclosed by the walls of the Roman fortress. Beneath the eastern part of the Roman fortress there is a terrace of limestone bedrock around ten or twelve meters below modern ground level. West of this terrace edge the underlying rock falls away sharply. A similar profile for the edge of this terrace is indicated by boreholes to the north of the fortress.[14] We know from other locations in the Nile Valley that the 0.75 km-wide channel of the river has a tendency to flow along the eastern edge of the valley, which is on average 10 km wide. Evidence from the boreholes in Old Cairo indicates that the edge of this limestone terrace (at 10–12 m MSL) represents the position of a paleo-channel formed as the Nile entered a period of bed erosion in the Late Pleistocene.

The Holocene floodplain of the Nile at Cairo is composed of stiff clay beds between 0.5–5.5 m deep, through which the river flowed in sandy channels that "interfinger laterally with silts and clays due to floodwaters that spill over the banks seasonally."[15] Below the clay beds are

Fig. 14. Nineteenth-century view (Lehnert and Landrock) of the Pyramids taken during the Nile inundation, showing how the flood waters sometimes extended as far west as the edge of the Giza plateau. © Lehnert and Landrock.

interbedded fluid sands (quicksands), fine above and coarse below, from which water for the city was drawn via wells in the past. Even the more conservative estimates of the rate of deposition would suggest that these beds are a geologically very recent feature probably dating back not more than five thousand years. As the clay beds deepened, the river would have flowed through them in sandy channels, adding to the banks on either side with every inundation. The beds are the mudflats left by the channels after the inundation, from which the water would gradually drain or evaporate. The floodplain thus created is convex in profile, formed by sediment overflowing the natural levees that mark the low water channel banks and which are a few meters higher than the seasonally inundated plain. The thickness of the clay deposits is variable, a local factor that either relates to already existing depressions below them or is the effect of different strengths of current and the creation of backwaters, as well as their distance from the Nile. Depressions in the surface of the clay beds would later become temporary lakes that would be filled during the inundation and would then gradually drain away through the rest of the year. Almost all of these lakes have now been buried beneath the modern city, but the names and general location of most of them are well established from various medieval texts. The distinctive trunk-like shape of the Birkat al-Fil (Lake of the Elephant), for example, was a familiar element of the topography of Cairo until the nineteenth century (fig. 2).[16]

Boreholes showing deep deposits of sand within these clay beds can thus be taken to indicate the position of former channels. Above the clay beds, the borehole logs show a variable but sometimes substantial layer of 'fill' or 'made ground.' These latter deposits constitute the archaeology of the city.

Environmental change provides a plausible explanation for the eastward shifting of the Nile channel and the consequent changes in settlement patterns. The deposition of the clay beds may be linked to a decrease in flood height and river volume, caused around five thousand years ago by a pronounced dessication that is recorded in the level of lake volumes in East Africa and the Sahara, as well as the greater absorption of the overflow from these lakes in the swamps that had formed in the Sudd basin in southern Sudan during the preceding wet period between 12,000–5000 BP.[17]

The consequent reduction in the volume of water in the Nile may have accentuated the natural tendency of the channel to follow the eastern edge of the valley. The arid period following the First Dynasty presumably also reduced the westward pressure on the Nile channel previously exerted by the Wadi Digla and the Wadi Hof (particularly the former) to the south of Old Cairo. At the same time, the constantly rising level of the riverbed may have elevated it above the gravel deposits laid by these wadis on the east bank, which had previously also impeded its flow and forced it to the west.

Before this the landscape of Cairo was characterized by a Nile channel that was more powerful and larger in plan form and which tended to hug the eastern edge of the valley, where its course is shaped by the contours of the bedrock.[18] To the south of Old Cairo this eastward tendency was counteracted by the inflow of water and the deposition of gravels from the Wadi Digla and the Wadi Hof, which combined to force the main channel westward. The higher flow rate also suggests the head of the Delta lay further to the south and that downstream of this point it divided into many channels or distributaries.[19] The course of one of these channels during this long wet period may be reflected in the deep sand deposits found beneath the clay beds in Cairo. At the end of the early Holocene the dynamics of the Nile's course changed. South of Old Cairo the decreased rate of flow of the river, as well as the reduced influx of water and gravel (and therefore westward pressure) from the wadis caused the main channel to shift to the east, while the configuration of the bedrock when it reached Old Cairo in turn forced it westward. This has remained the pattern ever since, with only the actual position of the main channels affected by natural and human changes in the environment.

The boreholes in Old Cairo suggest that the edge of the 10–12 m MSL limestone terrace may mark two major geological features. First, it is the edge of the early Pleistocene floodplain, at which time the Nile contained much more water but flowed at a lower absolute elevation. This is marked by massively thick (20 m+) deposits of clay, the top of which lie at around modern sea level. It is also the position of the early Holocene Nile channel described above. The existence of this channel is posited on direct geotechnical evidence from the boreholes, supplemented by other archaeological observations.[20] The course of the Holocene channel is indicated in the borehole logs by a 10 m-deep bed of sand, the top of which is found at around 11 m MSL.[21] This sandy layer is found directly against the edge of the limestone terrace, passing over the top of the deeper impermeable clay beds of the Pleistocene floodplain.[22] Its western edge is not well defined, although a single borehole on the present Nile Corniche in Old Cairo showed only fill and no sand above 22 m of silty clay between 11 m and minus 11 m MSL. Such a result may reflect the Holocene incision of the river into the floodplain as a result of heavy floods and the increased permanent flow that occurred in this period.

The course of the channel through Cairo is indicated by a number of sources. Bowden Smith's research in the 1920s indicated that the clay beds did not extend all the way to the edge of the Muqattam in the area of the city, while in the flat plain to the north he noted evidence for a sand-filled channel near the line of the state railway between 'Ayn Shams and al-Khanka.[23] Other ostensibly later features in the topography of the city may also indicate the course of the paleo-channel.[24] The identification of the canal known as the Bahr al-Libeini as the former main stream of the Nile, for example, has led to the suggestion that at the beginning of the fourth millennium BC the position of the eastern branch of the Nile north of the contemporary Delta apex can be approximated by projecting the line of what was later to become the Canal of Trajan southwest toward a junction with the Bahr al-Libeini.[25]

Immediately south of Old Cairo the buried limestone terrace forms the lower edge of the promontory variously known as al-Rasad, Istabl 'Antar, or Kom Ghurab. From here the borehole evidence indicates this terrace edge continues northward on a line running approximately through the middle of the fortress of Babylon, at least as far as the Mosque of 'Amr.[26] To the northeast of this point the limestone starts to rise toward the limestone outcrop of Gebel Yashkur, where the limit of the ancient floodplain once more swings out to the east following the edge of the limestone formation. In terms of the modern topography the edge of this formation therefore appears to run just to the east of the Mosque of Zayn al-'Abidin and to the west of rocky hill known today as Qal'at al-Kabsh.

Since the construction of the Aswan dams, and particularly the completion of the High Dam in the early 1970s, it has been harder to appreciate the central position occupied by the Nile flood in all aspects of life in Egypt from at least the third millennium BC.[27] Cultivation, settlement, and civilization in the Nile Valley and Delta alike owed their existence to the seasonal rise of the river and the inundation of the low-lying land around it. Fortunately the detailed accounts of travelers from the nineteenth century and supplementary evidence from ancient and medieval authors allow us to visualize the cycles in the life of the river and to regain some of this lost intimacy with its rhythms.

Man's relationship to the river created a sharp distinction between cultivated and inhabited land.[28] Both needed to be drawn from a finite supply of land, so there was no space for isolated farms and houses outside of settlements. The latter had to be located on natural or artificial rises or levees so as to be above all but the highest of floods. Cultivated land near the river was above the level reached by the inundation, partly as a result of manuring and other cultivation methods that gradually increased the height of these areas, but also because this land was intensively watered by artificial means to produce more than one crop, unlike fields more distant from the flood, which would have been watered just once at the time of the inundation via irrigation canals leading from the river bank. Analyses of the Roman-period Nilometer at Elephantine and more recent geoarchaeological observations indicate that both the bed of the river and the general level of the valley floor have risen by an average 13 cm per century, although clearly this has not been a constant accretion but one affected by environmental and local factors.[29]

Each year when the river, fed by monsoon rains over Ethiopia, began to rise in the middle of June (around the time of the summer solstice), the irrigation canals were cleaned out and then closed with an earth dam. They were opened only when the Nile was nearly at its height around the end of September (around the autumnal equinox).[30] High Niles could be as disastrous as low ones on account of the destruction they wrought, and plague too was sometimes a consequence of a high Nile flooding inhabited areas and not draining away rapidly enough. From the end of September the level of the river would fall, reaching about half the amount of its initial rise by the end of December and then more gradually for the following six months. As soon as the river began to fall the canals were closed again so that the water of the inundation was retained and not allowed to drain off too quickly.[31]

Geoarchaeological research into the history of the Nile flood combined with textual evidence from ancient Egypt has indicated that disastrously low floods occurred around 2200 BC. It has been argued that this 4.2-kiloyear aridification event and the consequent ecological results may have played a role in the end of the Old Kingdom and the upheavals of the First Intermediate Period, just as they may have contributed to the fall of the Akkadian Empire in Mesopotamia and the Umm an-Nar civilization in Arabia.[32] Climatic conditions during the Middle and New Kingdoms appear to have been generally wetter than those in modern times, and it has been suggested that high Niles may have contributed to the social disorder associated with the Second Intermediate Period (1700–1550 BC).[33] Wetter conditions persisted until around 1150 BC, when low Niles and droughts again coincided with a period of great instability toward the end of the New Kingdom. Thereafter the Nile flood assumed the pattern recorded in the modern period, although more exceptionally high floods appear to have occurred in the ninth to seventh centuries BC, the fifth century BC, the first centuries AD, the period AD 600–1000 (especially the early years of the ninth century), and in the seventeenth century AD. These indications are clearly significant when we consider the archaeological evidence for patterns or periods of settlement in the low-lying alluvial land such as that occupied by Old Cairo and the Roman fortress.

The size and power of the river has the potential to fluctuate widely, and as a consequence, the course of its main stream has not been constant. Recent research indicates it may move laterally at rates of up to nine kilometers every thousand years.[34] The huge quantity of suspended matter in the water of the river, particularly during the flood, meant that any changes to the course had profound consequences for the patterns of deposition of this material. Much of the river's load would sink to the bottom, so the level of the river in absolute terms has risen steadily, changing and obscuring its former relationships with earlier landscapes. The river has also responded to riverside settlement. Changes to the stream have been caused by dumping in the river or intensive use of the riverbank at a particular point. The formation and changing shape of islands has been another significant indicator of movement in the Nile channel.[35] Texts and historical maps show, for example, how successive changes in the course of the Nile channel from the thirteenth century first turned the medieval port area of Bulaq, originally on the west bank, into an island and then moved it to the east bank of the river.[36] From historical documents and archaeological observations we can try to fix changes in the course of the Nile stream in relation to surviving buildings (some of which can be closely dated) like the Roman fortress (AD 300), the monasteries of Abu Sayfayn and Abu Mina, and the Nilometer at the southern tip of the island of Roda (AD 751).

Major shifts of the main Nile channel and the location of the apex of the Nile, where it divides into its Delta branches to flow through the alluvium fan to the sea, have occurred since the medieval period. For ancient times other major shifts can be reconstructed from archaeological and geotechnical evidence (pl. 20). The effects of these changes on the topography of the ancient city of Memphis, nine kilometers southeast of Old Cairo on the west bank of the Nile, provide a useful comparison and a wider context for the situation in Old Cairo.[37] At the end of the fourth millennium BC, during the Early Dynastic period, the main Nile channel probably followed the course of the canal known today as the Bahr al-Libeini, which now flows along the western edge of the modern Nile floodplain at the edge of the Giza plateau. The Early Dynastic settlement of Memphis along the river lay close to the royal tombs of North Saqqara. By the end of the Third Dynasty, the settlement and tombs were abandoned (this area of tombs was not reused until the Hellenistic period), and the river had begun to cut a channel further to the east. Although Early Dynastic cemeteries survive from Saqqara in the south to Gebel al-Nahya in the north, little evidence of the related Early Dynastic or Old Kingdom settlements has ever been found *in situ*, which suggests that they may have lain on the eastern side of the ancient river course and were swept away as the river moved eastward.[38] It has been proposed that the line of the Ismailiya Canal (largely a reworking of Trajan's Canal, see Chapter 2) should be projected southwest to give the apex of the Nile Delta at the beginning of the fourth millennium. Thus the later line of the canal reflects the easternmost branch of the Delta in the early fourth millennium in the same way as the Bahr al-Libeini does for the main channel south of the apex.[39]

Changes to the riverine environment and the course of the main channel caused by lower flood levels and reduced rainfall may have been factors in the spread of the Old Kingdom settlements which have been noted between 12–15 m MSL at Giza, Abu Rawash, Ausim, and beyond into the western Delta.[40] These appear to be single-phase settlements, with no link to earlier occupation, and were possibly related to the huge pyramid and temple building programs taking place at the edge of the limestone plateau. Significantly, they do not continue to be occupied beyond the end of the Old Kingdom, by which time the Bahr al-Libeini course had dried up as the main channel of the river shifted eastward, although it may have continued for some time after as a minor channel.[41] It is also significant that the practical and ceremonial possibilities of the Bahr al-Libeini and the lakes fed by it were exploited only during the late Third and early Fourth Dynasties. Subsequently, building and cultivation took place on land reclaimed as the channel shifted to the east. This movement can be detected in the archaeological record. By the Ramesside period (1279–1213 BC) we know from the evidence of the new temple and palace complexes laid out at Memphis on virgin soil that the river had moved substantially to the east.[42]

New Kingdom (c. 1567–1085 BC) activity around Heliopolis in the northeast of the Greater Cairo area gives a further indication of the changes that had occurred in the landscape since the end of the Old Kingdom. Texts and archaeological investigations indicate that New Kingdom Heliopolis lay at the edge of the floodplain, on the end of a promontory projecting westward along the edge of the 16 m contour into the valley.[43] Most of the city is raised on a mound or tell between 17–20 m MSL. This is similar to the general threshold level (18 m MSL) found throughout Ramesside Memphis.[44] Heliopolis and the contemporary settlement at Tell al-Yahudiya both follow the edge of the floodplain and are located where a spur of the higher ground above the reach of the Nile flood comes down to the edge of the floodplain. From here the edge of the same floodplain continues to Bilbeis and into the Wadi Tumilat.

By the New Kingdom a number of intriguing questions regarding the relationship of settlement to the course of the Nile channels present themselves. Was Ramesside Heliopolis, for example, located on the easternmost delta branch of the river, with contemporary Memphis on the west bank of the main channel? Or does textual evidence indicate that Ramesside Heliopolis was not at that time on the Pelusiac branch of the Nile that defined the eastern edge of the Delta, but rather lay on the *Jtj* Canal, a feature that began north of Old Cairo, coinciding partly with the line of Trajan's Canal and partly with that of the modern Tewfikiyya Canal before rejoining the Pelusiac branch of the Nile at Tell al-Yahudiya?[45] Like Old Cairo, Heliopolis is situated at the edge of the higher limestone terrace forming the edge of the floodplain, so in either case the canal or channel on which it stood probably also reflected the remains of the earlier Holocene channel following the limestone terraces that form the edge of the valley. The indications we have for the nature and use of the Ramesside landscape in Cairo suggest that some settlement could have existed at the mouth of the *Jtj* Canal, but notwithstanding the fragment of a stele from the reign of Tuthmosis III from Shaft HC1, no stratified material was noted during our recent work to identify Old Cairo with such a settlement.[46] The possible location of this ancient channel/canal has also been indicated by boreholes carried out along the railway (now the Metro) line.[47] During the New Kingdom it may have functioned as a way of irrigating the large natural bay between Heliopolis and Siriaqus, which became known later as the Birkat al-Hagg.[48]

The locations of the Ramesside towns at the very edge of the eastern Delta, together with the evidence from Memphis, appear to confirm the ecological indications of a wetter landscape after 1800 BC. Given that the abandonment of Early Dynastic Memphis coincided with a decrease in the level of the average flood, the effects on settlement patterns of environmental change and consequent alterations to the position and flood level of the Nile should not be underestimated. As we have seen, it has been argued that drought and a series of exceptionally low Niles contributed to the end of the Old Kingdom and ushered in the First Intermediate period (c. 2181–2050 BC). It is also significant in this context that, following this, the Middle Kingdom rulers based themselves in Upper Egypt at Thebes. Only from the New Kingdom do we find the apex of the Delta once again the scene of large-scale settlement and activity. Much of this seems to have been based on the re-establishment of links to the north and east for the purpose of trade and military expeditions. The landscape of Cairo played an important part in land routes to the Red Sea, with a caravan route from Heliopolis and others from Gebel Ahmar through the Darb al-Hamra and the Darb al-Tuwara.[49]

Like Heliopolis, Old Cairo is situated where a spur of higher ground projects into the floodplain, in close proximity to a large natural bay eminently suited to large-scale irrigation (the seasonal lake known as the Birkat al-Habash in the medieval period now within the area of Dar al-Salam). The area of the Roman fortress has, however, produced almost no archaeological material earlier than the Late Period. Significantly, this Late Period material appears to lie at a lower absolute elevation than the chronologically earlier Ramesside remains at Heliopolis and Memphis. The remains noted to the south of Old Cairo at Athar al-Nabi appear to date from the Late Period and the Ptolemaic-Roman period, notwithstanding the *ex situ* find of a monumental statue of the New Kingdom king Merenptah.[50] We may conclude that in the second millennium BC the wetter prevailing conditions meant that the future Babylon lay within the floodplain or perhaps even within a still functioning paleo-channel. Only with the lower floods from the beginning of the first millennium BC did it become feasible to settle there.[51] A wider reoccupation of the Cairo area during the Late Period is implied by inscriptions, found on the West Bank around Ausim, indicating building activity.[52]

The Earliest Settlements on the East Bank at Cairo

The archaeological evidence noted during the groundwater lowering project clearly indicates the existence of a settlement predating the Roman period. This settlement was probably founded during the Saite or Persian periods in the seventh or sixth century BC. None of the ceramic material recovered from the shafts excavated to the natural rock in the eastern part of the fortress area appears to be earlier in date than the Third Intermediate Period (1085–664 BC), and the nature of this material suggests a settlement with extensive trading contacts throughout the Levant and the Aegean. To provide a context for this settlement it may be useful to consider what else we know of the other components of the ancient landscape of Cairo. This landscape has been heavily obscured and increasingly modified by the presence of modern Cairo, but archaeological observations and consideration of ancient Egyptian geographical and historical texts allow a broad picture of some of its most significant elements to be drawn.

The presence of Predynastic and Early Dynastic activity in the area covered by modern Cairo is attested to by material of the Maadi-Buto culture found at Maadi in the south of the modern city. The evidence consists principally of cemeteries associated with this culture located on the edge of the alluvial plain at Heliopolis in the north, and Wadi Digla, Turah, and 'Omari (Helwan) in the south of the modern city.[53] Settlement at Heliopolis probably continued throughout the dynastic period too, since at least from the Twelfth Dynasty we know it was the beginning of the land route to Suez (along the line of the old railway to Suez).[54] This land route reflects one of the important reasons behind the location of the first settlements in the wadis connecting the valley with routes through the Eastern Desert. Recent finds from Giza confirm, however, that activity was not confined to the East Bank.[55] The location and elevation of the Maadi settlement on the north side of Wadi Digla (40 m MSL) and burial sites (30 m MSL) have been interpreted as pointing to a higher level of inundation and a moister climate in the Predynastic period. These first settlements and cemeteries are clearly also related to the courses of major and at least seasonally active wadis, leading into the valley.[56] It is significant that the two major later centers of occupation at Memphis and Heliopolis are situated on or opposite east bank wadis giving access to land routes across the Eastern Desert.

The Early Dynastic cemeteries on the west bank at Abu Rawash and North Saqqara are located on plateaus overlooking the cultivation. At Helwan and Maadi the Early Dynastic cemeteries are significantly lower than nearby Predynastic counterparts. The earliest of the dynastic cemeteries are the southern group, in which the Helwan tombs face across the valley to Saqqara, Abusir, and Abu Ghurab.[57] All these are on the edge of the agriculturally viable land, perhaps located to give the highest profile as seen from the adjacent valley floor and to be accessible from it.[58]

After the unification of Egypt, the first capital of dynastic Egypt was founded on the West Bank at Memphis around 3100 BC. Similarly, on the east bank, the prehistoric origins of On (Heliopolis) are reflected in its later mythological identification as the *benben* or primeval mound.[59] The importance of Heliopolis as one of the foremost cult centers of ancient Egypt probably contributed to the identification of the whole east bank as far south as the area facing Memphis as part of the city. For the southern "suburbs" of Heliopolis we know of the existence of a temple to Hathor related to the ancient quarries of Gebel Ahmar.[60]

The tremendous symbolic significance of the junction between the Nile Valley and the Delta was recognized and celebrated by the ancient Egyptians. The area was called *Kher-Aha*, "the battlefield," and was identified as the site of the mythical battle between Horus and Seth, perhaps a reflection of real battles between the peoples of Upper and Lower Egypt in the Predynastic period, such as those shown on the Narmer Palette. New Kingdom texts clearly identify Kher-Aha as the site of an important necropolis, and archaeological finds continue to confirm this use into the Late Period. These finds include the large fragment of a stele from the tomb of P'a-di-Pep, a high official of the Twenty-sixth Dynasty (664–525 BC), found in 2000 reused in the arch of the medieval city gate of Bab al-Barqiya with its text turned inward.[61] The stele contains lists of the gods of Heliopolis and Kher-Aha and religious festivals, confirming the funerary aspect of Kher-Aha but also indicating that it formed a related but distinct part of the wider cultic landscape of Heliopolis.[62]

Kher-Aha has long been identified with Old Cairo.[63] Since no firm evidence of a New Kingdom settlement has been noted at Old Cairo it may, however, be that the term Kher-Aha refers rather to the whole east bank area of cemeteries south of Heliopolis. The southernmost district of Heliopolis is referred to as Per-Hapi, a term that suggests the existence of a temple or cult center of the river god. Per-Hapi was first identified with the "temple" and statues discovered in the 1930s at Athar al-Nabi, two kilometers south of Old Cairo.[64] A more southerly location for Per-Hapi was subsequently proposed on the basis of the extent of the necropolis of Kher-Aha shown by work at 'Izbat al-Walda and Wadi Hof.[65] In addition, there are mythical texts from the *Book of the Dead* and the walls of the Chamber of the Nile in the temple of Edfu that center around the idea of a 'hidden' source of the Nile flood for Lower Egypt to match that of the island of Biggeh at the First Cataract in Upper Egypt.[66] Since the mythical Lower Egyptian source of the Nile was identified in these texts as being located at the beginning of the necropolis, the cult center of the god immanent in the flood, Hapi, may have been located at modern Helwan. This mythical Lower Egyptian source, the "Great Chamber" in which the river god Hapi stays hidden until the time of the flood, may have been the incorporation into myth of the natural springs of Helwan.[67] The proximity of Helwan and Memphis means that the Nilometer of Memphis described by Strabo at the end of the first century BC can then plausibly be located on either side of the river in the area of Helwan.[68]

As at Memphis there is no surviving Early Dynastic or Old Kingdom settlement known from Old Cairo. An "extraordinary spread" of Old Kingdom settlements has, however, been noted on the west bank and in the western Delta, leading to the suggestion that the continuous settlement on the original east bank from the Archaic period into the early Old Kingdom was "eradicated by the eastward drift of the Nile bed throughout historical times."[69]

The New Kingdom (1567–1085 BC) is represented in the archaeological record of the Cairo area only by isolated finds of *ex situ* sculpture, but the texts of these and others of the same period are of some value to our reconstruction of the ancient landscape of Old Cairo. A stele of Year 8 of

Fig. 15. Part of a stele of Tuthmosis III found 10 m below modern ground level in Shaft HC 1, apparently reused in the foundations of the Roman fortress. (Tim Loveless)

the reign of Rameses II found at Manshiet al-Sadr informs us that "(Ramesses) was promenading in the Desert of On, south of the Temple of Re, north of the Temple of the Ennead and in front of the Temple of Hathor, Mistress of the Red Mountain."[70] An association between Hathor and the whole area of the Gebel Muqattam is further suggested by the lunette of a royal stele dating from the reign of Tuthmosis III (1475–1425 BC) found in 2004 at a depth of 10 m below Shari' Mari Girgis during the excavation of shaft HC1 of the groundwater lowering project (fig. 15). In this stele the king makes wine offerings to Hathor. Although only the right edge of the cartouche is preserved, the prenomen shows that the king is Tuthmosis III, an identification supported by stylistic details of the carving on the stele. The label to the goddess reads, "She gives to you stability, power, and life, the desert, the Mistress of the Red Mountain, Lady of Heaven, Mistress of the Two Lands," while the text of the stele may contain a unique depiction of the Red Mountain itself, the small outcrop of red sandstone still known as Gebel Ahmar that rises above the generally white Muqattam formation to the southeast of Heliopolis and that was heavily exploited by Tuthmosis III.[71]

South of the Roman fortress at Athar al-Nabi, a Nineteenth Dynasty statue of Merenptah was discovered near the edge of the railway embankment in 1929.[72] The kneeling figure of the king holds a *naos* (a small box-like shrine), inside which is a figure of Re-Horus. At the time, the find was taken to represent the presence here of a sun temple in which Atum, originally the chief god of Heliopolis, was equated with Re-Horus. This putative temple was also linked with the "Temple of the Ennead" (Per Pesezet) mentioned in the Piankhi (Piye) stele of the Twenty-fifth Dynasty. Forty years earlier Professor W. Golénischeff had visited the same spot and seen a red sandstone sphinx with the cartouche of the Twenty-sixth Dynasty king Amasis II.[73] The combination of Golénischeff's description of the location of the sphinx and Hamza's photograph of the naos and other large decorated stones together suggest they derived from a building at the foot of the limestone cliffs below the massive nineteenth-century fort of Istabl 'Antar.

In the early 1990s the al-Fustat inspectorate of the Supreme Council for Antiquities (SCA), under the direction of Ibrahim Abdel-Rahman, recovered several inscribed blocks in this area.[74] These sculptured relief blocks appear to be of Ptolemaic or Roman date and to have come from an *in situ* building south of the Monastery of Dayr al-Malak (the Archangel Michael). The monastery and these earlier buildings are located near the head of the Bani Wa'il canal, which fed the large seasonal lake known as the Birkat al-Habash in the medieval period. The archaeological evidence recovered by the SCA suggests, however, that the origins of both the canal and the lake should be sought at a much earlier period.

Fragments of inscribed sculpture discovered at a number of sites suggest that the religious center of Heliopolis continued to be maintained into the Saite period, until its reported destruction by the Persian king Cambyses in 525 BC. Even then the destruction does not seem to have been total, for the early Ptolemies continued to build here. It would appear therefore that the total desolation and abandonment of the city described by the Greek geographer Strabo in 25 BC could only have occurred during the two hundred years preceding his visit. The decline of Heliopolis and the falling river levels on the east bank may both have contributed to the foundation of a settlement at Old Cairo during the Saite period. The discovery of the burial of a Saite "Governor of the Fortress" and "Chieftain of Heka-'Adj" (the Heliopolitan nome) among the Batn al-Baqara tombs to the east of Old Cairo might be taken to support such a view.[75]

The funerary aspect of the landscape at the eastern limits of Old Cairo was shown during the 1930s, when a number of these Late Period shaft tombs were noted during quarrying in the Batn al-Baqara area to the east of the Roman fortress.[76] The area immediately to the north and east of this quarry is now the Kharafa al-Kubra or the great cemetery, which is known to have been in use from the early Islamic period. The Late Period tombs may suggest that the origins of this vast cemetery are much more ancient.[77] Mention of the necropolis of Kher-Aha in the New Kingdom versions of the *Book of the Dead* appear to place its origins at a remote date, and it is worth noting that one at least of the 'Ayn al-Sira tombs noted in the 1930s was ascribed to the Old Kingdom.[78] A number of *Book of the Dead* texts are accompanied by schematic drawings of the mountain landscape of Kher-Aha.[79]

The Archaeology of the Ancient Landscape at Old Cairo

And one thing I shall tell of, which few of those who go in ships to Egypt have observed, and it is this:—into Egypt from all parts of Hellas and also from Phoenicia are brought twice every year earthenware jars full of wine

(Herodotus, *Histories* III. 6.)

Archaeological finds indicate that the existence of an ancient Nile stream at the edge of the limestone terrace influenced the location of the earliest settlement of the site and its later development. The earliest datable finds suggest that the beginnings of this settlement should be sought at some time in the Third Intermediate Period (late eleventh to mid-seventh century BC). Although the exact date of this first settlement is not yet clear, the ceramics from the deep shafts and drain trenches of the groundwater lowering project suggest continuous occupation throughout the Late and Ptolemaic Periods and into the Roman Period, when the ceramic material is supplemented by other archaeological evidence in the form of the massive stone structures described in Chapter 2. The repertoire of vessels reconstructed from this work suggests a context of settlement and trade rather than industrial, religious, or funerary activities.[80] The presence of fragments of amphorae originating either from Palestine/Phoenicia or from the Aegean throughout this period shows a connection with the trade in luxury goods (principally oil and wine) from the Levant and the Mediterranean. The former are often associated with deposits of the first Persian period in Egypt, while the latter, variously from the Greek islands Samos, Chios, Rhodes, and Kos, are broadly indicative of the same period but appear to have been rather longer-lived. Some types of amphorae are found in Egypt in contexts ranging from the sixth century BC to the second century AD.[81] One of the Rhodian amphora fragments can be closely dated by the stamp of the potter Sokrates II, who used a flaming torch as his motif and is known to have worked from 200 to 174 BC (fig. 16).[82]

The most important stratified archaeological evidence for the Late Period was found during work to the east of the Ben Ezra Synagogue and in Shaft HC2 immediately to the south of the surviving South Gate of the Roman fortress. The western edge of a 2–4m-thick firm clay bed lies some 10 m to the east of the southwest corner of the fortress. The top of the clay bed here is at around 14 m MSL and forms part of the substantial clay beds rising to the east. Around the area of Shaft HC2 in front of the South Gate of the Roman fortress the top of the clay bed rises quite sharply to above 16 m MSL. It is significant that this higher area of land is where the curving stone steps of the later Trajanic quayside appear to have

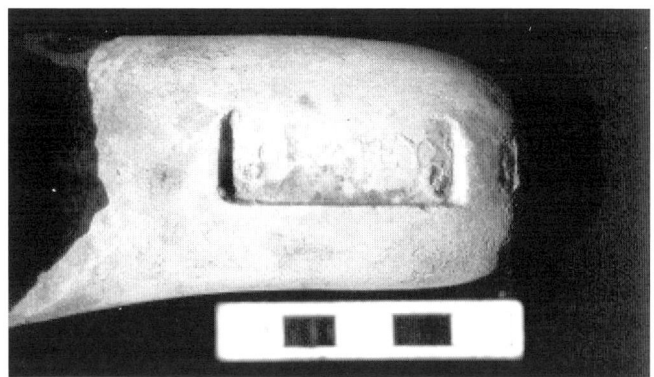

Fig. 16. Amphora handle stamped with the name and flaming torch motif of the potter Sokrates II. (Alison Gascoigne)

met the contemporary riverbank. The boreholes in this area generally show the bottom of this firm clay bed at between 10–12 m MSL, lying above a 10 m layer of sand that in turn lies above the massively thick underlying clay beds.

At the edge of this higher 16+ m MSL level, excavation indicated a 2-m-thick deposit dating from between the Late Period and the Persian Period (eighth–fifth centuries BC). The lowest ceramic sample recovered from within Shaft HC2 between 13–13.5 m MSL included material from the Third Intermediate Period. The composition of the deposit and the ceramic assemblage it contained indicates an intact stratigraphic sequence dating from the Late Period to the Persian Period including numerous sherds of Aegean amphorae, as well as material characteristic of deposits dated to the Persian Period (550–450 BC) from Buto. The material has made a valuable addition to the general picture of the location and stratigraphy of the Late Period/Persian Period riverbank previously gained from other Contract 102 locations. Sherds of Koan transport amphora (in use fourth century BC–first century AD), for example, have now been found at between 14.55–15.55 m MSL here and at other probable locations for the pre-Trajanic riverbank east of the Ben Ezra Synagogue and around Shaft 8 to the east of Qasriyat al-Rihan Church.

Whether this material represents *in situ* occupation or the deposition of material over the sloping side of the riverbank is not entirely clear. The elevation of this deposit relative to that of the level reached by the flood and the broad stratigraphic sequence discernible within it make a strong case for *in situ* occupation, as does the absence of any sign of water wear that might indicate material dumped into the water. This interpretation is supported by the finds of similar pre-Roman material at a similar elevation in the perforated drain excavation to the east of the Ben Ezra Synagogue, where it is associated with mud brick structures. The absence of material in Shaft HC2 for the period between the fifth century BC and the early Roman period (layers that were present in the deposits east of the synagogue) might indicate that these later deposits in the area south of the Hanging Church were then truncated during the creation of the Roman-period harbor.

These finds from the area in front of the South Gate, along with those made east of the synagogue in 2001, mark the first recorded trace of the settlement that can probably be associated with a number of Late Period shaft tombs noted in the 1930s during quarrying in the Batn al-Baqara area to the east of the Roman fortress.[83]

It might be tempting to see in the Eighteenth Dynasty stele found in Shaft HC1 evidence for settlement at Old Cairo going back beyond the Late Period, but the context of the find indicates it was redeposited much later, probably during the construction of a foundation raft for the southwest corner tower of the Roman fortress around AD 300 (see below). The base of the western flanking tower of the South Gate and the barracks east of the synagogue have both yielded evidence that the construction of the fortress utilized elements of earlier structures, and Late Period pottery was also found within the rubble raft laid to form the foundation of the southern round tower. The presence of *in situ* Late Period material in Old Cairo may indicate that the structures dismantled for reuse in the buildings of the Roman fortress also came from nearby. Similarly the finds from Athar al-Nabi may argue that the Late Period settlement indicated by the archaeological evidence from deep excavation in Old Cairo extended some way to the south.[84]

Both the areas in front of the South Gate and east of the synagogue produced double-rimmed bowls characteristic of deposits dated between 550 and 450 BC at Buto and Tell al-Maskhuta.[85] The presence of this Persian Period pottery is highly significant, given that this period saw the first cutting of the Red Sea Canal, the entrance of which was at Babylon in the Roman period (see Chapter 2). Ancient writers were explicit that the foundation of Babylon took place in the Persian Period. Josephus, in the first century AD, mentions that, "They took the road from Letopolis, at that time desert, afterwards the site of Babylon, founded by [the Persian king, 525–522 BC] Cambyses when he subdued Egypt."[86] The corrupt Ethiopic version of the original John of Nikiou text (seventh century AD), states that "Nebuchadnezzar [actually the Neo-Babylonian king c. 605 BC], king of the Magi and the Persians, was the first to build its foundations and to name it the fortress of Babylon."[87]

The location of Babylon at the southern limits of the city of Heliopolis (ancient On) has in more recent times suggested a derivation from the hypothetical *pr-H'pi n Iwnw* (the house [that is temple] of [the river god] Hapi in [the city of] On).[88] The first century BC accounts of Diodorus Siculus and Strabo of the foundation of Babylon have thus been considered to reflect ancient attempts to explain the etymology of Babylon, as having come about through the occidentalizing of an Egyptian toponym. However, both of these ancient authors' accounts show clearly that by 50 BC a view existed of the foundation which could very plausibly represent the establishment of a trading colony or military base by the Persian kings.

> It is said that the captives brought from Babylonia revolted from the king . . . and they, seizing a strong position on the banks of the river, maintained a warfare against the Egyptians and ravaged the neighboring territory. But finally, on being granted an amnesty, they established a colony on the spot which they also named Babylon, from their native land.[89] (Diodorus Siculus, Book I, ch. 56.3)

> In sailing up the river, we meet with Babylon, a strong fortress, built by some Babylonians who had taken refuge there, and had obtained permission from the kings to establish a settlement in that place.[90] (Strabo, *Geography*, Book XVII, ch. 1, 30)

These different explanations of the name of Babylon may not be mutually exclusive. The evidence of archaeology and etymology do not rule out the possibility of a Persian colony deriving its name from an already existing district of the city of Heliopolis/On. This was the period in which Egypt, ruled from the Delta, saw the influx of many groups of foreigners and the foundation by them of numerous colonies. Such colonies were seen and described at Memphis by Herodotus in the fifth century BC, and the archaeological material from Babylon could plausibly reflect just such a colony.

> Phoenicians from the city of Tyre dwell all around this precinct, and the whole place is known by the name of the Camp of the Tyrians.[91]

In terms of the extent of this settlement it is worth noting that little or none of this early material was noted in the shafts excavated to the north of the Roman fortress. Most of the earliest material was recovered from the shafts and trenches in the eastern part of the area inside the fortress. The more substantial and widespread recovery of the earliest material from a number of deep shaft excavations argues for the presence of stratified archaeological deposits from this earliest settlement of the site, perhaps going back as far as the Third Intermediate Period. Late Period ceramics were also found reused in the foundations of the southern round tower of the Roman fortress and in the "barracks" north of the northern round tower. The presence of this material, like the *spolia* in the foundations of the tower flanking the South Gate, is another indication of the profound remodeling of the site, which occurred first under Trajan around AD 110, and then Diocletian around AD 300.

Chapter 2

The River of Trajan

*And on the confines of Arabia and Aphroditopolis: Babylon, Heliopolis and the town of Heroum,
through which and the city of Babylon the River of Trajan flows.*
—Claudius Ptolemy, second century AD[1]

Introduction

Ancient and modern writers alike have linked the reign of the emperor Trajan (AD 98–115) with the Roman fortress of Babylon.[2] Although the archaeological evidence presented in Chapter 3 reveals that the fortress itself was not built until nearly two hundred years after Trajan, his reign does indeed constitute a defining moment in the making of Old Cairo and the topography of the entire city of Cairo. For at Old Cairo Trajan built a stone harbor and incorporated within it the entrance to a great canal named after himself, the Amnis Traianus. This canal linked the Nile with the Red Sea and thereby reopened a direct trade route between the Mediterranean and the East, just as the Suez Canal was to do eighteen hundred years later. In Cairo the canal survived into the modern period as al-Khalig al-Misri. The line of this canal formed the western edge of medieval Cairo and it remained a fundamental element in the topography of Cairo until much of it was filled in as a public health measure during an outbreak of cholera in 1896.[3] The origins of the canal of Cairo, however, and in particular the location of its original junction with the Nile, have remained obscure until recently.[4]

The origins of Trajan's canal lie in a much earlier Holocene eastern branch channel of the Nile that flowed through the Wadi Tumilat toward the depression of Lake Timsah and from there through the Bitter Lakes to the Gulf of Suez. The course of this channel in the Cairo area followed the limestone terrace that forms the eastern edge of the Nile Valley. Forming the east bank of this former channel is a band of firm clay between two and four meters thick lying over the bedrock between elevation 11 and 15 m MSL. Archaeological material recovered during the excavation of the deep shafts of the groundwater lowering project indicates that the first settlement at Old Cairo took place on these clay beds during the middle of the first millennium BC.

Ancient sources and archaeological evidence show that, at the same time (around the end of the Late Period (664–525 BC), existing natural depressions were joined for the first time by canals to form a waterway linking the Nile to the Red Sea. At the beginning of the second century AD the emperor Trajan revived and extended this Red Sea canal to form a new route between the Nile and the sea. At Old Cairo, where the entrance to the canal was located, he created a magnificent stone harbor. The massive walls forming the two sides of this entrance survive beneath two of the most ancient churches of Old Cairo, the Orthodox Church of St. George (Mari Girgis) and the Coptic Church of SS. Sergius and Bacchus (Abu Serga). The canal to the Red Sea continued in use throughout the Roman period and into the first centuries after the Arab Conquest, although by then the entrance at Old Cairo was no longer used and a new entrance had been cut further to the north. Even in later medieval times the canal continued to fulfill an important function, replenishing the underground water supply of Cairo during the annual Nile inundation and irrigating the agricultural land to the north of the city.

Connecting the Nile with the Red Sea

The economic attractions of a waterway connecting the civilizations of East and West via the Nile and the Red Sea exerted a powerful influence on the development of Cairo, for the location of the mouth of this canal and its course through the city have been fundamental topographical features since at least the second century AD. Ancient accounts

Fig. 17. Bourdon's 1925 plan and profiles of the ancient and modern canals linking the Nile at Cairo with the Red Sea at Suez. © The British Library Board (Ac.6042.d).

broadly agree with the idea that the canal was first dug during the transition from the rule of the Late Period pharaohs to that of the Persian kings, a time when Egypt was increasingly opened up to Mediterranean and Near Eastern trade. This is also the first period represented for which we have *in situ* archaeological material from Old Cairo.

A number of ancient authors give the historical background to the foundation of the canal against which we can consider the archaeological evidence.[5] Some, including Aristotle, writing in the fourth century BC, preserve the legend that a canal was first attempted by Sesostris (the Greek version of Senusret, the name of three Twelfth Dynasty rulers). Herodotus, writing in 450 BC when the canal was still in use, relates that Necho II (610–595 BC), the son of Psammetichus I, began but failed to complete a canal that would link the Pelusiac branch of the Nile from a point "a little above Bubastis" first to the Wadi Tumilat and then via Lake Timsah and the Bitter Lakes to the Red Sea. One of the major motivations for the first canal may have been the establishment of a new link for the incense trade with Punt (probably in the region of modern Somalia) to replace the land routes from the south that had been cut off by war and political change in the lands south of Egypt around 660 BC.[6] Another factor would have been the important trade links via Sinai to Syria and Palestine that are revealed in the ceramic record of this period. The great scale of the undertaking is indicated by the vast numbers of workers (more than one hundred thousand) that are reported to have died in digging the canal (fig. 1).[7]

Herodotus' near-contemporary account of the next major phase of work on the canal describes how it was completed by the Persian king Darius I (521–486 BC), second king of the Twenty-seventh (Persian) Dynasty. According to Herodotus, the canal in his day was wide enough for two triremes to pass each other and the journey from the Nile to the Red Sea through its course in the Wadi Tumilat took four days. Archaeological evidence for the achievement of Darius survives in a series of large granite commemorative stelae inscribed in hieroglyphic and cuneiform texts that were set up along the line of the canal. The text of one of these stelae makes the king's achievement in cutting the canal explicit.[8]

Saith Darius the King: I am a Persian; from Persia I seized Egypt; I gave order to dig this canal from a river by the name Nile which flows in Egypt, to the sea which

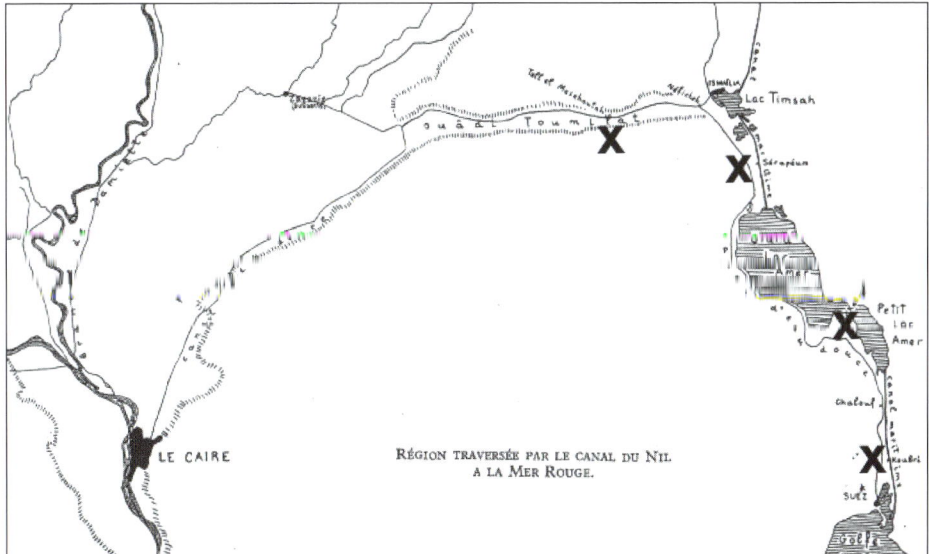

Fig 18. Posener's sketchplan showing the four find locations of the Persian stele.

goes from Persia. Afterward this canal was dug thus as I had ordered, and ships went from Egypt through this canal to Persia. (Kent 1950: 147; Scheil 1930)

Darius' canal appears to have been created by cutting through the ridge of Shalouf, thereby allowing seawater to fill the depressions that are now the Bitter Lakes and Lake Timsah. The evidence of the stelae is supported by archaeologically recorded settlement patterns in the Wadi Tumilat, which show a marked increase along the line of the canal in the Persian period.[9] Later authors like Aristotle, Strabo, and Pliny claim that Darius too had not completed the work for fear of introducing salt water into the Nile, but the archaeological evidence and the testimony of the stelae appear to show that these accounts linked the earlier failed attempts to cut the canal with Darius so as to give the credit for its achievement to the Hellenistic Ptolemies, who revived the route of the canal in the third century BC and gave it a new name, the Potamos Ptolemaios. The accounts of the Roman writer Diodorus Siculus (50 BC) and the Greek Strabo, as well as the Pithom Stone discovered by Naville at Tell al-Maskhuta, probably relate to a re-excavation of the silted-up route of the Persian canal through the Wadi Tumilat by Ptolemy II (284–246 BC).[10] A new feature at this time may have been the introduction of a lock system to prevent the mixing of salt and fresh water and allow the depressions of Lake Timsah and the Bitter Lakes to fill with fresh potable water from the Nile, allowing Ptolemy to found the city of Clysma (Arsinoe), either on the shore of Lake Timsah or more likely on the site of modern Suez.[11] Archaeological evidence from the Wadi Tumilat shows there were twice the number of settlements under the Ptolemies, at least half of them permanent settlements now represented by mounds, compared to under Persian rule.[12] This may relate to more sustained settlement and the use of the Wadi Tumilat for agriculture rather than merely as a trade route. Renewed interest in this route and use of the canal in the Ptolemaic period is also suggested by references to the extensive campaigns waged by Ptolemy II against 'pirates' in the Red Sea.[13] Strabo's account around 25 BC of the route of the canal shows that it had not changed from the time of Herodotus four centuries earlier:

> The canal which empties into Red Sea begins at Phacussa, a village, to which the Village of Philo is contiguous. Here are both the city Bubastis and the Bubastite Nome; and above it is the Heliopolite Nome. (XVII.I.27).

A review of the ancient sources suggests that the canal may have gone out of use by the time of the Roman occupation of Egypt after Augustus' defeat of Cleopatra and Mark Antony at the Battle of Actium in 31 BC. Plutarch says that after the battle Cleopatra tried to have her galleys dragged overland to the Red Sea, while there is no mention of the canal in the first century BC account of navigation and trade in the Red Sea, the *Periplus Maris Erythraei*.[14] In both cases, however, this may have been due to the fact that the canal was a seasonal feature that was only navigable in the period from September to December following the Nile flood. Strabo only refers to shipbuilding taking place at Cleopatris "on the old Nile canal."

The specific location given by Herodotus and Strabo for the point of departure from the Nile shows that no canal linked Old Cairo with the Red Sea either in the mid-fifth century BC or at the beginning of the Roman period. By contrast, the explicit reference by Claudius Ptolemy, writing in the second century AD, shows that between his account and that of Strabo a new entrance to the canal had been made some 60 km to the south at "Babylon . . . through which the river of Trajan flows."[15]

The late antique traditions for a shift of the canal mouth to Babylon are also explicitly preserved in one of the key ancient references to the history of Old Cairo, the seventh-century account of John, the Coptic Bishop of Nikiu:

> And the Jews who were in the city of Alexandria and in the province of Cyrene assembled and chose a leader named Lucuas to be their king. And when Trajan was informed and apprised of this movement, he sent against them an officer named Marcus Turbo with a numerous force. . . . And Trajan came to Egypt and built a fortress with a strong impregnable tower, and he brought water into it in abundance and he named it Babylon in Egypt. Nebuchadnezzar the king of the Magi and Persians was the first to build its foundations and to name it the fortress of Babylon . . . Nebuchadnezzar came to Egypt with a numerous army and made a conquest of Egypt, because the Jews had revolted against him, and he named [the fortress] Babylon after the name of his own city. And Trajan moreover added some buildings to the fortress and other parts in it. And he dug also a small canal—sufficiently large to convey water from the Gihon to the city Clysma. And he put this water into connexion with the Red Sea, and he named this canal Trajan after his own name.[16]

The elements of this account have a remarkable resonance with the archaeology of Babylon. Both associate the foundation of Babylon with Persian rule, although with Nebuchadnezzar, who conquered Egypt in 568 BC, rather than Darius, half a century later. Physical evidence for the explicit link between Trajan's activities at Babylon and the creation of the canal is preserved in the huge stone walls of the canal that lie beneath the churches of St. George and St. Sergius. At the end of the third century the circuit walls were indeed raised and the fortress was enlarged, not however by Trajan but by the emperor Diocletian. Thus the main events and principal protagonists have been conflated by the significant omission of the part played by Diocletian. Given the Coptic view of Diocletian as scourge and anathema to the early Church in Egypt (he is described by John of Nikiu as "the most wicked of all men"[17]), his absence from the account of the foundation of Babylon is perhaps not surprising.

The archaeology of the massive walls of the canal, the accounts of both Ptolemy and John of Nikiu, and various papyrological references all appear to place the first cutting of the canal in Old Cairo in the reign of the Emperor Trajan.[18] At the same time, the earliest archaeological material from Babylon and the ancient sources indicate that the first settlement at Babylon was broadly contemporary with the first cutting of a Red Sea canal in the sixth century BC. The explicit trade context of the archaeological material and its similarity to finds made at other sites along the known route of the canal makes a further case for linking the first settlement in Old Cairo to the first opening of the canal. The first canal to the Red Sea was therefore created in the context of a combination of political and topographical factors, the kind of response to changes in the riverside environment that characterizes the civilization of Egypt from the Early Dynastic period onward.

Reconciling these two trends suggests the existence of a first millennium BC precursor to that part of the Canal of Trajan that follows the line of the Holocene channel through the landscape of Cairo. Textual references indicate the existence of an earlier canal, the *Jtj* Canal, to the west of the city of On/Heliopolis during the New Kingdom.[19] Like Old Cairo, Heliopolis is situated at the western edge of the higher limestone terrace that forms the edge of the Nile floodplain, so it seems clear that this canal used the same relic Holocene east Delta branch channel later reused by Trajan at Old Cairo. By the New Kingdom, Heliopolis was not on the main east Delta branch, which lay further to the west of the city.[20] The *Jtj* Canal represented an important link from Heliopolis southwards to Memphis (one day's sailing) and northward (three days) to the Ramesside capital at Per-Rameses. The evidence of ancient texts and archaeology suggests that this canal followed the course of the Holocene channel dictated by the limestone formation north of Heliopolis, and, like Trajan's Canal, rejoined the river at the contemporary head of the Pelusiac branch at Tell al-Yahudiya. In the context of the later function of Trajan's Canal it is also worth noting that the *Jtj* Canal seems to have had some connection with the levying of tolls and customs duties on cargoes sailing between Memphis and Per-Ramses via Heliopolis.[21]

In addition to the possible continued existence of the *Jtj* Canal and its links to the city of Heliopolis, the other rationale for the Persian Period settlement at Old Cairo was its location on the east bank of the Nile at a strategic confluence of routes and a crossing-point over the river. The first millennium archaeological material is important in showing that Trajan's choice of Babylon as the location of the harbor and the entrance to the canal was not entirely *ex novo*. At each stage of the canal those who worked on its course showed a natural tendency to see themselves as breaking new ground, so that in later reworkings of the route of the canal Roman Babylon was linked with the Amnis Traianus and Arab al-Fustat with the "Canal of the Commander of the Faithful." The historical narratives and the material finds from Old Cairo suggest that Trajan's project may have taken the familiar Roman form of improving the riverside and harbor facilities at an existing location that was already firmly associated with the Red Sea canal route, but one that had not previously been the location of the actual entrance to the canal from the Nile.

One of the most ancient sites on the route of the Roman-era canal is Musturud, where the association of the Church of the Virgin with the sojourn of the Holy Family in Egypt has taken on a new significance following the discovery of the wall of the Canal of Trajan beneath another of the sites on the route of their Flight, the Church of Abu Serga in Old Cairo. To the south of Musturud, between Heliopolis and the Mosque of Sayyida Zaynab, the medieval version of Trajan's Canal, al-Khalig al-Misri, forms a remarkably straight line in the landscape. The position of the Fatimid enclosure of al-Qahira along its eastern bank shows that this line has remained unchanged for at least the last thousand years. Some information on the course of that part of the canal running south from al-Qahira to Gebel Yashkur and the area of Qal'at al-Kabsh is provided by the tenth-century description of the Moroccan traveler al-Muqaddasi.[22] To the south of Qal'at al-Kabsh the exact original course of Trajan's Canal becomes less certain, but the entrance to the canal between the two round towers of the later fortress provides a terminus, and the canal appears to have followed the edge of the buried limestone terrace between these two points. The southernmost part of the *khalig* that curves away to the west forms part of the new entrance to the canal cut following the Arab Conquest. The later westward movement of the Nile shifted the entrance toward the area now known as Fumm al-Khalig ('The Mouth of the Canal'), where a great intake tower and aqueduct was built by Sultan al-Ghuri in 1505 to supply the Citadel of Cairo (fig. 2).

The accounts of a number of medieval Arab authors from the ninth century onward make it clear that, after the Arab Conquest of Egypt in AD 641, the new rulers simply re-excavated and brought back into use an existing feature.[23] Since the position of the northern part of the canal can be fixed from its relationship to the tenth century enclosure of al-Qahira, it seems reasonable therefore to suppose that this straight northern section is close to the original line of the Canal of Trajan.

The Coptic churches and chapels of the Harat Zuwayla are located on the eastern bank of the *khalig* within the area of this Fatimid enclosure. This anachronistic presence is clearly a survival from earlier times, and the presence of churches here can probably be used to fix the line of the canal from at least the first century after the Conquest.[24] If the line given by this northern part of the *khalig* is continued to the southwest it arrives at Old Cairo between the massive 6 m wide stone walls set parallel to each other forty meters apart beneath the churches of St. George and St. Sergius in Old Cairo.[25] Another indication that the *khalig* originally continued straight to Old Cairo is the survival into the modern period of seasonal lakes (Birkat al-Fil and Birkat Baghala) along this course. These are probably to be identified as remnants of the former straight course of the canal and/or the earlier Nile channel.

The position shown for the mouth of the canal at Fumm al-Khalig on historical maps dates back at least to the medieval period, while the situation in the early sixteenth century is marked by the great hexagonal water tower built by al-Ghuri. For the earlier medieval period we have evidence in the form of historians' and travelers' accounts, as well as several buildings that survive as topographical markers. Al-Muqaddasi, writing in AD 985, describes how the great mosque built by Ahmad Ibn Tulun on Gebel Yashkur in 876–79 dominated the entrance to the canal in his time.[26] The course of the southern end of the canal and its relation to the ruin heaps of al-Fustat shown on eighteenth- and nineteenth-century maps also indicates its position by the Fatimid period. At the mosque of Sayyida Zaynab (the granddaughter of the Prophet Muhammad) a *mashhad* (shrine) has existed over what was believed to be the site of her tomb from at least the Fatimid period.[27] The interests of the Fatimid dynasty in establishing legitimacy through building at ancient sites linked with figures of early (especially Shi'i) Islam might suggest that the origins of the mosque probably go back at least to the time of her death in al-Fustat in AD 680.[28] In any event, the presence of the mosque suggests that the position of this southern end of the canal goes back to the very beginnings of al-Fustat.[29] Like Harat Zuwayla within Fatimid Cairo, the Coptic Church of Mari Mina is another useful marker for the early medieval topography of the city.[30] Later medieval historians preserved the tradition that an earlier Church of Mari Mina had been destroyed prior to its rebuilding around AD 725.[31] It may be that like the Mosque of Sayyida Zaynab, the original church can be dated to the period when the canal was re-dug in the period immediately following the Arab Conquest. Like several of the churches of Old Cairo, this would place the foundation of Mari Mina in the period immediately following the Arab Conquest between 644–85, when al-Fustat was growing and the Copts were experiencing a revival after the persecution of the last ten years of Byzantine rule. It seems clear that the later ban on the construction of new churches was not a feature of the early Islamic period. We also know from al-Muqaddasi's tenth-century account that the Copts still made up the majority of the population, and he even remarks on their haughty comportment.[32] Given the great popular significance associated in later times with the ceremony of the Opening of the Canal, the location of important religious buildings like Mari Mina and the Mosque of Sayyida Zaynab may reflect the position of the entrance to the canal in the first years after the Conquest.[33]

The location of the crypt of Abu Serga Church over the eastern wall of the canal in Old Cairo and the veneration associated with this place may reflect a similar ancient significance associated with the original entrance to the canal. The present crypt was built much later, probably during the tenth or eleventh centuries, as part of a larger church extending out over the former line of the canal, which by that time had long been filled in. Nevertheless, the relationship of the crypt of the Church of St. Sergius and the Orthodox Church of St. George to the two sides of the canal may be significant. It is worth noting that the façade of Abu Serga lies in the very centerline of the filled-in canal. Its conversion into an important road lined with churches and leading to the main congregational mosque of the new city suggests that some echoes of the ceremonial significance associated with the original entrance to the canal may have continued.

For Old Cairo all this shows that the canal running between the massive stone walls built by Trajan went out of use at some time between 300, when Diocletian built a fortress to guard the entrance to the canal, and the Arab Conquest in 641, by which time a new entrance to the reopened canal had to be dug to the north to allow the construction of the central quarters of al-Fustat over the original line of the canal through and to the north of the former Roman fortress, an event for which we have both historical and archaeological evidence.[34]

Trajan's Canal and the Harbor of Old Cairo

To link far distant peoples by commerce so that the natural products of any place now seem to belong to all.
—Pliny the Younger, on Trajan's construction of new harbors, *Pan.* 29.2

Trajan's reign has been characterized as one of reforms "generated by a visionary speculation that conceived of a unified political, economic and military system for the Roman empire."[35] There is clear evidence in the Letters of Pliny the Younger for a series of poor harvests in Italy between AD 97–107, and these may have stimulated capital investment and reforms to the administration of the grain supply of the city of Rome, the *annona*, in which Egypt played an essential role.[36] The *cura annona* was both a major function of Roman government and its largest shipping operation, and the prefect appointed to run it held one of the most important administrative posts from the reign of Augustus onward.[37] Under Augustus, Rome received twenty million *modii* (around 130,000 metric tons) of grain a year from Egypt, while another ancient source says the Egyptian grain tribute fed Rome for four months. Tacitus's wry comments reveal how important this operation was to the very survival of Rome:

> But no one makes any proposal about the fact that Italy is dependent on supplies from abroad, that the life of the Roman people is tossed every day at the mercy of wave and wind.[38]

Storehouses for the grain supply were located at Rome and its harbors (Ostia, Puteoli, and from AD 42, Portus), as well as in the primary producing provinces of Egypt and Africa. A third century papyrus describes the loading of a sealed sample of grain onto two riverboats in Middle Egypt for transportation under armed escort to Alexandria.[39]

The construction of harbors to facilitate the grain supply and trade in general seems to have been an integral part of Trajan's vision and a concrete expression of his good works or *beneficium*. New harbors were also needed to cope with the increasing volume of seaborne traffic and the size of individual ships. In Italy these new harbors included most notably Portus but also Civitavecchia and the harbor of Ancona with its great triumphal arch dedicated to the emperor and his family. The inscription on the arch at Ancona is dated to 115 and specifies the commercial nature of the harbor.[40] For the construction of Civitavecchia we have the valuable eyewitness account of Pliny, written while staying at the emperor's villa nearby: "[A] natural bay is being converted at the moment into a great harbor. The left arm has already been secured with a mole of solid masonry, and the right is now being built."[41]

At Portus the huge hexagonal basin of "Trajan's auspicious harbor" (Portus Traiani Felicis, built between 106–112), with each side of the hexagon 358 m long, was linked to the Tiber and Rome by a 40 meter-wide canal. Mooring points for over a hundred ships and individual numbered berths were provided along the 6 meter-wide quay. Set back from the quayside were substantial storehouses or *horrea*. The appearance of the harbor was completed by large monolithic columns at the angles of the hexagon and a colossal statue of the emperor, while other buildings on the northwest side have been interpreted as an imperial residence.[42] Aelius Aristides' extravagant second century AD eulogy of Rome as the emporium of the world provides a vivid picture of the volume of Roman maritime trade produced by the measures of Trajan and others:

One can see so many cargoes from India, or, if you wish, from Arabia Felix, that one may surmise that the trees there have been left permanently bare, and that those people must come here to beg for their own goods when they need anything. . . . Egypt, Sicily and the civilized parts of Africa are your farms. The arrival and departure of ships never ceases, so that it is astounding that the sea—not to mention the harbor—suffices for the merchantmen. . . .[43]

The reopening of the Red Sea canal by Trajan was connected to strategic and commercial interests in the eastern empire and was related to Trajan's annexing of the kingdom of Nabatea in AD 106 and his campaigns against the Parthians in Mesopotamia, preparations for which appear to have begun around 111.[44] The annexation of Nabatea was an important event in Trajan's reorganization of the eastern provinces, for it allowed the construction in 111 of the Via Nova Traiana, an adaptation of the ancient trans-Levantine trail running from Aqaba to Damascus known in later times as the King's Highway (fig. 1).[45] Inscriptions along the road show that it and the reopening of the Red Sea canal route formed part of a unified approach to create a network of new trading and military routes for the eastern provinces, replacing the ancient caravan trails from the Tigris and Euphrates valleys disrupted by war with the Parthians:

After reducing Arabia to the status of a province, through the agency of Gaius Claudius Severus, imperial legate with rank of praetor, opened and paved a new road from Syria to the Red Sea.[46]

The annexation of Nabatea was therefore an important step, for the problems occasioned by Nabatean "pirates" had been one of the major factors in preventing the Ptolemies from exploiting the full potential of the Red Sea link to the Nile.[47] Eutropius, writing of the reign of Trajan in 363, suggests an additional motivation for the works carried out by Trajan to revive the Red Sea link: "On the Red Sea he established a fleet, so that he might ravage the (outlying) territories of India with it."[48] Trajan may have also envisaged a military purpose for the canal in pursuing his campaigns against the Parthians by sea as well as by land.[49]

A specific date for the works on the canal and the construction of the harbor at Old Cairo is provided by a tax receipt on an ostracon from Thebes dated to September 2, 112, which refers to the payment of four drachmas levied on the entire Egyptian population for work on the Potamos Babylonos.[50] The latest date for the beginning of the works would therefore be the spring of 112, before the Nile began to rise that year. The wording of the receipt and the absence of others like it suggest this tax was a single payment connected with the reopening of the canal by Trajan rather than an annual levy related to its maintenance.

Trajan's Canal appears to have followed the route of the ancient Persian and Ptolemaic canals through the Wadi Tumilat, but west of the entrance to the wadi it followed an entirely new route south toward Heliopolis and Babylon, utilizing at least in part the old relic channel of the Nile. Remains of the canal banks have been noted in the Wadi Tumilat.[51] Within and on the edge of Cairo the Roman canal appears to have been subsumed into Shari' Port Said and the Sweet Water Canal in 1896 and 1855 respectively, but in 1925 Bourdon noted a long stretch of the canal running west of the latter between the villages of Kafr Hamza (15 km north of Cairo) and Gawarni (at the entrance to the Wadi Tumilat) (fig. 17).[52] The reason for this new course appears to have been the continued silting-up of the Pelusiac branch of the Nile, a process that had been ongoing since the Twenty-first Dynasty and that caused the shift of the royal capital from Avaris to Tanis.[53] The new section of the Roman canal appears to have been wider than its predecessors.[54] Combined with the cutting of a new entrance at Babylon this would have increased both navigability and the amount of potable water flowing into the Wadi Tumilat and the lakes of the Isthmus of Suez.

Road schemes like the emperor's renewal of the Via Appia between Brindisi and Rome, reorganization of the imperial post, and the creation of new harbors all contributed to a more 'global' view of communications and trade in which "Trajan consciously favoured the application of new solutions to old problems, and it was his surveyors who were responsible for the major feats of engineering."[55] The units responsible for the related projects of the Red Sea Canal and the Via Nova Traiana appear to have been the Legio III Cyrenaica, already stationed at Alexandria and probably the Legio II Traiana Fortis, founded in 105 and transferred from Dacia after its annexation. Legio II Traiana Fortis took part in Trajan's campaign against Parthia in 115–117 and succeeded III Cyrenaica at Alexandria in 125, remaining as the main force in Egypt until the fifth century.[56]

The strong and almost constant north wind prevailing in the Gulf of Suez governed the principal direction of traffic along the canal, which was of use primarily to ships sailing south into the Red Sea. Rather than tacking against this strong wind, at least some of the traffic in the other direction would have involved trans-shipment overland to the Nile Valley from ports further south along the Red Sea coast, like Myos Hormos (Quseir al-Qadim) and Berenice, and thence down the Nile to Alexandria, routes explicitly mentioned during the early part of the Roman period by Strabo around 25 bc and again by Pliny the Younger at the very beginning of the second century AD.[57] Strabo's account shows that the canal had played little or no part in this trade in the early years of Roman rule at the end of the first century BC:

> At the present time (the cargoes of aromatics) are for the most part transported on the Nile to Alexandria; and they are brought from Arabia and India to Myus Hormus, and they are conveyed by camels over to Coptus in the Thebaid . . . and then to Alexandria.[58]

The archaeological evidence for a relative decline in the importance of the Red Sea ports from the third century AD onward suggests, however, that the canal and its associated land routes played an increasingly dominant part in all trade coming through the Red Sea.[59] The availability of waterborne transport must have provided a considerable stimulus to the exploitation of the porphyry and other mineral resources at sites along the Red Sea coast like Mons Claudianus and Mons Porphyrites, as well as the mineral resources made available by the annexation of Sinai.[60] Certainly the reign of Trajan saw the first intensive exploitation of these quarries for use in the western empire on prestigious projects like the portico of the Pantheon,[61] and the attraction of transporting large monolithic stones by water rather than dragging them on sledges overland from Myos Hormos (Quseir) to Koptos seems clear.

Even before the construction of the canal, the account of Pliny at the end of the first century AD reveals how much the trade with India would have justified such a large capital investment: "In no year does India absorb less than 50,000,000 sesterces of our Empire's wealth, sending back merchandise to be sold with us at a hundred times its original cost."[62]

The harbor at Babylon would thus have played an important role in the transport down the canal and south into the Red Sea of the more bulky types of goods exported in return for Indian spices and luxury goods, in particular perhaps the amphorae filled with Mediterranean and Egyptian wine for which abundant archaeological evidence survives from Old Cairo.[63]

Archaeological Evidence from Old Cairo for the Canal and the Harbor of Trajan

New archaeological evidence for the existence and the position of Trajan's harbor and the canal in Old Cairo was gathered during the groundwater lowering project between 1999 and 2005. This evidence derives from geotechnical borehole logs, deep shafts sunk in Shari' Mari Girgis, and the drainage trenches excavated under the Greek Orthodox Church of St. George and the Coptic Church of Abu Serga. All these indicate that the line of the northern section of al-Khalig al-Misri once continued straight through to Old Cairo.

The most compelling new evidence for the mouth of the Canal of Trajan being located in Old Cairo lies in the massive six-meter-wide stone walls found beneath the churches of St. George and Abu Serga during the groundwater lowering project. These walls predate the Diocletianic fortress and run parallel to each other some forty meters apart, forming a channel leading off to the northeast from the ancient course of the Nile that is marked by the western wall of the fortress.[64] The direction of this channel is consistent with that of the former line of the *khalig* west of Fatimid Cairo. The beginning of the western wall of Trajan's Canal at Old Cairo lies under the Late Roman tower now surmounted by the Church of St. George. Here the wall forms a rounded junction between the riverfront and the entrance to the canal. The western wall of the Roman fortress thus indicates the position of the east bank of the Nile at the beginning of the second century AD, with the river now represented by the modern Shari' Mari Girgis and the Metro line.[65] Much of the Early Roman material found in the shafts in Shari' Mari Girgis along this western edge of the fortress appears to represent debris dumped or fallen into the water along the edge of the harbor. The Late Roman tower beneath the Church of St. George is built over and partially within the curve of this section of the wall. Mooring holes for tying up boats were noted along the inner face of the Trajanic wall north of the tower. Regularly spaced walls projecting perpendicularly from its inner face were a feature of this quayside. Greek letters carved into the top of these stone walls may relate to the division of the quayside into specific sections (fig. 19. and pl. 15).

Archaeological investigations carried out during the course of the groundwater lowering project showed that although the southern round tower of the fortress is part of Diocletian's building campaign at Babylon around AD 300, the massive masonry of the earlier Trajanic wall continues immediately south of the tower. The southern round tower thus appears to have been added to the northern end of the existing harbor wall, narrowing the entrance to the canal. The boreholes and micro-tunnels carried out in Shari' Mari Girgis during 2005 provided valuable new information on the position, condition, and original depth of the western wall of the Trajanic harbor over a distance of more than 30 m south of the round tower in the garden of the Coptic Museum. Significant evidence for the position of the Nile, the function and appearance of the wall, and the date of its construction was provided by an unscheduled addition to the operations of the groundwater lowering project. Most

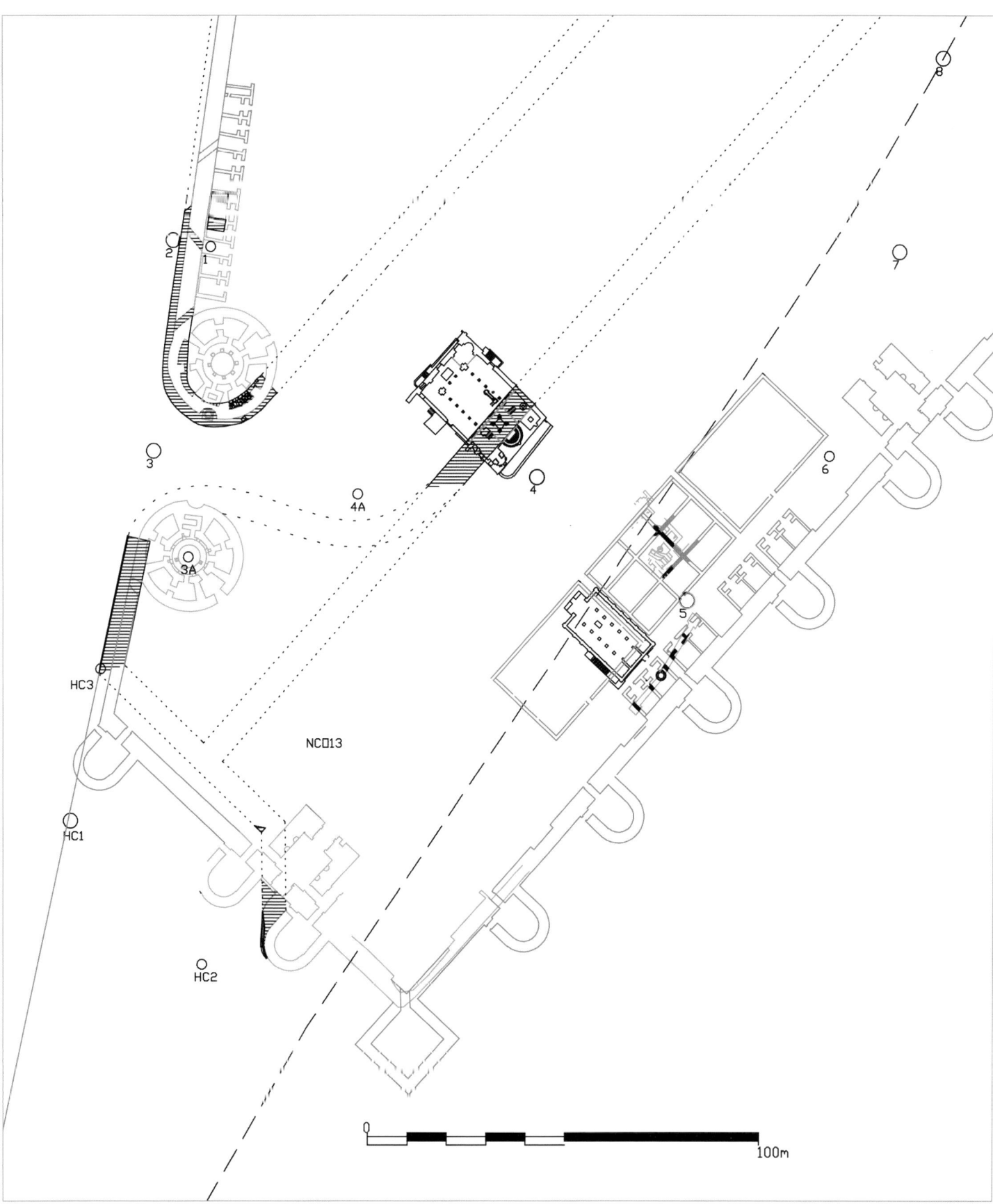

Fig. 19. Reconstructed plan of the Roman fortress of Babylon showing the areas (shaded) where the Trajanic harbor has so far been recorded. The approximate location of the 10 m contour broadly equating to the edge of the limestone terrace forming the eastern bank of the Holocene relic channel is shown as a dashed line. Shaft and borehole locations mentioned in the text are also shown (Peter Sheehan). From D.A. Agius, J.P. Cooper, A. Trakadas, and C. Zazzaro, eds., *Navigated Spaces, Connected Places: Proceedings of Red Sea Project V held at the University of Exeter, 16–19 September 2010* (Oxford: Archaeopress, 2012).

Fig. 20. The stepped Trajanic quayside below the eastern tower of the South Gate at Babylon. (Peter Sheehan)

Fig. 21. Slots for the swallow-tailed bronze cramps that originally joined adjacent blocks and are a distinctive feature of the Trajanic work. (Peter Sheehan)

important of all, it showed the position of the southwest corner of the harbor, where the wall turns and runs eastward. In the summer of 2004 the micro-tunneling machine used to connect the collector shafts became stuck during the laying of pipes between Shafts 3 and HC3. The position of the machine, adjacent to the Metro line and in the middle of a major tourist street, could not have been more inconvenient. The consequent obtaining of permits and wrangling between authorities meant that not until nearly a year later was it possible to sink another shaft to rescue the machine and change the line of the micro-tunnel. The massive stone blocks of the Trajanic quay wall appeared in the eastern half of the shaft from 17.3 m MSL (9 m below the modern street level) and continued to the end of excavation at between 13.15–13.81 m MSL. The distinctive cramp slots on the top surface of these stones and the character and appearance of this masonry were the same as that preserved under the eastern flanking tower of the South Gate of the Diocletianic fortress (figs. 20 and 21). This wall preserves a series of steps allowing access from the top of the quayside to boats moored alongside it, a feature also echoed by divers' descriptions of the wall encountered in Shariʿ Mari Girgis during the sinking of Shaft 2 and actually visible beneath the eastern flanking tower of the South Gate of Babylon.[66] The stepped face of the wall would have allowed the use of the quayside to reflect the changing level of the river through the course of the year.

The blocks recovered from Shaft HC3 included one of the most memorable and important finds made during the course of Contract 102, a long stone block 1.8 m long laid as a header and terminating in a lion-headed mooring post at the quayside level of the wall. The grooves in the stone worn around the projecting head of the lion by mooring ropes provide an evocative glimpse of the Roman riverfront. Vitruvius's description of the harbor at Ostia tells us that there would have been cranes, operated by *professionarii de ciconiis*, and the riverfront would also have bustled with *saccarii* (sackmen or stevedores) and *urinatores* (divers), employed to recover goods lost overboard during loading and unloading (fig. 22 and pl. 19).[67]

Unfortunately the lion lay just beyond the northern side of Shaft HC3, and the left side of its face had been removed by the diver during the work to clear obstructions from beneath the cutting edge. Blocks from seven or eight successive courses of the wall between these levels were dismantled by machine, carried out in conjunction with a group of divers acting as subcontractors and engaged in breaking the part of the stone blocks lying directly under the cutting edge of the shaft and loosening others so that they could be removed by machine. Reconstructing the condition of the wall before this work, the position and elevation of the blocks recovered from below the water level by a combination of jackhammer and the toothed bucket of the excavator represents something of a three-dimensional puzzle, the resolution of which depended on the observations made during the sinking of the shaft, discussions with the divers, and the elevations of other parts of the Trajanic harbor noted elsewhere in Old Cairo. When the first stone was encountered, thirteen of the 0.6 m-deep rings of the shaft and 0.30 m of the cutting edge were below the 25.9 m MSL benchmark on the concrete collar of the shaft. About a further 0.4 m of ring 14 had also been sunk, indicating that the bottom of the cutting edge resting on the highest preserved point of the Roman wall was at around 17.4 m MSL. This level can be compared with the top of the Trajanic harbor wall noted variously at 17.05 and 17.4 m MSL during the work beneath Mari Girgis Church in 2002, 17.24 m MSL in the stepped quayside at the South Gate and 17.22 m MSL in the eastern side of the Canal of Trajan revealed beneath the east end of the Church of Abu Serga in 2004. The next fixed elevation was provided by one of the blocks, which the divers' information and monitoring of the excavated material indicated came from the sixth course of excavated stonework. This stone block retained a circular impression in the stone where the cutting head of the micro-tunnel machine had finally come to rest embedded 0.06 m below the top surface of the block of the sixth course of the wall (fig. 23). From our knowledge of the elevation of the top of the micro-tunnel machine we can deduce that the top of this block was at about 14.71 m MSL. The blocks from the courses above this level are all 0.40–0.45 m in height. Taking 0.42 as an average height and 17.24 as the original elevation of the top of the wall, this would mean that the micro-tunnel machine had become stuck between the seventh and eighth courses below the top of the Trajanic harbor wall. Our observations suggested rather that this block was from the sixth course recovered during the sinking of the shaft. Adding five blocks of 0.42 m each to the 14.71 m of the block in which the micro-tunnel machine became stuck gives an elevation of 16.86 m MSL for the top of the first complete course excavated in Shaft HC3. This is the same as the first step down in the quayside beneath the eastern flanking tower of the South Gate and would indicate that the top course of the Trajanic quay is missing in parts, an impression that is reinforced by the boreholes in this area, which show the top of the stone layer ranging from the intact 17.23 m MSL to 16.23 m MSL. On the other hand, the survival of at least parts of the wall to the original top elevation is indicated both by the top surface of the lion-headed mooring stone and direct measurement of the first stone encountered beneath the cutting edge of the shaft. The information provided by the form of the blocks recovered from Shaft HC3 was, however, of great importance in showing not only that they belonged to a stepped quayside like that preserved beneath the eastern flanking tower of the

Fig. 22. Relief from the Torlonia museum in Rome showing the unloading of amphorae from boat to quayside. Fototeca Unione, American Academy in Rome.

Fig. 23. The stone block from the Trajanic harbor wall recovered from Shaft HC3 that shows where the micro-tunnel machine head came to rest. (Peter Sheehan)

South Gate (and from the divers' accounts also in Shaft 2), but that the point at which the micro-tunnel machine had become stuck was in fact the southwest corner of the Trajanic harbor wall where it curves and turns to the east. The outer faces of the blocks from the third/fourth course have been angled to form this curve and some of the blocks are wedge-shaped to allow a closer fit at the corner. This corner has a profound influence on our understanding of the relationship between the harbor of Trajan built around AD 110 and the fortress of Diocletian added nearly two hundred years later. The position of this corner in relation to the

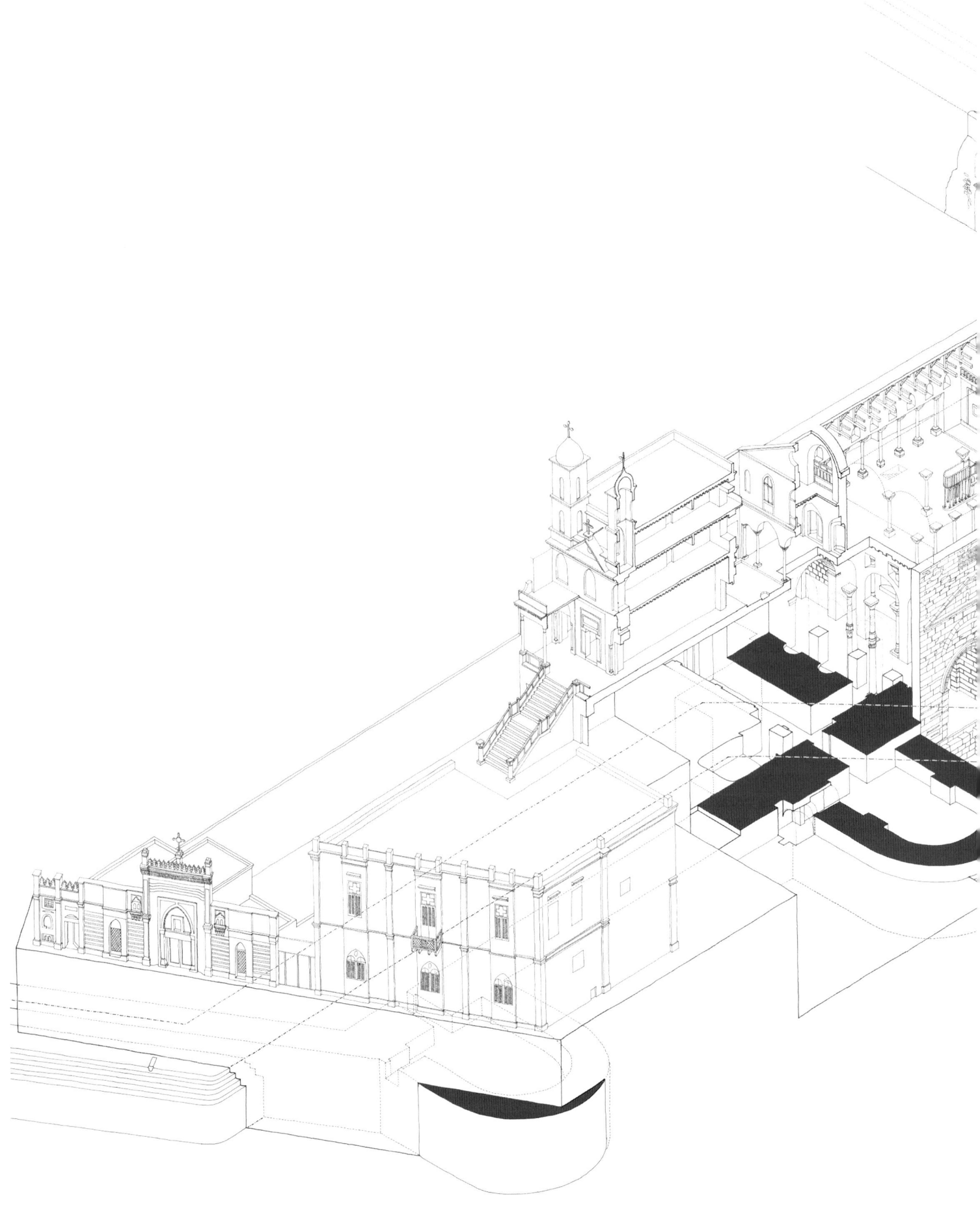

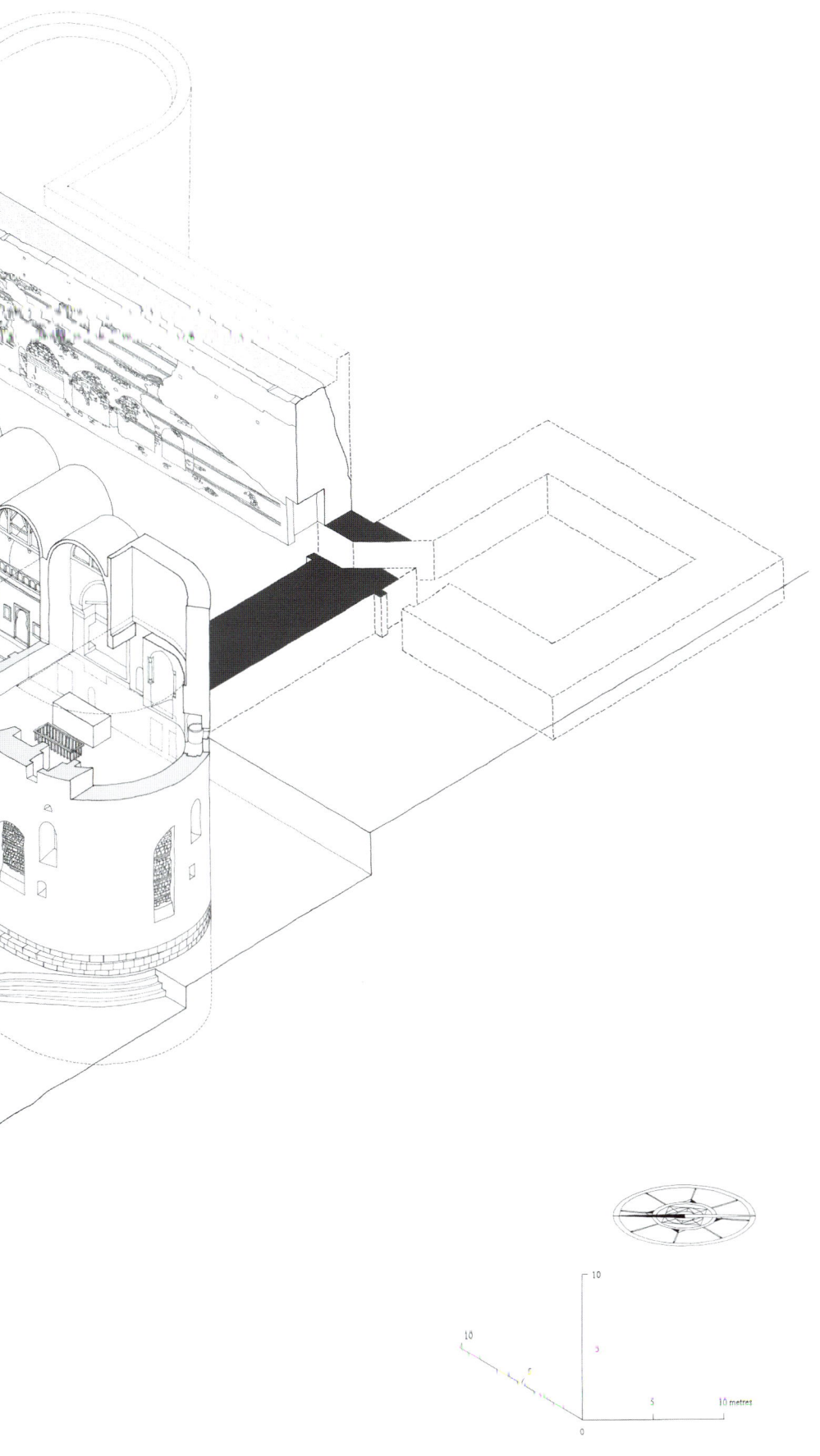

Fig. 24. Axonometric of the southwest corner of the Trajanic harbor and the later fortress, also showing the relationship of these structures to the Hanging Church. (Nicholas Warner/George Dawes)

western flanking tower of the South Gate and the U-shaped corner tower beneath the nineteenth-century al-Barati house shows that these towers and the south wall of the fortress between them were set forward about 3.7 m to the south of the old Trajanic quay. The presence of the foundations necessary for these Diocletianic constructions were confirmed by the limestone in the micro-tunnel samples from Shaft HC1 to Shaft PS3. Whether the loss of control over the micro-tunnel machine was due to it entering a void between the northern edge of these foundations and the stepped face of the Trajanic wall or the difference in resistance between the limestone rubble of the tower foundations and the limestone blocks of the quay wall, it seems to have been no coincidence that the machine should have been stopped at the very corner of the Trajanic harbor.

This corner shows that the south wall of the Trajanic harbor runs parallel to that of the fortress 3.7 m to the north. It must therefore have formed the base for the massive Roman wall still visible north of the western flanking tower of the South Gate which in turn supports the stairway to the Hanging Church. A continuation of the line of the preserved section of the stepped Trajanic quayside wall beneath the eastern flanking tower of the South Gate would join the south wall of the harbor at the corner of the massive wall that lies beneath the Hanging Church stairway. The relationship of this wall (which supports the stairway to the Hanging Church) to the western flanking tower had previously been hard to understand. It now appears to have been built over the angle of the earlier Trajanic quayside wall that survived the truncation east of this point caused by the later construction of the Roman gate. We can conclude therefore that the two sections of wall in Shari' Mari Girgis and beneath the South Gate were once connected, and that the part of the wall between them formed the southern edge of the Trajanic harbor. It seems likely that the part within the gatehouse was removed during the construction of the gate by Diocletian. Whether the part to the west of the gate was also dismantled or continued in use as part of the inner harbor of Babylon awaits further investigation. Blocks with clamp slots that probably come from the quay can also be seen reused in the foundations of the tower built by Diocletian flanking the gate to the west (fig. 24).[68]

Reconstructing the appearance of Trajan's harbor at Old Cairo is aided by this eloquent nineteenth-century description of the remains of the harbor of Portus, built by the emperor in the same period:

There is no doubt that, in ancient times, no hydraulic work was considered perfect unless it joined to the skill of engineering the beauty of architecture. What I mean is this: we are satisfied, for instance, with fixing to our wharves iron rings and old guns as moorings: in ancient times, the rings (dactylia) were cut in stone or marble, in the shape of a lion's head, or dolphin—and the columns were costly marbles, and bore inscriptions in praise of the constructor of the harbor. We fence the space allotted to commercial transactions with iron railings; the ancients enclosed it with colonnades of Oriental marble. We enter the docks, or the line of customs, through an iron gate; the ancients entered through triumphal arches, such as the well-known Arch of Trajan on the eastern pier of the harbor of Ancona. For the storing of merchandise, we make use of wooden and iron sheds, and, in exceptional cases, when we want to impress the stranger with our magnificence, we build brick warehouses. I wish the reader could see, as it has been my privilege to see, the beauty of the docks and warehouses of Porto, the perfection of their reticulated masonry, their cornices and entablatures, carved and moulded in terra-cotta, their mosaic pavements, their system of drainage and ventilation![69]

The stones forming the outer curving face of the quayside were joined for additional strength with iron swallow-tailed cramps. Slots for these cramps have been found in all the areas where the quayside wall was built with a curved face; beneath the Greek Orthodox Church of St. George, inside Shaft HC3, and in front of the South Gate of the fortress (pl. 21). The hard white mortar used in the walls of the Trajanic harbor is distinctly different from the mortar used two hundred years later in the walls and towers built by Diocletian. Sunk into the stonework at the curved entrance to the canal there is a massive limestone column base, perhaps echoing the monolithic columns set in the angles of the hexagonal harbor of Portus (pl. 22). This column was probably raised to mark the entrance to the canal part of the Trajanic phase, and was subsequently retained and enclosed within a semicircular niche when the northern round tower was built by Diocletian.

The borehole evidence within Old Cairo and the area to the north of the Mosque of 'Amr indicates the presence of a buried channel of the Nile following the edge of a limestone terrace of the Muqattam formation along the 11 m contour. In Old Cairo a borehole and a shaft (4A) sunk in the garden of the Coptic Museum revealed a sequence of sand and silt layers below 17 m MSL, which is approximately the level of the Roman quayside structures. The position of the canal walls suggests that this shaft was located toward the center of the channel, and the sequence of layers strongly suggests cycles of waterborne deposition. It may even reflect periodic cleaning and dredging.[70] Similar deposit sequences and a complete absence of structures below around 17 m MSL were noted at Shaft 10. Boreholes in the area of the former Church of the Virgin (Qasriyat al-Rihan) showed sand between 7 and 15 m MSL. To the north of the fortress, further points along the course of the canal appear to be indicated by boreholes in the area between Shafts 19 and 21. Comparison with the Roman foundation levels noted in the eastern and western parts of the fortress makes it clear that no Roman structures ever existed in this central part of the fortress, with buildings only springing up here after the canal had been filled in and converted to a road running north. Work to the east of the Wedding Hall of the Church of St. George appeared to confirm this, for Late Roman structures were only noted to the east of the line of the canal.

A seven-meter-long section of the similarly massive eastern wall of the canal was revealed by recent work within the crypt and beneath the sanctuaries of Abu Serga church. The stones that we saw along the western side of this wall (which runs along the line of the sanctuary screens of the church) showed wear that could be consistent with use of the canal frontage for the mooring of boats. The same wall was encountered twenty meters south of the crypt of Abu Serga during micro-tunneling operations between Shafts 4 and 4A. Records of the excavated material produced by the tunneling machine showed that it had passed through a wall of the same massive thickness and on the same alignment as the wall in Abu Serga. Archaeological evidence and parallels with the great harbor works carried out by Trajan at Portus suggest that the stone entrance to the canal was probably preceded by a small harbor in the southwest corner of the area contained within the later fortress. It may be significant also that the hexagonal harbor at Portus had a constant depth of around 6 m, just as at Old Cairo.

The presence of a narrow band of clay below the Trajanic foundations is confirmed by boreholes and excavations around the northern round tower. A borehole located inside the western flanking tower of the South Gate, below a ground level of around 18.4 m MSL, showed the tower is built on 5 m of limestone and brick foundations, ending at 13.4 m MSL. Below this a thin 1 m band of silty clay lies over 8.5 m of sand, probably representing the position of the early Holocene Nile branch channel. At 3.9 m MSL this sand gives way to firm gray clay, which continues down for at least 6.5 m and is no doubt the same very deep deposit of clay noted in other boreholes in the garden of the Coptic Museum.

An important element of the Roman riverscape concerns the evidence for a bridge via the island of Roda to the west bank. The layout of the Late Roman fortress shows that an important street crossed the fortress from the East Gate to another gate situated just beyond the junction between the Trajanic riverfront and the northwest walls of the Diocletianic enclosure. If the line of the river, indicated for the Early Roman period by the walls of the harbor beneath Shari' Mari Girgis, continued to the north, then the angle of the riverfront wall would leave a space in front of this presumed West Gate.[71] A number of factors suggest that this point probably marked the eastern end of a bridge crossing to Giza, which marked the beginning of the great land route west to North Africa. The massive scale of the harbor works carried out by Trajan reminds us that such an undertaking would have been well within the scope of military engineers at almost any point throughout the entire period of Roman rule in Egypt. A number of first-hand accounts, ranging from Julius Caesar to the fifth century, can be cited to illustrate Roman familiarity with and expertise in the building of bridges:

> River channels are bridged by the Romans with very great ease, since the soldiers are always practicing this operation, like any other military exercise, on the Danube, the Rhine, and the Euphrates.[72]

Accounts of the Arab siege of Babylon in 641 suggest that there was another fortification on the southern part of the island of Roda that complemented that of Babylon on the east bank.[73] Lane describes seeing what he took to be the "remains of a massive Roman wall (which is said to have surrounded the whole island): it supports the bank" in the middle of the nineteenth century.[74] These fortifications may have been related to a bridge spanning the river from Babylon via the island to a western bridgehead around Giza. Al-Muqaddasi, writing at the end of the tenth century, tells us that a bridge of boats across the river had been in place at the southern end of Roda until a few years before his account. It was destroyed at the time of the Fatimid conquest of Egypt, and it seems more likely that this was done to impede the Fatimid army arriving from the west than by the Fatimids, as al-Muqaddasi relates.[75] The power and annual rise of the Nile probably dictated that any Roman bridge would have been of the floating type, although again it is interesting to note that Trajan's reign saw the construction in 106 of the famous bridge on piers across the Danube at Drobetae (Turnu-Severin, Romania), which is still visible at low tide and which has inspired wonder in both ancient and modern writers.[76]

> Trajan constructed over the Danube a stone bridge for which I cannot sufficiently admire him. Brilliant, indeed, as are his other achievements, this surpasses them. For it has twenty piers of squared stone 150 feet in height above the foundations and sixty in width, and these, standing at a distance of 170 feet from one

another, are connected by arches. How, then, could one fail to be astonished at the expenditure made upon them, or at the way in which each of them was placed in a river so deep, in water so full of eddies, and on a bottom so muddy? . . . This, too, then, reveals the magnitude of Trajan's designs.[77]

The area around the West Gate of Babylon is really the only position that was both available and suitable for a bridge that would span the river from Old Cairo via Roda. As we have seen, south of this point lay the harbor and the entrance to the canal, and it would not have made any sense to block either of these with the construction of a bridge. It is not clear from al-Muqaddasi's account how much of the modern riverside area of Old Cairo between the fortress and the present riverbank had already formed by the tenth century, although the earliest monuments preserved along the modern Corniche date from the fourteenth century. The date of the shift of the riverbank westward remains a matter of conjecture, but given the ninth-century references in Arabic sources to a stepped quayside it may be that the position of the river and the use of the Roman quayside continued for some time after the Conquest and that the shift occurred relatively quickly, perhaps in consequence of the exceptionally high floods that occurred at the beginning of the ninth century.[78] In this case the change in the topography of the modern riverside area of Old Cairo may reflect the position of the eastern part of the bridge or its piers, which may have silted up to become a kind of artificial peninsula or 'mole.' Clearly such a process would have forced the course of the Nile channel westward.

How the canal functioned remains to some extent open to speculation and further research, as does its relationship to other installations of the Roman riverside and the harbor.[79] It may have been that the canal was filled during the inundation and then blocked at each end to retain the water. In this way it would remain navigable for longer. A papyrus dating from 710 warns the headman of the village of Aphrodito to send certain items for the ships in Clysma before the level of water in the Potamos Traianos falls and he has to send them by land.[80] At the Red Sea end of the canal the ancient accounts speak of Ptolemy's innovation of a lock, and a similar arrangement may have existed in Old Cairo.[81] The width and depth of the canal would also have dictated the size and type of vessel used, and goods were probably trans-shipped from Nile boats to smaller flat-bottomed craft more suitable for this purpose, as was the case at Ostia.[82] The arrangements for traffic along the canal and the specialist craft used on it must have contributed further to the complexity of the Roman harbor. One of the key functions of the port of Cairo down to the medieval period was as a staging post for the different kinds of boats serving Upper Egypt and the Delta, with different parts of the harbor used for mooring boats from these two areas.[83] This function may have had its roots in the Roman harbor at Old Cairo, in which case the bridge across the river may have served as a logical division between the two areas.

One of the most intriguing questions to arise from this is the effect of the canal and the physical impression made by the period of Roman rule on the topography of the city of Cairo. Did the Roman canal stimulate the growth of Babylon in the same way as its continued presence clearly did for its Arab successor in the seventh and eighth centuries? There is some archaeological evidence for the explosive growth of al-Fustat around the former Roman fortress in the first hundred years after the Arab Conquest of 641.[84] In contrast, very little evidence of Roman or Byzantine settlement or even activity has been noted in al-Fustat or in the deep shafts sunk to the north of the fortress of Babylon. This evidence may have been swept away by later activities in the same way as Fatimid resettlement largely effaced the earlier buildings of al-Fustat dating from the first century after the Conquest.[85] Even this thorough removal to bedrock left traces of earlier activity, however, so the lack of archaeological evidence appears to show that at least no large Roman town sprang up around the mouth of the canal. Of course this is not to say that no settlement existed on the East Bank. As we have seen, there are ancient references to a city of Babylon and the survival of settlement at Heliopolis. In the Byzantine period textual references and the evidence provided by the surviving Christian churches and monasteries may represent the beginnings of an urban center that foreshadowed and formed the later core of al-Fustat. We know, for example, that there was a Bishop of Babylon at the Council of Ephesus in AD 431.[86]

The major difference between Roman Babylon and Arab al-Fustat, however, seems to lie in the fact that the Amnis Traianus and the stations along its route were, like many other aspects of Roman Egypt, conceived as a means of refining the supply and enrichment of Rome. The construction of the canal also took place within a securely held province in which the movements of the population were closely controlled. This may have been even more the case after the military reorganization of the province by Diocletian, in which the fortress of Babylon played a pivotal role.[87] What was needed at Babylon was military control of the junction of important trade and supply routes. Of course the same military and strategic considerations informed the Arab Conquest and their reuse of the canal, but once the conquest had been achieved, impetus to the massive expansion of al-Fustat was given by the fortunately compatible desires to consolidate the hold over the source of "cereals giving life to the Hijaz" and the need to settle large numbers of land-hungry warriors.[88] With the Arab Conquest the focus of Egypt's trade and politics turned definitively from Alexandria and the Mediterranean eastward to the Red Sea via al-Fustat.

Archaeological Evidence for the Wider Roman Landscape of Cairo

The importance of its produce, the circumstances of its conquest, and its subsequent unruly history all combined to give Egypt throughout the period of Roman rule a markedly military character.[89] This military aspect appears to characterize the Roman landscape of Cairo, certainly insofar as we know it from archaeological evidence. Strabo tells us that, "The prefect has the rank of the [former] king."[90] This accords well with the view that the Romans kept Egypt deliberately un-urbanized, except for Alexandria and a few other existing cities. Much of the evidence for the Roman landscape of Cairo consists of previous descriptions of structures or features that have now disappeared. Into this category, for example, comes Lane's mid-nineteenth century mention of Roman fortifications on the island of Roda.

Strabo's description of the legionary encampment at Babylon in 25 BC is the first indicator of a Roman military presence in the landscape of Cairo.

> At present it is an encampment for one of the three legions which garrison Egypt. There is a mountainous ridge which extends from the encampment as far as the Nile. At this ridge are wheels and screws by which water is raised from the river, and one hundred and fifty prisoners are employed.[91]

The location of this first encampment was much discussed by antiquarians at the end of the nineteenth century. Butler, who examined this subject more closely than most, came down clearly on the rocky hill of al-Rasad to the south of Old Cairo as the location for the legionary encampment.[92] It is important to remember that there need not have been any link between the position of the first legionary encampment under Augustus and the works of Trajan and later Diocletian. Three legions are mentioned by Strabo as being in Egypt in 26–24 BC, with one of them at Babylon. One legion left in AD 23, while of the two that remained, one was stationed permanently at Alexandria and the other was most likely to have been stationed in the south of the country, particularly after the revolt in the Thebaid of AD 29.[93] It seems probable therefore that the legion stationed at Babylon by Augustus had left less than fifty years later.

Evidence for other Roman sites is equally inconclusive. On Gebel Yashkur, site of the Mosque of Ahmad ibn Tulun that dominated the entrance to the canal in the Tulunid and Fatimid periods, there is "massive limestone masonry forming the lowest courses of the mosque temenos wall. . . . suggesting perhaps, that an earlier Roman or even Pharaonic structure may have occupied the rock outcrop before the mosque was built."[94] Likewise, the massive masonry of the Qal'at al-Kabsh (the Fort of the Ram) led Lane-Poole and others to suggest that it was built "probably on an ancient foundation." In any event it certainly seems likely that the first legionary encampment occupied a more elevated and strategic location than the later fortress of Babylon.

The layout of the Late Roman fortress described in Chapter 3 gives indications of other features existing in the landscape to which the fortress appears to have been oriented when it was built in AD 300. It is perhaps significant that the line of the *cardo decumanus* or *via praetoria*, the main north–south street of the eastern enclosure of the Roman fortress, leads directly to the area known later as the Rumayla. This was famous in medieval times as the mustering point for the army and was located at the northern end of a hippodrome.[95] The origins of both the Rumayla and the hippodrome may therefore be related to a military function in the Roman period. The orientation of the East Gate of the fortress indicates the position of the *cardo maximus* or *via principalis* corresponded to a route leading toward the Late Period tombs of 'Ayn al-Sira and also perhaps to land routes east through the desert wadis. The continuation of this road westward across a Nile bridge would have connected it to Giza and thence to outposts on the west bank.[96]

The location of parts of this west bank and the continued use of Memphis into the Late Roman period are both attested to by an extant area of the riverside wall.[97] Similarly, the first accounts of the construction of the Nilometer at the southern tip of Roda in the eighth century indicate that its predecessor at Memphis (possibly on the east bank opposite Memphis at Helwan) continued in use. Other elements in the strategic landscape were watchtowers or *burgi* like that of Abu Rawash located to control trade routes westward into the desert.[98]

The Heritage of the Canal and Its Importance to the Later Topography and Development of the City of Cairo

The canal clearly played a large part in opening access and increasing traffic between Egypt and the East—it was said that 'Amr ibn al-'As himself knew Egypt from having visited it for trade prior to the Arab Conquest in 641, and a tradition is preserved in the ninth century *Futuh Misr* of the historian Ibn 'Abd al-Hakam that ships were traveling in it to al-Hijaz until just before the Conquest.[99]

The presence and possibilities of the canal also clearly played a major part in the decision to locate the new Arab capital at Old Cairo instead of the Mediterranean port city of Alexandria. The early medieval Arab sources agree that the re-excavation of the canal took place in the period immediately following the Arab Conquest. Ibn 'Abd al-Hakam quotes a letter to 'Amr from the caliph Omar in which he commands that the canal be re-dug as a matter of urgency so that Egyptian wheat can be sent to feed famine-struck Arabia.[100] The passage is also interesting in revealing Egyptian opposition to the re-excavation of the canal, no doubt founded on previous experience that the canal had been a tool of the country's economic exploitation. Al-Farqan adds the detail from the exchange that the canal, "although filled by sands, should be re-opened," and Ibn Duqmaq, probably drawing on al-Kindi's lost tenth-century work *al-Jund al-gharbi*, relates that the work took only six months and started just two years after the conquest in 643.[101] Both accounts show that the work consisted almost entirely of re-excavation of the existing Roman canal, now renamed *Khalig Amir al-Mu'minin*, or the Canal of the Commander of the Faithful.[102] The increased importance of the canal in connecting and supplying Arabia was also no doubt a major factor in the spectacular growth of Fustat following the Conquest. It may have gone out of use at the end of the Ummayad period either around 750, when parts of the southern part of the city may have been sacked and burned to avoid it falling into Abbasid hands or in 767/8, when the Arab sources suggest that it was closed by the caliph al-Mansur to prevent supplies reaching rebels in Madina.[103] It is interesting to speculate that the prodigious floods experienced shortly after this period (at the beginning of the ninth century) may have also played a part in the demise of the canal as a waterway.[104]

The primacy of the canal in the strategic thinking of the first years of the Arab empire continued for several centuries after the conquest of Egypt. Al-Muqaddasi's description in 375/985 of cereals being exported to the Hijaz shows that the route of the canal was still active, even if the actual waterborne link between Cairo itself and the Red Sea may have stopped functioning in the mid-eighth century.[105]

The innovation to the route of the canal as re-excavated after the Arab Conquest involved cutting a new entrance north of Babylon in the area of Sayyida Zaynab Square. Although we have no direct historical evidence for the date of this new entrance, the re-excavation of the canal after the Arab Conquest seems to provide the most likely impetus. Certainly by the time of al-Muqaddasi's visit at the end of the tenth century the entrance to the great canal was dominated by the Mosque of Ibn Tulun, the prime mosque of the "upper" *(fawqani)* part of the city.[106] The archaeological evidence from Old Cairo suggests the shifting of the entrance was a deliberately planned measure to allow the foundation of the new city of al-Fustat around a nucleus formed by the Roman fortress. This involved the conversion of the southern part of the canal into a major route running through the former fortress and into the central administrative district of the new city, a route now vestigially preserved as 'Atfat Mari Girgis.[107]

Archaeological analysis of the two great round towers shows that the entrance to the canal continued to be used after Diocletian's construction of the fortress in AD 300. At that time there was no wall between the towers, and ships entering the canal would have passed in and northward through the massive stone revetments. At a later point this entrance was, however, blocked with a similarly massive stone wall (pl. 23). Beneath the southern side of the Church of St. George this massive stone wall between the two Roman towers clearly abuts both the underlying "riverside wall" masonry *and* that of Diocletian's round tower built over it. Further evidence for this wall between the towers was provided during drilling for one of the sand/gravel "filter walls" of Contract 102. Where this filter wall crossed the line of the wall between the towers, the drilling log showed it to be more than 3 m wide and still present at 11 m MSL, some 15 m below modern ground level. What was the function of such a massive wall? We have seen that it is stratigraphically later than the northern round tower (and therefore the southern tower also), while the different construction technique of the wall makes it unlikely that it represents a Roman dike built between the two towers, to be partially dismantled and rebuilt during the filling of the canal. The wall was built to block the space between the two towers and appears to be part of a later phase when the former entrance from the river was blocked, either to prevent the flood waters from entering or to complete the circuit of the fortifications. In either case, the closure of the entrance to the canal from the river would have been accompanied by the filling in of its former course through the fortress. The first buildings in the central area of the fortress—including the earliest foundation of the Church of Abu Serga—thus date from the period after this closure and this filling in of the canal.

The buildings currently surviving above ground within the former line of the canal include the Mamluk Wedding Hall of the Church of St. George and a number of Ottoman buildings. A substantial earlier brick building, probably dating from the tenth/eleventh century, was also noted beneath the Wedding Hall. Archaeological work in Abu Serga showed at least three major building phases within the line of the former canal before the construction of the present church, which probably dates to the thirteenth century (see Chapters 4 and 5). The second of these phases appears to be a colonnaded church similar to the present building, while the nature of the earliest building below this is not clear. Historical sources for the Church of Abu Serga point to its foundation in the immediate post-Conquest era (around 690). If the colonnaded paleo-church is identified with this foundation, the filling in of the canal in Old Cairo must have occurred before this date. The position of the present façade of the church on the centerline of the canal is also probably significant in indicating either that it is contemporary with the creation of the street, or more likely that it follows an earlier street line created by the filling in of the southern end of the canal. The façade of the present church therefore reflects the western edge of all the earlier building phases on the site, the first of which is probably contemporary with the filling in of the canal and its conversion to a road.

The line of this road north to Cairo via the Mosques of 'Amr, Abu Su'ud, and Ibn Tulun survived into the first maps of the post-medieval period.[108] Projecting this street northward from its beginning in Old Cairo, it arrives at the junction where Shari' al-Khalifa becomes Shari' al-Surugiya (the Street of the Saddlers), which in turn becomes Shari' al-Khiyamiya (the Street of the Tent Makers). From the point where it passes through the gate of Bab Zuwayla this street becomes the *Qasaba*, the central highway of medieval Cairo and its main road to the north (fig. 2).

Al-Muqaddasi's 989 description of the newly founded al-Qahira underlines its strategic location at the point where this and earlier routes from the south of the city converged:

> The castle of the government occupies the centre of the town . . . it is situated on the great route to Sham and no one can get to Fustat via any other way, because the two towns are located between the mountain and the river.[109]

The foundation of the Mosque of 'Amr along the line of the filled-in canal indicates that this road was already functioning shortly after the Arab Conquest. The main façades and formal entrances of the churches of Abu Serga and Qasriyat al-Rihan gave on to this road at least into Fatimid times, just as the church of St. Barbara did with the older via praetoria. The precise location of these façades in the center of the former canal and the labor and effort required to fill in the canal and block its entrance with a massive stone wall all indicate that the conversion of the canal to a major road was a coordinated and deliberate step. Such a major piece of town planning seems most likely to have been associated with the creation of a new capital with a large native Christian population in the years 644–685.[110]

The Roman land routes complementing this road and the new course of the canal were another major influence on the topography of the city. In the Roman period when the canal was still functioning, the major northward route would probably have been a continuation of the via praetoria of the Roman fortress running toward the foot of the citadel. Where this road probably joined the ancient route (now Shari' al-Khalifa) that skirts the necropolis it is interesting to note the presence of early topographical markers in the shape of the Fatimid tombs built between 1110 and 1113 over what were believed to be the graves of descendants of the caliph 'Ali, who had come to Egypt in the seventh century.[111] Use of the older via praetoria was probably discontinued after the abandonment of much of the eastern part of al-Fustat, perhaps as early as the eighth and certainly after the eleventh century, when the link to the southern part of the city was blocked by the ruin heaps of the abandoned areas that soon became the dumping ground for a population that had relocated northward to al-Qahira.

At the crossroads between Shari' al-Khalifa and Shari' al-Surugiya, these roads are joined by another clearly ancient road leading east to the Rumayla. To the west this road (Shari' Ibn Tulun) now ends at the Tilul Zaynhum, the huge rubbish mounds of the medieval city. The twin presence of a canal and a land route leading to the northeast is thus a constant feature of the topography of the city from the most ancient times. In the most distant past we have the names at least of the *Jtj* Canal and the Road of Sep, although we know little about either of them. With the Roman period, however, the association between the Amnis Traianus and the roads leading north out of the Roman fortress becomes an explicit feature in the landscape. These two aspects dictated and constrained the location of the Fatimid enclosure of al-Qahira and continued their relationship into the medieval period as the *khalig* and the Great Road to Sham.

The silting up of parts of the canal and changes to its line failed to stop this traffic. In Old Cairo the topography of the medieval buildings shows that the line of the canal after it was filled in usurped the earlier Roman roads and became an axial route fronted by important buildings—the Church of Abu Serga and the Mosque of 'Amr, for example. Further to the north of the city a similar phenomenon occurred. In the later medieval period when the northward extension of the canal beyond the city had long silted up, the site where it ended became a lake known as Birkat al-Hagg, which was the starting point for the pilgrimage caravans to Mecca.

Chapter 3

Diocletian and the Roman Fortress of Babylon

Live in harmony, enrich the soldiers, and scorn all others.
—Reported to be Emperor Septimius Severus' (AD 193–211) dying words to his sons[1]

The previous chapters have provided a broad picture of the development of both the natural and human landscape of Old Cairo up to the end of the third century AD, when the present fortress of Babylon was built during the visits of the Emperor Diocletian to Egypt. As we have seen, the most striking features of the pre-Diocletianic landscape (and the one for which we now have substantial evidence) were the great stone river walls forming the harbor of Old Cairo and the entrance to the Amnis Traianus. Other settlement and building probably lay along the eastern edge of the canal leading to ancient Heliopolis and the north.

The Building Campaign of Diocletian in Context

The construction of the fortress should be seen in the context of three major developments already well advanced by the reign of Diocletian. The first two of these were closely connected, being the reorganization of the administrative and military aspects of the empire and a reform of the fiscal system needed to finance new defense measures.[2] These changes were a reaction to the series of political and military crises that throughout the third century threatened to destroy the Roman empire and turn it "from Military Monarchy into Military Anarchy."[3] External threats from across the Rhine and the Danube and from the Sassanian Persians in the East drained the wealth of Rome and concentrated its power in the hands of the frontier armies. The inevitable civil wars that resulted as these armies sought to influence the imperial succession further undermined the economic base that had underpinned the Pax Romana of the second century. The fifty-year period before the accession of Diocletian saw twenty-one emperors created by the provincial armies of the Danube, the Rhine, or the East, as well as numerous other unsuccessful candidates. This anarchy had tangible benefits for the soldiery, for at his accession each new emperor (if he was wise) granted a generous donation to the army in return for their support. The long line of soldier-emperors created by the army contributed to an autocratic style of rule more akin to oriental monarchs than that of earlier emperors. Diocletian, for example, was addressed as *dominus noster*, or "our lord," while Augustus and Trajan had merely been *primus inter pares*, or "first among equals."

The third major development in this period consisted of changes in Egyptian civil and intellectual society, in particular the growing importance of Christianity. The significance of the advent of Diocletian to the history of the Egyptian Church is reflected in the dating of the first year of the Coptic era (*Anno Martyrorum*—the Year of the Martyrs) from his accession in AD 284.

Though they focus on the emperor's persecution of Christians, the accounts of contemporaries such as the Christian writer Lactantius (250–325) reflect in a more general way a realization that the themes of Diocletian's reign had combined to create a new and troubling era: "In his greed and anxiety he [Diocletian] turned the world upside down."[4]

These changes in Egyptian society and administration at the end of the third century had far-reaching effects. Higher taxes and conscription, as well as religious persecution and a general feeling of insecurity, contributed to a flight from society to the desert fringes and thus to the spectacular growth of Egyptian monasticism, the model for many of the later European monastic communities. Changes to the defense and the internal order of Egypt, reform of the tax system, and the conflict between paganism and Christianity combined to produce a watershed in the history of the country. Contemporaries saw the link between these themes of Diocletian's reign. Lactantius, while deploring the treatment of the Christians, also laments the increase in taxes, the cost of his building program, and the greed of Diocletian. Pagan sources pass over his treatment of the Christians but repeat these other features of his reign.

Diocletian seems to have visited Egypt twice between 296 and 302 to deal with a variety of problems that reflected the already agitated state of the province at the end of the third century.[5] These included a peasant rebellion in Upper Egypt (suppressed by Galerius, Diocletian's Caesar and nominated successor in the East, in 294), incursions by the Blemmyes of the Eastern Desert and most significantly, a revolt by the usurper L. Domitius Domitianus in Alexandria in June/July 297(6?).

Later sources, such as the seventh-century chronicle of John, Bishop of Nikiu, give a Christian perspective on the reasons behind the emperor's activities in Egypt:

> And when Diocletian the Egyptian became emperor, the army turned to give its help to this impious man and persecutor of the faithful and the most wicked of all men. But the city of Alexandria and Egypt declared against him and refused to submit to him.[6]

Following the reimposition of imperial order, Diocletian appears to have spent as much as a year in Egypt reorganizing the borders and the military defenses of the province. This formed part of a much greater project, the reorganization of the eastern borders (*limes*) of the empire from Egypt to Persia. The efficacy of these measures was recognized by ancient commentators like Zosimus, writing in the first half of the fifth century:

> [T]he Roman Empire was, by the foresight of Diocletian, everywhere protected on its frontiers . . . by towns and fortresses and towers, in which the entire army was stationed; it was thus impossible for the barbarians to cross over, there being everywhere a sufficient opposing force to repel their inroads.[7]

In Egypt the dual policy of control over the province and defense of its borders involved the abandonment of the settlements of the Dodecaschene south of a new frontier at Aswan, and the construction of a string of key strategic fortresses along the length of the Nile Valley at Nag' al-Hagar (north of Aswan), Luxor (the fort here was built around Luxor temple), Babylon, and Nicopolis (Alexandria), as well as smaller outposts in the Fayyum at Qasr Qarun and on the Red Sea Coast at Abu Sha'ar.[8] It also included the formation of a new legion, the Legio III Diocletiana, to garrison these fortresses along with the existing Legio II Traiana Fortis (which had probably been involved, along with the Legio III Cyrenaica, in the construction of the Roman harbor and the entrance to the Red Sea Canal by Trajan around AD 110).[9] The *Notitia Dignitatum* mentions eight legions in connection with Egypt, most of them Diocletianic in origin. At Luxor, inscriptions on one of the tetrastyles date the construction of the fort to the end of 301 or the beginning of 302, while it has also been suggested that the *adventus domini* paintings in the 'chapel of the ensigns' at Luxor Temple depict a subsequent second imperial visit to the completed fort.[10] An inscription on the other tetrastyle gives a date of 308/9. Inscriptions like these from the Luxor fortress and from contemporary and later Coptic textual sources provide valuable circumstantial and chronological detail to supplement and provide a background to our archaeological observations in Old Cairo (pl. 26).

The economic crisis affecting the Roman Empire at the end of the third century was famously marked by Diocletian's largely unsuccessful 301 edict limiting the prices of goods and services.[11] Other fiscal measures had already included the abolition of the old tax system and the issue of a new coinage in 296. Land and manpower were the bases of the new tax system, and both were to be reviewed, at first every five years and, from 312, every fifteen years.[12] Essentially the new system sought fixed returns in place of the earlier system of quotas under which revenues varied year by year. To achieve these fixed returns, certain occupations were made hereditary, and people were increasingly tied to the land.

In Egypt an edict of the Prefect Aristius Optatus (AD 297) details the change from the ancient system, in which tax was based on the amount of land inundated each year, to a global sum based on the previous year and a cadastral valuation of the productivity and quality of land. The official cadastral survey on which all subsequent tax was levied was made at high Nile in the years between 297 and 302. The valuation of the land was then combined with a reading of the Nile level on a particular date at the beginning of the flood season. The prefect informed the emperor of this Nile level, on which the calculation of the year's tax was to be made. Once calculated there was to be no appeal or easing of the tax burden should the estimate prove greater than the actual yield. In this way the Nilometer became an active tax tool rather than merely an indicator of the expected yield.[13] The contrast with the earlier system "based on the true state of the actual rising" is shown by the edict of the Prefect Tiberius Julius Alexander from AD 68:

I have even before this checked also the excessive power of the state accountants, because everybody inveighed against them for entering numerous assessments on the basis of analogy—the result of which was they were getting rich and Egypt was becoming a wasteland. . . . A malpractice of the same kind is the so-called collection [of taxes] according to estimate, based not on the actual rising of the Nile but on a comparison of certain risings of former times, although nothing seems to be more just than the true facts. I desire men to live in confidence and cultivate with zeal, assured that the collection will be based on the true state of the actual rising and of the inundated land, and not on the trickery of those who enter assessments according to estimate.[14]

Similarly the tax moratorium of Hadrian from AD 135–36, providing a revised payment schedule for different areas based on relative hardship, shows that good governance could temper the desire to raise revenue:

> Since I have been informed that this year again, just as it did last year, the Nile has risen rather insufficiently and incompletely—even considering the fact that during the preceding years it produced successive rises that were not only full but even almost higher than at any time before, and that, flooding the entire country, it caused the production of most beautiful and abundant crops—nevertheless I have deemed it necessary to bestow a benefaction on the farmers, although I hope—may this be said with divine favor!—that any present deficiencies will be restored in the coming years by the Nile itself and the earth; [for such is] the nature of things, changing from productivity and abundance to scarcity, and from scarcity to plenty.[15]

The fiscal reforms of Diocletian had a fundamental effect on the relationship of the farmer with the Nile flood by removing its direct connection with taxes, which were now based on a more theoretical combination of land value and estimated yield. One effect was to give no chance for the small farmer to pay a reduced tax in a bad year. Inevitably this led to the formation of great estates owned by merchants or men with a source of income independent of the land.

A specific role for the fortress in the execution of these fiscal reforms cannot be ascertained from its archaeological remains. It is very likely that the Trajanic harbor at Old Cairo had always functioned as a trans-shipment and customs or duty point between vessels from Upper Egypt going not only to the Delta and the Mediterranean but also via the Amnis Traianus to the Red Sea. The location of a Nilometer for official readings of the Nile level in at least one of the great round towers is certainly a strong possibility. Strabo's description of the Nilometer at Elephantine shows how aptly the towers could have functioned in this way:

> The Nilometer is a well on the bank of the Nile constructed of ashlar masonry on which are indicated the greatest, least and mean rises of the Nile; for the water in the well rises and drops with the river. Accordingly there are marks on the wall of the well, measures of the full rises and of the others. Now, watchers inspect these and give out word to the rest of the people for their information; for long beforehand they know from such signs and the dates what the coming rise will be, and they predict it. This is useful both to the farmers with regard to water control, embankments, canals and other such matters, and also to the prefects with regard to the revenues; for the greater rises mean also greater revenues.[16]

The medieval writers Ibn Duqmaq and al-Maqrizi speak of a Nilometer in the area of the Melkite (Greek Orthodox) Church of St. George. These medieval authors seem to have inferred such a use for the great column that survives within the niche on the south side of the tower, while the accounts from the eighteenth and nineteenth century show that the stair chamber of the northern round tower was by this time being erroneously identified as the Nilometer.[17] It has been claimed that evidence for the Nilometer in the northern tower was found during work there in the early twentieth century, but no archaeological record of this work appears to survive.[18]

Notwithstanding a potential fiscal role, the part played by the fortress in Diocletian's military reorganization of Egypt is clear. The fortress fortified and enclosed the mouth of the canal and dominated the land and sea routes between Upper and Lower Egypt. Its size and scale allowed it to function as a potent symbol of the power of the emperor without the need to maintain a substantial land army. This was a major issue at the end of the third century when the recruitment of troops for the hard-pressed eastern *limes* had become a matter that could only be addressed by an improved and permanent organization of strongholds and frontiers rather than by force of arms. The harbor and the entrance to the canal had not been fortified by Trajan because there had been no need for such measures before the crises of the third century; the rise of the Parthian and Sassanian threats from the East made the political and military situation very different. John of Nikiu's seventh-century account does link Trajan's excavation of the Red Sea Canal to the fortification of Babylon. There is, however, no archaeological evidence for any fortification of Old Cairo before Diocletian, and it is more likely that this account conflates the fortifications of

Diocletian still existing in the seventh century with the earlier massive project of Trajan to renew the Red Sea Canal.

The crisis facing the army was connected with the question of the Christians, the other great theme of this period and in particular the reign of Diocletian. Systematic persecution of the Christians had occurred for the first time in 250–51 under the emperor Decius.[19] At a time when the very existence of the empire appeared to be in grave doubt, a need was perceived for solidarity in army and society alike based on "traditional" Roman values. As a public demonstration of this solidarity all citizens (but particularly those suspected of being Christians) were required to sacrifice to the Roman gods. The suffering and martyrdom that resulted from refusal to sacrifice would come to be one of the defining characteristics of the Egyptian Church. The targeting of the Christian leadership during these early persecutions increased the importance of martyrdom in the Church's identity.[20] The Decian persecutions were short-lived however, and the Church enjoyed a long period of peace until the last great persecution of the Christians started under Diocletian in 303. In the early part of his reign Diocletian may have simply favored the old gods and despised the Christians, but a major factor in instigating active persecution was again the perceived conflict of loyalties for Christians serving in the army between their beliefs and the ancient model of empire that Diocletian was seeking to restore. In March 302 he published a significantly worded edict at Alexandria condemning Manicheans to death for crimes "against what has been decided and fixed by the ancients."[21] The Christians were also increasing in number, a trend that must have seemed potentially disastrous. It is significant that these persecutions started in the army, and again the first wave consisted of threats to purge the army and the imperial administration of those who would not sacrifice to the Roman gods. In the Egyptian context it is also probably significant that the persecutions occurred only after Diocletian had been in Egypt for the second time in 302.[22] The Christian writer Eusebius of Caesarea was a witness to these events and he writes that in the following year, apparently at the instigation of Galerius, Diocletian's Caesar and successor in the East:

> Imperial rescripts were promulgated everywhere, commanding that the churches be brought to the ground and that the Scriptures be destroyed by fire, and proclaiming publicly that those who had attained honor (i.e., Christians in the army or the imperial administration) would become dishonored. . . . Such was the first edict against us.[23]

More edicts of increasing intensity and violence followed the retirement of Diocletian in 305 and the succession of Galerius as emperor in the East. Lactantius memorably describes Galerius as "more evil than all the evil men who have ever lived."[24] The clergy were imprisoned, tortured, and executed. A short amnesty was granted by Galerius in 311, but in the same year the persecution resumed in the East under his successor Maximinus Daia. For the Egyptian Church, the execution of Patriarch Peter of Alexandria in this period was the culmination of its early development, "shaped by this discourse of martyrdom."[25]

These events and the background of martyrdom are obviously important for the history of Old Cairo and the foundation and development of its churches. Archaeological information from Luxor and the evidence gleaned from Coptic martyrologies and hagiographies suggest that the fortresses built by Diocletian may have functioned as centers both for the fostering of the imperial cult and later for the persecution of its opponents.[26] In these accounts of good versus evil, Diocletian is portrayed as the malefactor, but it is usually a governor who carries out the execution of the martyrs. Forty-one of these passions mention Diocletian, while only four concern Maximian. It is probable that all of these were composed before 600. Included in some of the accounts is a recurring theme of overturning the throne of the emperor, suggesting the action was believed to have taken place inside a throne room or basilica. Other trials are sometimes mentioned as having been held in a theatre. The history of the Alexandrian church also indicates a preference for the construction of *martyria* on the site of former tribunals from the end of the fourth century onward.[27] The location of churches within former fortresses after the final triumph of Christianity in the later part of the fourth century would clearly have represented a highly symbolic victory.[28] Two of the churches and the convent are dedicated to St. George, Roman soldier and "the Prince of Martyrs." All three are built over earlier buildings of the Roman fortress. Another of the churches is dedicated to the soldier martyrs SS Sergius and Bacchus and another to the martyr St. Barbara of Nicomedia, the location of Diocletian's imperial court. On the other hand, the primacy of the cult of martyrs in the Egyptian Church also created other church complexes in Cairo, such as the Monastery of St. Mercurius and the Church of St. Menas. These are similarly dedicated to soldier saints but have no apparent connection with the sites of Roman persecution. It is also worth noting that the first references to the cults of St. George and SS Sergius and Bacchus do not appear until the fifth century, and in both cases it has been argued that they relate more to the short period of renewed persecution during the reign of Julian the Apostate between 361 and 363 than to the reign of Diocletian.[29]

Pl. 1. Aerial view of Old Cairo looking north. Note the Metro line showing the course of the Nile in the Roman period and the modern Nile at top left. (Rajan Patel)

Pl. 2. Aerial view of Old Cairo looking southeast showing the various monuments within the Roman fortress walls and the cemeteries to the north and east. (Rajan Patel)

Pl. 3. Aerial view of the Mosque of 'Amr looking east. To the north of the mosque is a Muslim cemetery and to the northeast the squatter settlement of Izbat Abu Qarn and beyond this the archaeological site of al-Fustat. (Rajan Patel)

Pl. 4. Aerial view of the Mosque of 'Amr, Old Cairo, and the Nile looking southwest toward the Pyramids of Giza. (Rajan Patel)

Pl. 5. Façade of the Ottoman-period sabil or public drinking fountain at the east end of the Harat Dayr Mari Girgis. The dedicatory inscription over the window from which the water was dispensed was stolen in the early 1990s. At the bottom right is the inlet from where the cistern below the building would have been filled. (Peter Sheehan)

Pl. 6. A general view of the church of Qasriyat al-Rihan looking northeast, taken in 2000 shortly before its demolition. The church was heavily damaged by fire in 1979. (Peter Sheehan)

Pl. 7. Ceramics workroom at the Supreme Council of Antiquities inspectorate in al-Fustat, with Alison Gascoigne and Mohammed Khalifa recording finds from the project. (Peter Sheehan)

Pl. 8. The groundwater level under Mari Girgis Church before the project began work there in 2002. (Peter Sheehan)

Pl. 9. Groundwater level in the crypt of Abu Serga Church in 2004 before works began. (Peter Sheehan)

Pl. 10. Part of the complex and well-preserved medieval drainage system below the Convent of St. George. (Peter Sheehan)

Pl. 11. Mari Girgis: The northern round tower (right) and the 1940s arcade, looking east. (Tim Loveless)

Pl. 12. Mari Girgis: The northern round tower (left) and the 1940s arcade, looking west. Note the stone blocks of the Roman barracks in the lower center of the photograph. (Tim Loveless)

Pl. 13. Material excavated during a night shift at Shaft 7 to the north of the Church of St. Barbara. In cases like this, ceramics and other finds recovered from the excavated material could be assigned only to a certain depth range. (Peter Sheehan)

Pl. 14. A Roman stone wall 2.5 meters below the modern ground surface in Shaft 5 immediately to the north of the Ben Ezra Synagogue. This was the first of the internal structures of the Roman fortress to be encountered during the groundwater lowering project. (Peter Sheehan)

Pl. 15. The massive stone wall forming the eastern side of the Amnis Traianus revealed in the crypt of Abu Serga Church. The column forms part of the late medieval remodeling of the crypt. (Tim Loveless)

Pl. 16. Medieval wall paintings in the southern apsidal sanctuary of Abu Serga Church after conservation. The painting depicts Christ enthroned, surrounded by the four living incorporeal creatures and flanked by the sun and moon. The style of the paintings helps us to date the addition of the apse to a date before AD 1230. (Tim Loveless)

Pl. 17. Detail of the Abu Serga wall paintings during the conservation work. The damaged areas occurred when a plaster layer that had covered the paintings was roughened to receive a subsequent layer. (Tim Loveless)

The Building Campaign of Diocletian: The Topography of the Roman Fortress of Babylon

The existing limits of Diocletian's fortress form a five-sided figure enclosing a roughly rectangular area of some three hectares. The outline of the fortress would form a rectangle but for the western wall of the fortress. This section of the walls runs almost directly north–south for around 220 m and forms an angle of about 33° to the rest of the enclosure. Unlike the partially preserved southern and eastern walls it has no projecting towers but instead two massive round towers (29 m in diameter) set 22 m apart at a tangent to the inner face of the wall. The northern of these round towers is set exactly at the center of the western wall. The southern wall is a hundred meters long, with a monumental gateway flanked by U-shaped towers toward its eastern end (pl. 26). This southern wall forms a right angle with the preserved eastern fortifications, which extend for some 190 m northward and are composed of the remains of four separate U-shaped towers linked by stretches of curtain wall. Beyond the last of these individual towers comes another tower that is actually the southern flanking tower of the East Gate of the fortress. Much of the original 10–11 m height of the eastern wall has been buried by the buildup of centuries of debris, and over the last hundred years the eastern fortifications have been engulfed by the Christian cemeteries of Old Cairo. The northern wall is entirely missing above ground and even its position is unknown, although there are some indications to suggest it was visible in the area north of the present day Shari' al-Imam until the 1940s.[30]

The Roman Riverside and Fortification of the Existing Trajanic Harbor

The alignment of the fortress was derived from the existing riverside walls of the Trajanic harbor and in particular the direction of the Amnis Traianus. The canal formed the median line of the fortress, and the eastern and western walls formed two enclosures of equal width on either side of the canal.

The southwest corner of the fortress does not owe its apparently peculiar configuration to the truncation of an original corner by a shift in the line of the river. Instead the line of the wall here marks the position of the river at the beginning of the second century AD, when the harbor and the entrance to the Red Sea Canal were built by Trajan. The position of the river appears to have been broadly unchanged two hundred years later when the fortress was built.

A Diocletianic date for the fortress appears certain based on a combination of criteria, including its technique of construction and particular architectural features such as the plan-form of the U-shaped towers of the eastern and southern enclosure walls and its gates with internal courtyards. Both these elements are characteristic of Late Roman military architecture, with close parallels in a group of fortifications built between 293–308 in Lower Moesia (the area of the Lower Danube in modern Bulgaria), Arabia, and Egypt.[31] The most notable Egyptian example is the enclosure of Luxor Temple, converted to a legionary *castrum* around AD 297–98.[32] The presence in Egypt at this time of Roman legionary forces that had previously been in Moesia may be a sufficiently convincing explanation for this similarity.[33] Labor for the construction of the fortress may have been conscripted from more populous areas of Egypt. A papyrus from July 299 relates to one Aurelios Unephris of Theadelphia in the Fayyum called up to work for one month at Babylon, after which time he was to be replaced by another.[34] The round towers on the western side of the fortress are unique structures without parallel in Roman military architecture.[35] The rationale for their construction is therefore to be sought in more specific terms of function and location, that is, defending the entrance to the canal.

The techniques of the Diocletianic phase were twofold—massive construction in large limestone blocks combined with widespread use of *opus mixtum* using large flat tiles and small limestone blocks. The use of these two complementary techniques throughout the fortress clearly indicates that the round towers and the rest of the fortress above ground are the work of a single constructional phase. Apart from the remains of the Trajanic riverside walls, the fortifications show no evidence of having incorporated earlier structures or of having been restored or added to. Even the barrack blocks (see below), although clearly built against an existing interior face of the curtain wall, appear identical in method and material of construction to the walls of the fortress.[36] They were therefore probably added immediately after the circuit of the fortress wall had been built.

This combination of methods and materials produced a structure of great strength, allowing it to survive in large parts more or less intact for seventeen centuries. Massive limestone blocks were used in the substructure of the southern round tower to create a structure independent of the adjacent Trajanic work that would resist the force of the river. Similar massive blocks were also used in the façade of the South Gate and the foundations of its western flanking tower. These huge blocks are further found in the internal buildings of the fortress used as lintels, thresholds, and in stairways. They were also used as the outer circular skin for the rubble foundations of the two massive concentric walls of the northern round tower, exclusively in the spoke walls of both towers, and as capping stones for deep rubble-filled foundation trenches on which the barracks and other internal buildings were built. To these structural elements the rest of the buildings were added in a strong, flexible, but much lighter (and faster) system of coursed rubble faced

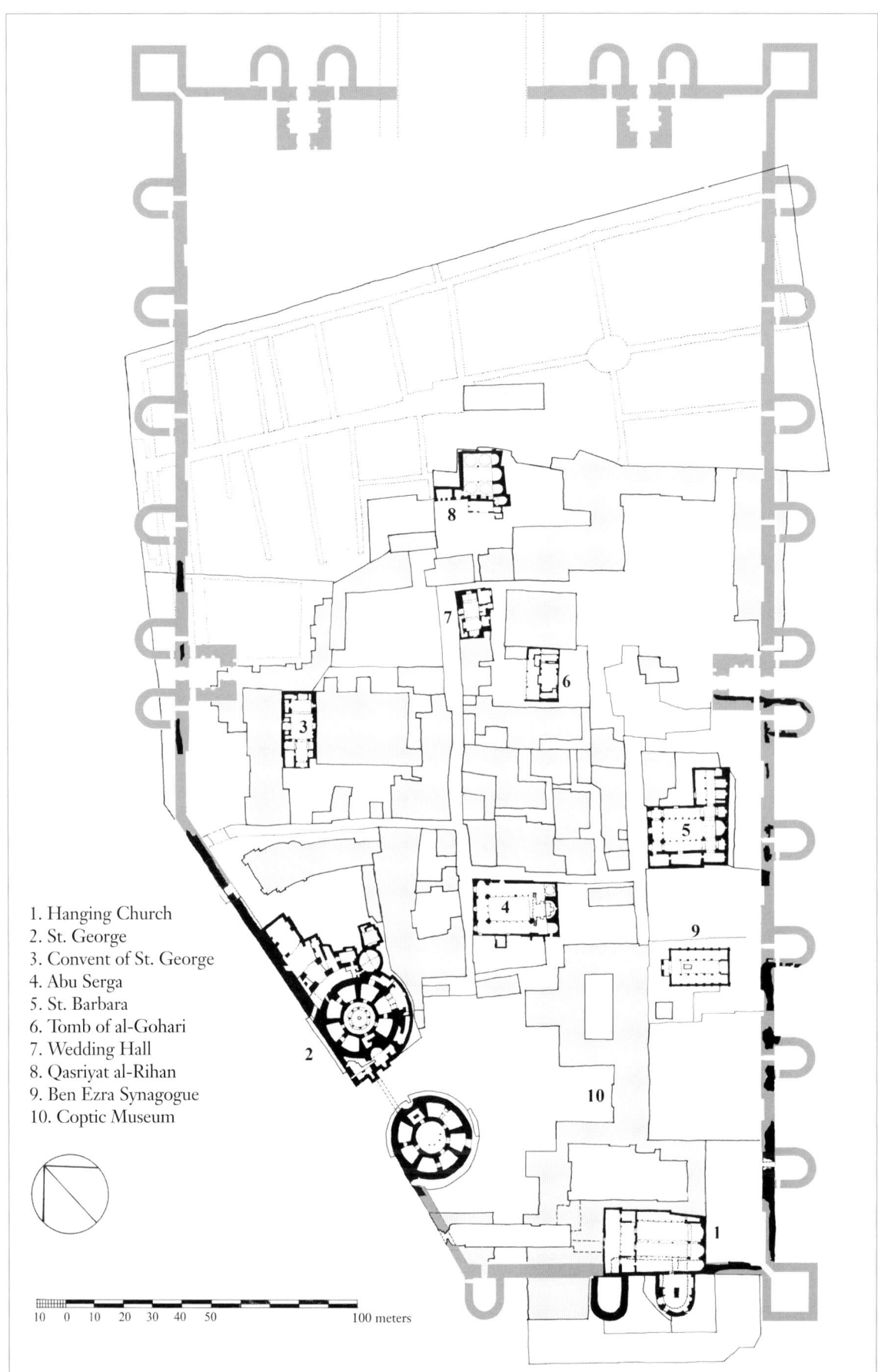

Fig. 25. Plan of Old Cairo showing existing buildings and the areas (shaded) of the Roman fortress standing above ground or revealed by excavation. The plan also shows a conjectural layout of the northern part of the fortress. (Nicholas Warner)

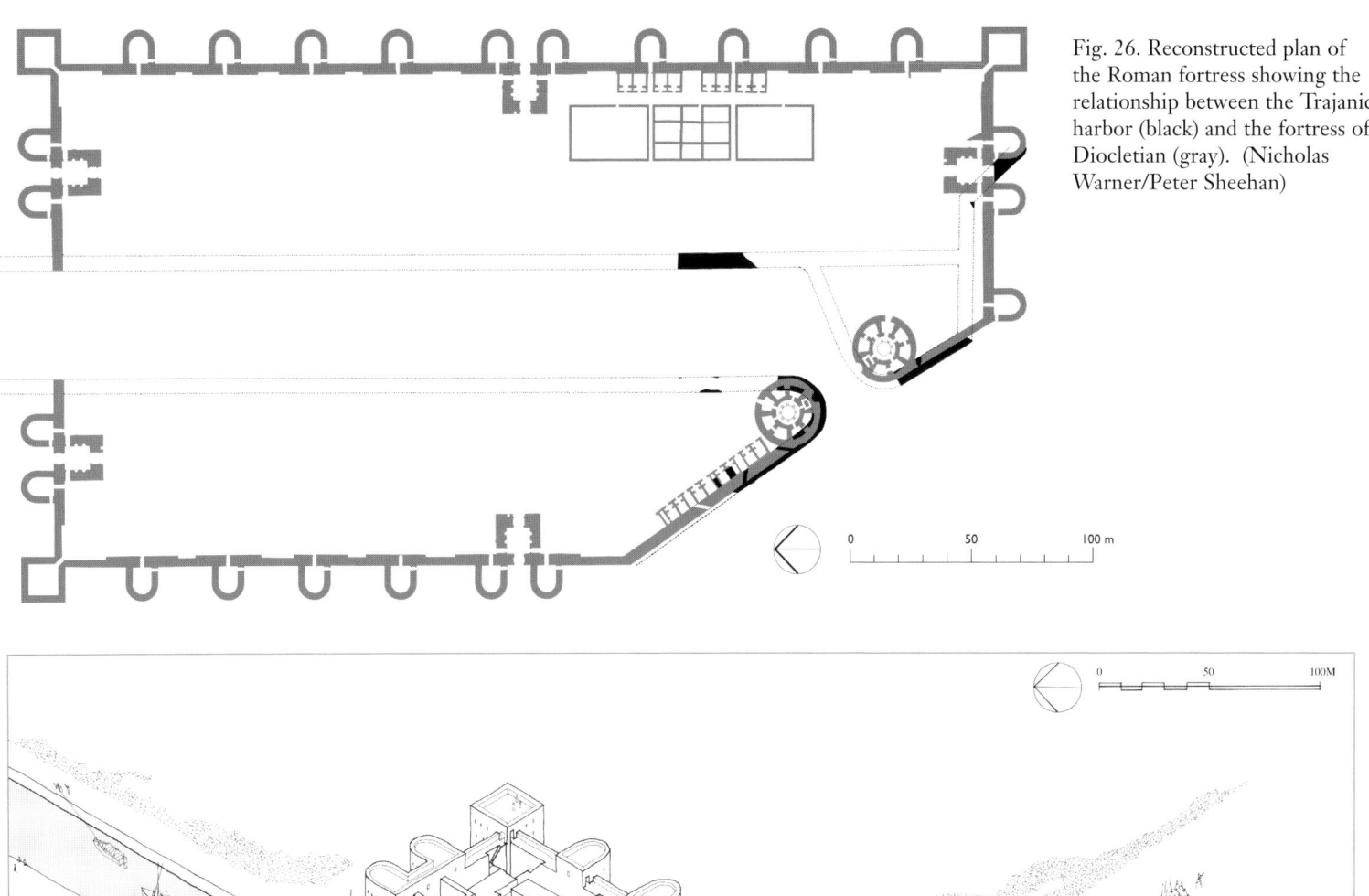

Fig. 26. Reconstructed plan of the Roman fortress showing the relationship between the Trajanic harbor (black) and the fortress of Diocletian (gray). (Nicholas Warner/Peter Sheehan)

Fig. 27. Axonometric reconstruction of the Roman Fortress of Babylon and the entrance to the Amnis Traianus c. AD 300. Note how the earlier inlet in front of the South Gate has been filled in and also the position of the West Gate opening on to the bridge that led via Roda to the west bank of the Nile. (Nicholas Warner)

Fig. 28. The surviving southern side of the East Gate in an early-twentieth-century photograph from the Comité archive.

with smaller dressed limestone blocks. Generally the arrangement of this *opus mixtum* follows a system in which every five courses of limestone alternate with three courses of broad brick tiles passing right through the thickness of the wall. This was the technique used in the curtain wall, but also extensively in the upper part of the barrack walls, as well as in substantial constructions like the inner gatehouses of the South and East Gates. Other distinctive constructional techniques noted during the recent works were the mortared rubble foundations of the northern round tower (used also to support the massive stone-block stairway chamber in the south tower) and the dense limestone rubble used in the foundations of the barracks. After construction, the ground in the barrack buildings in the east of the fortress and the southern round tower appears to have been leveled with a loose mixture of small limestone chippings, much of which was probably produced as work on the walls proceeded upward. A layer of these chippings 0.7 m deep was also found in front of the southern wall of the fortress during Contract 102 work in 2005. This layer had been deposited over an area that had previously formed an inlet from the river to the south wall of the Trajanic harbor, and appears to indicate the abandonment of this part of the harbor and its conversion into the approach to a land gate of the fortress. The presence of redeposited ceramic material in this layer ranging from the Old Kingdom to the First Intermediate Period shows that it is also similar to the rubble base laid within the former harbor around AD 300 to provide a base for the southern round tower.

The layer of chippings shows that the southern quay of the Trajanic harbor went out of use in or before AD 300 and that the area in front of it was converted into an approach to the land gate of the new fortress. The 1m difference in level between the threshold of the gate and the earlier quay wall may have been intended to raise the former above the generally higher level of the Nile, although other Late Roman structures in the western riverside area of the fortress (notably the round towers) were built at the same level as the existing Trajanic quay. This fact seems to confirm the continued use of parts of the Trajanic harbor, while the higher level in the areas of new construction like the eastern enclosure may reflect the presence of a low tell either created by earlier settlement on the site or left after the demolition of earlier buildings of this settlement. The level of the chippings layer is the same as that found within the Late Roman buildings in the west of the fortress (the round towers), even if it is nearly 1 m lower than the threshold of the South Gate. The difference in level between the top of the chippings layer at 17.4 m MSL and the threshold of the South Gate at 18.36 m MSL may simply indicate that the chippings sloped away from the gate from north to south and that the higher area was entirely removed during subsequent periods, in particular the excavation of the area in front of the gate by the Comité in 1901 (see Chapter 6).

The façade formed by the towers and the southern wall of the fortress lies about 10 m to the south of that of the existing Trajanic quay. The reason for this massive construction appears to have been the desire to create both a fortified inner harbor and an imposing façade that would be immediately visible to anyone sailing north as they rounded the bend in the river at Babylon. Parts of the earlier structure were dismantled to be reused in the wall—at least one block fragment with the distinctive swallow-tailed cramp marks of the Trajanic construction can be seen reused in the foundations of the western flanking tower—but it is possible that much of the southern wall remained in use as the quay of an inner harbor, protected now by the walls of the fortress. At the same time as the construction of the southwest corner tower, the western quay of the Trajanic harbor was extended southward. Such an extension of the quay would have acted as a retaining wall for the material dumped into the former inlet of the harbor. The presence of this wall in one of the groundwater project shafts (HC1) provides more evidence that the Late Roman construction of the U-shaped towers and curtain wall marked the definitive filling-in of the inlet in front of the south quay and its conversion into an approach to the South Gate.

The stone rubble used in the foundations of the southwest corner tower and the extension of the western quay southward included a royal Eighteenth Dynasty stele of Thutmoses III recovered from between 10–11 m below present street level (15.7 m MSL). The use of the same rubble raft foundation system for the southwest corner tower and the southern round tower indicates they are contemporary features, both forming part of Diocletian's remodeling of Babylon around AD 300, when the fortress was built to defend and enclose the early Roman harbor and the entrance to the Red Sea Canal.

The use of different foundation systems seems to have been dictated by which parts of the Trajanic harbor remained in use and which needed to be modified or removed by the new requirements. We can see from the layout of the fortress and the absence of a wall between the two great round towers that the stone sides of the canal not only continued in use but formed the principal axis around which the eastern and western enclosures of the fortress were symmetrically arranged. The northern round tower was thus built over the rounded end of the existing canal entrance in such a way as to permit its continued use.

The remarkable similarities in size and layout between Babylon and the legionary fortress at Luxor suggest both may have been the work of the Legio III Diocletiana, whose involvement is recorded at Luxor by inscriptions on the tetrapylons.[37] Both fortresses comprise a pair of enclosures each 100 m wide, aligned to and laid out symmetrically either side of a major existing topographical feature some 40 m wide. At Luxor the existing feature was the temple of Amenhotep III and Rameses II (and the Avenue of Sphinxes connecting it to Karnak), while at Babylon it was the Canal of Trajan. At the latter site the fortress takes its general alignment from the canal but also incorporates the Trajanic alignment to the main Nile channel. If our reconstruction of the original size of the Fortress of Babylon based on the East Gate being in the center of the east wall is correct, then it was substantially longer (380 m versus 235 m) than the fort at Luxor, which is, perhaps significantly, the same length as that part of the Diocletianic fortress added to the north of the earlier Trajanic harbor. Apart from the association with the Legio III Diocletiana, the remains of the fortress at Luxor suggest that the main axes of the Roman fortress at Babylon would have been related to the gates in the two parallel enclosures and that tetrapylons would have stood at the intersections of these colonnaded axes (pl. 27).

The building campaign of Diocletian created three distinct sectors in the fortress. The first of these comprised the existing riverside wall and the entrance to the canal, now fortified by the two massive round towers. To the east and west of the canal the construction of the outer walls of the fortress created two rectangular fortified "enclosures." These two enclosures must have been joined by one or more bridges, since seasonally, at least, they would have been partly separated from each other by the canal. Examination of the plan shows that the imposing South Gate of the fortress is set centrally within the separate eastern enclosure rather than within the overall southern façade of the fort.

There appear to have been important differences in the topography of these areas. Enough archaeological evidence exists from the eastern enclosure to indicate a regular array of barracks and administrative buildings set either side of the north–south via praetoria. In this eastern enclosure the ground level was also one meter higher than that of the western towers and their barracks. This may have been due to an existing higher ground level caused by the demolition of earlier buildings on the bank of the canal. This difference in ground level is preserved within the modern urban fabric of Old Cairo, as the ground rises noticeably east of the line of the canal. The presence of reused material within the Diocletianic fortress at the South Gate, the buildings east of the synagogue, and the stele of Thutmoses III all rather tend to the idea that, as at Luxor, existing structures were quarried for building material.

A number of important archaeological and related historical questions immediately arise. Were the massive stone walls forming the harbor and the mouth of the Amnis Traianus still visible and in use when the fortress was built? If so, was Diocletian's purpose to enclose and fortify the mouth of the canal? Two factors suggest this was at least partly the case. The first of these is the precise alignment of the fortress to the earlier walls, and in particular to the direction of the canal. The second factor is the absence of any wall or gate between the great round towers on its western side. Excavations carried out here in the late 1940s found no trace of such a gate.[38] Since we know that the western wall marked the position of the river at the time of Trajan, it follows that if this was still the case in AD 300, then the water of the Nile would have passed in through the entrance between the towers. If the river had moved to the west by this time, then we should expect that the entrance to the fortress would have been blocked by a wall between the two towers. That no such wall or gate between the towers existed under Diocletian is shown by the fact that at some time subsequent to the construction of the towers the decision was taken to block this entrance with a massive wall (pl. 23). Even then this wall may have been a construction partly dismantled each year during the inundation to allow the Nile to flow into and fill the canal, as was the case with the medieval version of the canal, al-Khalig al-Misri.[39] Although the northern round tower is cut into the thickness of the Trajanic river wall, the exterior face of the earlier wall would not have been affected. The entrance to the northern tower is also situated within the line of the great river wall as it turns northeastward. Some changes did take place, for the former quays along the inner face of the Trajanic river wall north of Mari Girgis were incorporated into the foundations of the barracks built against the inside of the fortress wall here. Another indication that the canal was still in use is that no trace of any internal buildings of the Late Roman fortress have been noted within its course. The effort needed to construct the southern round tower in such a careful relation to its northern twin also argues that the position of the northern tower relative to the Trajanic entrance to the canal was still significant. The semi-circular niches in the towers, perhaps filled with honorific columns or statues of the emperor, suggest that the space between the two towers marked an entrance to the fortress. Such a large undefended space can only have been feasible if this was the entrance directly from the river, perhaps closed by a lock that would allow passage between the towers while retaining the water in the channel.[40]

The curious appearance of the fortress plan thus conceals a layout of great precision, arranged symmetrically on either side of the Amnis Traianus, which ran between the massive walls revealed during our recent work beneath Mari Girgis and under the sanctuary of Abu Serga. The axis formed by the center of the canal passes through the western end of the southern wall of the fortress, and the outer walls of the western and eastern enclosures that form the rectangle of the fortress were each built 100 m from this centerline. The distance from the centerline of the canal to the eastern wall of the fortress is thus equal to the length of the southern wall of the fortress. It is also the same as the distance from the centerline of the canal to the wall of the Diocletianic western enclosure where it joins the northern end of the Trajanic river wall.

The archaeological evidence from Mari Girgis shows that the program of Diocletian did involve modifications to the Trajanic quayside. The barracks against the curtain wall north of the round tower are built over earlier massive stone rectangular "wharves" built out perpendicularly from the inner face of the river wall. The surface of these shows drainage channels and Greek letters cut into the stone, the latter a feature probably related to the storage of goods or the division of activities along the quayside. The area may even have originally given directly onto the canal, with the wharves allowing goods to be trans-shipped directly from the river to the smaller boats plying the canal. In any case, the archaeological sequence shows that the area within the rounded end of the river wall was perhaps filled in and certainly remodeled by Diocletian at the time of his construction of the fortress. We know that the river still ran along the western wall, however, for the barracks within this area were built so as to allow passage via arched posterns through the thickness of the curtain wall and out onto the riverfront.

Fig. 29. Excavations in the southern round tower at the entrance to the Coptic Museum in the late 1940s. Comité archive.

The most convincing interpretation of the archaeological evidence is that the canal was still in use, but that Diocletian's modifications responded to changes in the topography of the riverside and the entrance to the canal which had occurred in nearly two hundred years since its construction. More evidence for the continued use of the canal comes in the form of a papyrus from Oxyrhyncus dated to 332. It refers to an unskilled laborer called up for work on the Potamos Traianos, with the context suggesting this was a paid levy, with each village or group of villages providing labor.[41] Later papyrus references from the 420s suggesting the existence of a standing group of paid workers concerned with the upkeep of the canal show the canal was still in use.[42] We have no indication in any of the historical sources that the location of the entrance had been changed since the time of Trajan.

More extensive modifications to the Trajanic harbor were carried out around the southern entrance to the fortress. The arrangement of the South Gate as built by Diocletian is extremely unusual. Although it has the classic appearance of a land gate, a stepped quayside lies beneath the eastern flanking tower. Slots for the iron swallow-tailed cramps joining the stone blocks of the stepped quay show that it belongs to the same phase of Trajanic work noted elsewhere under the Church of Mari Girgis and in Shari' Mari Girgis at Shafts 2 and HC3. The difference in level between the threshold of the gate (18.5 m) and the quay (17.4 m) is another indication that the latter forms part of the Trajanic work. Obviously this quay cannot be later than the flanking tower built over it, so previous suggestions that "at some later period, the Nile was brought up to the gateway" and a quay built cannot be admitted.[43] This fundamental stratigraphic relationship shows that the quay is not a subsequent addition but a part of the Trajanic work incorporated into Diocletian's fortress as a foundation for the eastern flanking tower of a land gate to the new fortress.

Examination of the structure shows that the masonry beneath the western flanking tower and the massive stone foundation of the gate itself were built as part of the Diocletianic construction phase. The masonry in the foundations of the western flanking tower includes reused blocks with relief sculpture, as well as other fragments showing the slots for swallow-tailed cramps like those used in the Trajanic work (fig. 30). A borehole sunk inside the western tower showed that it is not built over the solid river wall, but like other elements of Diocletian's fortress (including the southern round tower) on a massive 4 m-thick rubble raft. The façade of the gate itself was first built in massive limestone blocks similar to those used elsewhere in the Diocletianic fortress for doorways and façades. The upper parts of the flanking towers were clearly added later

Fig. 30. Decorated blocks reused in the foundations of the western flanking tower of the South Gate. (Peter Sheehan)

on either side of the gateway, as was the internal gatehouse with its second arched entrance. This relationship is similar to the barracks inside the fortress, which were built later than the fortress wall but should be seen as forming part of the same constructional phase. There is therefore little doubt that the gateway itself is part of Diocletian's work. The position of the gate in the very center of the Diocletianic eastern enclosure is another indication that it forms part of this phase. There had to be a gate at the southern end of the axial via praetoria. Gates were a highly significant element of Roman architectural symbolism, particularly so during the Tetrarchy, for a number of the coins of the period show the four Tetrarchs sacrificing in front of a turreted fortress or city gate.[44] The new southern façade of the fortress gave onto the river, so the gate could have been seen and admired from afar by boats coming downstream. The *adventus domini* painting from the Roman *castrum* at Luxor suggests the personal presence of the emperor in Egypt during the construction of the legionary bases on the Nile at Luxor and Old Cairo. We know that he came to Egypt, probably on two occasions between 297 and 302, so it is highly likely that he visited the fortress during or after its construction. The emperor may even have stayed at Babylon during these visits, and some of the internal buildings of the fortress may also have been built so that it could function as a fortified imperial palace of the kind to which he eventually retired at Split in modern Croatia.[45] The massively thick walls of the Roman building noted beneath the Convent of St. George in 2005 may indicate that such high-status buildings, or perhaps the *principia* of the fortress, lay in this area.

One other factor lay behind the construction of the imposing South Gate. Diocletian's fortress deliberately enclosed and dominated two routes of fundamental significance to the early history of Cairo; the Red Sea Canal at its junction with the Nile and the east bank land route to Lower Egypt and to the north along the eastern edge of the floodplain at the point where it joined a major crossing point of the Nile. In the same way that the round towers marked the beginning of the canal, the South Gate of Babylon marked the beginning of this land route northward.

The unrecorded excavations and soil injections carried out during restoration work in 1998 inside the Roman gate meant that an opportunity to investigate the construction sequence of the gate was sadly missed. It seemed clear from viewing the excavated fill of the gatehouse that these excavations did not meet solid masonry, which would have indicated that the Trajanic quay continues under the gateway. As with the northern round tower, the whole gateway seems to have been cut through the earlier work in such a way that parts of the Trajanic structures were removed or modified by Diocletian. These changes did not, however, alter the fundamental relationship to the river, which continued to flow alongside the western wall of the fortress.

Our work in Old Cairo identified three areas of the Trajanic riverside from which we can attempt to reconstruct its original configuration and to understand the changes made by Diocletian during his construction of the fortress. These three areas are the riverside wall of the harbor of Trajan running along the line of modern Shariʿ Mari Girgis (incorporating the western wall of the entrance to the canal), part of the eastern wall of the canal under the sanctuary of Abu Serga, and the parts of the quayside revealed beneath the western and southern walls of the fortress in Shariʿ Mari Girgis and below the Hanging Church (fig. 19).

The 220 m length of the riverside wall is divided in two by the rounded entrance to the Amnis Traianus from the Nile, surmounted by one of the round towers of Diocletian's fortress and the Church of Mari Girgis. This rounded end of the Trajanic wall forms the north side of the entrance to the canal. From here the wall of the canal straightens out and starts to run to the northeast, although at this point the inner face has been partially cut into to allow the circle of the Diocletianic round tower to be completed.

In 2004 our archaeological observations beneath and around Abu Serga Church revealed the presence of another section of the eastern wall of the canal parallel to the Trajanic wall running northeast from Mari Girgis. This wall forms the ancient floor of the crypt of Abu Serga and underpins the entire sanctuary end of this church. The 6 m width of the wall here was exposed and recorded over a distance of some seven meters during the work in the crypt. Micro-tunnel logs from the groundwater lowering project enabled us to trace this wall for another twenty meters southeast of the church. This wall showed little evidence of having been modified by the Diocletianic changes to Old Cairo, but as we have seen, it gives the eastern enclosure of the fortress its orientation and forms its western edge.

The southern half of the western wall of Trajan's harbor can be traced again at the junction with the outer curve of the southern round tower of Diocletian's fortress. At the point where the curve of the Diocletianic tower begins, the end of an earlier massive section of masonry was noted below foundation level in one of the chambers of the tower (pl. 20). This stonework was already worn and eroded at the time of its incorporation into the Diocletianic tower. As with the other round tower, the presence of a postern south of the tower leading out onto the riverfront is another indication that the broad earlier river wall continues here beneath Diocletian's fortress, and that a 2-m-wide strip along the edge of the earlier quay wall was left after the construction of the 4-m-thick fortress wall. Boreholes indicated the presence of this wall to the south of the southern round tower, again offset 2 m from the line of the fortress wall above. The presence of this wall was confirmed when the Contract 102 tunneling machine head became stuck within it in June 2004 while traveling from Shaft HC1 towards Shaft 3. The extra shaft (HC3) sunk to retrieve the machine and allow a change of direction was excavated through the entire depth of this wall, revealing a lion-headed mooring stone built into the face of the wall. We can now see that the western wall of Diocletian's fortress was built on the existing riverside wall, while the alignment of the canal was adopted for the fortress enclosures added to the east and west of it. It seems unlikely that the southern round tower is built over an earlier Trajanic wall. Certainly no 6-m-wide earlier wall, corresponding to that in the northern tower, was noted during installation of pipes in the northwest chambers of the southern round tower. The absence of this wall and the massive foundations of the southern tower suggest therefore that the entrance to the canal may originally have been somewhat wider and that the southern round tower represents a slight narrowing of this entrance and a reduction in the size of the inner harbor, rather than merely the fortification of its southern edge.

This southern section of the Trajanic river wall originally created a small harbor at the entrance to the canal and may have provided additional wharves and quays like those preserved to the north of Mari Girgis and beneath the eastern flanking tower of the South Gate. The sinking of Shaft HC3 revealed that the micro-tunnel machine had in fact become stuck as it met the corner of the stepped face of the Roman quayside. As the masonry was brought to the surface we could see that in technique and appearance it was identical to that preserved under the eastern flanking tower of the South Gate. This wall preserves a series of steps that would have allowed access from the top of the quayside to boats moored alongside it at the different levels of the Nile during the year. Seeing this masonry reminded us of the divers' accounts of the wall encountered at Mari Girgis during the sinking of Shaft 2 at the beginning of the project in 2000. At the South Gate the Trajanic quayside was truncated and converted into a foundation during the construction of the gate, while blocks from the quay can also be seen reused in the foundations of the tower flanking the gate to the west. In fact, only one of the towers of the south wall of Diocletian's fortress was built over the former quay (where this was made possible by a southward bend in the quayside), while the other two towers were built on rubble and masonry rafts constructed against the face of the quay.

The Archaeology of Diocletian's Fortress
The Round Towers

The most impressive remains of Diocletian's building work are the two massive round towers set some 22 m apart at a tangent to the inner face of the western wall of the fortress. The northern tower now carries the Greek Orthodox Church of St. George (Mari Girgis), while the southern tower now lies within the garden of the Coptic Museum. In plan each tower forms an almost exact mirror image of the other, at least above ground level. Above this ground level (17.4 m MSL) the towers are 16 m high, three-story constructions, each story composed of eight roughly trapezoidal chambers formed by walls projecting radially from an inner concentric wall around a central colonnaded space (pl. 24).

Work on the South Gate of the fortress in the last years of the nineteenth century led the members of the Comité de Conservation des Monuments de l'Art Arabe (CCMAA) to believe that a similar gate existed between the two round towers. Some investigations to this end were made when the buildings over the southern round tower were cleared between 1946 and 1951. These investigations showed that a wall (shown on the Comité plan of 1946) did exist between the two towers, strengthening the idea that this was indeed the location of the West Gate of the fortress. However, examination of the archaeological evidence for this wall shows that it is a later construction that runs up and over the southern end of the earlier Trajanic river wall before abutting the northern round tower of Diocletian.

As we have seen, a major result of our recent work has been the archaeological evidence to demonstrate that the Roman tower beneath the Church of St. George is built over an earlier massive stone riverside wall. This wall was clearly noted by the Comité during the work in the northern tower in the early twentieth century, and the space between the towers is even marked on their unpublished drawings as "harbor entrance."[46] The final depth of the wall has not been definitively ascertained, but a number of observations indicated that it may continue to around 11 m MSL.

Around AD 300 the riverside wall or harbor was incorporated into Diocletian's new enclosure. This building phase saw the construction of both round towers, clearly conceived and executed as a single project. Archaeological evidence shows that no wall connected the towers at this time. The conclusion is that at both the earlier and Diocletianic phases the space between the two towers was open to the passage of water and waterborne traffic, and thus that the opening between the towers continued to form an entrance from the Nile. Facing each other across the entrance, the outer circumference of each tower is marked by a broad niche, the northernmost of which contains a huge column base, probably a column or statue surviving from the Trajanic harbor and marking the entrance to the canal.[47]

In the northern tower, Diocletian's architects first raised or more likely reinstated the top of the earlier riverside wall to 17.4 m MSL with massive blocks set in the distinctive pink mortar used in other parts of the fortress. Below this top course the stones are set in a harder white lime mortar similar to that noted in the wall beneath Abu Serga. Protected from the river by the massive earlier wall, the two concentric circles defining the northern tower in plan could be built as wide casemate walls filled with coursed and mortared rubble, linked and strengthened by spoke walls of solid masonry. The innermost concentric wall is wide enough to carry both a three-storied circular arcade and the circular wall dividing the central area from the side chambers (pl. 28).

Although above ground the two towers are identical in plan, the construction of their foundations is very different. Unlike the northern tower built over the Trajanic harbor wall, the southern tower has massive stone foundations and was constructed over a rubble raft. The earlier Trajanic harbor wall was incorporated into the tower and continues to the south, but the tower itself appears to have been a completely new construction built in a manner that could withstand the force of the river. The southern tower is composed of three concentric circles rather than the two noted in the northern tower, with the additional difference that these three concentric walls, as well as the spokes connecting them, are composed of solid block masonry. In the southern tower the use of a rubble core is confined to the chamber containing the stairway. Test pits dug in the tower showed this solid masonry continuing to at least 14.6 m MSL, while other observations in the area of the towers suggest its final foundation level may be around 11 m MSL. The key information regarding foundation levels for both the Trajanic harbor and the southern round tower is the wall built at a later date between the two Roman towers. The relative date for this wall is shown by the fact that it is built over the riverside wall and abuts both the southern round

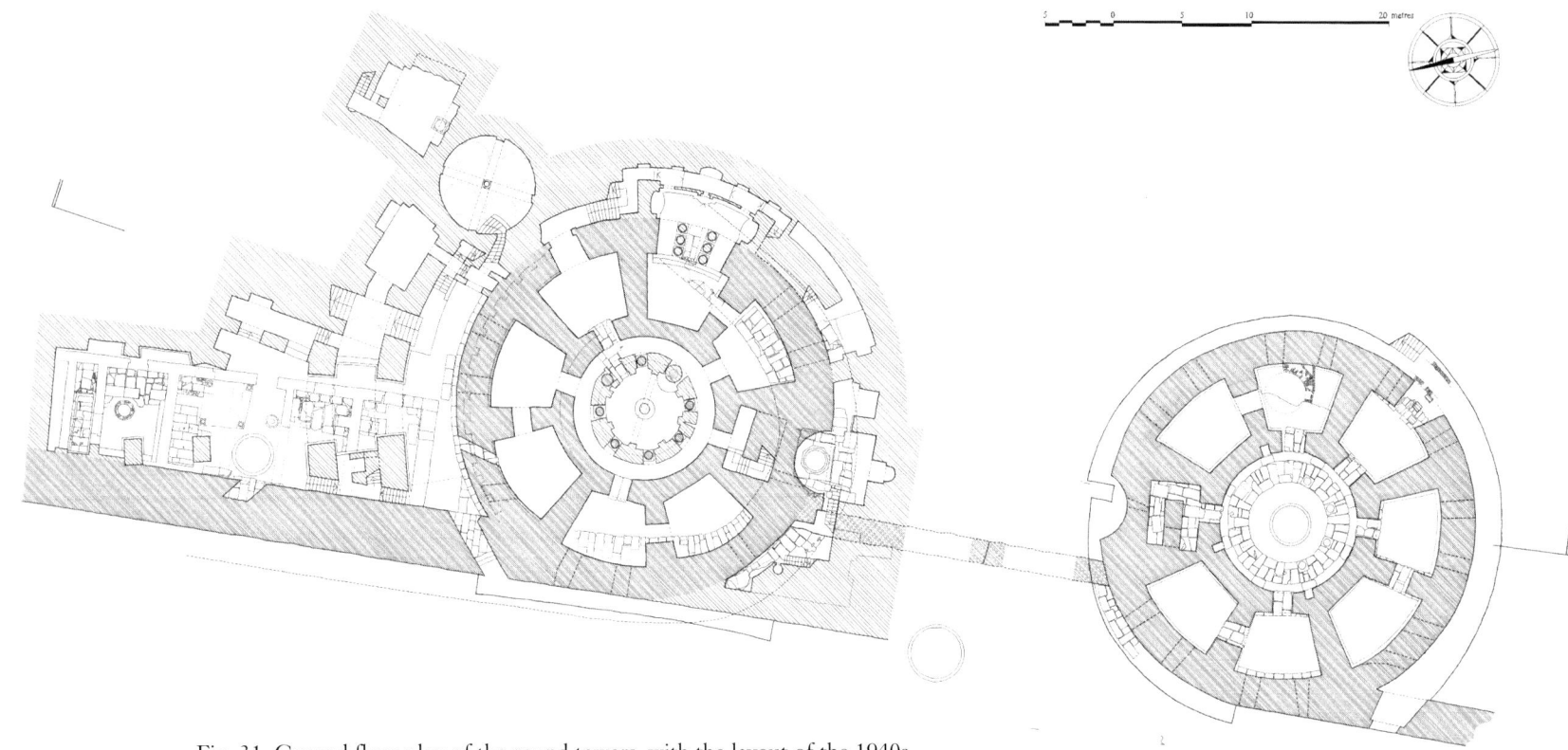

Fig. 31. Ground floor plan of the round towers, with the layout of the 1940s Greek Orthodox Church of St. George around the northern tower also shown. (Nicholas Warner/Peter Sheehan)

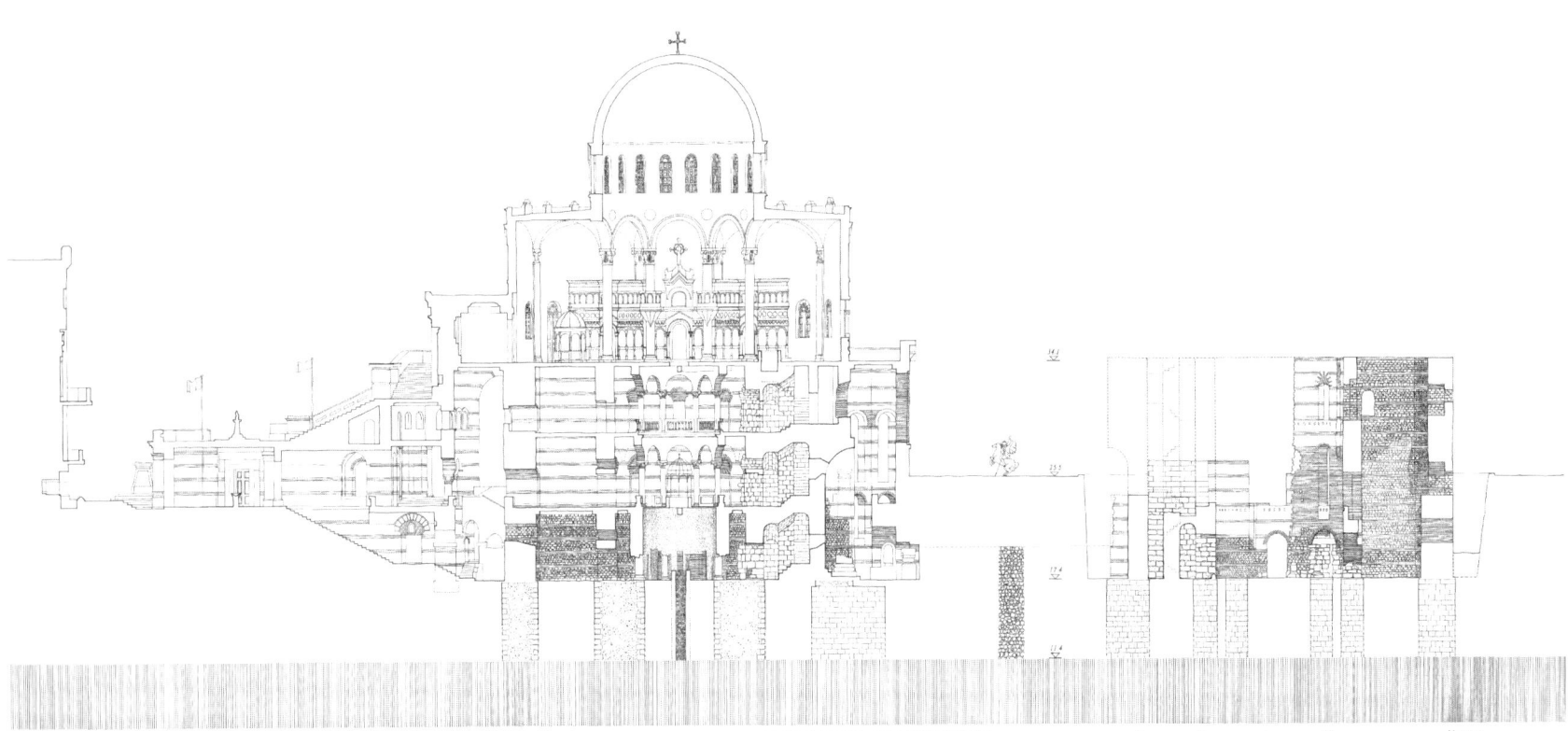

Fig. 32. Section through the round towers and the Greek Orthodox Church of St. George. Note the different types of foundations encountered in the two towers, and the rubble wall subsequently built to block the entrance to the canal between them. (Nicholas Warner/George Dawes)

Fig. 33. Axonometric view of the northern round tower. (Nicholas Warner)

Fig. 34. The original stonework of the entrance to the southern round tower before the recent restoration. (Peter Sheehan)

tower and the tower beneath the Church of St. George. The sand- and gravel-filled piles forming a "filter wall" between Shafts 3 and 4A of the groundwater lowering project had to be cut through this later wall between the towers from around 18 m MSL to a depth of around 11 m MSL. The later wall blocking the space between the two Roman towers is unlikely to be deeper than the adjacent original structure, so it can be assumed that the foundations of the riverside wall and the two towers also continue to the same depth of around 11 m MSL.

The excavation of Shaft 3A in the center of the southern round tower provided useful information regarding foundation levels within this phase. At 15 m MSL (excavation was continued to 13.88 m MSL) we encountered for the first time small-to-medium gravel and large chunks of broken Roman brick. The absence of any comparable change in the stone structure of the tower at 15 m MSL suggests this is the top of the backfilled foundation, extending to at least 13.88 m MSL (and probably to 11 m MSL).

Subsequent boreholes carried out in Shari' Mari Girgis immediately to the west of the southern round tower indicated limestone at 8.5 m below street level in an area immediately west of the tower (that is 17.3 m MSL, well above the foundation level). This appears to indicate the presence of a 2-m-wide offset between the edge of the Trajanic quay and the wall of the tower similar to that encountered in the northern round tower.

A circular arcade of eight evenly spaced columns occupies the center of each tower, the columns of this arcade being placed at the junction of the innermost concentric wall with each of the spoke walls. The spoke walls thus receive the thrust of the columns. Several column bases of the ground floor arcade survive *in situ* in the southern tower. All these bases, together with the lower third of their limestone columns, survive in the northern tower. Original access to the towers was via doorways on the northeast and southeast side respectively (pl. 29 and fig. 34). From here one passed through one of the chambers into the central arcaded area. At ground floor level, access from the arcade to the lateral chambers was gained through four additional doorways, one leading to the stair and the others each providing access to two chambers via a connecting door. The upper floors were reached from a newel stairway placed in the chamber behind the facing niches of each tower. Unlike the ground floor, the lateral chambers of the upper floors are not connected for the most part and communicate directly with the central space.

The massive column base in the niche of the northern round tower remains an intriguing detail (pl. 22). It is made from a type of numulitic limestone noted elsewhere only in two massive single stones reused immediately to the east of the crypt of Abu Serga and the river wall upon which the latter is built. The presence of massive limestone monumental blocks found only in close association with these two areas of the Trajanic harbor is perhaps significant. Close examination of the base shows that it was definitely cut into the earlier river wall. Less definite is the relationship with the niche itself, which may have been built around it. This stratigraphic sequence of river wall, column base, and tower is supported by the different alignment of the base in relation to the newel stairway chamber behind it. The arrangement suggests the niche and this part of the tower have been fitted in around the existing column base. If the column base is pre-Diocletianic it is intriguing to consider what it carried to mark the entrance of the Amnis Traianus. If, on the other hand, the column base is contemporary with Diocletian but was merely erected before the tower, it is more likely to have borne a statue of the emperor or an honorific column of the type known from a number of other Egyptian sites in this period.[48]

It was suggested in Chapter 2 that the towers were positioned at the head of a bridge or a bridge of boats crossing the Nile via the island of Roda and linking Giza and Memphis on the west bank with Heliopolis on the east.[49] Analysis of the Roman topography shows that such a bridge is more likely to have been located on a continuation of the east-west axis running through the fortress. The round towers therefore functioned primarily to guard the entrance to the canal, although additionally they may have been connected to other features related to the periodic closure of this entrance, such as locks or a dam. The position of the towers, their great depth, and the nature of their construction also suggest that either of them could also have functioned as Nilometers to measure the height of the annual flood.

Internal Layout: The Archaeology of the Eastern and Western Enclosures of Diocletian's Fortress

Diocletian constructed a great land fortress to enclose and protect the harbor, the entrance to the canal, and the adjacent land route to the north. Within its walls the fortress housed the manpower, the administration, and the storage facilities needed to fulfill this strategic role.

The circuit of the fortress was defended by a massively thick (4 m) and high (15 m) curtain wall. The eastern wall was punctuated at 22 m-intervals by U-shaped towers projecting 14 m from the outer face of the wall. At the southern corner archaeological evidence and contemporary parallels suggest instead the presence of a square tower, although at the western end of the southern wall (at the junction of the southern and western arms of the Trajanic river wall) cartographic evidence and old photographs indicate the use of the same type of U-shaped tower as those flanking the South Gate.[50]

The U-shaped towers were three stories high, with brick-vaulted internal chambers. Evidence from the South Gate indicates that each of the towers on the landward side was provided with a small postern gate to allow the defenders to counterattack as the opportunity arose, another distinctive and datable feature linking this phase of the fortress quite firmly with the Later Empire. Similar posterns let through the wall north and south of the round towers allowed defenders access to the riverside wall.

The entrances to these U-shaped towers appear to have dictated the internal plan of the fortress. Roads leading out perpendicularly from the via praetoria to the towers divided the fortress buildings into regular blocks or *insulae*. This shows the strong military rationale behind the layout of the internal buildings of the fortress, allowing quick and easy access to the towers in the event of attack. Rapid reaction was further served by a perimeter road, the via sagularis, running around the interior circuit of the fortress in front of the barracks built against the curtain walls.

The South Gate probably had a ceremonial or symbolic status related to its position facing the river. The arrangement of the fortress either side of the Amnis Traianus and comparison with the plan of the *castrum* at Luxor suggest that at least a further four to six gates would have existed in the Diocletianic fortress, two in the northern wall and one or perhaps two in each of the eastern and western enclosures.[51] Of these gates, only the southern half of the East Gate can be seen today. Remains of the northern half of this gate were noted below modern ground level in 1994.[52] Despite their different functions the arrangement seems similar to that of the South Gate—flanking bastions enclosing a monumental double-arched entrance leading to an interior gatehouse. As with the South Gate, there is evidence here for pairs of semicircular arched niches set into the walls of the gatehouse, possibly holding statues of the Tetrarchs.

At the western end of the east–west via principalis we can expect there to have been another gate, especially if this area contained the mercantile and unloading facilities around the head of a bridge or behind the western extension of the earlier harbor. Archaeological evidence for the remains of this West Gate survives as a blocked-up gap in the Roman circuit wall, still visible within the Greek cemetery. The subsidence of the modern boundary wall here suggests the weight of modern tour buses is causing a settling of the looser fill between the flanking towers of the gate.

The gates in the northern wall would have lain at the end of the two major north–south roads running equidistant from and parallel to the canal. These roads continued the ancient land route along the edge of the flood plain and were destined to continue in use long after the end of Roman rule, forming the main road through al-Fustat to the north along which its successors would grow. Projected northward, the

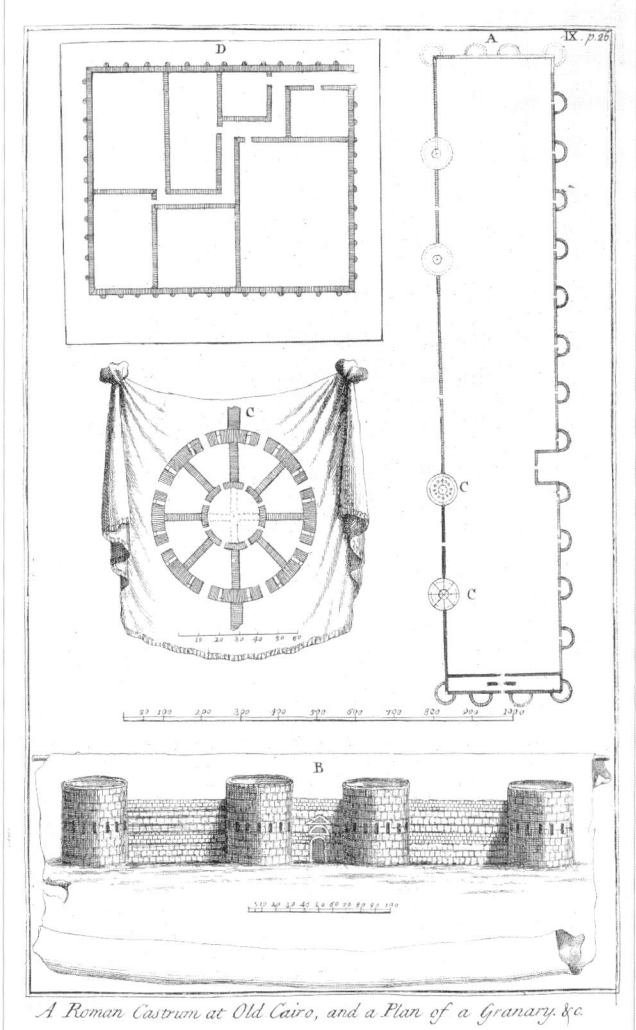

Fig. 35. Pococke's 1734 plan and other details of the Roman fortress.

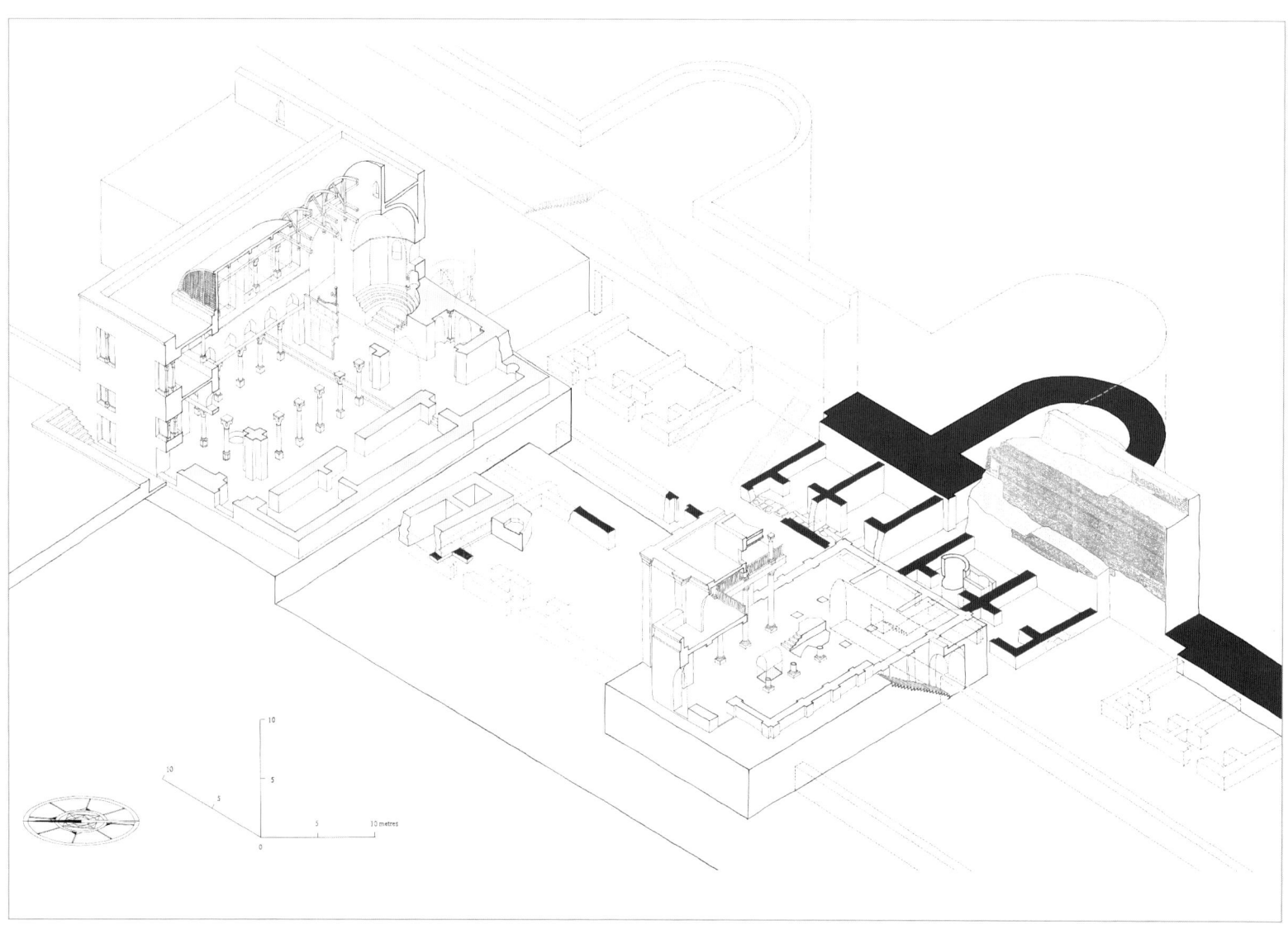

Fig. 36. Axonometric reconstruction of the Roman barracks in the area east of the present Ben Ezra synagogue showing the relationship of the Roman buildings to the synagogue, the Church of St. Barbara, and other medieval features. (Nicholas Warner)

patriarch Dioscorus, an increasingly violent conflict ensued between the Byzantine state and church (with their own rival patriarch of Alexandria) and the mainstream anti-Chalcedonian Egyptian Church (led by the successors of Dioscorus).[66]

These conflicts and the disruptions caused by the short period of Persian Sasanian rule between 619 and 629 left both Egypt and the wider Byzantine Empire divided and ripe for conquest at the time of the Arab invasion. The Arab Conquest ushered in even more far-reaching changes. Political and cultural focus turned toward the East rather than the Mediterranean and the West. Demographic changes began with the massive influx of settlers to the new foundation of al-Fustat around the nucleus of the Roman fortress, while the religion of Egypt's new rulers was gradually embraced by much of its people. In short, the Conquest marks the end of ancient Babylon and the beginning of its transformation into medieval Old Cairo.

Part 2
The Making of Old Cairo

Chapter 4

Al-Fustat and the Making of Old Cairo

From Fortress to City: Babylon as the Nucleus of al-Fustat and Its Role in the Development of Medieval Cairo

Throughout the Hellenistic and Roman periods Egypt was an integral part of the wider Mediterranean world, and for nearly a thousand years this relationship was channeled through, and dominated by, the great port city of Alexandria.[1] In AD 641–42 Egypt was conquered by an Arab army under the command of 'Amr ibn al-'As.[2] For seven months over the winter of 641 and the spring of 642 the Arab army laid siege to the strategically vital Roman fortress of Babylon. The death of the Byzantine emperor Heraclius, who had previously wrested back Egypt and much of Syria from the Sassanians, presaged the fall of the fortress by a matter of days. From this point on, Egypt became an integral part of the Muslim and Arab world. The focus of Egypt's rulers and the destination for its grain and its wealth changed from the Mediterranean and the West to Arabia and the East. The strategic value and economic importance of Egypt had attracted eastern rulers throughout the first millennium BC. After the first Assyrian conquest of the seventh century BC, successful attempts at eastern control had taken place during the 27th (Persian) dynasty (525–404 BC) and the Second Persian Occupation (345–332 BC).[3] A continuing desire to control Egypt is demonstrated by the later struggles between the Roman and Parthian/Sasanian empires and by the Third Persian occupation of Egypt, AD 619–29.[4] The "empire" of early Islam was able to take advantage of the power vacuum caused by the mutual exhaustion of the Byzantine and Sassanian regimes to achieve lasting control of Egypt, Syria, and Palestine with barely a struggle.[5] The historical connection of the Red Sea Canal with the Persian king Darius, historical accounts of the foundation of Babylon, and our archaeological evidence all indicate that from the eastern perspective, Babylon was an ideal location from which to achieve this aim. It seems clear that this was a view inherited by the Arabs.

After the conquest of Egypt and the expulsion of the Byzantine armies, the city of al-Fustat was founded around the site of the siege-camp of Babylon.[6] The settlement was also known by the Arabic word for 'camp', *misr* (pl. *amsar*), a name which continues to be used for the city and which from very early in the Islamic period was extended to refer to the entire country of Egypt.[7] In the first century of its existence the city grew at a phenomenal rate, mirroring the development of other 'camp cities' founded by the Arab armies in this period, such as Basra, Kufa, and Wasit in Iraq. From al-Fustat/Misr the existing links by land with the East and along the Amnis Traianus to the Red Sea enabled it to replace Alexandria as the administrative and economic capital of Egypt.

In this first century after the Conquest the explosive growth of al-Fustat took place on the *amal asfal*, the alluvial plain of the Nile around the Roman fortress and harbor, as well as on the rocky terraces, the *amal fawq*, rising to the east.[8] Archaeological evidence from both these areas shows that building in this period appears even to have outstripped the supply of materials, with houses constructed out of stone, red brick, mud brick, and generally whatever lay to hand.[9] Settlement on the rocky plateaus was made possible by the construction of aqueducts to bring water from the seasonal lake of Birkat al-Habash (to the south of al-Fustat) and by deep cisterns cut into the rock. Babylon was the

Fig. 37. One of the early Islamic aqueducts revealed by the IFAO team on the plateau of Istabl 'Antar that would have supplied the city with water from Birkat al-Habash. (Peter Sheehan)

nucleus of this new city, and the fortress fundamentally influenced the layout of the buildings constructed around it, in particular the center of the new city around the congregational mosque founded by 'Amr ibn al-'As (fig. 37).

As with the initial influx of Arab settlers after the Conquest, however, another major wave of new immigration arrived in Egypt from Baghdad and the East following the Abbasid conquest in 750.[10] Egypt was the final victory in the Abbasid campaign to wrest control of the Muslim empire from the Umayyads of Syria, and it was now ruled from their capital at Baghdad.

To the north of al-Fustat the Abbasids founded al-'Askar, a 'royal' or administrative area, deliberately distinct from the rest of the city. Two more of these separate enclosures were founded to the northeast of al-Fustat during the next two hundred years.[11] The second of these separate enclosures was al-Qata'i', built by Ahmad ibn Tulun after he was sent from Baghdad to govern Egypt for the Abbasids in 868. After his secession from Abbasid control, al-Qata'i' became the capital of his own short-lived Tulunid dynasty. Its major features were the great palace and mosque of Ibn Tulun on the hill of Gebel Yashkur, dominating the alluvial plain of the Nile. As with the earlier Umayyad settlements on the *amal fawq*, al-Qata'i' was provided with water from Birkat al-Habash via an intake tower and a great aqueduct, the southern part of which still survives in a very poor condition in the area of the modern city known as al-Bassatin.

Like the earlier Abbasid satellite district of al-'Askar, the area of al-Qata'i' was gradually subsumed and largely obliterated by the continued growth of al-Fustat, and this process was probably hastened by the destruction wrought on al-Qata'i' during the Abbasid reconquest of Egypt in 905. The same fate did not, however, overtake the third royal enclosure, al-Qahira, founded in 969 by the Shi'a Fatimid dynasty from North Africa. This endured to become the core of medieval Cairo, the richest, most famed, and most populous city in Africa and the Middle East. The Fatimid conquest was accompanied by another large influx of population, this time from the Maghreb countries, including large numbers of Jews.

The position of all these royal enclosures continued the fundamental relationship with the great canal that had characterized Babylon and was inherited by al-Fustat. In 985 the North African geographer and traveler al-Muqaddasi describes the great Mosque of Ibn Tulun as dominating the entrance to the great canal.[12] The enclosure of al-Qahira, laid out by the Fatimid commander al-Gawhar after his conquest of Egypt in 969, displays an even more explicit relationship with the canal running along its western edge. The main road within the walled enclosure of al-Qahira, the Qasaba, now became the successor to the ancient land route beside the canal running north from Old Cairo and the Roman fortress. The walls of al-Qahira therefore not only protected the caliph and his court, but also defended al-Fustat against attack from the north:

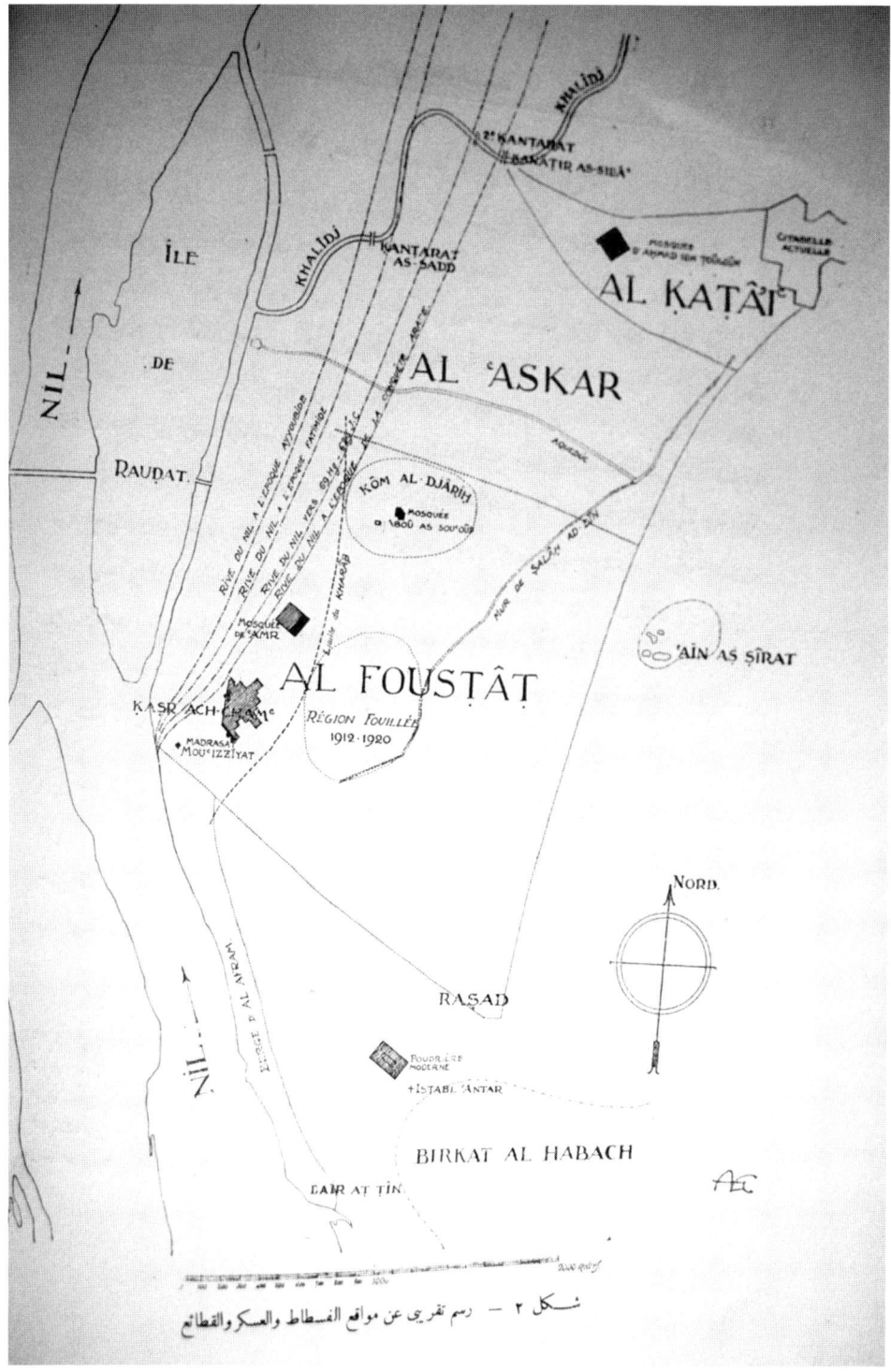

Fig. 38. Plan showing al-Fustat, al-'Askar, al-Qata'i', and other topographical elements of the city; taken from Bahgat Bey's 1921 *Fouilles d'al-Foustat*. Courtesy Mohammed Fahmy.

... the castle of the government occupies the center of the town ... it is situated on the great route to Sham [Syria/Palestine] and no one can get to Fustat via any other way, because the two towns are located between the mountain and the river.

—al-Muqaddasi, 985[13]

Although the foundations of al-'Askar and al-Qata'i' were later subsumed into Fustat, the writings of later medieval commentators, like al-Maqrizi and Ibn Duqmaq in the fourteenth century, show that a clear distinction existed between al-Qahira and the surviving areas of the older southern part of the city, al-Fustat–Misr.[14] These accounts reflect the historical and physical separation of the two areas caused by the abandonment of much of the southern part of al-Fustat in the latter part of the eleventh century and the movement of much its population to al-Qahira. The abandonment of al-Fustat was a consequence of a series of natural disasters suffered by the Egyptian capital in the long reign of the caliph al-Mustansir (1036–94)—low Nile levels, plague, famine, earthquakes. The effect of these disasters was aggravated by the unrest and anarchy that followed in their wake.[15] The end of al-Fustat was effectively recognized by a 1072 edict of the vizier Badr al-Gamali, which allowed the citizens of Cairo to remove building material from the abandoned parts of the city.[16] From the end of the eleventh century al-Fustat was extensively robbed for building material, and over almost a thousand years much of it became a vast dumping ground used for industrial activities and occupied only by squatters. Although the areas of the city to the north and east of the Roman fortress were largely abandoned, part of the ruin field was enclosed in the Ayyubids' great project to create al-Qahira al-Mahrusa (the Well-Protected) at the end of the twelfth century by building a wall around the entire city.[17] The inclusion of Old Cairo within this scheme shows its continued significance, although the scale of the Ayyubid city walls preserved in al-Fustat suggests they had a symbolic rather than military character. They were thus much less imposing than the fortifications in the northern part of the city, where attack by an army invading from the north had been shown to be a real possibility by the Fifth Crusade and the events leading up to the creation of the Ayyubid dynasty. One of these events was the famous "Burning of al-Fustat" in 1168 to prevent it falling into Crusader hands, although since much of the city was already abandoned by this time, it has been suggested that the event has been conflated with the large-scale disorders that had occurred in the reign of al-Mustansir, or even with the burning of the city by the Umayyads as they retreated from the Abbasid armies in 750.[18] The wall enclosing al-Fustat also carried an aqueduct supplying the Citadel of Cairo, built by the Ayyubids as the new seat of royal power. The creation of the citadel accentuated the demographic shift toward al-Qahira from the end of the twelfth century, as the former royal areas of the Fatimid city were subsumed into the urban mass and converted to public and private use.

Archaeological Evidence for the Making of Old Cairo

The medieval period encompasses the 'making' of much of Old Cairo as it is preserved today, and the archaeology of this period reflects the gradual transformation of the ancient harbor and the Roman fortress into a medieval landscape within the wider urban setting of al-Fustat and Cairo. Following the Arab Conquest and the foundation of al-Fustat, the fortress lost its military role and was divided up and incorporated into the urban fabric of the new city. The archaeology of the medieval period thus presents a more complex set of relationships and problems than those presented by material remains of both major phases of the Roman period, which essentially concern understanding the plan layout of large single-phase building projects. Unlike these Roman structures, the key relationships preserved in the archaeology of the medieval period are those that show vertical sequences of activity over time. Analysis of this stratigraphic information, allied with changes to the plans of buildings, demonstrates how Old Cairo was made and transformed in the medieval period. The complexity inherent in the post-Roman fragmentation of the fortress and the development of individual buildings also makes the conclusions to be drawn from medieval archaeology more local and sometimes less certain. On the other hand, our understanding of the medieval period is aided by an increase in the amount of historical information available and the greater availability of cartographic and documentary evidence, as well as by the continued survival of much medieval building fabric above modern ground level.

The medieval transformation of Old Cairo can be approached both chronologically and thematically. Chronologically we have divided the period into three phases on the basis of a combination of archaeological evidence and documented historical and political events. The first phase, called here *early medieval*, covers the period from the Arab Conquest of Egypt in 642 to the abandonment of al-Fustat that occurred during the reign of the Fatimid caliph al-Mustansir (d.1094). The *medieval* phase (1094–1517) deals with events in Old Cairo from the abandonment of al-Fustat to the Ottoman Conquest of Egypt. The *post-medieval* period (1517–1890) continues the story of Old Cairo through the centuries of Ottoman rule until its "rediscovery" by antiquarians around 1890. A number of important sites worked on during the groundwater lowering project, notably the Church of Abu Serga and the Convent of St. George, preserve archaeological sequences covering all three phases.

Archaeological material encompassing some or all of these sequences was encountered in almost every location excavated during the groundwater lowering project. The nature of this material allowed a number of distinct themes in the making of Old Cairo to be identified. The reuse of Roman buildings, either in their entirety or as foundations, is one of the most recurring of these themes. The type of reuse varied widely. Some Roman buildings were simply quarried for their stones while others were preserved entirely and merely adapted to new uses: ecclesiastical, domestic, or industrial. Other recurring types of archaeological features were the complex systems of water supply and drainage across the area. The ubiquity of these systems underlines the importance of the provision of fresh water and the disposal of sewage in the medieval city. In Old Cairo the supply of water became a major focus of medieval activity as the riverfront moved further from where it had been in the Roman period. Another theme arising from archaeological and documentary evidence is industrial activity, in particular the production of pottery. Industrial activity increased in scale and importance after the abandonment of al-Fustat, when its ruin heaps became a convenient location (downwind of medieval Cairo) for noxious industrial installations such as pottery kilns, lime kilns, and tanneries.

Our archaeological sources include the standing buildings of Old Cairo—its churches, monasteries, mosques, synagogues, and tombs. Historical information about these buildings allows us to use them as temporal markers in the landscape. The evidence provided by archaeology for numerous restorations and repairs reminds us that individual buildings developed over time and were not simply products of particular periods. The process of tracing the first appearance of the buildings of Old Cairo and their subsequent changes is greatly aided by church histories and travelers' descriptions, supplemented as we enter modern times by maps and then photographs.[19] Although relatively late in date, the cartographic evidence preserves topographical elements that clearly go back to much earlier periods. To all this historical information, travelers' accounts, and traditions concerning the foundation of the churches and monuments of Old Cairo, we have now added a significant archaeological aspect. Our archaeological information from Old Cairo adds to that gained during exploration of different parts of the ruin fields of al-Fustat over the past eighty years. The earliest work was that of Bahgat Bey in marshalling the *sebakhin*. These were a particular phenomenon of the nineteenth and early twentieth centuries, and consisted of large gangs of laborers who devastated many ancient sites in Egypt in their search for material to be salvaged or ancient mud bricks and organic material which could be used as *sebakh*, or fertilizer. Their systematic exploitation of the ruin fields, however, provided some overview of the archaeology of this part of al-Fustat in the period before its abandonment in the eleventh century.[20] George Scanlon and Wladyslaw Kubiak continued the work of Bahgat in the areas of al-Fustat scheduled to go under public housing schemes during the 1970s.[21] The recent work of the IFAO team under Roland Gayraud on the higher terraces to the east of Old Cairo has thrown important light on the nature of the early settlement of al-Fustat.[22] The sites and buildings within Old Cairo preserve evidence from some or all of the various sources—historical, cartographical, and archaeological. To take one example, although we have little archaeological information to support it, the existence of an earlier medieval road running through the ruin fields of al-Fustat between the Mosques of 'Amr, Abu Su'ud, and Ibn Tulun can be inferred from looking at maps from 1736 onward.[23] Within the walls of Old Cairo, however, there is persuasive archaeological evidence to show that the same road, dating from the early medieval period, is in fact the filled-in line of Trajan's Canal.

Despite the abandonment of much of al-Fustat at the end of the eleventh century, a narrow strip along the Nile survived into the periods of Ayyubid and Mamluk rule that comprise the medieval period in Old Cairo. The area still occupied included the interior of the fortress, which continued its ancient links with the port of the city to the west of Old Cairo and around the island of Roda. The ancient roads from Babylon north to Cairo and to the massive cemeteries on the eastern edge of al-Fustat continued to pass through the ruin fields.

The Ayyubid period saw significant architectural and decorative changes to the Church of Abu Serga, changes that were probably echoed in other churches of the area including the Church of the Virgin (Qasriyat al-Rihan). Archaeological evidence for Old Cairo during Mamluk times survives in entire standing buildings such as the *qa'a* or hall within the Convent of St. George and the 'Wedding Hall' (Qa'at al-'Irsan) of the Church of St. George, as well as elements of other buildings like the northern *haykal* (sanctuary) of Abu Serga. From the fourteenth century, tensions between Muslims and an increasingly minority Christian community contributed to the exterior aspect of the churches becoming plain and unostentatious, in marked contrast to their original appearance.[24] A rich background to the archaeology of the medieval period is provided by the accounts of European merchants and pilgrims, as well as by the detailed topographic compendia of the Egyptian historians al-Maqrizi and Ibn Duqmaq and the documents of the Cairo Geniza.[25]

The Ottoman Conquest of Egypt in 1517 provides a convenient cutoff point for the end of the medieval and the beginning of the post-medieval phase. The connection between the interior of the former fortress and the riverfront areas of Old Cairo continued, although with the growth of Bulaq as a new port further to the north, the importance of the port of Old Cairo finally began to decline. At the beginning of the eighteenth century Old Cairo was transformed by a major program of building and renovation, and the same period saw almost the entire northern half of the surviving part of the fortress converted into the walled Convent of St. George. The cemeteries that are today such a feature of the northern and eastern edges of Old Cairo also began to proliferate from the eighteenth century onward. Throughout the nineteenth century Old

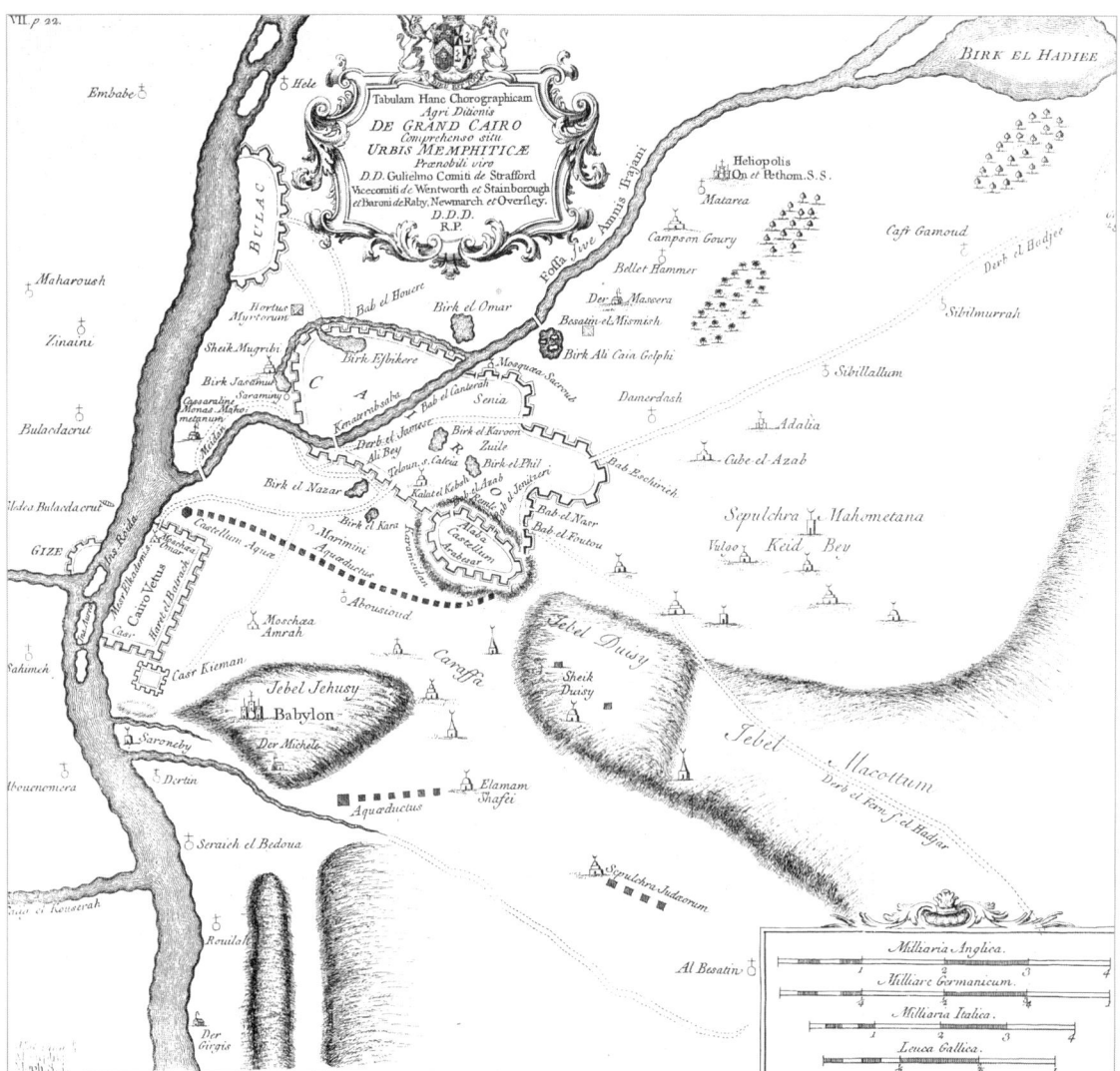

Fig. 39. Pococke's 1734 'Chorograph of Grand Cairo' showing the salient features of the city in the early eighteenth century, including a road leading north of the fortress, described here as Casr Kieman, clearly a corruption of Qasr al-Sham'. Note that Pococke still refers to the canal as the *Amnis Trajani*.

Cairo declined once more, until the simultaneous arrival of the railway and antiquarian interest in the 1890s led to the 'rediscovery' of its ancient churches and the beginning of the modern cycles of restoration. In this post-medieval period, church histories and the accounts of travelers are complemented by legal documents dealing with land ownership, as well as by the first appearance of detailed cartographic maps and views.

Combined with historical information, the archaeological record throws new light on a number of important questions relating to the changing landscape of the Egyptian capital in the first centuries after the Arab Conquest. How did the area of the former Roman fortress function within the new Egyptian capital? What happened to the fortifications and the internal buildings of the Roman fortress after the Conquest? When were the first churches founded in Old Cairo and what relation do these earliest structures bear to the present churches? What happened to the canal after its entrance ceased to be located in Old Cairo?

In addressing these questions we now have detailed archaeological information from a number of previously unexplored locations and buildings within the fortress. The general picture provided by the archaeology is that Old Cairo shared in the fortunes of al-Fustat—early organic growth, large formal building projects between the ninth and the eleventh centuries, followed by abandonment and robbing at the end of this period. The Ayyubid and Mamluk buildings suggest that many of the earlier buildings survived as ruins until they were razed to the ground to make way for new building projects during the period when the power of the sultans and Mamluks was concentrated in the massive citadel built in the 1240s on the southern tip of the nearby island of Roda.[26] As the seat of power in later Mamluk times shifted back to the Citadel of Cairo, the prosperity of Old Cairo brought by its proximity to Roda declined. The extent of this decline is revealed by historical sources and the documents of the Geniza, and is illustrated *de facto* by the need for the regeneration of the area during the 'Coptic Revival' at the end of the seventeenth century.[27] At this time Old Cairo was rebuilt and reorganized as part convent and part Christian enclave through the intervention of wealthy and well-connected Coptic notables of the Ottoman court.

Al-Fustat and the Early Medieval Making of Old Cairo

The early medieval history of Old Cairo begins with the foundation of al-Fustat in the second half of the seventh century and ends with the final abandonment of most of the southern part of the city, especially the areas to the north and east of the fortress, by the end of the eleventh century. Over this period the archaeology of Old Cairo indicates intense building activity both inside and immediately around the perimeter of the fortress. Inside the fortress, archaeological evidence from a number of locations testifies to the first reuse of Roman buildings. This reuse can also be inferred from the survival of complete buildings such as the round towers and the South Gate.

Our investigations, allied to previous archaeological work in al-Fustat, suggest that this early medieval phase can be further subdivided into three main phases of activity. The first of these comprises buildings erected during the hundred years or so between the Arab Conquest and the Abbasid capture of the city in 750. Following this earliest phase there is also historical and archaeological evidence of Abbasid building activity during the eighth and ninth centuries and a further extensive program initiated around the end of the tenth century, after the Fatimid conquest of Egypt in 969.[28]

Our archaeological investigations at Abu Serga and observations at other sites in Old Cairo suggest that most of the churches of Old Cairo were founded at the beginning of the early medieval period. This view finds support in the historical information available for the churches and in the impression that the years 644–715 constituted a revival of the Coptic Church under the twin stimuli of the end of Byzantine persecution and the tolerance, and even patronage, of Egypt's new rulers.[29] Notwithstanding the influx of new settlers from Arabia, the creation and administration of a new city around the former fortress also required a substantial component formed from the native Christian population. The physical transition from fortress to city was probably effected in a way familiar from other former Roman garrison sites.[30] The southern part of the fortress perimeter wall was retained, while the northern wall, contiguous to the center of the new settlement around the Mosque of 'Amr, was demolished. This move allowed the concentration of the native Christian population and its churches to take place within the southern part of the former fortress, as well as the area of Kom Ghurab immediately to the south.

Although the foundation of the first churches in Old Cairo probably dates to some point within the initial fifty years after the Arab Conquest, evidence derived from Abu Serga and supported in other locations suggests that the general form and plan of the present churches of Old Cairo was the result of a major rebuilding phase under Fatimid rule in the eleventh century. Investigations east of Abu Serga, north of the Ben Ezra Synagogue, and beneath the Convent of St. George and the Wedding Hall of St. George have revealed the existence in this same period of large buildings with sophisticated provision for water supply and drainage. A number of early medieval travelers' descriptions assist our archaeological understanding of topographical change in this period, and our impression of life within Old Cairo is greatly amplified from the tenth century onward by the documents of the Geniza archive.[31]

Topographical Influences on the Foundation of al-Fustat: The River and the Canal, Ancient and New Roads

As we have seen, the Red Sea Canal had played a large part in opening access and increasing traffic between Egypt and the East in the period before the Arab Conquest. The existence of the canal also clearly influenced the decision to locate the new Arab capital at Old Cairo in place of the Mediterranean port city of Alexandria. The twin traditions preserved by Ibn 'Abd al-Hakam, that ships were traveling along the canal to the Hijaz until shortly before the Conquest and that it was re-dug on the orders of the caliph Omar (633–44), combine to suggest that the entrance at Old Cairo may have continued in use until the breakdown of the administrative apparatus required to maintain it, perhaps during the hiatus produced by the Sassanian occupation of Egypt (619–29) and its subsequent recapture by the Byzantine emperor Heraclius.[32]

The silting-up of the entrance to the canal at Babylon and the decision to create a new urban center immediately to the north of the former fortress probably influenced the decision to cut a new entrance further to the north. Reopening the canal would also have provided a relief channel to reduce the effects of flooding on the newly settled central areas of Ahl al-Raya and Hamra.[33]

The cutting of a new head for the canal and the final filling in of the former entrance and its initial course within the fortress in Old Cairo therefore both appear to be features of the formative first half-century of the foundation of al-Fustat. The first buildings in the central area of the fortress formerly occupied by the canal, including the earliest foundation of the Church of Abu Serga, thus date from the same period. Historical sources for the Church of Abu Serga also support its foundation in the same post-Conquest era, around 690. Our archaeological work in Abu Serga revealed that the present floor of the church lies about 1.85 m above that of a large colonnaded church that appears broadly similar in size and layout to the present building.

Furthermore, the alignment of the façades of the earlier churches and the other buildings along the eastern edge of Harat Dayr Mari Girgis and 'Atfat Mari Girgis mark the centerline of the former canal, indicating that it was deliberately converted into an important north–south street, parallel to the existing via praetoria in the eastern enclosure of the fortress, and linking the area of the fortress with the new quarters laid out around the Friday mosque of al-Fustat, founded by 'Amr ibn al-'As.[34]

The location of the church façades in the center of the former canal, as well as the labor and effort required to fill in the canal and block its entrance with a massive stone wall, indicate that the conversion of the canal to a major road was a coordinated and deliberate step. Such a major piece of town planning seems most likely to have been associated with the creation of a new capital, including a sizable area set aside for the large native Christian population, in the years 644–715. The axial relationship between this road and the positioning and alignment of the main mosque suggests a much more formal layout of the central quarter of al-Fustat than has previously been proposed.[35]

The line of the road formed by the filling-in of the canal ran parallel to the earlier Roman roads of the fortress and was later continued northward to Cairo. Its course via the mosques of 'Amr, Abu Su'ud, and Ibn Tulun survived into the first maps of the post-medieval period. Projecting this road northward from its beginning in Old Cairo, it arrives at the junction where Shari' al-Khalifa becomes Shari' al-Surugiya (the Street of the Saddlers), which in turn becomes Shari' al-Khiyamiya (the Street of the Tent Makers). From the point where it passes through the gate of Bab Zuwayla this street becomes the Qasaba, the central highway of medieval Cairo and its main road to the north. The ancient combination of the canal and a land route leading to the northeast thus continued to be a feature of the topography of the new city, with the Amnis Traianus and the continuation of the via praetoria north of the Roman fortress now replaced by the Canal of the Commander of the Faithful (al-Khalig al-Misri) and the Great Road to Sham (the Levant) (fig. 2).

Even after the filling in of the canal in Old Cairo and its conversion to a road, the ancient roads leading north from the Roman fortress continued to exert a major influence on the topography of the early medieval city. Where this road probably joined the ancient route (now Shari' al-Khalifa) which skirts the necropolis it is interesting to note the presence of early topographical markers in the shape of the Fatimid tombs built between 1110 and 1113 to mark the graves of Muhammad al-Ga'fari, Sayyida 'Atiqa, and Sayyida Ruqayya, all members of the family of the Caliph 'Ali who came to Egypt in the seventh century.[36]

Although the former line of the canal had been converted to a road, the massive wall used to block its entrance between the round towers of the Roman fortress shows that the course of the main Nile channel and the location of the harbor remained unchanged. The continuing use of the Roman waterfront is indicated by references as late as the eleventh century to an "embankment, in the form of at least seven steps, probably made of stone, which allowed mooring at different levels according to the changing water level," and was called *al-ma'aridj*.[37] The description is surely that of the Trajanic harbor wall and river revetment, and we have already considered in the last chapters the evidence that the latter continued north beyond its junction with the northwest wall of the fortress.

The Reuse of the Roman Fortress

The most obvious survivals of the Roman fortress are its walls and towers, which defined and protected Old Cairo throughout its medieval transformation. Large parts of the walls are now buried by the gradual rise in the ground level inside the fortress. The accumulation of domestic rubbish and rubble created by constant building and rebuilding has raised the ground level inside the fortress by up to four meters above that of Roman times. Outside the walls, the rise in ground level has been accentuated by the vast dumps of rubbish and building material deposited in the medieval and modern periods. In Shari' Mari Girgis, for example, alongside the western wall of the fortress, the modern street is more than eight meters above the level of the Roman quayside.[38]

The Roman fortress, however, comprised much more than its perimeter wall and towers. Information on the internal layout of the Roman fortress developed from our recent archaeological work shows how closely the medieval development of Old Cairo derived from the internal layout of the Roman fortress. The influence of these internal buildings can immediately be seen simply by considering the streets of Old Cairo. All but one of the current streets are probably Roman in origin, as were a number of others that have gone out of use only in recent times. The line of the former canal later converted to a road is now represented by Harat Mari Girgis and 'Atfat Mari Girgis, while the north–south section of Harat Sitt Barbara is the via praetoria of the eastern enclosure. The entrance to the Convent of St. George lies on the line of the axial north–south street (known in other fortresses as the Via Quintana) that bisected the western enclosure of the fortress. This street joins the perimeter street against the western wall (via sagularis) north of the round tower beneath Mari Girgis Church, from where a postern gate led out onto the quayside. (figs. 3 and 25)

The position of other former Roman streets has left a mark in the urban fabric of Old Cairo. The north and south sides of the major east–west road of the fortress (via principalis) are shown by the positions of the Church and the Convent of St. George respectively. Both of these lie over substantially preserved Roman buildings. This east–west thoroughfare probably continued in use at least until the end of the early medieval period and the abandonment of al-Fustat.[39] It was later replaced as the main east–west route through the fortress by the present main entranceway to Old Cairo, the Harat Dayr Mari Girgis. Even this road may have its origins in an east–west Roman street dividing the southern half of the western enclosure halfway between the Via principalis and the northern round tower, although clearly the door at its western end is a later feature punched through the curtain wall.[40] In fact, of all the streets of Old Cairo only the part of the Harat Sitt Barbara running along the northern side of Abu Serga Church appears to have no obvious connection with the layout of the Roman fortress. The position of the western edge of the perimeter road running along the eastern fortifications (via sagularis) is now shown by the east walls of the Church of St. Barbara and the Ben Ezra Synagogue. What appears to be the eastern wall of the synagogue is actually part of its late-nineteenth-century rebuild, designed to enclose the subterranean passage leading to the so-called Well of Moses.[41] The real eastern wall of the building, following the line of the Roman building below, forms the western side of this passage (fig. 36). The continuation beyond the via praetoria of another Roman road running east–west from the U-shaped tower to the east of the synagogue later became the 'Atfat Abu Serga. Part of the façade of this medieval street, buried during the construction work for the Coptic Museum in the 1930s, was exposed again briefly in 2000 during excavation for the new toilet block of the museum.[42]

Another visible survival of the Roman fortress in the modern topography is the appreciably higher modern ground level within the eastern enclosure east of the canal, a product in its turn of the originally higher Diocletianic Roman ground level in the eastern enclosure of the fortress. This rise in ground level is apparent and palpable to anyone passing the eastern end of Abu Serga along the Harat Sitt Barbara. Partially as a consequence of this higher ground level, the Roman buildings in the eastern enclosure are preserved to a higher level, between two and three meters above their original ground level of 18.5m MSL (pl. 31).

The earliest post-Conquest reuse of parts of the Roman fortress can be inferred from the intact survival of its walls and towers. Two of the churches of Old Cairo surmount the South Gate of the fortress and the northern round tower, the Coptic Church of the Virgin (al- Mu'allaqa/The Hanging Church) and the Greek Orthodox Church of St. George respectively. Beneath these churches both the northern round tower and the South Gate are preserved above ground to their full height and are largely intact. Unfortunately little evidence of the medieval modifications to these buildings survived the clearance and subsequent restoration of the interior of the Roman structures that took place from the beginning of the twentieth century onward.

Like the synagogue and the Church of St. Barbara, the eastern or sanctuary end of the Coptic Church of St. George now lies over a Roman building. This would originally have formed the northern corner of a major crossroads in the eastern enclosure between the north–south via praetoria and the east–west via principalis. The evidence of blocked doorways in the Roman building beneath the Church of St. George indicates that the first reuse of Roman buildings occurred at a time when the configuration of the Roman fortress was still visible and its buildings were still largely standing. A similar pattern of reuse of standing structures was also noted in the buried Roman barrack buildings east of the Ben Ezra Synagogue, where ceramic evidence confirmed that this phase predated the eighth/ninth centuries. Many of these Roman buildings may have continued in use until a relatively late date, judging from the tenth/eleventh-century date for the huge dumps of pottery and other debris found within the largely intact barrack chambers all along the eastern wall of the fortress.

The massive scale of the fortress and historical accounts of the siege of Babylon in 641–42 suggest it was captured largely intact.[43] We know then that the disappearance of the northern walls and the buildings of the northern part of the fortress must have taken place between the seventh and the seventeenth century, when the present outline of the northern limits of Old Cairo appears for the first time in our cartographic sources.

While nineteenth-century accounts bemoaning the destruction of the fortress indicate that much more of it survived into relatively recent times, it seems likely that these complaints related to the parts held by the various communities within the preserved southern half of the fortress:

> [W]ith the British occupation came a sense of security which has led to the most deplorable destruction. The need of a fortified enclosure having vanished, Copts, Greeks, and Jews vied together in demolishing the walls. . . . It is the simple truth that in the last eighteen years more havoc has been wrought upon the Roman fortress than in the previous eighteen centuries.[44]

For the northern wall, however, it seems more plausible that the demolition occurred at the very beginning of the early medieval period, and actually formed an integral part of the transition from fortress to city. The striking contrast between the southern flanking tower of the East Gate, preserved to its full height, and the northern tower, razed to the ground, suggests that the absence of the northern walls above ground may have resulted from a deliberate act of planning. Given the scale of the preserved walls it is clear that the demolition of even one side would also have produced a vast amount of building material for use in the new town.

The fate of the fortress north of the via principalis may reflect either a different character of the Roman buildings in this area or the nature of their reuse in the early medieval period. We have briefly considered the possibility that part of the Diocletianic fortress may have functioned as a kind of imperial residence or palace analogous with the emperor's famous retreat at Split in modern Croatia.[45] We also know that the central quarter of al-Fustat around the Mosque of 'Amr, the district known as Khittat Ahl al-Raya, was the preferred district for aristocratic residences from the very beginnings of al-Fustat.[46] Thus the conquerors may simply have removed the north wall and annexed the former imperial quarter of the fortress for the use of their elite within the 'new' settlement north of the via principalis. Although the existence of imperial or public buildings in the northern part of the fortress has not been proven by excavation it seems likely that at the very least the fortress north of this point was appropriated for new buildings at the foundation of al-Fustat. The via principalis would have made a logical dividing line for the extension of settlement, for, as we have seen, its relationship to the bridge across the Nile made it perhaps the most important route of the fortress. This link to the west bank of the Nile was made even more important by the location at the western end of the bridge of an important and often overlooked part of al-Fustat, the fortified 'suburb' of Giza.[47] The fortifications of this area were essential to the protection of the bridge and, like the bridge itself, were no doubt Roman in origin. The numerous churches, monasteries, and a large ancient synagogue mentioned in the historical sources make it clear that Giza, like Babylon, was part of the same ancient settlement situated on either side of the river crossing.

Whatever their origins, the disappearance of the early medieval buildings in the north of the fortress can probably be dated to the period after the eleventh-century abandonment of much of al-Fustat. The central part of the early medieval city became a quarry for the buildings of Cairo, and the former center of the elite of al-Fustat must have provided a rich harvest. That the churches of Old Cairo survived this robbing is another indirect proof that the northern area of the fortress had been annexed for the use of the new Arab elite at the time of the Conquest, for unlike these former palaces, abandoned as the center of power moved northeast, the buildings of the southern area were not robbed out because the churches and synagogues remained in use and were tended by their communities.

The Archaeological Evidence for the Foundation of the First Churches in Old Cairo

No archaeological evidence has been recorded in the churches of Old Cairo for a foundation during the fourth- and fifth-century transition from paganism to Christianity. The reason for this is probably that Babylon continued to be primarily a strategic military post guarding the confluence of important routes by land and water, and not "a medium-sized fortified town" as has previously been suggested.[48] We have already noted the first appearance of the cult of martyrs at the end of the fourth century and the beginning of the fifth, as well as a general preference for a symbolically triumphal location on the site of former tribunals. The earliest archaeological evidence in Egypt for the cult of martyrs is the basilica built in the first half of the fifth century at the shrine of Abu Mina near Alexandria.[49] Other surviving churches that may date to the fifth or early sixth century include the main church of the White Monastery at Sohag and the basilicas at Dendera and al-Ashmunayn.[50] None of these, however, were located within fortresses that continued to fulfill an important military and strategic role, as we know Babylon did right up until its final siege and capture in the seventh century. Of course this is not to say that no churches or chapels for the garrison existed within the fortress from the fourth century to the seventh, but neither archaeological nor historical evidence for these survives.

In Old Cairo there are seven 'ancient' churches, four of which are dedicated to martyrs. Two of these are Coptic and Melkite churches dedicated to St. George. In addition to these there are the Coptic churches of SS. Sergius and Bacchus and St. Barbara. The latter, however, may have been dedicated to St. Barbara only after the transfer to it of the relics of the saint in the eleventh century; before this it appears to have been dedicated to the martyrs Abu Qir and Yuhanna.[51] The first appearance of the cults of all of these individual martyrs does not seem to have taken place before the middle of the fifth century.[52]

It is often held that new churches were rarely built after the Arab Conquest, but this may reflect a situation much later in the medieval period, when the Copts were becoming a minority and attitudes toward *ahl al-dhimma*, the subject peoples 'protected' by Islam, were very different from those in the immediate years after the Conquest.[53] Egypt remained very much a Christian country until well into the medieval period. Al-Muqaddasi's description of the "haughty comportment" of the Copts as late as the tenth century is revealing as to perceptions of their own status and position.[54] It also seems probable that no new Coptic churches were founded during the repression by the Byzantine and Chalcedonian (Melkite) Church and the imperial authorities from the second half of the sixth century, particularly within military bases of the Byzantine administration.[55] This background, as well as traditions preserved by a number of Church sources, indicates that the origins of the Coptic churches of Old Cairo should be sought in the immediate post-Conquest era.

The Church of SS. Sergius and Bacchus is located approximately in the center of the existing remains of the Roman fortress of Babylon. It is a building of great significance on account both of its great antiquity and central importance in the history of the Coptic Church. It receives particular veneration as one of the locations at which the Holy Family is believed to have stayed during the Flight into Egypt. It is also a building of intense archaeological complexity and interest. The constructional sequence shown by recent archaeological work in the church has thrown new light not only on the history of the church, but on the wider questions of the foundation and development of the churches of Old Cairo and the topography of the area itself.

One of the most interesting aspects of the recent archaeological work in the church has been the chance to compare archaeological observations with the relative wealth of medieval and later written sources relating to the church. These include descriptions by medieval European pilgrims, the accounts of native Egyptian geographers, the annals of the Coptic Church, and antiquarian research from the eighteenth century onward.[56]

The cult of Sergius and Bacchus, particularly the former, first appears in Syria around 425 and was very popular throughout the fifth and sixth centuries. This fact alone suggests that the foundation of the church could not have occurred before the mid-fifth century at the very earliest.[57] St. Sergius is the major protagonist in the story of these martyrs, and the church is popularly known as Abu Serga, a name that appears only in Arabic sources of the medieval period (fourteenth century) onward.[58]

The earliest securely dated written source mentioning the Church of Abu Serga is a reference to the church in 969 from the Geniza archive. The church is also mentioned in in the account by George the Archdeacon, a contemporary witness, of the life of the Coptic patriarch Isaac, who held office in 689–92. In this account the church is mentioned as one of the locations for the election and enthronement of the Coptic patriarch, in itself a strong indication that it may have been the first Coptic church to be built in the fortress.[59] The enthronement of the patriarch was shifted to the Hanging Church from 977, but the Church of Abu Serga remained important as the seat of the bishop of al-Fustat–Misr.[60]

Another early tradition concerning the construction of the churches of Old Cairo is contained in the *Annales* of Eutychius, who was the Greek Orthodox patriarch of Alexandria from 877–940. This tradition places the construction of two churches in Old Cairo in the period from 685–705. One of these is the Church of St. Barbara (at that time dedicated to the martyr Abu Qir), and the other is named variously in different manuscripts as either the Church of St. George or that of St. Sergius. The work is said to have been carried out by a secretary (variously called Athanasius, Aninas, or Andre in surviving accounts) of the then governor of Egypt, 'Abd al-'Aziz ibn Marwan.[61]

Our recent work below the present floor of the Church of Abu Serga indicated at least two major building phases within the line of the former canal *before* the construction of the present church, which probably dates to the tenth or eleventh century. While the nature of the earliest building phase is not clear, the second of these phases appears to be a large colonnaded basilican church similar to the present building. The floor level in this earlier church lies at 18.15 m MSL, some 1.85 m below the present floor, and three of the column bases of the colonnade dividing the nave from the south aisle survive *in situ* in a line 1.75 m to the north of the present southern colonnade. There is some evidence that the floor of this church may have been at least partially paved with marble. A north–south wall bearing a much larger and apparently reused Roman column base may represent the transition from the nave to the *haykal* (fig. 42). No evidence for this earlier church was noted during our work within the present crypt, and the small difference in level between the church floor and that of the canal wall (17.4 m MSL) makes it hard to see how the latter could have formed part of this phase. On the other hand, the existence of the canal wall was known, for fragments of walls probably belonging to this phase were founded directly onto the Roman stonework (fig. 40).

The date range for the foundation of this earlier church is constrained by a number of topographical and historical factors. One of these is the date of the cult of SS. Sergius and Bacchus, which makes a date of before 450 very unlikely. If the earlier colonnaded church is identified with the church reported by Eutychius as having been built in the 690s, then the first phase of buildings below Abu Serga should probably be dated to the filling in of the canal immediately after the Conquest. The position of the present façade of the church (and a number of other medieval buildings along 'Atfat Mari Girgis) along the centerline of the canal indicates that it follows the earlier street line

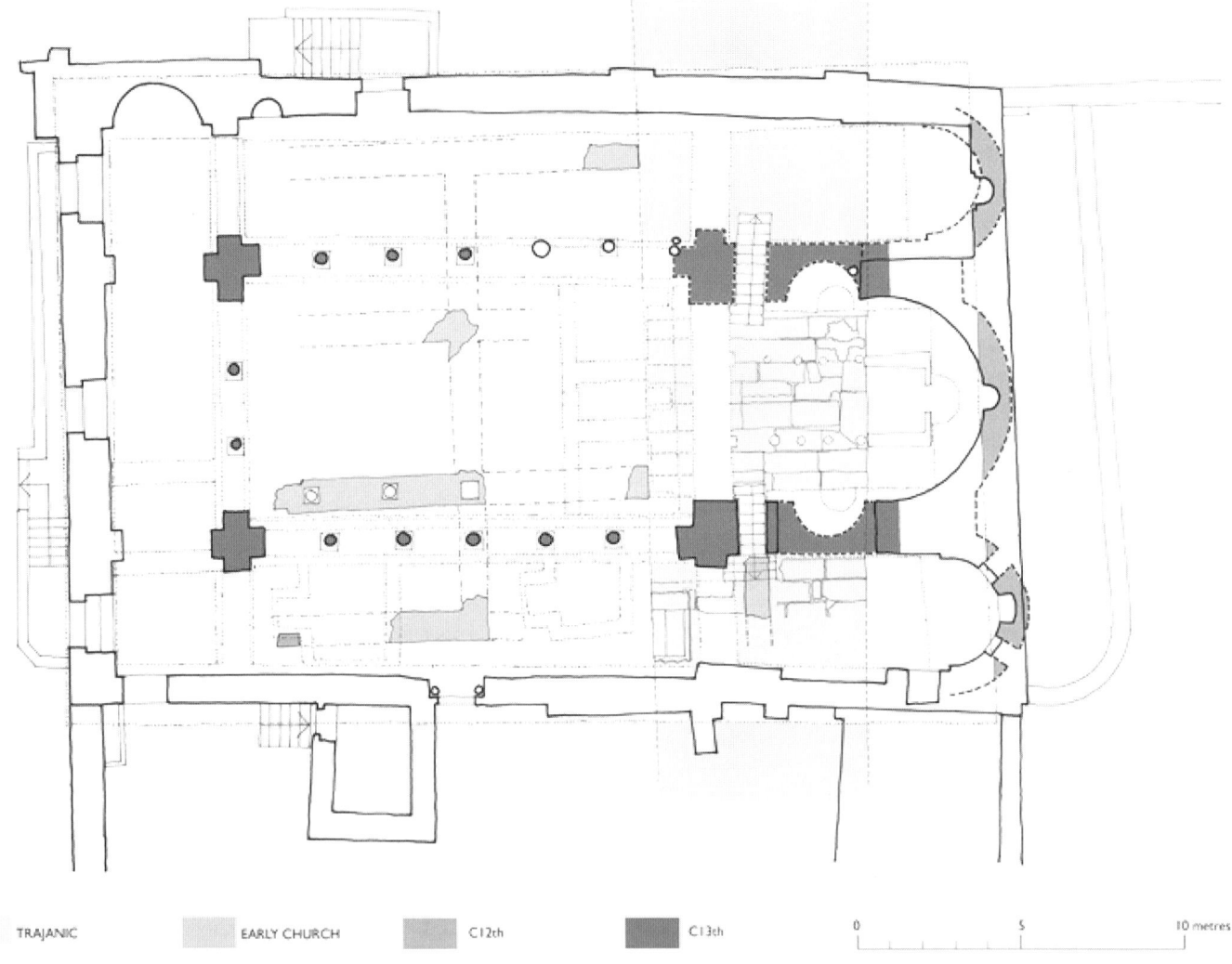

Fig. 40. Plan of Abu Serga Church showing the phase of its development revealed during the groundwater lowering project. The unshaded parts of the building show the main layout of the church constructed in the tenth/eleventh century. (Nicholas Warner)

frontage created by the filling-in of the canal and its conversion to a road.

Little direct archaeological evidence can be adduced for the foundation date of the other churches of Old Cairo. Most existing copies of the account of Eutychius mention the Church of St. George rather than that of St. Sergius as having been constructed at the same time as the Church of Abu Qir and Yuhanna (the current Church of St. Barbara), but the archaeological evidence makes it seem more likely that the tradition of the construction of two churches at the end of the seventh century relates to Abu Serga and the Church of St. Barbara rather than the present Coptic Church of St. George.[62] We have seen that a Roman building lies beneath the eastern end of the Church of St. George. This church was largely rebuilt at the end of the nineteenth century, although the eastern end of the church with its fine brick sanctuary clearly survived the fire that destroyed the rest of the church. This eastern end is built on a thick rubble raft laid over a well-preserved Roman building. The ground level represented by the top of this raft, as well as details of the brickwork and the mortar used in the sanctuary, suggest a tenth- or eleventh-century date for the building. The fact that much of the Roman building continues through into the structure of this Fatimid period sanctuary might suggest that if there was an earlier phase of the church it took place within a surviving Roman building.

Material evidence of the earliest Church of St. Barbara may be indicated by the carved sycamore and pine doors discovered in the main façade of the church during restoration work in the 1920s and now in the Coptic Museum.[63] These have been variously dated on art historical grounds to between the fourth and sixth centuries.[64] At any rate, these doors appear to have been reused in the rebuilt church of the eleventh century. Previous writers have suggested that the chapels dedicated to Abu Qir and Yuhanna in the north transept may represent the original core of the

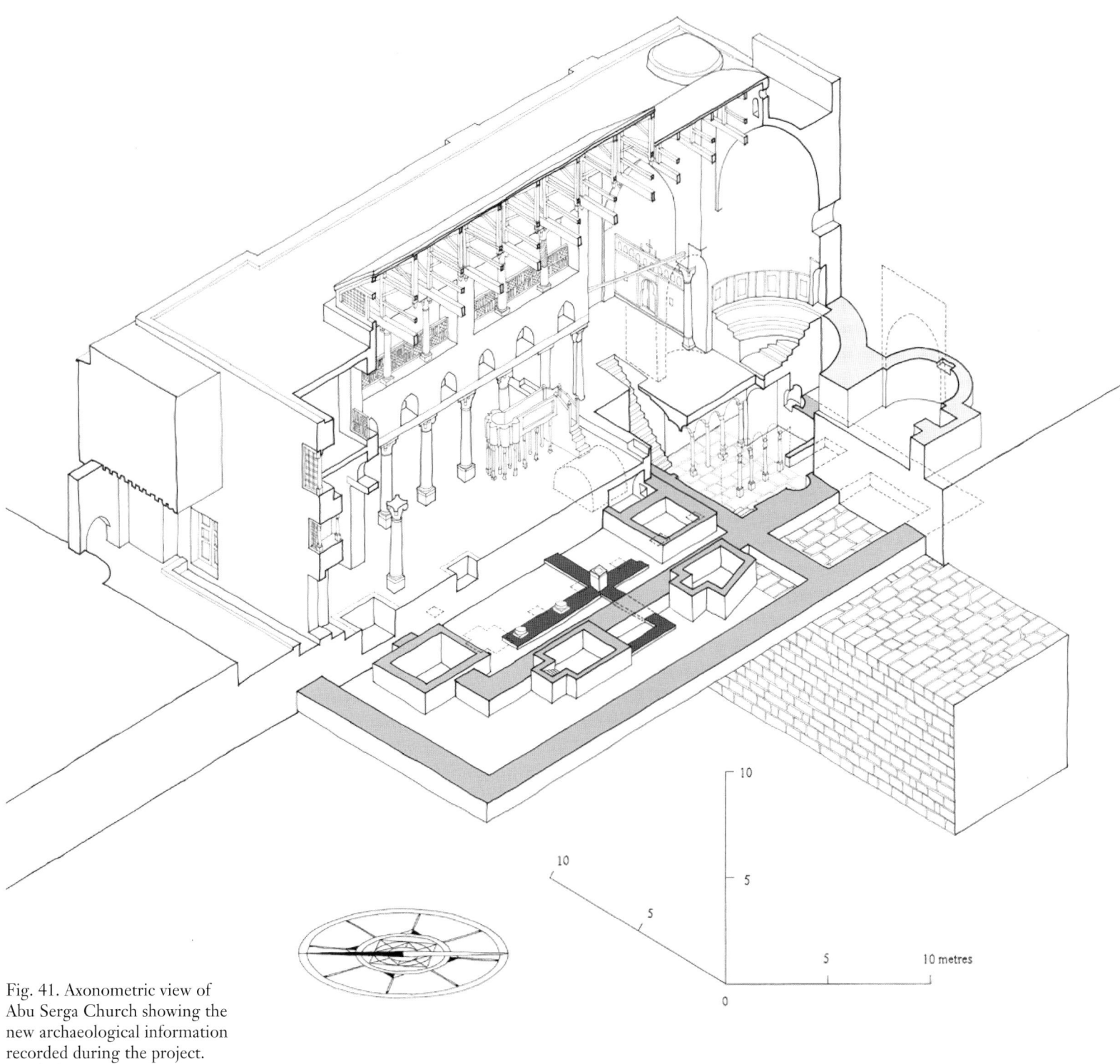

Fig. 41. Axonometric view of Abu Serga Church showing the new archaeological information recorded during the project. (Nicholas Warner)

Fig. 42. Abu Serga proto-church: Part of the colonnade of the early church revealed below the floor of the present building during the groundwater lowering project. On either side of the brick wall carrying the column base are marble slabs forming the floor of this church. At the top left of the picture is part of the concrete reinforcement added during the restoration of the church in the early 1990s. (Peter Sheehan)

church, subsequently enlarged into the present building.[65] However, Monneret de Villard and Patricolo, who carried out restorations and excavations in the 1920s, believed this part of the church to date from the fourteenth century.[66]

The Rebuilding of Old Cairo from the End of the Tenth Century

Archaeologically, almost all the surviving medieval buildings of Old Cairo show evidence of having undergone a major program of rebuilding between the tenth and mid-eleventh century. The same period also saw the extensive rebuilding of large parts of al-Fustat to the east of the Mosque of 'Amr.[67] As far as building work on the churches and synagogues of Old Cairo is concerned, it is worth noting that this period coincides with the advent of Fatimid rule and the end of a theocratic Abbasid regime, under which restrictions on church building had been in place from the reign of al-Mutawakkil in the mid-ninth century.[68] The thirteenth-century Egyptian Christian writer Abu al-Makarim makes no mention of the churches of Old Cairo but records that the nearby Church of St. Mercurius in the monastery of Abu Sayfayn (still in the area of Old Cairo but to the north of the Roman fortress and to the west of the Mosque of 'Amr) was restored during the reign of the Fatimid al-'Aziz bi-llah (974–96), having long been in ruins and latterly used as a sugar cane store.[69] The Shi'a Fatimids, new rulers of what had been up to then firmly Sunni Egypt, cultivated the other minorities and were consequently sympathetic to the Christian and Jewish communities.[70] Cairo became a haven for members of these communities displaced by war and upheaval in North Africa and Syria. Devastating earthquakes known to have occurred in the second half of the ninth century may also have been a factor in the large-scale rebuilding operations that took place under the Fatimids.[71] Detailed archaeological evidence for this phase survives primarily from the Church of Abu Serga and the Convent of St. George. Another large building of this phase was recorded beneath the Wedding Hall of the Coptic Church of St. George, and, as noted above, the eastern sanctuary end of this church appears also to be a survival from this era. Observations made during the restoration of the Church of St. Barbara in the 1920s indicated that the form of the present church also dates to the second half of the eleventh century.

One of the most important archaeological conclusions to come out of our recent work was that the crypt of Abu Serga is not the remains of an earlier structure at a lower level but was built at the same time as much of the present church. The date of this construction is indicated by a number of factors. In the first place, a *terminus ante quem* for the church and crypt is provided by the first appearance of the legend of the Holy Family in the accounts of western pilgrims at

Fig. 43. Remains of the vaulted tombs in the nave of Abu Serga church truncated by the concrete floor added in the 1990s, with the wall bearing the columns of the south aisle pierced (bottom right) by a perforated drain line inserted at the same time. (Peter Sheehan)

the end of the thirteenth century.[72] More detailed descriptions of the cave of the Holy Family from 1320 onward clearly refer to the present crypt beneath the sanctuary, so the mention of the church in association with the Holy Family in earlier documents probably allows us to infer that the present crypt structure (although not necessarily details such as the arrangement of columns within it, see below) was in place at the latest by 1300.

The thirteenth-century wall paintings recently revealed in the southern sanctuary (see Chapter 5) also help in pushing back the date of the crypt and the church to a point before 1200. The curved apse on which they are painted forms part of an extension of the church eastward beyond the original end wall of this sanctuary. The earlier original back wall of the southern sanctuary—without an apse—was revealed below ground during the recent work, when it could be seen to form part of the same constructional phase as the crypt and the walls carrying the colonnades of the church. In the northern sanctuary, remains of an identical original arrangement were found, although it had been truncated when the *haykal* of the northern sanctuary was completely rebuilt in the Mamluk period. In the tenth/eleventh-century structure, a number of bricks found with fragments of painted plaster adhering to them may have been reused from the earlier basilica. The brick building technique in this phase of the church, which employs alternating courses of headers and stretchers, is also strongly reminiscent of buildings throughout al-Fustat whose construction has been securely dated to the Fatimid period before the abandonment of that area in the second half of the eleventh century.[73] All these factors lead us to believe that the plan form of the present church was put in place at some time during the late tenth or early eleventh century.

Before the construction of the church and crypt, the previous church and perhaps other adjacent buildings over the canal wall were razed to the ground (around 18.15 m MSL) and sealed with a layer of sand. The ground level of the new building was similar to that of the present day (just below 20 m MSL) another indication that this phase of the church dates from the end of the early medieval period rather than its beginning. The rise in level from the previous church allowed the creation of the crypt (with its floor founded at 17.4 m MSL on the Trajanic canal wall) below the main sanctuary. Within the main church a complex subterranean arrangement of vaulted tombs was also built, with some of these vaults springing from the same walls that carry the columns (fig. 43). In areas where no subterranean crypts were built, the bases of the columns within the earlier church were not removed but were left in place. Access to the tombs in the nave was via vertical slots let into the floor, from which a short flight of steps led to the vaulted burial chamber itself. The construction of these tombs, contemporary with that of

Fig. 44. The early medieval building revealed beneath the floor of the medieval hall of the Convent of St. George. The structure in the center is a tank or fountain set within the central hall of the medieval *qa'a*. (Peter Sheehan)

the church, suggests that they were perhaps intended for a long-term future use for the burial of important church figures. The creation of these tombs may have been related to Abu Serga's role at this time as the seat of the bishop of al-Fustat–Misr.[74] They may have been intended for the burial of the patriarchs of the Church, for the seat of the patriarchate was shifted from Alexandria to Old Cairo in the middle of the eleventh century. Since the enthronement of the patriarch took place thereafter in the Hanging Church and not as previously in Abu Serga, it may be that a patriarchal link with Abu Serga was retained by the construction of these crypts, particularly given that the structure of the Hanging Church, suspended over the Roman gateway, precluded any provision for burials. It may be that these questions will be answered by future historical research. Although the burial environment inside the church has been severely affected by the high groundwater levels of recent years, it was seen that where they had not been destroyed by the work of the 1980s the burials survived, and a number of finds of exceptional quality, including a bronze cross (fig. 12) that would have been mounted on a staff and a silver signet ring with an inset precious stone, pointed to an ecclesiastical identity for the deceased. The surviving parts of these tombs were recorded but left undisturbed during the present work. These finds and the structure of the tombs also seem to confirm that they were intended expressly for interment and were not ossuaries or structures in which the relics of martyrs were housed.

The form and function of the crypt itself in this eleventh-century church raises a number of intriguing questions. Was it originally a funerary chapel associated with the vaulted tomb structures, which came to be associated with the Holy Family only from the thirteenth century? Another interesting point is how access was originally gained to the crypt. The first actual mention of stairs dates to 1384, although Pipinus de Bononia's 1320 description of the chapel beneath the main altar might lead one to believe that a similar arrangement was already in place by then.[75] The existence of two flights of stairs leading to the crypt is first mentioned in 1420, which at least shows that neither flight was added during the extensive post-medieval changes to the church and therefore that both are probably part of the original arrangement. It is possible that the large hole we noted cut into the central part of the stone floor was a feature of the first crypt, and that the Roman blocks missing from this area were removed to allow the interment of relics or for some other purpose related to the function of the funerary chapel. Previous buildings below the eastern end of the crypt (beyond the inner edge of the canal wall) were leveled and used as the base for the brick floor of the crypt (pls. 32 and 33).

It was suggested above that the palaces of the ruling elite were located in the northern part of the Roman fortress from the time of the Conquest onward, and it is likely that the use of this area for "royal" or high-status buildings persisted into the Fatimid period. Recently, archaeological evidence for the existence of high-status constructions in Old Cairo around the end of the Early Islamic period was revealed beneath the Convent of St. George (fig. 53).

A large and well-preserved brick building that probably dates from the end of the Early Islamic period (that is, the tenth or eleventh century) was exposed beneath the great hall and the *majlis*, or reception area, of the medieval house that survives within the convent (fig. 44). The brick building shows a number of parallels in constructional techniques with others from the end of the Early Islamic period previously noted in Old Cairo and al-Fustat. The use of alternate courses of headers and bricks laid on edge as a distinctive feature of foundations is a technique, for example, also seen in the crypt walls of Abu Serga. It may well be that the Fatimid-period carved panels reused in the huge seven-meter-high cedar doors of the medieval house derive from this earlier building.

The part of the building revealed during the recent work comprises a range of four approximately square (3 m x 3.3 m) rooms along the western side of a rectangular courtyard. Running between the walls of these rooms and the somewhat wider wall of the courtyard is a narrow (0.65 m) but deep (more than 1.5 m) drain with a brick floor. The remains of a well noted beneath the *majlis* and the cistern still preserved within the 'old church' area of the convent may also date from this phase of the building.

One of the most notable features of the building is a complex and well-preserved system of water supply and drainage. Ceramic pipes built into the western wall of the courtyard may have connected the well and the cistern, while the walls of the chambers along the western side of the courtyard are all built with arched openings allowing water to drain through them into the main drainage channel.

Along the northern edge of the building there appear to have been further rooms, separated from the courtyard by a narrow internal passage. The space between the two walls forming this alley was, later in the medieval period, at least partially filled with rubble to provide a solid foundation for the great arch leading into the northern *iwan* of the medieval hall. Like the medieval *qaʻa*, this building also clearly extended further to the east, and the remains of a plastered tank in the northernmost bay of the current entrance passage are valuable not only in giving some clue as to the nature of the structure in this area, but also in showing that the massive Roman wall that had previously existed here had already been truncated by the Early Islamic period.

Although we have little direct archaeological evidence from the Hanging Church, the Church of St. Barbara, and the Ben Ezra Synagogue, all of these buildings seem to share architectural features or historical circumstances which link them with the reconstruction of Abu Serga in the Fatimid period. The architectural similarity between Abu Serga and the Church of St. Barbara is particularly striking, so it is interesting to note a document from 1629 that indicates a date prior to 1072/73 for the construction or enlargement of the church to receive relics of St. Barbara that had formerly been housed in the Hanging Church.[76] It is possible that at this time the church had an extra southern aisle in the space now occupied by storerooms and the stairway to the women's gallery. A similar division of the nave into four sections by rows of columns is paralleled at the Hanging Church in Old Cairo and the Church of the Virgin in Harat Zuwayla, which probably both also date from this period.[77]

Archaeological observations made during the Comité's restoration of the Church of St. Barbara between 1918 and 1922 were published by Patricolo in *La Chiesa di Santa Barbara al Vecchio Cairo*.[78] They dated the original church on the site to a period between the fourth and fifth centuries on the basis of the carved doors found during the restoration. In the existing building they identified two phases, placing the construction of the outer walls in the second half of the eleventh century and the nave, aisles, and narthex later, at the beginning of the thirteenth century. Our recently acquired archaeological evidence points to a broadly similar phasing for the Church of Abu Serga as it is preserved today.

To the south of the Church of St. Barbara is the Ben Ezra Synagogue. Although the current synagogue building dates from the end of the nineteenth century, test pits carried out in 1989 indicated at least one earlier phase of the building on the same alignment.[79] By the time this alignment had been arrived at, it seems that some of the topography of the Roman fortress was no longer apparent, for the northern wall blocks the line of the Roman road leading from the via praetoria of the fortress toward the U-shaped tower east of the synagogue. On the other hand, the major topographical elements of the fortress continued to influence the footprint of later buildings as late as the tenth or eleventh century. As we have seen, the eastern walls of the Church of St. Barbara and the Ben Ezra Synagogue both clearly follow the western edge of the perimeter road running along the eastern edge of the fortress.[80] Other parts of the fortress were reused on account of the depth and strength of the Roman foundations, as with the medieval wells sunk within the northern round tower and in the former barracks buildings east of the synagogue.[81]

While documents from the Geniza archive suggest that the first foundation of the synagogue took place in the mid-tenth century, they also provide convincing evidence for a major restoration or rebuilding in the period 1037–41. A number of detailed documents relating to this work survive, including a bill of quantities for the work on the *haykal*, which gives a good idea of the nature and organization of these medieval building projects.

> For the work at the heikal of the synagogue: gypsum, polishing the pillars, 15,150 bricks including their handling, the pipe and two walls of the new compound, 28 loads of black clay, 24 qintar [around one ton] lime, inclusive of transportation, ashes, slaking, water for slaking, building the pipe and whitewashing the interior of the new compound. Two himls [around 80 kg] oakum, 16 loads of yellow clay.[82]

For much of al-Fustat, the building boom that began with the Fatimid conquest and continued into the first half of the eleventh century was the final act. Decline and abandonment from the 1070s onward turned the southern and eastern parts of the city into a wasteland for a thousand years. The parts of the city along the river were never abandoned; this fundamental relationship to the Nile, as well as its ancient roots and sacred associations, ensured that, having been the nucleus around which the first city formed, Old Cairo would continue to share in the development of its medieval successor.

Chapter 5

Cycles of Decline and Revival
Ayyubid, Mamluk, and Ottoman Old Cairo

Introduction

We have seen in the previous chapters how the archaeology of Old Cairo reflects the area's fundamental role in the origins of the city and its strategic importance to Roman rule, as well as its central position in the foundation and development of al-Fustat/Misr in the early medieval period. The events of the eleventh century and the abandonment of al-Fustat left Old Cairo physically isolated from the new center, but this did not stop subsequent development from being shaped by the same political and economic conditions that underpinned urban formation processes in the rest of the medieval city. Thus the area inside the former Roman fortress shared in the surge of building that accompanied the Ayyubid (1169–1250) and the early Bahri Mamluk (1250–1382) periods and that saw the construction of two new citadels and the city walls, as well as a host of new madrasas built to reintroduce Sunni orthodoxy in Egypt.[1] Similarly, the relative economic stagnation of the later Mamluk period and the first two centuries of Ottoman rule is reflected in the lack of archaeological evidence for building activity in Old Cairo, as well as what we can extract from the historical and cartographic sources that become increasingly numerous from the sixteenth century onward.[2] By the mid-seventeenth century, the increasing independence of the *bey*s, native dignitaries who sat on the ruling council with the Ottoman pasha, allowed them a greater control over taxation revenue. Instead of being sent to Istanbul, some of this revenue contributed to a renewed phase of patronage and building activity in the city. Coptic notables who served the *bey*s were able to share in the benefits of wealth and power, much of which they directed toward the restoration of churches and monasteries, including those of Old Cairo, throughout the eighteenth century.[3] At the same time, its ancient religious buildings and associations gave Old Cairo a unique status within the religious life of both Egyptians and the increasing number of foreigners coming to Egypt from the medieval period onwards. This status modulated the political and economic context, with the result that the area was equally affected both by the religious persecutions of the fourteenth century and by the Coptic cultural revival at the beginning of the eighteenth.

In contrast to the earlier history of Old Cairo, which we have presented based primarily on archaeological information, one of the problems of interpreting its development in the medieval period stems from a lack of archaeological data commensurate with the relatively rich array of documentary material. This material includes a range of primary and secondary written sources, supplemented by early maps and views from the end of the fifteenth century onwards. For Old Cairo these written sources include the accounts of European pilgrims and travelers, as well as the detailed topographical descriptions provided by the Egyptian writers Ibn Duqmaq and particularly al-Maqrizi in the early part of the fifteenth century.[4] This secondary material is supplemented by primary written sources in the form of the numerous and varied documents detailing the daily life of the Jewish community of Old Cairo from the Geniza archive.[5]

Cartographic evidence on Pagano's 1549 map *Descriptio Alcahirae Urbis quae Mizir, et Mazar dicitur* shows that by the time of the Ottoman Conquest of Egypt in 1517 the metropolis of Cairo had taken on a form that is still recognizable today (pl. 34).[6] Comparison of this, and other sixteenth-century maps derived from it, with the later *Description* plan of the city produced by the Napoleonic

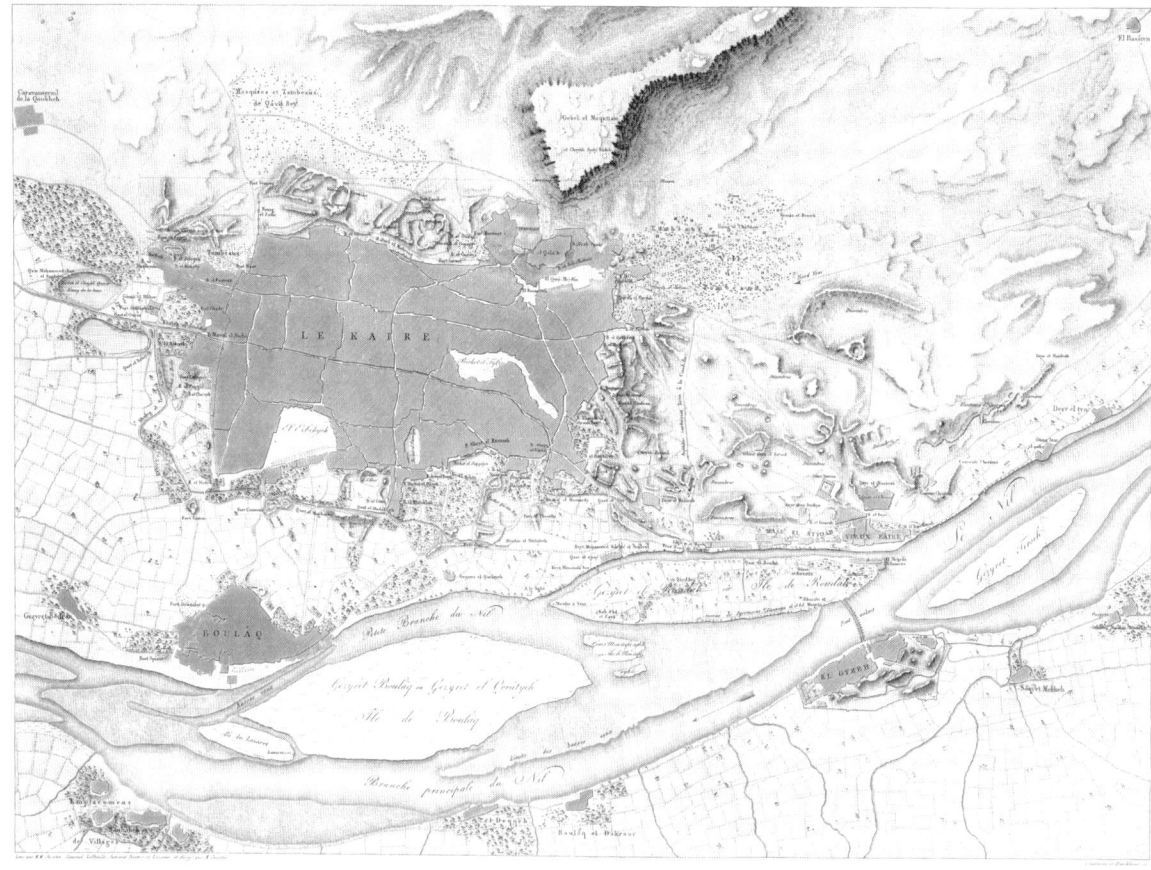

Fig. 45. Cairo in 1809. "Plan général de Boulâq, du Kare, de l'île de Roudah, du Vieux-Kaire, et de Gyzeh," from the *Description de l'Egypte, Etat Moderne I*, pl. 15, 1809. Courtesy Nicholas Warner.

expedition of 1798–1801, reveals how little the broad outline of the city changed under Ottoman rule, with the changes that did take place being largely a matter of increasing the density of the urban fabric (fig. 45). These early maps show the continued but distinct presence within the metropolis of previously integral areas of the city, such as Old Cairo and Giza, which had survived the ruin of al-Fustat. They also provide valuable clues as to how this landscape had formed in the period from 1100 to 1500, from which no maps survive.

What archaeological sources we have comprise the evidence retained in existing buildings such as Abu Serga Church and the medieval hall preserved in the Convent of St. George, as well as those that stand no longer, such as the Church of the Virgin (Qasriyet al-Rihan), demolished in 2000. Supplementary information was obtained during recent subsurface work at various sites in and around the fortress, primarily within Abu Serga and the Convent of St. George, and in the area around the Wedding Hall of the Coptic Church of St. George. The constructional sequences recorded in Abu Serga Church and in the Convent of St. George constitute our baseline for the medieval archaeology of Old Cairo. This sequence is supplemented by additional archaeological information from the churches and the other buildings of the area, as well as by observations made during the sinking of the shafts of the groundwater lowering project. A wider background to the archaeological evidence is provided by contemporary documents and travelers' descriptions, as well as modern scholarly research into Mamluk and Ottoman architecture and urbanism in Cairo. In part, the paucity of archaeological data for the medieval period is a consequence of the peculiar conditions pertaining inside the walls of the Roman fortress. Unlike the area outside the walls, there has not been a massive buildup of rubbish and building material. In consequence, the medieval archaeology is much closer to the surface and has been disturbed or truncated to a greater extent in recent times, unlike the more deeply stratified Roman and early medieval layers. We noted substantial truncation of the medieval deposits, for example, in the area of the Ben Ezra Synagogue, which was extensively remodeled at the end of the nineteenth century. In consequence of the removal of medieval deposits, the archaeological sequence preserved around the synagogue now comprises material from the end of the nineteenth or early twentieth centuries superimposed directly over early medieval layers. Similarly, antiquarian investigations and "restoration" of the monuments of Old Cairo from the first years of the twentieth century onward, coupled with a number of disastrous fires, combined to sweep away much of the accumulated medieval evidence within buildings like the Hanging Church or the Greek Orthodox Church of St. George. We are fortunate that, for the later medieval period in particular, the absence of archaeological evidence in many of the buildings of Old Cairo is partially offset by the relatively large number of travelers' descriptions.

The development of Old Cairo in the medieval period took place in the context of profound political, social, and economic changes occurring in the Egyptian capital. Within the walls of the Roman fortress these changes were manifested most clearly in the fortunes of its churches, and we will consider the evidence for these buildings both individually and collectively below. First, however, we will examine the wider changes to the topography of the city and the position of Old Cairo as a physically detached yet integral part of the medieval metropolis.

The Changing Medieval Topography of Cairo and the Position of Old Cairo within the Metropolis

The disasters suffered by the Egyptian capital during the long reign of the Fatimid caliph al-Mustansir (1036–94) had led to the abandonment of large areas of al-Fustat by the end of the eleventh century. Archaeological evidence from the areas of al-Fustat excavated in the 1920s and those of Istabl 'Antar from the 1980s onward provides a physical link with the decree of the vizier Badr al-Gamali from 1072 that allowed the residents of Cairo to remove building material from the houses of al-Fustat.[7] The further abandonment and depopulation of most of the southern part of the city was hastened by a major earthquake in 1138 and perhaps too by the infamous burning of al-Fustat at the time of the Crusaders' attack on Cairo in 1168.[8] Much of the southern part of the city around Old Cairo was abandoned for nearly a thousand years, becoming a vast dumping ground downwind of medieval and modern Cairo and utilized only for noxious industries such as tanning, dyeing, pottery, and quicklime production.[9]

The presence of its churches and its proximity to the river ensured that Old Cairo was not abandoned in the same way. Archaeological evidence illustrates the continuing importance of the area inside the fortress through the remains of great houses that were later incorporated into the Convent of St. George and the Wedding Hall of St. George. At both these sites Ayyubid and Mamluk activity seems to mirror the replacement of earlier Fatimid buildings that occurred around this time in Bayn al-Qasrayn, the area of the former great palaces of the royal enclosure of al-Qahira.[10]

The archaeological evidence from Old Cairo suggests that a major change of axis had occurred from that used in

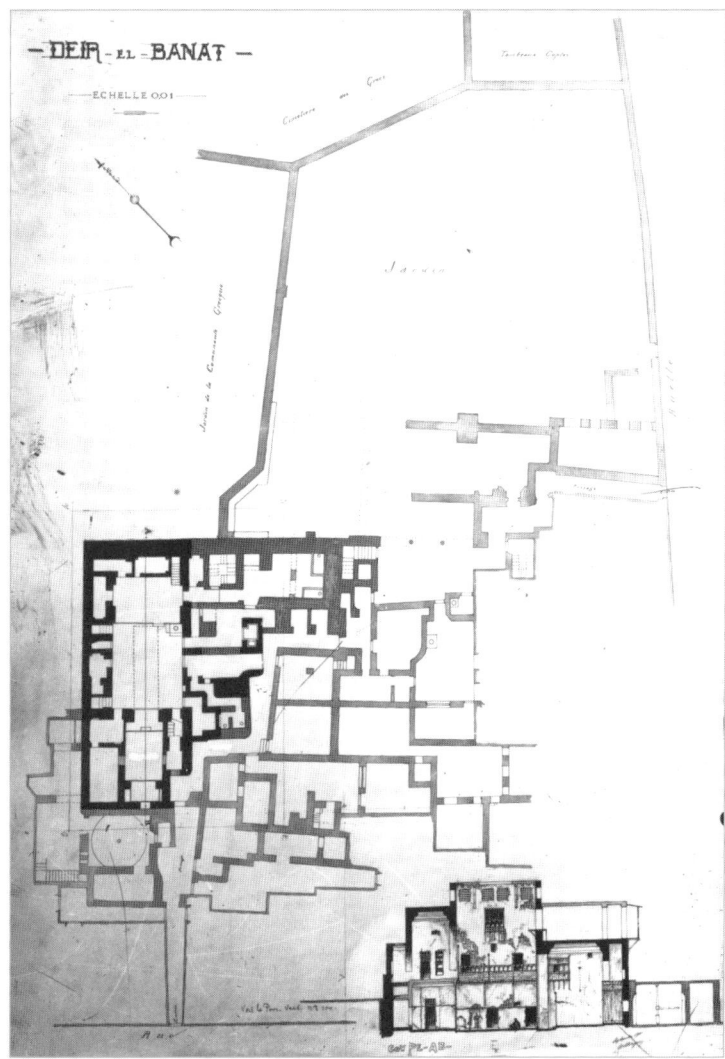

Fig. 46. The 1906 Comité plan of the Convent of St. George showing the approach from Harat Mari Girgis. The plan also shows the parts of the building to the east of the great hall that were later removed during the construction of the present convent. The elevation shows the appearance of the galleries fronting onto the great hall from these eastern rooms. Comité archive.

Byzantine and early medieval times. The main east–west axis of the fortress along the via principalis had gone out of use by the time the great *qa'a* now located within the convent of St. George was built, for this building was entered via a bent axis approach from Harat Mari Girgis to the south. As we have seen, it is possible that the end of the via principalis was hastened by the destruction of the earlier bridge across the river. It is worth noting, however, that the approach to the building from Harat Mari Girgis still used the line of the former north–south Roman street dividing the western enclosure of the fortress. By the time of the construction of the *qa'a* of St. George, Harat Mari Girgis and its extension westward had become the primary route leading from Old Cairo toward the river and the Ayyubid and Mamluk citadel at the southern end of Roda (fig. 46).

annual processions that were intended to underlie their religious legitimacy.[12] There is certainly archaeological evidence for the existence of high-status Fatimid buildings in Old Cairo, such as the large building recently revealed beneath the Convent of St. George, from which the carved panels in the huge seven-meter-high cedar doors of the medieval building on the same site probably derive.

A contemporary corollary to the demolition and redevelopment of the former centers of Fatimid power, and at the same time one of the most important elements in the formation of the topography of the medieval city, was the Ayyubid project to create a new center of government at the citadel and to enclose the city, creating al-Qahira al-Mahrusa (Cairo the Well-Protected) within a comprehensive system of city walls. The project was initiated by Salah al-Din in 1186 and completed by his Ayyubid successors in the mid-thirteenth century. Both Old Cairo and the ruined areas of al-Fustat were included within this comprehensive scheme, which combined a defensive wall with an aqueduct to bring water from the Nile south of Old Cairo to the new Ayyubid citadel. In al-Fustat significant archaeological information is provided by the fact that the line of the wall clearly cuts through the surviving houses in this part of the city. This shows both that the inclusion of this abandoned part of the earlier city within the *intra muros* area was largely dictated by the line of the aqueduct, and that it never led to the resettlement of this area.[13]

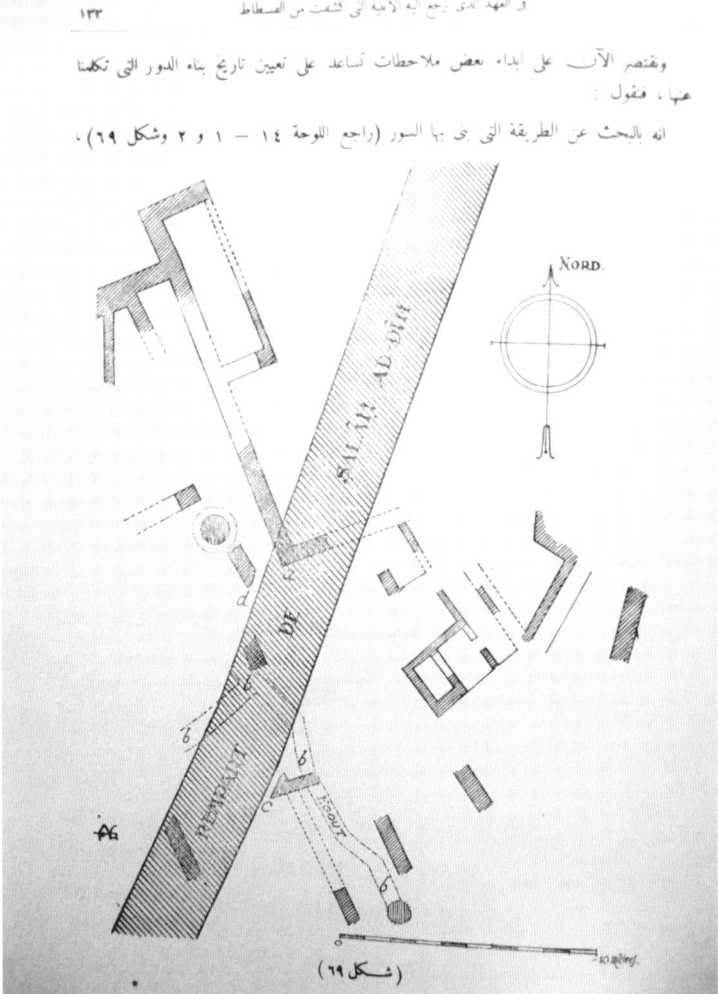

Fig. 47. Plan from Bahgat Bey's 1921 *Fouilles d'al Foustat* (figure 69, page 133), showing how the line of the Ayyubid wall cuts through the earlier houses of Fustat. Courtesy Mohammed Fahmy.

The end of Fatimid rule in 1171 and the transition to the Ayyubid dynasty founded by Salah al-Din was marked by a number of important topographical developments that emphasized the change of dynasty and a return to Sunni Islam after the period of Fatimid Shi'a rule. One of these was the demolition of the Fatimid palaces of al-Qahira and the remodeling of the central area of the former "royal" city.[11] Within the former Roman fortress in Old Cairo there is archaeological evidence for a similar leveling of large areas of the existing Fatimid buildings. It was suggested in the previous chapter that the palaces of the ruling elite may have been located in the northern half of the former fortress from the time of the Arab Conquest onward, and it is likely that the use of this area for royal or high-status buildings persisted into the Fatimid period. The high esteem in which the Fatimid rulers held the Mosque of 'Amr and the old city is revealed by the role both of these played in archaizing ceremonies and

The ancient strategic importance derived by Old Cairo from its proximity to the Nile and the harbor of the city was reinforced by the construction of another citadel on the southern end of the island of Roda by the last of the Ayyubid sultans, al-Salih, in 1240. Even after the fall of the dynasty, this citadel continued to be used as the seat of power till 1280 by the Bahri Mamluks (who ruled Egypt from 1250–1382 and took their name from this *bahri* or riverside location). Nothing remains, at least above ground, of the Roda citadel, but its construction provided an impetus to redevelopment that is still reflected in the layout of streets connecting the area within the fortress walls to the part of Old Cairo now located along the river bank. From the earliest maps we can see that these two areas together defined Old Cairo in the medieval period, and in fact continued to do so until they were effectively isolated from each other by the construction of the Cairo-Helwan Light Railway (now the Cairo Metro) in the last years of the nineteenth century (fig. 48).

The Nile remained the major influence on the topography of the medieval city and its constituent parts. Fortunately the Ayyubid walls around the earlier Fatimid enclosure survived long enough to appear on the earliest maps from the fifteenth century, and from the westernmost

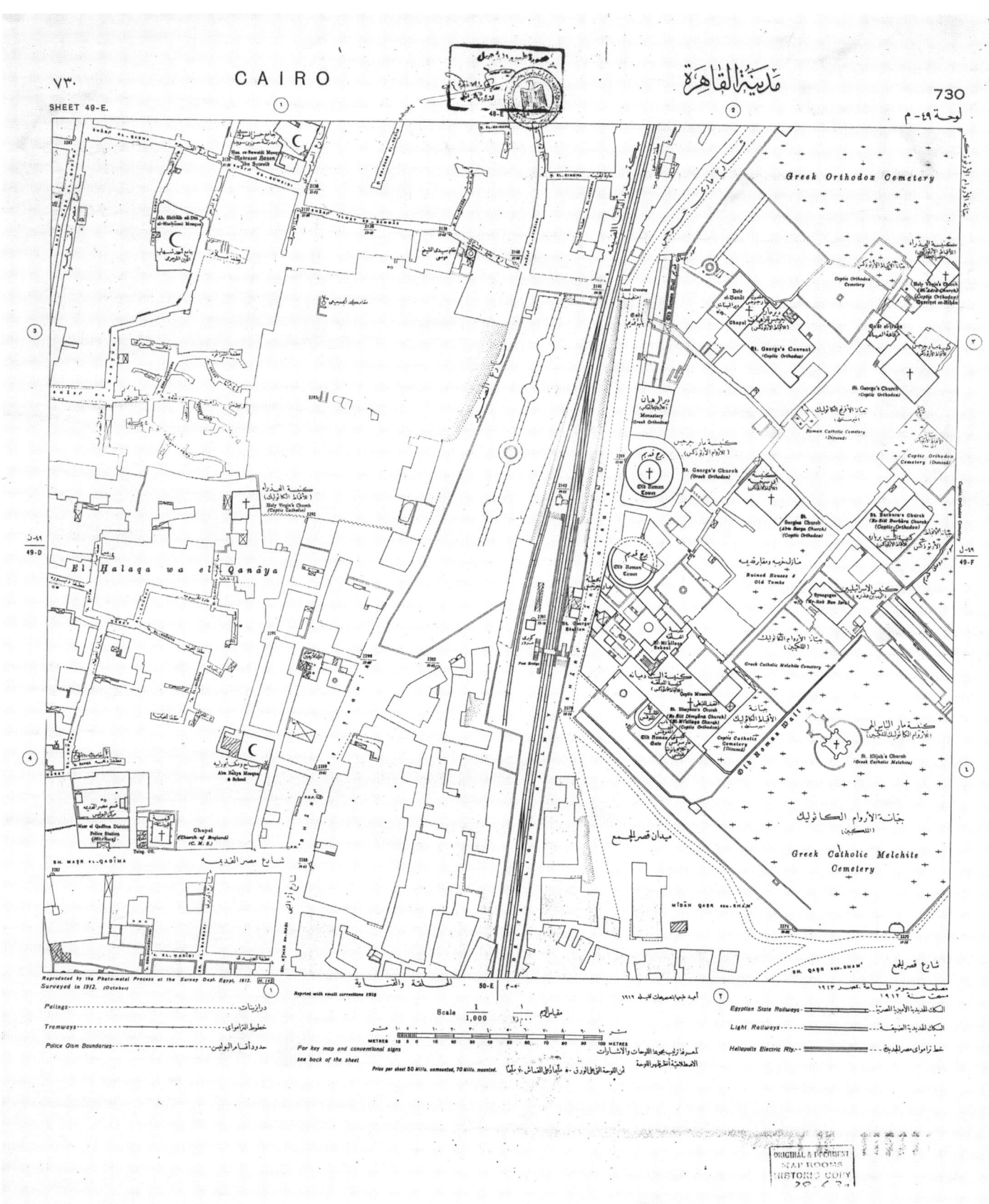

Fig. 48. The 1918 Survey of Egypt plan showing the relationship of the riverside area of Old Cairo to the fortress, and how this relationship was severed by the coming of the railway.

extent of the northern walls of the city we can infer the position of the Nile in the thirteenth century.[14] Despite some errors and omissions created largely by the perspective views chosen for the city, the European cartography of the sixteenth century is a rich source for topographical change in Cairo between the mid-thirteenth century and the beginning of the sixteenth century.[15] Before considering these changes it would be as well to examine briefly the political and economic conditions influencing the urbanization of the Egyptian capital during the Mamluk period.

Several distinct aspects of the Mamluk period represent a key to understanding the medieval development of both Old Cairo and the wider metropolis. One of these is the nature of the slave-soldier Mamluks as "outsiders in the city," who were first brought in by the penultimate Ayyubid ruler, al-Salih Najm al-Din al-Ayyub, in an attempt to circumvent the inherent problems of a dynastic system occasioned by the ruler's distrust of his own tribal or family base.[16] Despite the efforts of a number of Mamluk sultans to create heirs, the Mamluk system was generally seen by contemporaries to function in a non-hereditary way. Contemporary admirers like Ibn Khaldun saw this as the secret of Mamluk vitality and the reason for the longevity of the system over two and a half centuries.[17] Certainly one of the effects of the Mamluk military victories over the Mongols and Crusaders in the thirteenth century was a renewed trust in Islamic political and territorial unity.

For the urbanization of Cairo one of the most distinctive features of the medieval (and the later Ottoman) period was the use of the *waqf* as a tool for urban development and/or renewal.[18] The waqf can be defined as a perpetual and inalienable endowment to finance a religious institution. In the classic Ayyubid and early Mamluk scenario these endowments would consist of commercial or residential properties (*mawqufat*), located around the religious institution to be financed by their revenue. In many cases this system provided the conditions for urban renewal or development, for the *waqif*, the person endowing the religious institution, could buy an area of ruined buildings, which would then be removed to allow the construction of new religious buildings with which the Mamluks could assert their individual piety and the legitimacy of the system. The survival of the houses and palaces of the great and good through their conversion into religious buildings is another well-known phenomenon of medieval Cairo, and there is also a long tradition of the houses of their patrons being built adjacent to religious buildings. In the Mamluk period the institution of the waqf system led to many houses being converted into *madrasa*s as a means of keeping them under the control of the founder's family (*waqf ahli*) as a matter of expediency at difficult times.[19] Contemporaries like al-Suyuti saw the ultimate contradiction in the system: if Mamluks were slaves, how could they own land with which to endow institutions?[20]

The waqf system and the Mamluk desire to emphasize their legitimacy to rule through architectural display, amply funded by the revenue from taxes on agricultural land, combined to create a series of building booms in the Egyptian capital in the thirteenth and fourteenth centuries.[21] After the prime land created by the dismantling of the Fatimid palaces in al-Qahira had been developed, a recurring lack of space led to the creation of new urban centers from the mid-fourteenth century onward. These included the area south of Bab Zuwayla and the zone to the west of al-Khalig al-Misri, between it and the new canal excavated by Sultan al-Nasir Muhammad in 1324–25. Most of these urban developments took place under more effective and consequently longer-lived Mamluk rulers like Barquq, al-Mu'ayyad Shaykh, Barsbay, Qaytbay, and al-Ghuri.[22] The negative effects of these booms on the ancient urban fabric were not lost on contemporaries and in fact were the inspiration of writers like Ibn 'Abd al-Zahir, whose *khitat* was an attempt to record the core of Fatimid Cairo that was being transformed in the mid-thirteenth century.[23] This theme is later repeated by the most pre-eminent of the Mamluk historians, al-Maqrizi, whose 1440 *Khitat*, "a unique exploration into history writing through the chronicling of buildings and topography," has as its stated aim the recording of streets and buildings before their imminent destruction through late Mamluk mismanagement.[24] For al-Maqrizi, the twin highpoints in the development of Cairo were first the Fatimid period and then its position as the capital of the mid-thirteenth century Mamluk empire. His view of the cyclical rise and fall of power has its culmination in what he considered to be the disastrous and rapacious rule of the early Burgi sultans, especially Farag ibn Barquq (1399–1412).[25] Again, however, the wider political scene provides a telling context, for as with Late Roman Egypt, many of the economic difficulties endured during the reign of Farag ibn Barquq were consequent upon wars needed to defend the frontiers, this time those of the Mamluk empire against Tamerlane.

The Mamluk period also saw a number of lasting setbacks to the development of the city. One of these was the arrival of the Black Death in the middle of the fourteenth century (1353).[26] The population of the city fell by a third, and there were twenty other outbreaks of plague between 1347 and 1517. Depopulation was also exacerbated by a series of crop failures throughout the fourteenth century. The economic hardships of the fifteenth century must have accentuated al-Maqrizi's laments for the loss of the early Mamluk pageants, the religious processions, and the general feeling of plenty that had existed in the thirteenth century. Relations with the Christian European powers worsened following invasions of Egypt during the Fifth Crusade in 1219–21 and again by the French king Louis IX in 1249–50. On the other hand, as we discuss below, the loss of Jerusalem to the Mamluks led to an increase of European merchants in Cairo, which became the new center for western trade with the Orient.

One of the most important influences on the landscape of later medieval Cairo was the canal excavated by the sultan al-Nasir Muhammad ibn Qalawun in 1324–25. The relation of this canal to the eastern (Roda) channel of the Nile, and the westernmost point of the northern Ayyubid walls of Cairo at the River Gate, Bab al-Bahr, shows that the course of the canal of al-Nasir Muhammad largely reflects the position of the earlier east bank of the main Nile channel, which had silted up as the river shifted westward. As with Trajan and the Amnis Traianus, the re-excavation of an earlier natural channel was the most logical and effective means of controlling the Nile and directing its flood. The shift of the river westward can be followed in the historically documented development of the area of Bulaq from its original formation as a sandbank in the late thirteenth century.[27] In the early fourteenth century the sandbank had become permanent enough to attract a settlement. Medieval maps show that by the end of the fifteenth century at the latest, Bulaq had arrived at its present position on the east bank of the main channel, connected to the city via a causeway across the marshy area that was left by the silting-up of the former eastern arm of the Nile. This marsh was subsequently gradually reclaimed and incorporated into the city from the late Mamluk period onward. The reasons for the silting-up of the earlier medieval channel, its shift westward, and the creation of the Bulaq sandbank can all be linked to the narrowing of the Roda channel. This in turn appears to be related to the gradual lengthening northward of the island of Roda caused by the depositional action of the river.[28] The date of these changes to the river suggests that building works associated with the creation of the Ayyubid citadel at the southern tip of the island may have played a significant part in this process. As we have seen in the previous chapter, the archaeological evidence from Old Cairo suggests that the destruction and abandonment of the bridge from Giza via Roda to the east bank at Old Cairo may have contributed to the formation of the present riverside area of Old Cairo from the beginning of the Fatimid period onward. The date of the monuments preserved in this area gives some indication of the timescale for this process, for they show that the river had shifted to its present position by the middle of the fourteenth century at the latest. On the present Nile corniche in Old Cairo are the remains of the oldest building in this area, al-Madrasa al-Kharubiya, built in 1349, while further to the east along the roads connecting the waterfront with Old Cairo and the Mosque of 'Amr are the Mosques of al-Suwaydi (begun 1420) and Muhammad al-Saghir (1426). Immediately to the north of Old Cairo the limit of the westward movement of the river by the end of the fifteenth century is shown by the extension of the aqueduct supplying the Citadel and its massive hexagonal water intake tower, the Burg al-Saqya, built at Fumm al-Khalig by Sultan al-Ghuri in 1508.

The excavation of the canal of al-Nasir Muhammad had the effect of creating a large area of newly drained land west of the old Khalig al-Misri, which may have first been intended for cultivation but was increasingly built on in the later Mamluk and Ottoman periods. The Pagano map and its variants show this area as less built up than that east of the Khalig, with more open *maydan*s and lakes visible at the beginning of this process of urbanization.[29] Development of this area took the usual Mamluk form of new quarters constructed around pious foundations.

Another significant land reclamation measure was the fourteenth-century construction to the south of Old Cairo of the dike known as the Gisr al-Afram by the amir Ghandar al-Afram.[30] It was said that this powerful amir owned one-eighth of Egypt, and al-Maqrizi relates that al-Afram profited from the rent of land created by the recession of the Nile westward. It is also worth considering, however, to what extent the construction of this dike might actually have caused or contributed to the westward movement of the Nile.

The combined causes and effects of the narrowing of the Roda channel and the silting-up of the former eastern arm of the Nile certainly contributed to the waning importance of the harbor of Old Cairo from the fourteenth century onward and its replacement as the main port of the city by Bulaq. That it continued in use as an entrepot for produce from Upper Egypt is shown by the survival of the wheat market and the grain warehouses shown as the *Greniers de Joseph* on the French *Description* map of Old Cairo. Edward Lane, writing in 1825, also describes how many vessels from Upper Egypt still unloaded here, and how numerous ferry boats plied between Old Cairo and Giza.[31] On the other hand, the settlement along the east bank of Roda shown on the earlier medieval maps had largely disappeared by the time of the *Description* map and the slightly earlier (1774) map of Carsten Niebuhr.[32]

An important indicator for the shift of the river westward from the line of the Roman waterfront of Old Cairo is the industrial use of this area in the medieval period. One of the most important archaeological sites for this aspect of medieval Old Cairo is the southern round tower of the fortress, which has retained extensive evidence for the industrial reuse of the Roman fortress buildings. Remains of a kiln revealed in one of the lateral chambers of the tower showed it to have been built over a thick dump of polychrome-glazed 'Fayyumi' pottery

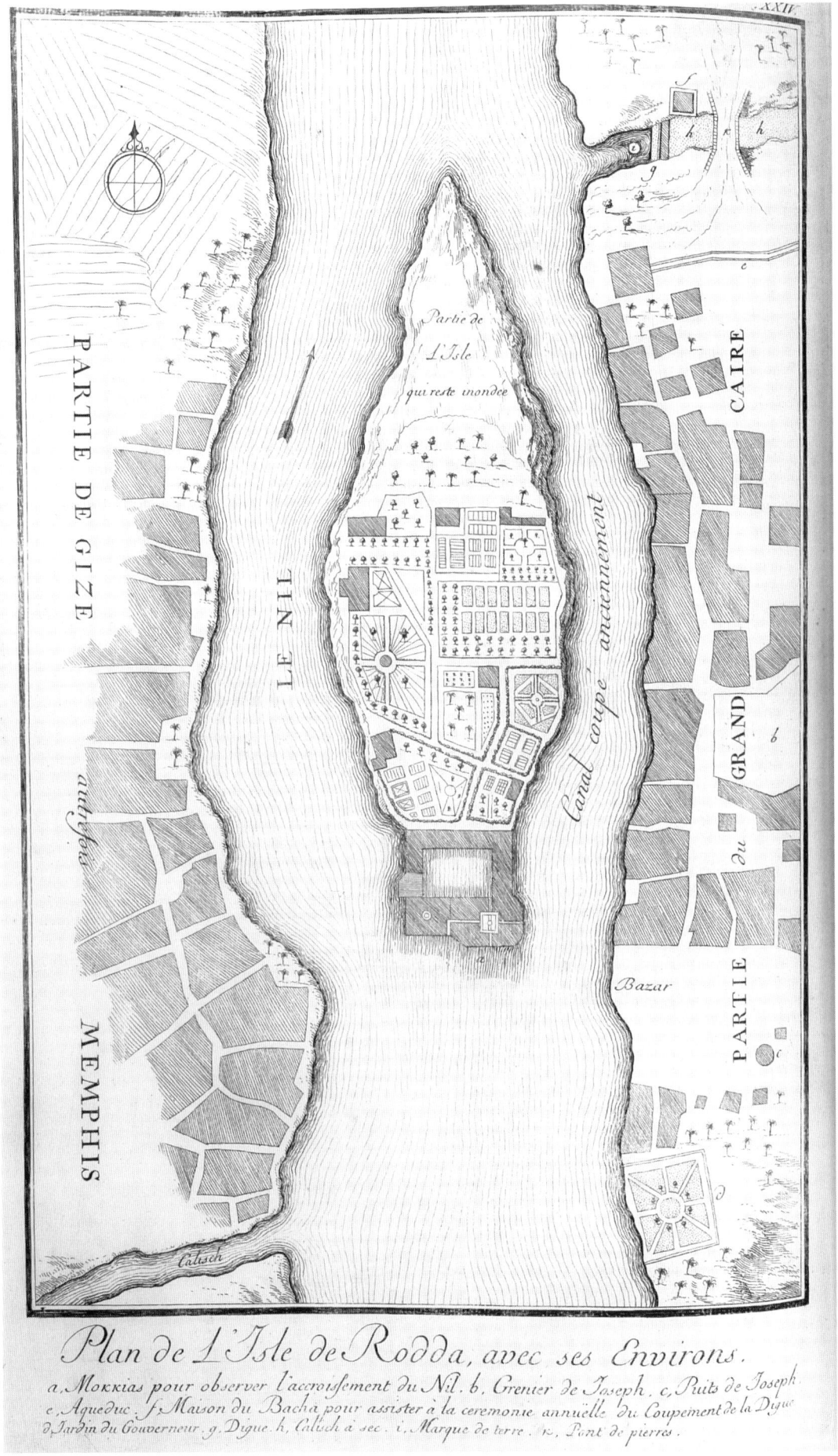

Fig. 49. Frederik Norden's plan of the island of Roda from 1757. Apart from the detail of the riverfront of Old Cairo and the dike at the mouth of the al-Khalig al-Misri which would be broken at the annual 'Cutting of the Canal' ceremony, the plan is interesting for its depiction of the northern part of the island, which suggests it was gradually formed by the depositional action of the Nile.

Fig. 50. Niebuhr plan of Cairo, 1774.

dating from the ninth and tenth centuries.[33] The presence within this dump layer of pots of various stages of manufacture, including wasters, as well as several items of kiln furniture, must indicate the presence of an earlier kiln, and that the existing kiln was probably built on top of rubble and debris from the earlier emplacement within the same broad phase of activity. There was also some possible evidence for metalworking or perhaps glassmaking in the deposits under the kiln. Remains of associated buildings and a water channel related to this kiln were noted around the eastern exterior of the tower. Another similar kiln survives immediately north of the Roman tower beneath the Church of St. George, suggesting the whole area of the former Roman waterfront may have been used for industrial purposes from a relatively early point in the medieval period. The position of the latter kiln beneath the Church of St. George, against the western face of the great wall built to block the entrance to the canal between the two round towers, clearly shows that by the time of its construction the river was no longer adjacent to the western wall of Babylon.

The Churches and the Medieval Archaeology of Old Cairo

Despite the assertive Sunni rule of the Ayyubids and the absence of a patriarch from 1216 to 1235, the thirteenth century was an active and vibrant period for Coptic culture.[34] The tolerance generally enjoyed under Fatimid rule continued into the Ayyubid period, largely because the new Sunni rulers concentrated their initial efforts on combating the Shi'a doctrine of the Fatimids, a program that found architectural expression in the construction of madrasas or religious colleges by a series of powerful patrons. The fourteenth-century Egyptian writer Ibn Duqmaq lists twenty-seven madrasas in al-Fustat–Misr by the end of the fourteenth century, of which nine are known to be Ayyubid foundations, and eleven Mamluk.[35] The religious dynamics created by the madrasas and their effect on Egyptian society were soon afterward to have a significant negative impact on Christian Egypt, but under the Ayyubids the Coptic churches appear to have shared in the extensive program of reconstruction which took place throughout the city. The twenty-year reign of the sultan al-Kamil (1218–38) probably represents the high point of Ayyubid tolerance toward the Copts, and may have been related to his peaceful overtures to the Crusader kingdoms of Palestine.

The building and reorganization that accompanied Ayyubid rule allowed a continuing role for influential Coptic lay people, the *arakhina* (derived from the Greek word *arkhon*), in financial and administrative affairs. Like their Muslim counterparts, their social role included the patronage of architecture, the arts, and literature. Building and other activities, however, found expression within the inter-confessional cultural orientation with which a number of recent writers have characterized the material culture of the medieval Middle East.[36] In religious literature, for example, the Coptic revival personified and patronized by the brothers known as

Fig. 51. Engraving of the Battle of the Pyramids, July 21, 1798. This illustration contains a great deal of topographical information for the condition of Cairo by the early nineteenth century, including the formation of the island of Roda and the relationship of the canal of al-Nasir Muhammad to the earlier eastern channel of the Nile. Courtesy Jose Santos.

the Awlad al-'Assal between 1230 and 1260 took place in Arabic, rather than in Coptic.[37] In the building and decorative arts, the use of forms and decorative motifs was similarly more indicative of prevailing architectural or decorative idioms than of ethnic or religious origin.

Major recent projects combining conservation and study carried out by ARCE have illuminated the building work and in particular the painted program of the *zographos* or 'painter of life' Theodore and his team, carried out at the Red Sea Monastery of St. Antony between 1232–33, as well as a similar program in the same period at the nearby monastery of St. Paul.[38] In both places the power of patronage at the beginning of the Ayyubid period was able first to return the monasteries from the Syrian church into Coptic hands and then to finance the extensive building and decorative programs carried out in them.[39]

To these insights we can now add archaeological information and the evidence of the paintings discovered in January 2004 during the course of the groundwater lowering project at Abu Serga and conserved by ARCE in October 2005.[40] The wall paintings revealed in the apse of the southern sanctuary of Abu Serga Church are a significant contribution toward our understanding of the development of Old Cairo at the beginning of the medieval period, for they form the most visible part of the scattered evidence for a major period of activity that took place within the walls of the Roman fortress during the thirteenth century. The Abu Serga paintings appear very similar to the thirteenth-century decorative program at the Church of St. Antony in the Monastery of St. Antony at the Red Sea, where the evidence of the painted plaster decoration from the 1232–33 program indicated that the entire sanctuary was probably added at the eastern end of the church at this time, with the *khurus* (choir) now occupying the place of the original sanctuary.[41] At St. Paul's the archaeological evidence indicates that the early thirteenth century also saw the creation of the present sepulchral church around the tomb of the saint (pls. 16 and 17).[42]

At Abu Serga the archaeological evidence suggests that medieval changes to the crypt-church took place in 2 phases, which we tentatively date to the twelfth/thirteenth and fourteenth/fifteenth centuries (figs. 40 and 41). Elements of both these phases have survived either within the fabric of the building or formed part of the archaeological record below ground.

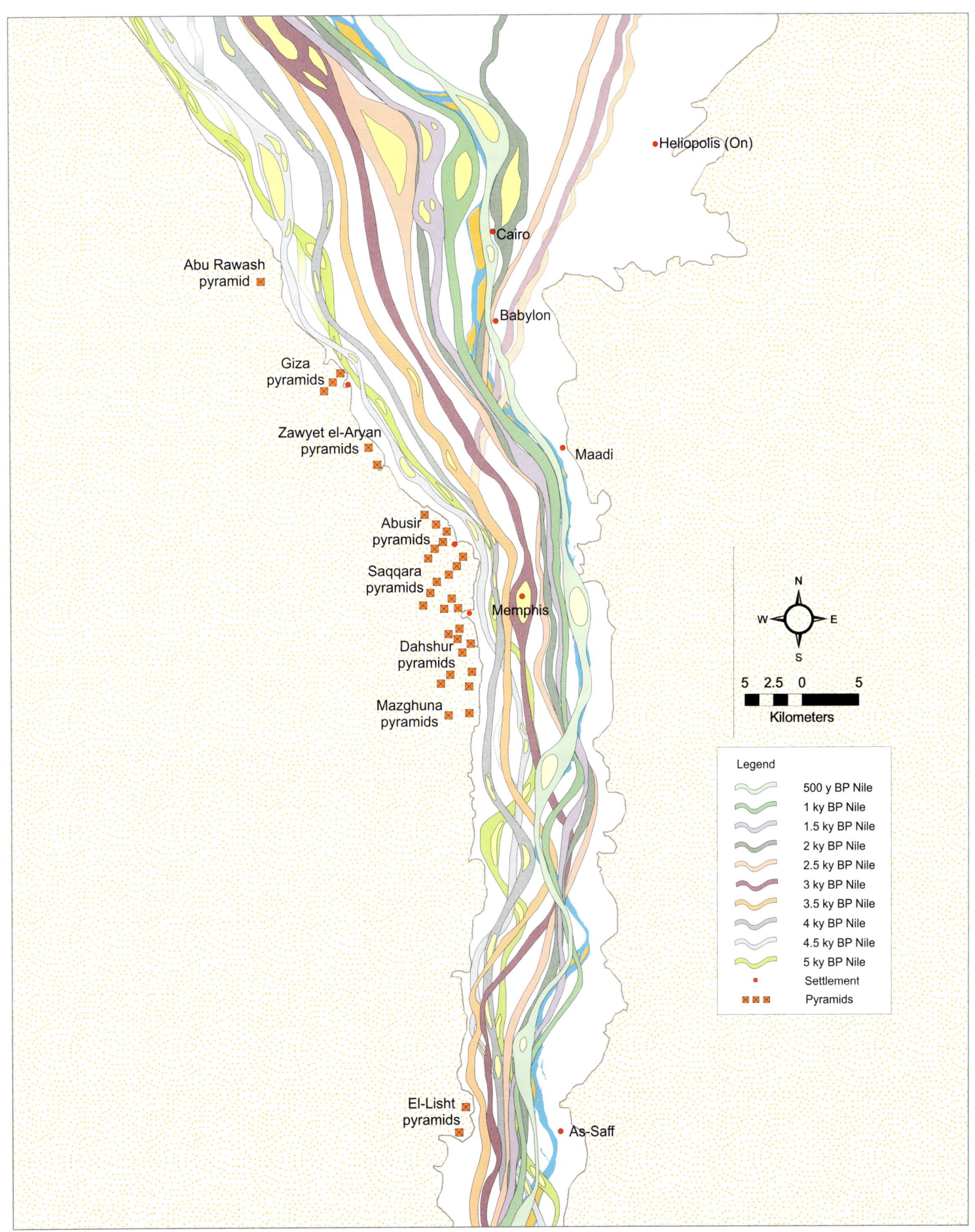

Pl. 18. Shifts in the course of the main channel of the ancient Nile in the Cairo area from 5000 to 500 BP. Reproduced with the kind permission of K Lutley and J Bunbury.

Pl. 19. The lion-headed mooring post from the Trajanic harbor wall coming to the surface during the excavation of Shaft HC3 in Shari' Mari Girgis in 2005. In the background is the monumental entrance to the Hanging Church. (Mohammed Khalifa)

Pl. 20. The north end of the earlier Trajanic quay wall revealed in the westernmost room of the southern round tower. Note how the blocks of the tower foundation abut and run over this earlier wall. (Peter Sheehan)

Pl. 21. The curving outer face of the quayside wall beneath Mari Girgis Church, with the slots in the blocks showing how they were originally joined by swallow-tailed bronze or iron clamps. On the right is the massive wall that was probably built around the end of the seventh century AD to block the entrance to the canal between the two round towers. The steps on the left form part of the presentation of the area carried out by the Greek Orthodox community in the 1940s. (Tim Loveless)

Pl. 22. The huge stone column base within the niche of the northern tower. This column was probably set up to mark the entrance to the canal. (Tim Loveless)

Pl. 23. The massive stone wall built between the round towers of Babylon to block the entrance to the canal, probably built around the end of the seventh century AD. In the background is part of a pottery kiln subsequently built against this wall as part of the industrial use of this area in the ninth to tenth century AD. (Tim Loveless)

Pl. 24. The central arcade of the southern round tower of the Roman fortress after the insertion of the collector shaft 3A. Note how the concentric stone rings of the tower are tied together at the points where the column bases of the central circular arcade are located. (Tim Loveless)

Pl. 25. Fragment of an Oxyrhyncus papyrus of 208 mentioning the Canal of Trajan.
Courtesy Imaging Papyri Project, University of Oxford and Egypt Exploration Society.

Pl. 26. The South Gate of the Roman Fortress of Babylon. In the right lower foreground is the stepped quayside of the Trajanic harbor that was used as a foundation for the eastern flanking tower when the fortress was built c. AD 300. On the left are blocks from other parts of the harbor broken up and reused in the foundations of the western flanking tower. (Tim Loveless)

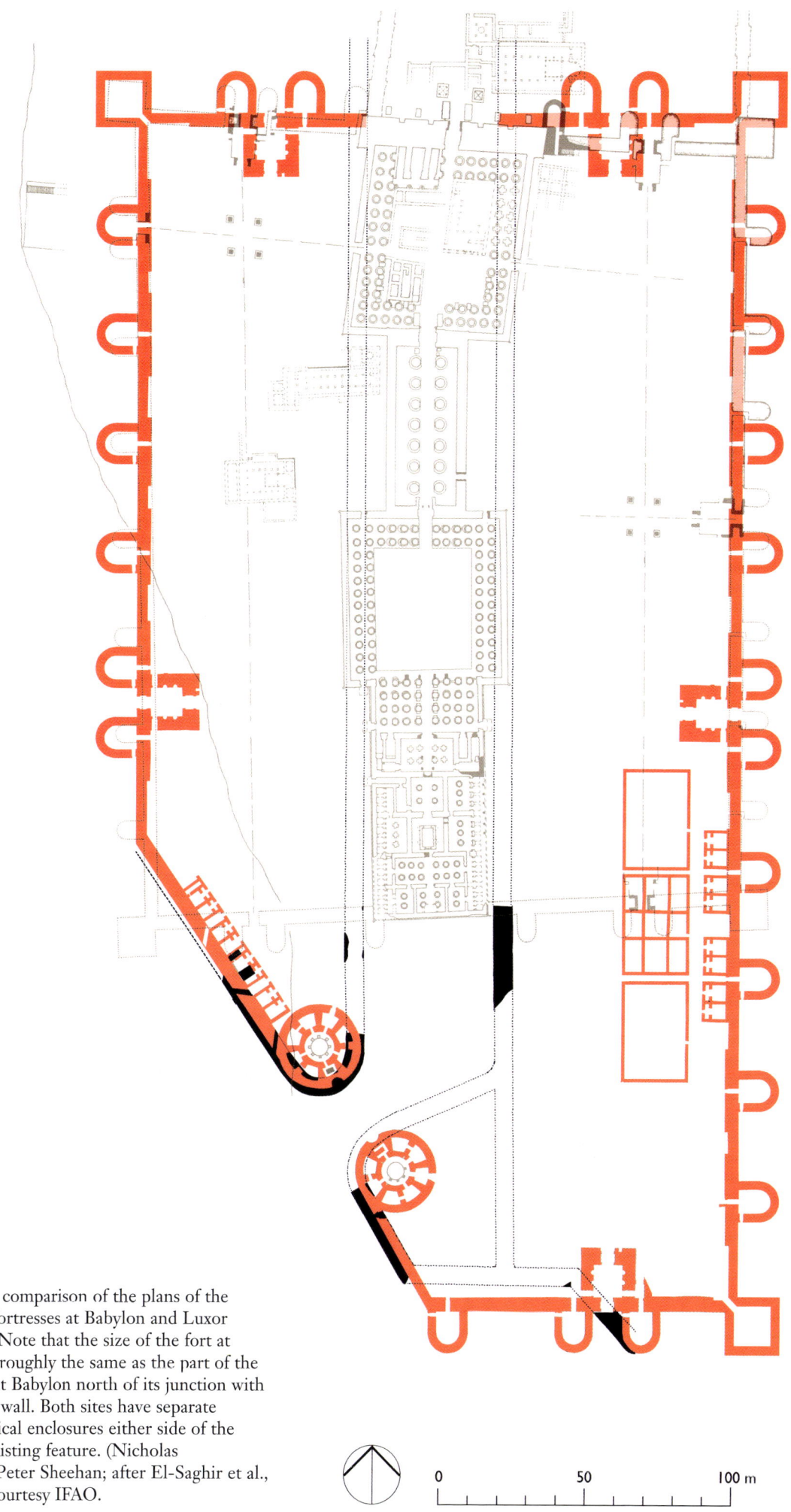

Pl. 27. A comparison of the plans of the Roman fortresses at Babylon and Luxor Temple. Note that the size of the fort at Luxor is roughly the same as the part of the fortress at Babylon north of its junction with the quay wall. Both sites have separate symmetrical enclosures either side of the earlier existing feature. (Nicholas Warner/Peter Sheehan; after El-Saghir et al., 1986). Courtesy IFAO.

Pl. 28. Detail of one of the columns in the central arcade of the northern round tower. Like the other columns, this was truncated to form a base for the foundation of the medieval wall visible in the top of the picture. (Tim Loveless)

Pl. 29. The original entrance to the northern round tower, restored in the 1940s. In the medieval period the ground floor of the tower was already buried, and the wall on the right is actually the external wall of the Mamluk cistern shown in pl. 41. (Tim Loveless)

Pl. 30. The first floor arcade in the northern round tower of the Roman fortress, now part of the Greek Orthodox Church of St. George (Mari Girgis) (Tim Loveless)

The date of the wall paintings in the southern *haykal* show that the first of these medieval phases had occurred before the 1230s. The presence of earlier layers of painting and plaster could take this date back to as early as the second half of the twelfth century and relate the changes in the church to the extensive damage to the churches of al-Fustat in the 1160s described by Abu Salih, that included 'a church named after the Nativity of Our Lord Jesus Christ in the Flesh:'

> The Ghuzz and the people of Cairo pillaged it, and broke the pillars of the apostles, and part of the roof was burnt. In consequence of this the restoration was undertaken by the Shaikh ath-Thikah Gabriel in the caliphate of al-'Adid (1160–1171) and it was consecrated afresh.[43]

One of the key elements in this medieval transformation of the church was the partial demolition of the eastern end of the crypt-church and the addition of a new curved apsidal end to the southern and central *haykal*s. A similar curved apse was probably also added in the northern *haykal*, but this area was completely rebuilt in the fourteenth or fifteenth century and no trace of the earlier medieval phase was noted here. In the southern *haykal* the foundations of the medieval apsidal end of the church are much shallower than the earlier eastern wall of the crypt-church—without an apse—that was revealed below ground during the work of the groundwater lowering project. This earlier wall forms part of the same building phase characterized in the previous chapter as the crypt-church, of which the crypt and the subsurface walls carrying the colonnades of the present church survive.

The squared wooden ties inserted within the brickwork of the apse windows in the southern sanctuary suggest that the external walls of the church above ground may have been largely rebuilt at this time, for the same distinctive technique was reused (presumably based on the construction method already used in the wall) for the reconstruction of the western and northern facades by the Comité de la Conservation des Monuments de l'Art Arabe (CCMAA) in the early twentieth century. Similar ties were noted (and some still survive) in the external walls of the Church of St. Barbara during the restoration works from 1918–22.[44]

In the central *haykal* another element of this first medieval phase survives in the form of the base of a large plastered brick platform, perhaps an altar, over the center of the vault of the crypt. The floor of the sanctuary is preserved as fragments of stone paving around the edge of this altar. Part of a herringbone-pattern limestone pavement survives to the south of the altar platform, and fragments of what appears to be the same pavement laid over an identical mortar bedding in the southern *haykal* form part of this phase. We know that these pavements postdate the crypt-church

Fig. 52. The Church of Abu Serga. Remains of the tall medieval niche on the north side of the central sanctuary preserved at its junction with the curved apse and tribune with its rows of marble benches for the clergy. (Peter Sheehan)

because the demolition layers over the original east wall of the southern *haykal* run under this pavement too.

The medieval changes to the church appear to have been closely related to the twin concerns of the roofing arrangements of the church and access to the crypt, and it may be significant for the date of these changes that the first association of the crypt with the Holy Family in Coptic sources dates from 1247 and in European sources during the same century.[45] Another major component of this first medieval phase appears to have been the re-erection of the arcade columns, which now terminated in massive cruciform masonry piers. Two of these piers were erected at the southwest and northwest corners of the crypt, with stone staircases inserted above the brickwork of the crypt-church. The archaeological evidence shows that the southern stairs at least are a later addition, and it is likely that both were added at this time. In any case the historical sources indicate that both stairways to the crypt were in place by 1420 at the latest, while the first actual mention of stairs to the crypt dates to 1384.[46] East of the stairs, these piers were continued eastward to abut the original apse of the crypt-church, with a tall niche set centrally between the stairs and the apse.[47] Most of this arrangement has been truncated or obscured by later changes within the sanctuary, but traces of the curving plastered face of the northern niche were discovered during the installation of a new stainless steel floor over the roof of the crypt in 2004 (fig. 52).

The position of the columns carrying the first-floor galleries in relation to the earlier subsurface walls of the crypt-church upon which they are built suggests they too were re-erected in this twelfth/thirteenth-century phase, and this impression is reinforced by details of the structural woodwork preserved within the church. It is likely that the original parts of the barrel-vaulted wooden roof date from this period, a date suggested both by their method of construction and perhaps also by the first appearance of the concept of the roof as an inverted version of the Ark in Coptic texts of the thirteenth century.[48] The painted wooden impost boards above the colonnades dividing the nave from the aisles and narthex are painted with designs familiar from the thirteenth century in Egypt, and the *mashrabiya* screen of the central sanctuary appears to be of a broadly similar date. As at the church of the Red Sea monastery of St. Antony, the eastward shift of the sanctuary at Abu Serga was no doubt motivated by changing liturgical needs. The presence of the stepped marble *opus sectile* tribune in the central sanctuary was another feature of this new liturgical space, which may have also been influenced by the processional possibilities of the twin stairways to the crypt. The nature and the scope of these medieval changes to Abu Serga show the continued importance of the church, the strength of its community and patrons, and, perhaps most significantly, the importance of its new identification as one of the places where the Holy Family stayed on their return from Upper Egypt.

Recent evidence from the Red Sea monasteries suggests that the power of Coptic patronage continued at least to some extent throughout the thirteenth century, if such a conclusion can be deduced from the Pantocrator cycle of wall paintings (1291–92) at the Monastery of St. Paul and the work of the "Ornamental Master" at the Monastery of St. Antony, which has been dated to within half a century after 1233.[49]

The Ornamental Master's decoration of the wooden beams of the *khurus* vault at the Church of St. Antony with arabesque and geometric motifs and *naskhi* inscriptions from the Psalms provides an important link with the decorated ceilings of another important medieval archaeological site in Old Cairo, the great hall preserved within the Convent of St. George, commonly known as Dayr al-Banat. The most recent consideration of this building placed its construction within the period 1275–1325.[50] Our recent archaeological work in and around the building has thrown much new light on its constructional history as well as the topography and chronological development of this part of Old Cairo (fig. 53).

The Convent of St. George is located within the western part of the Roman fortress of Babylon. The convent lies on the north side of the Harat Dayr Mari Girgis, which is reached via the steps leading down into the fortress area from Shari' Mari Girgis (fig. 4). No precise historical sources survive to indicate the foundation date of the convent. The earliest historical references to it are from the second half of the seventeenth century, and even these relatively late sources do little more than indicate the presence of a convent for Coptic nuns within the walls of the Roman fortress of Babylon.[51]

The hall or *qa'a* of a medieval palace or great house survives within the western part of the convent. The *qa'a* is composed of a large central hall, or *durqa'a*, flanked to the north and south by reception areas or *iwan*s. This building takes the form of a *majlis-iwan*, with the main reception area being the T-shaped southern *majlis*, with a simple *iwan* to the north of the central hall. This particular architectural groundplan, with its *majlis al-hiri bi kummayn* or 'two sleeves,' is used in buildings after 1150, gaining in popularity from 1250 to 1350 and then declining rapidly.[52] The high ceilings of the *qa'a* were designed for cool summer living, with *malqaf*s (windcatchers) to draw the cool north wind down through the hall. Along the western side of the *qa'a* a series of smaller vaulted rooms carries a first-floor passage or gallery that gave onto the hall through wooden *mashrabiya* windows or a wooden balcony. This type of *aghani*, or singers' gallery, is known from other fourteenth- and fifteenth-century halls.[53] Similar rooms with a gallery to a first-floor balcony and *mashrabiya* windows at second-floor level on the eastern side of the *qa'a* are shown in a 1906 elevation drawing made by the Comité. The surviving rooms along the western side were thus originally paralleled by other rooms on the eastern side of the building in the area of the modern arched passageway. The southern *majlis-iwan* of the medieval building is separated from the central hall by a pair of huge seven-meter-high folding wooden doors with eleven pairs of elaborately carved panels set vertically in each leaf and a further twenty-five in the outer frame. These rooms are currently used as a *mazaar* or visiting place with relics associated with the martyrdom of St. George. The carved cedar panels of these doors have been dated to the second half of the eleventh century, and are similar to an eleventh-century example reused in the Qalawun complex in Cairo and the sanctuary doors of several monasteries in the Wadi Natrun.[54]

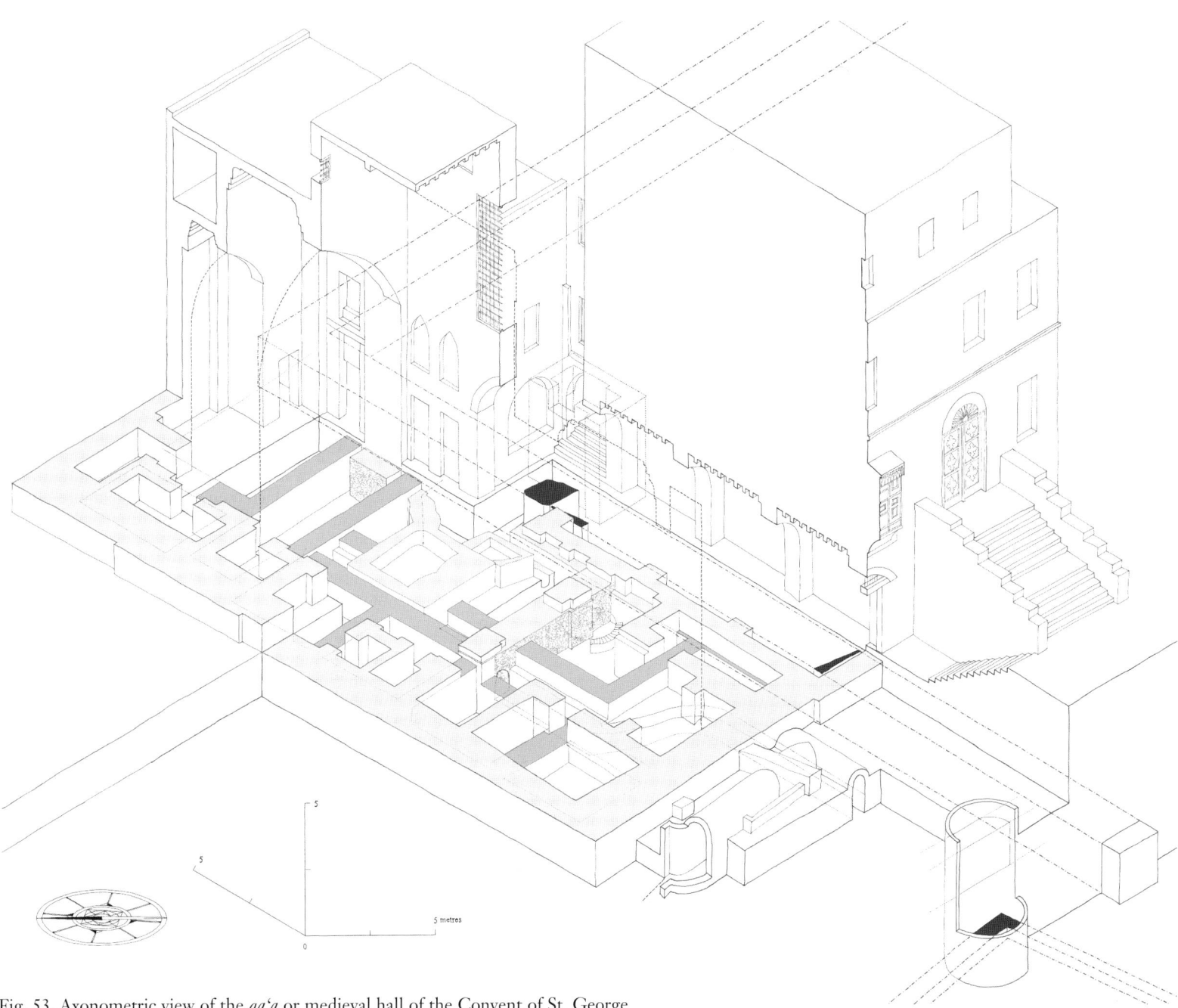

Fig. 53. Axonometric view of the *qa'a* or medieval hall of the Convent of St. George showing the new archaeological information recorded during the project. The plan of the earlier brick building from the Fatimid period is shown in dark gray and fragments of surviving Roman masonry in black. (Nicholas Warner)

As we have seen in the previous chapter, a large and well-preserved brick building of the Fatimid period was also exposed beneath the medieval *qa'a*. The plan of this Fatimid building is quite different from that of the building above ground, and it is abundantly clear that the southern end of the *qa'a* does not represent the survival of part of the earlier structure, even if it is possible that the carved panels of the great doors may have come from this earlier building. Before the *qa'a* was constructed, the Fatimid building was leveled, with some of its walls being reused as foundations. Most of the walls of the current building, however, were built on distinctive limestone rubble foundations, with the stone probably coming from earlier Roman structures on the site. Where necessary, these rubble foundations were cut down into the brick walls of the earlier building. The alley to the north of the courtyard in the Fatimid building was filled with rubble to provide a solid foundation for the great arch leading into the northern *iwan* of the medieval hall.

The vaulted drain running along the western side of the Fatimid courtyard was blocked by the limestone foundations of the wall that divides the great hall from the *majlis*. (pl. 36) The drain continued in use, but the direction of flow was reversed to drain water to the north from a new feature of the medieval building, a plastered basin or fountain placed centrally within the *durqa'a*. This fountain was supplied with water by ceramic pipes built into a wall leading from the large cistern of the earlier building, which remained in use. The water of the central fountain or basin was drained by other ceramic pipes flowing into a brick-vaulted tank to the east, and when these became blocked through use, this arrangement was replaced by channels cut into the brickwork of the fountain itself. Although the part of the earlier vaulted drain running through the hall and the *majlis* was blocked, the rest of the system was modified to receive a new drain carrying waste water from the area to the east of the hall. Although most of this eastern part of the building was removed in the early twentieth century, parallels with other surviving examples of the medieval Mamluk *qa'a* suggest that the rooms to the east of the hall may originally have had domestic or washing functions, an analogy which is supported here by the presence of the cistern in this area, extensive remains of canalization, and even the disposition and appearance of the rooms on the plan of the building made by the Comité in 1906. Against the southern exterior wall of the *qa'a* we noted other medieval brick buildings employing reused limestone paving stones (almost certainly from the Roman street) for their foundations. These buildings also incorporated subterranean vaulted drains that fed into the earlier system.

The apparent size and complexity of the demolished brick building makes for an interesting parallel with the destruction by the Ayyubids of the Eastern Fatimid palace in al-Qahira, which also displays a quite different orientation to the Ayyubid madrasa built over it.[55] A number of architectural features support a date within the second half of the thirteenth century for the construction of the *qa'a* of the Convent of St. George, although there are few examples of the pre-Mamluk *qa'a* with which to compare it; in fact, the only examples are the *qa'a* of al-Dardir (heavily modified in the Ottoman period) and that of Sultan Salih, built in 1240 within the Roda citadel next to the Nilometer, a building which is known only from the plan contained in the Napoleonic *Description*.[56]

The ornamentation on the ceiling of the *majlis* and the northern *iwan* supports an Ayyubid or Bahri Mamluk date for the building, particularly the combination of Kufic and *naskhi* script for the inscriptions from the gospels in the ceiling of the northern iwan, the *naskhi* inscription taken from Psalm 91 in the *majlis*, the winged lions of the northern *iwan*, and the stucco birds within the outer frame of reciprocal polylobed arches in the *majlis*. This ceiling frame is very like that of the Mosque of Ulmas al-Hajib, built in 1329–30 on the Qasaba to the south of Bab Zuwayla.[57] Similarly, the extensive use of vaulting within the building is a feature of the Ayyubid or earlier Mamluk period, since all the extant examples of the Mamluk *qa'a* from the 1330s onward, for example those of Bashtak Alin Ak and Qawsun, have flat wooden ceilings.[58] A related earlier feature is the court, which was originally open, a fact that can be deduced from the presence of the great doors to keep out the dust, as well as the need to provide adequate lighting in the majlis.[59] Finally, the arrangement of the reused Fatimid carved panels in the great doors finds a nearby parallel in those that probably came from the doors to the baptismal chapel of the Hanging Church, which were acquired by the British Museum in 1878, and have been dated to 1300.[60]

The similarity of the ceiling frames and the stucco decoration also link the *qa'a* of the convent to another site of thirteenth- or fourteenth-century activity in Old Cairo, the Wedding Hall of the Church of St. George, located a mere sixty meters to the east. The stucco medallions in the Wedding Hall have been likened to those of the tomb of Kujuk (1343) in the Mosque of Aqsunqur.[61] Our recent work shows that the Wedding Hall, like the medieval hall of the convent, was also constructed on limestone rubble foundations over a substantial earlier brick building. The fact that this earlier building was razed to the same 19.5 m level as that beneath the convent presents a strong argument for an extensive rebuilding program over large areas of the former fortress (fig. 54).

We were able to record more circumstantial evidence for the thirteenth-century revival in Old Cairo during the demolition in 2000 of the Church of the Virgin, Qasriyat

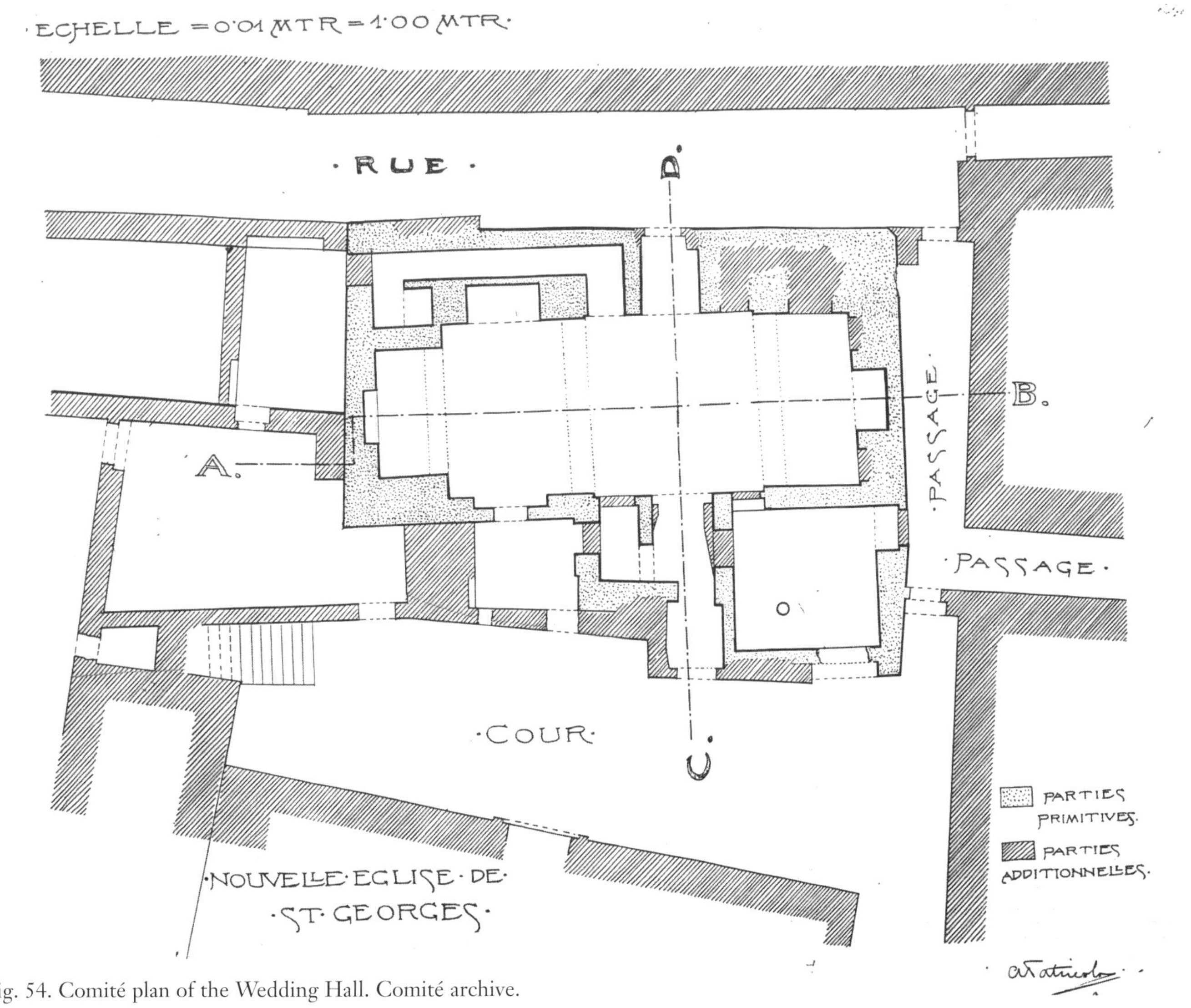

Fig. 54. Comité plan of the Wedding Hall. Comité archive.

al-Rihan.⁶² The first references to this church are from the ninth century, an early date which is supported by the low elevation of the floor of the church relative to its surroundings. During the demolition of the church it was noted that the brickwork construction of the semi-domes appeared similar to those of the Ayyubid Madrasa of al-Kamiliya, built in 1225.⁶³

Archaeological observations made during a major restoration of the Church of St. Barbara carried out by the Comité from 1918 to 1922 provided more evidence for the renewal of the area around the thirteenth century. In the existing building, two phases were identified during this work, with the construction of the outer walls taking place in the second half of the eleventh century and the nave, aisles, and narthex rather later, at the beginning of the thirteenth century.⁶⁴ The dates of both these separate phases are strikingly similar to those provided by our archaeological investigations for the construction of the crypt-church of Abu Serga and the later medieval rebuilding of the church above ground. In contrast to Alfred Butler, who had believed the north transept of the Church of St. Barbara to be the original structure, subsequently enlarged into the present building, Patricolo ascribed the construction of this part of the church to a period not before the fourteenth century.⁶⁵ This phase also finds a contemporary parallel at Abu Serga with the rebuilding of the north sanctuary. According to Patricolo and Monneret de Villard, the upper rounded part of the central apse of the Church of St. Barbara, as distinct from the lower seven-sided aspect noted by Butler, also belonged to this fourteenth-century phase. They also identified a number of other elements as belonging to the same medieval phase, including the painting of the lower surface of the wooden architraves carried on the nave columns and the addition of the chapel to the south.

Fig. 55. The Ben Ezra Synagogue: The medieval mastaba revealed during conservation work by the Canadian Centre for Architecture (CCA) in 1999.

The churches were not the only religious buildings of Old Cairo to experience renewal in the thirteenth century. At the Mosque of 'Amr, Ibn Duqmaq relates that the northwest wall (one of the oldest surviving parts of the present building) was rebuilt by Sultan Baybars (1260–77).[66] The inscriptions on the reconstructed Holy Ark of the Ben Ezra Synagogue, found in the Geniza by Solomon Schechter and now in the Jewish Museum in New York, refer to rebuilding of the sanctuary and other parts of the building by the al-Ma'ali and al-Amshati families, both related to the famous contemporary Jewish scholar Moses Maimonides, around 1220.[67] In situ archaeological evidence for the medieval synagogue is confined to the *mastaba* located in the center of the building, which was revealed beneath its modern marble revetment in 1999. The work carried out at this time showed the *mastaba* to be a tall (at least 1.73 m) stone structure, plastered to resemble a medieval vaulted tomb and founded at a level that is below the floor of the present building and thus presumably on the medieval floor.[68] As far as the architecture of synagogues is concerned, the *mastaba* seems to be unique, and its construction seems therefore most likely to be connected with the increased medieval interest and veneration of Old Cairo, at which time it was probably erected as a reaffirmation of the Jewish presence at the site from earliest times (fig. 55).

We have seen from the layout of the medieval *qa'a* of the convent that the former east–west route through the fortress to the river along the via principalis was shifted south in the medieval period to take its present form as Harat Mari Girgis. The ancient routes northward from the fortress, however, continued to function. The main façades and formal entrances of the churches of Abu Serga and Qasriyat al-Rihan, both apparently rebuilt in the Ayyubid period, continued to give onto the great early medieval road leading north which had been formed by the filling-in of the ancient canal. Similarly the façade of the Church of St. Barbara still gave onto the older via praetoria, while the continued importance of the terminus of this road at the Rumayla or parade ground of the later Mamluks suggests that the use of at least parts of the route probably survived the abandonment of al-Fustat.

Despite all the evidence of their continued vitality throughout the thirteenth century, the position of the Copts of Egypt had begun to worsen appreciably, probably even before the advent of Mamluk rule in 1250. Official measures and popular agitation against the Egyptian Church began within fifteen years of this date. Sultan Baybars is recorded as having threatened to burn all the Christians in 1262 and sumptuary laws were imposed on Christians and Jews in 1268.[69] The erosion of a long tradition of tolerance and coexistence may have been one of the unwanted side effects of the program of madrasa building begun by the Ayyubids. The second half of the thirteenth century also saw a revival of the debate over the nature of the conquest of Egypt and in consequence the status that was to be enjoyed by Christians. Those who came to the conclusion that the Christians and Jews were subject groups by virtue of armed conquest argued that churches and synagogues should be demolished because they had all been reconstructed or rebuilt at some time after the Conquest, in spite of such building works being expressly forbidden to a subject people.[70] The passions ignited by the Crusades contributed to this problem, as did the influx of Muslim refugees from the Maghreb and al-Andalus and others fleeing the Mongol sack of Baghdad in 1258. Another major complaint was that Christians in the administration were using their influence with the amirs to further the aims of their community, a charge that was no doubt influenced by the extensive church building and decoration that had indeed been carried out under the Ayyubids. Church buildings were therefore a natural focus for disorder, although it is worth noting the contemporary document showing that after a riot against the Christians in Qus (Upper Egypt) in 1307 the authorities took the side of the Christians.[71] The consequence of these grievances seems to have been frequent, and therefore probably largely unheeded, Mamluk edicts against Christians, including exclusion from state service.

The prosperity enjoyed by the Christian population under the Fatimids had largely continued into Ayyubid and early Mamluk times, buoyed by the major reconstruction of the city and the wealth engendered by military success and the consolidation of a new Islamic empire stretching from Egypt into the Levant. Political and religious issues combined with the success of the Ayyubid and Mamluk armies lent new weight to the idea of Islamic unity, while tolerance of the Christians within this community declined and the rate of conversion to Islam correspondingly increased.[72] On the other hand, the fourteenth-century Italian traveler Pietro de Pennis comments on the devotion of ordinary Muslims at Santa Maria de Cava, the name often given by western travelers to the Church of Abu Serga.[73] It should also be noted that even under the Ayyubids, the Coptic churches in Old Cairo had endured early travails. The Hanging Church, for example, was closed during part of the reign of the Ayyubid sultan al-Malik al-Kamil (1218–38), and apparently pillaged at some point between 1240 and 1259.[74] Al-Maqrizi, writing in the early fifteenth century, relates that the church was also sacked during the reign of Khalil Salah al-Din al-Ashraf (1290–93). All the churches of Old Cairo suffered closure in 1301 and again from 1320–23, and on both occasions many other churches in Egypt were destroyed.[75] As the residence of the Coptic patriarch, the Hanging Church naturally attracted more attention than others, and the authorities closed it again in 1316. In 1321 it was nearly burned down by a Muslim mob, a disaster averted only by the intervention of the amir Aydagmash.[76] The Irish pilgrim Symon Semeonis, in his description of the Hanging Church between 1322 and 1324, clearly refers to the sufferings of the Coptic Church at this time and the beginnings of the hopes of the faithful for deliverance: "[T]here is a white marble column, from which they say that Mary spoke to a Copt about the liberation of the Christians."[77]

The repeated closures and attacks and the declining importance of Old Cairo resulted in the abandonment by the Coptic patriarch of his residence in the Hanging Church after 1320 and the relocation to the Church of the Virgin at Haret Zuwayla in Cairo.[78] This move marks a key moment in the subsequent decline of the area and the shift by the elite of the Christian and Jewish communities to Cairo. We know also that from the end of the eleventh century the synagogue neighborhood was in decline and that by the end of the fifteenth century the restored Ben Ezra Synagogue was used only on the Sabbath, while for the rest of the week, "the Jews hire a servant to stand there and guard it."[79]

By the middle of the fourteenth century, often considered to be a turning point in Egyptian religious history, the increasingly hostile and implacable position of the Mamluk authorities had created the most fundamental crisis for the Egyptian Church since the persecutions of Diocletian. This was a period that saw the destruction of churches, many of which were never rebuilt. The historian al-Sakhawi reports that in 1447 the sultan Jaqmaq ordered the demolition of the Melkite Church of Qasr al-Sham' on the grounds that it had been restored without permission. The pulpit, or *bima*, of the Ben Ezra Synagogue was also destroyed by the authorities in 1442.[80] Measures were put in place to ensure the compulsory conversion of Copts in governmental posts—the *musalima*— in 1293, 1301, 1321, and 1354, the last of which involved special measures to ensure the *musalima* really were practicing Muslims.[81] The significance of these demographic changes is indicated by the fact that thirty-six out of 163 viziers in the Mamluk period (1250–1516) were converts to Islam.[82] The period is also notable for nonviolent Coptic resistance, including the execution of forty-nine "voluntary" martyrs in the 1380s and 1390s.[83]

Another effect was the increasing change to the previously Christian and Jewish character of Old Cairo. Ibn Duqmaq, writing in the fourteenth century, records eighteen mosques in the area of the fortress.[84] The surviving columns in the gatehouse of the South Gate of the fortress, as well as the walls removed by the Comité in 1915, might even have formed part of the mosque known as the Gami' al-Qubba, described in 1336 as being underneath the church. According to this description the mosque had an arched entrance with three *mihrab*s, a niche, and a *maqsura* (portion of the mosque separated by a screen and set aside for the use of the ruler or imam) with a small recess. The account continues: "go in and dig to the depth of a man, you will find a trapdoor . . . lift it and you will descend into a cave which extends under the mosque called Gama' el-Qobbah."[85] The description of the cave may refer to the great drain under the floor of the Roman gateway, which was revealed by the Comité and apparently destroyed during the recent installation of perforated drains in this area.[86]

Repairs to the churches and synagogues were strictly monitored and several instances are recorded of fines and destruction carried out after restoration work had exceeded the limits allowed by the Muslim authorities. A court document from 1473 contains references to a survey of the dilapidated synagogues of Old Cairo apparently carried out as a result of a request by the Jewish community to repair the buildings.[87] At the Hanging Church there are records of a 1384 examination of the church by the courts, followed by the order to destroy the reconstruction work recently carried out in the church.[88] On the other hand, these instances are significant in showing that building work and repairs continued even through the difficult times of the Mamluk period, for by 1488 Obadiah of Bertinoro reports that "there is a very beautiful synagogue built upon great pillars."[89]

The northern sanctuary of the Church of Abu Serga with its distinctive *muqarnas* vault was also probably rebuilt in the fourteenth century. There is no historical information as to the reasons for this rebuilding, but since it involved the complete removal of the northern apsidal extension added in the early thirteenth century we may suspect structural failure of the latter, perhaps in relation to the great earthquake recorded in 1303. Our recent work in the church suggested that the Trajanic canal wall underpinning much of the crypt and the south sanctuary has been truncated in the area beneath the northern sanctuary, and the absence of this massive stonework may have had consequences for the stability of this part of the church. Alternatively the closure of the churches of Old Cairo from 1320–23 may have been a consequence of the damage and fires suffered during the attacks of 1321, and this part of the church may have required rebuilding. Damage or collapse of the northeast corner of the church may be further indicated by the way in which the northern aisle ends abruptly at the entrance to the northern sanctuary, with its painted wooden architrave cleanly cut through and the northern sanctuary now independently roofed.[90] In any event, the Mamluk-period work involved the construction of a substantial new square stone foundation for the dome. Archaeological work in the northern sanctuary revealed that the same period also saw at least one burial in a vaulted brick tomb with a floor made of wooden boards. In this connection it is interesting to note that Vansleb in 1672 describes seeing the epitaph of a "Gentil-homme Européen" in the crypt of the church: *Hic jacet Nobilis Petrus Louys IX Neapollonies, qui obiit M.CCCCII die XI, Februarij*.[91]

For the churches of Old Cairo the decline of the power of Coptic patronage was partially offset by the influence of European Christians, for the final Mamluk expulsion of the Crusaders from the Holy Land in 1291 brought European merchants (especially Italians from the great trading cities of Venice and Genoa) to Cairo in search of a new base for the spice and luxury trade with the East. It is from this time that Old Cairo begins to be much visited, venerated, and described by European travelers, a trend stimulated by the inclusion of a visit to the Monastery of St. Catherine within the itinerary of pilgrims to the Holy Land.[92] This veneration was based largely on the association of the Church of Abu Serga with the Holy Family, an association that, as we have seen, appears to have become the focus of the church as rebuilt in the thirteenth century. The first European account of the sojourn of the Holy Family in the crypt of Abu Serga Church dates from the early thirteenth century, but the number of European travelers increased greatly in the following century. One of the earliest and fullest accounts of the church and crypt of Abu Serga by a western traveler is that of Franciscus Pipinus de Bononia in 1320:

> I was in the city of Babylon in Egypt where there was a house in which the Blessed Virgin and her son lived when they fled to Egypt. There is an old and beautiful church which they call Saint Mary of the Cave and under the main altar of this great church is a covered chapel which they say was the place where the Glorious Virgin lived with her son and Joseph when they were in Egypt. The Christians gather at this place to worship the Saviour Lord who lived here with the Blessed Virgin.[93]

Fig. 56. Abu Serga: Marble cross from the medieval floor of the crypt re-set in the niche of the south aisle by the Comité. (Peter Sheehan)

Fig. 57. Abu Serga: The importance of the church to Catholic pilgrims is also shown by the surviving Terra Santa crosses preserved during the Comité restoration—one inside the sanctuary and this one on the main façade of the church. (Peter Sheehan)

Travelers' descriptions help us to trace the architectural development of the crypt through the medieval period.[94] In the second half of the fourteenth century the crypt is described as "a dark vault" and "a cave of stone."[95] Altars in the crypt are mentioned from the fourteenth century onward, with the central altar marking the position of a large marble stone engraved with a cross.[96] The central niche at this time is described as inlaid or revetted with marble. During the course of the groundwater lowering project we were able to record archaeological evidence for a number of the features mentioned in the medieval accounts. Crosses engraved on marble blocks were found in the niches in the central "sanctuary" and the south aisle of the crypt. These appear to have been reset there during the Comité restoration of the church in the early twentieth century, when a new marble floor was laid in the crypt (fig. 56). We found other slabs of decorated marble facedown beneath the altar of the central sanctuary, while numerous smaller fragments and plainer pieces had been reused in the makeup of the Comité marble floor. Columns in the crypt make their first appearance in a traveler's account at the end of the fifteenth century (1485), although archaeological data and travelers' descriptions indicate that the present arrangement of columns probably dates from the seventeenth century (see below).[97] Although the walls of the crypt sanctuary were almost entirely rebuilt by the Comité, a tiny area of marble *opus sectile* similar to that preserved (although much restored) in the central sanctuary of the medieval church survived below the twentieth-century floor to suggest that the corresponding part of the crypt may have been similarly decorated. The medieval access to the crypt appears to have continued the original arrangement, although the first explicit mention of stairs to the crypt dates to 1384 and the presence of two stairs to 1420. This is valuable in showing that neither of the stairs was added during the extensive post-medieval changes to both the crypt and the eastern end of the church.

One of the factors involved in the importance of the crypt to European pilgrims and travelers seems to have been the increasing presence and influence of the Franciscans. Francis himself is believed to have met with Sultan al-Kamil during the siege of Damietta by the Crusaders in 1219. Symon Semeonis reports that the sultan al-Nasir Muhammad had granted custody over the Christian holy places of Egypt to the Franciscans around 1330, and a number of accounts from 1324 through to the end of the nineteenth century testify to the rights of the Franciscans to say Mass and carry out baptisms in the crypt.[98] Other indicators of the Roman Catholic presence in Old Cairo continued into the nineteenth century in the form of a Franciscan hostel (in the area of the modern bazaar) and a small Roman Catholic cemetery located just to the north of the church, now built over.[99] Another Catholic cemetery (recently demolished) lay to the east of the Hanging Church (fig. 57).

Abu Serga was not the only church in Old Cairo to receive foreign attention. It has been argued that carved panels from the Hanging Church, including one showing a wholly Byzantine subject (the *Anastasis*), indicate the presence of Greek artists or a Byzantine sponsor.[100] The panels, which retain traces of gesso for gilding or painting, have been reconstructed on paper as having been an arrangement of paired scenes (like the doors of the Convent of St. George) on doors probably located at the entrance to the baptismal chapel of the church. The chapel may have been renovated in 1301–02 in association with an embassy from the Byzantine court. In the same part of the church (built over the tower flanking the Roman gate), the *haykal* screen of the chapel to the fourteenth-century Ethiopian saint Takla Haymanot has doors with inscriptions from Psalm 117 in *naskhi* script and, above this, Byzantine icons connected with Christ's infancy.[101]

The date of the increased European and Byzantine interest in Old Cairo coincides with a wider ecclesiastical and ecumenical initiative and unity between the Roman and Orthodox Churches produced by the new Islamic hegemony in the Near East. The scope of this initiative extended beyond Egypt and into Ethiopia, as the chapel of Takla Haymanot shows, and the continued importance of the Red Sea monasteries in this link southward is demonstrated by the presence of the abbot of the monastery of St. Antony at the Council of Ferrara-Florence in 1440 and the use of the monasteries as Arabic language schools for Catholic missionaries until well into the seventeenth century.[102]

Early Ottoman Decline and the Eighteenth-Century Revival under the "Sultan of the Copts"

The European cartographic sources examined earlier in this chapter indicate that after the Ottoman Conquest in 1516 the broad limits of Cairo remained largely unchanged for much of the next four centuries. Changes to the urban fabric consisted mainly of reworking or adding to its density rather than expansion into new areas. A notable exception was the port area of Bulaq, which naturally expanded as the new rulers set about the process of directing the wealth of the new province northward to Istanbul.[103] The hiatus in the growth of the city was therefore largely a consequence of Egypt's shift from the center of Mamluk power to a province of the Ottoman Empire. The historical and archaeological evidence from Old Cairo does not contradict this broad picture: the poverty of the area during the sixteenth and seventeenth centuries was symptomatic of a decline that had already begun under the later Burgi Mamluks and was clearly not alleviated by the increasing importance of Bulaq as the port of the city.

By the early eighteenth century, however, the decline of the central Ottoman administration produced more local autonomy for the *bey*s of Egypt, and the Coptic community saw a return to the earlier medieval situation, with its notables (the *arakhina*) once again assuming influential positions as secretaries and administrators. Archaeological work and archival photographs have now revealed that a major cultural and building revival took place in the Coptic churches of Egypt throughout the eighteenth century.[104] As with the medieval period, the archaeological evidence from Old Cairo complements that gained during the ARCE projects at the Red Sea monasteries.[105] These monasteries saw extended programs of renewal and revival, beginning in 1701 and continuing throughout most of the century.

Throughout Egypt the buildings of the churches, monasteries, and convents were restored, decorated, and provided with new endowments for their upkeep. Within the churches, what constituted a cultural and artistic renaissance manifested itself in the production of icons and the copying of manuscripts. Using the mechanism of the waqf endowments, the revitalization of the area probably took a similar form to that of the extensive building programs in a number of other locales in Cairo in this period (pl. 37).[106]

In Old Cairo much of the revival appears to have been financed and organized by one of the most influential Coptic figures of the early modern period, Ibrahim al-Gohari, and later by his brother Girgis. Their influence and patronage contributed to the restoration of churches and monasteries in a number of different locations throughout Egypt. On one of the screens in the eighteenth-century Church of St. Mercurius at the Red Sea monastery of St. Paul, Ibrahim is even given the epithet "the Sultan of the Copts."[107] Ibrahim al-Gohari died in 1795 and was buried in the tomb he had built for himself in Old Cairo adjacent to the Coptic Church of St. George.

The archaeological survival of a number of buildings or fragments of this phase testify to a program of restoration and rebuilding that extended throughout much of the area within the walls of the fortress. The archaeological information is supplemented by archival photographs from the early twentieth century, when much more of this phase survived intact than now. Most of the surviving archaeological evidence for the "Ottoman revival" in Old Cairo is now concentrated in the group of buildings located along the central route of ʿAtfat Mari Girgis and its southward extension, but fragments of buildings from this phase survived until recently along much of the length of the former via praetoria running through the eastern enclosure of the Roman fortress, and to the west and north of the Church of Abu Serga (pls. 38 and 39).

As with other parts of Cairo, one mechanism for urban revival was the process of *istibdal* or "exchange," whereby properties originally forming part of the inalienable endowment of a religious building could be sold and redeveloped if it could be proved that they were neglected and not generating adequate income.[108] That *istibdal* was practiced among the Christian communities of Old Cairo is suggested by Ahmad al-Higazi in 1470, who refers to Mari Girgis al-Muʿallaqa (that is, the Church of St. George 'suspended' over the Roman tower) "which is now Melkite having been Coptic."[109] This reference and the present close relationship between the property boundaries of the Orthodox and Coptic communities in the western part of Old Cairo give the impression that the tower may have come into the hands of the Orthodox Church during the fifteenth century, perhaps in exchange for what is now the Coptic Convent of St. George (Dayr al-Banat).

In Old Cairo, Ibrahim al-Gohari may have purchased many of the existing properties with the specific intention of creating new endowments, particularly for the Convent of St. George. We know that the convent already existed at this time, and can infer that it was in need of renewal, from the account of Vansleb, visiting Egypt in 1672 and 1673: "I saw the convent of Coptic nuns, called Deir el Banat, or the Monastery of the Maidens . . . but it is a place so horrible that I couldn't stay there for even a moment."[110]

Archaeological and cartographic evidence exist for the eighteenth-century creation of a large walled enclosure around the convent, which in effect took up most of the northern part of the fortress. This includes the areas now occupied by the social club of the Church of St. Barbara and the area to the north of Abu Serga (fig. 9 and pl. 35).[111]

The *Description* plan, published in 1821, shows the limits of Old Cairo, called here "Deyr al Nasara," or monastery of the Christians, at the end of the eighteenth century.[112] The existence of roughly the same boundaries can be inferred from the view of the area drawn by Claude Sicard in 1715, in particular the irregular line of the northern wall that now divides the area of the convent and the Church of the Virgin from that of the Greek Orthodox cemetery.[113] The extent to which the wall of the convent defined late medieval Old Cairo can be seen from the French plan, on which the route northeastward from the "Bab al Deyr" to Cairo and the Qarafa closely follows the northwest walls of the convent.

The towers shown on these two illustrations at the northern edge of Old Cairo may have been remaining elements of the Roman fortress or medieval features, but most of the extant parts of the boundary wall, such as, for example, the repairs to the flanking tower of the East Gate, appear to date to the enclosure of the convent grounds, perhaps at the beginning of the eighteenth century. It was probably at this time that the surviving U-shaped towers of the eastern wall of the Roman fortress began to be used as tombs. However, Butler's plan of 1884 reveals that the towers at the northern edge of Old Cairo shown on the 1715 and 1821 illustrations had by then disappeared under the Greek Orthodox cemetery. Parts of them may have been incorporated into the western end of the Church of the Assumption, which now stands within the cemetery.

Together with the surviving archaeological evidence, these two cartographic indicators, separated in time by a century, give us a good idea of the limits of the convent and its eighteenth-century layout. The key element in this layout was the Coptic Church of St. George, which before its partial destruction by fire in the middle of the nineteenth century almost certainly functioned as the main convent church.114 Significantly, access to this church from the main residential area of the convent was still along the route of the Roman via principalis. To reach the church the nuns would have crossed the 'Atfat Mari Girgis and passed through the vaulted entrance passage that survives on its eastern side and would have led into the courtyard that is now defined by the southwest corner of the church and the tomb of al-Gohari. During the recent work in 'Atfat Mari Girgis to lower the groundwater level affecting the Wedding Hall of the Church of St. George, archaeological evidence indicated that the western edge of the street in the medieval period was actually much further to the east than at present. The medieval 'Atfat Mari Girgis crossed by the nuns to reach the Church of St. George was therefore substantially narrower, and would probably have been more or less entirely enclosed by the overhanging corbelled upper stories of the buildings on each side.

The *Description* plan of the fortress reveals the extent of the convent by 1800, and shows only the single main entrance to its enclosure at the junction of Harat Mari Girgis and 'Atfat Mari Girgis. The major access road through the fortress involved passing around the southern edge of the convent enclosure and down the old via praetoria past the Jewish quarter to the *hara* (quarter) north of the Hanging Church. An alternative route that entered the fortress through a gate south of the round towers led into the *hara* located around the Church of Abu Serga. Another entrance to the *hara* of Abu Serga from Harat Mari Girgis survives in the form of the low arch at the northwest corner of the church.115

At this time the eastern end of Harat Mari Girgis and thus the main entrance to the convent was marked by a *sabil*, or drinking fountain, the façade of which survives, including the inlet for filling the cistern located under the building.116 The location of a *sabil* at a corner or intersection is a typical feature of Ottoman architecture; this one, at the entrance to the convent and the end of the road for the thirsty visitor coming from the Nile, appears to have been a highly visible symbol of the al-Gohari brothers' heritage of good works (pl. 5).

By the eighteenth century the main entrance to the convent was certainly through the arched doorway leading from Harat Mari Girgis into 'Atfat Mari Girgis, the latter being the ancient route along the line of the canal, which functioned as the main street of the enclosed area of the convent. This doorway into the convent would have been guarded by day and kept closed and locked at night.117 Another Ottoman entrance to the convent area was until recently (1998) still standing at the northeast corner of the Church of St. George.118

Other elements of the later medieval topography of Old Cairo can be gleaned from travelers' accounts. The account of Vansleb's 1677 visit to Old Cairo is particularly useful in assessing the condition of the various buildings he saw. In contrast to his rather disparaging remarks on many of the churches and monasteries of Old Cairo, he found at the Hanging Church: "la Maa'llaca, église fort ancienne, magnifique, et très claire."119 This church too shared in the activity at the beginning of the eighteenth century, for a restoration under Patriarch John XVI (1676–1718) is described in a manuscript dated to 1704.120 The date and the involvement of the patriarch may even indicate that the restoration of its medieval seat was intended to act as the catalyst for the renewal of the whole area.

Medieval Coptic sources indicate a link between the Hanging Church and the Church of St. Barbara that had been created by the transfer of some of the relics of the saint to the latter church at some time before 1072.121 Al-Maqrizi in the early fifteenth century described the Church of St. Barbara as large and much venerated by the Copts, and Vansleb's description in 1677 supports the view that, like the Hanging Church, it had fared better than others in the intervening two centuries: "Elle est grande et fort claire, et à cause de sa clarté, elle me semble plus agréable que toutes les autres."122 Like the Hanging Church, the archaeological work carried out during the 1920s in the Church of St. Barbara indicated that this church too was substantially modified in the eighteenth century.123

The tombs of the former Coptic Catholic cemetery in the southeast corner of the Roman fortress (an area still known as the Muqauqas, see Chapter 3), which were recently cleared away during the Coptic Museum restoration project, can probably also be dated to this period. The inscription over one of these tombs showed that this cemetery was in use until at least 1878, but pilgrim medals found in archaeological work here in 1994 indicated that the origins of the cemetery went back at least to the middle of the eighteenth century.124 The provenance of the medals from Cologne and other pilgrimage starting points in southern Germany and Austria suggests that at this earlier date the tombs were intended for the burial of European pilgrims who died during the course of their stay in Egypt and were buried near the crypt of the Holy Family. From the sixteenth century onwards there are historical and cartographical references to a Catholic hospice and another Catholic cemetery, adjoining the Convent of St. George and to the north of Abu Serga, a plot that may then have been acquired for the Convent of St. George by the endowments of Ibrahim al-Gohari.125 The Catholic material from the Muqauqas cemetery may therefore represent the choice of an alternative burial ground for these pilgrims in response to the expansion of the Convent of St. George in the middle of the eighteenth century. In seeking the earlier medieval use of this area before the cemetery it is perhaps significant that historical references to the second synagogue of Old Cairo, the Synagogue of the Babylonians that seems to have been located near the Hanging Church, cease after the sixteenth century.[126]

The presence of a Greek convent in the northern round tower of the Roman fortress is explicitly indicated by the descriptions of writers of the seventeenth century, starting with Thevenot in 1652:

> . . . this monastery is inhabited by Greek nuns, it is very old and well built and right at the top there is a place from which one can see for miles around.[127]

and then Le Brun in 1674:

> . . . this church belongs to a cloister of Greek nuns, it is very old and pretty well built; it is very high and above it there is a platform from which you can see a long way.[128]

The second account appears to have been largely copied from Thevenot, but the mention of a platform (that is, the top of the Roman tower) adds a valuable detail.

The brief account of the fastidious Vansleb in 1677: "le Monastère est fort sale aussi, et fort mal propre" ["the monastery is also very dirty and really horrible"]; and that of Soderini in 1671: "nella cima vi era una povera chiesa de Greci. . . . Credo che questo sia uno hospitale dei Greci poveri, perche ne viddi tutte le stanze piene et anco addimandano tutti la elemosina" ["At the top there is a poor church of the Greeks. . . . I believe this is a hospital for poor Greeks, because I saw all the rooms full of these people all asking for alms"] are valuable for the wider reflection of the post-medieval decline of Old Cairo on the eve of its eighteenth-century revival.[129]

The outward appearance of the Greek church and convent of Mari Girgis is given by the *Description* plan of the area from 1800 and the drawing of Fairholt from the 1860s.[130] The plan shows that both the huge Roman round towers of the western fortress wall had been so obscured by later building as to have been invisible to the French surveyors around 1800 (figs. 6 and 9).

Alfred Butler's 1884 account of his descent by candlelight into the lower levels of the northern round tower provides us with an evocative image of the appearance and use of the interior of the tower before it was transformed, first by fire and then by the restorations of the twentieth century:

> The compartments between the Roman circles are also divided by Arab walls, lightened generally by high pointed arches, but forming together a ring; so that altogether round the well-shaft are ranged in four concentric circles two Arab and two Roman walls.[131]

Little remains of these "Arab walls" inside the building, with the most substantial survival being the rubble wall founded over the circular Roman arcade in the center of the tower. This wall was only retained during the twentieth-century restoration because it carries the concrete floor inserted at that time at first-story level. The columns of the Roman arcade had been neatly leveled to form a base for this dividing wall, while the construction of the wall, the contemporary ground level at the time it was built, and the presence of reused architectural fragments within it suggest that this work formed part of the late medieval or post-medieval operations, perhaps only after the tower had come into the hands of the Melkite church. It seems probable that the large numbers of huge ceramic jars displayed around the twentieth-century arcades of Mari Girgis were found during the clearance of the tower in the early twentieth century, a find that might suggest its use as a storage cellar for communion wine, just as the lowest rooms in the ancient towers of the Red Sea monasteries of St. Paul and St. Antony continue to be used to this day (pls. 41 and 42).

At the Church of Abu Serga the seventeenth and eighteenth centuries saw important changes in the crypt and

Fig. 58. Abu Serga crypt: A detail of one of the patches of limestone medieval floor surviving around the edge of the crypt and the brick rubble makeup layer beneath it. (Peter Sheehan)

118   Cycles of Decline and Revival

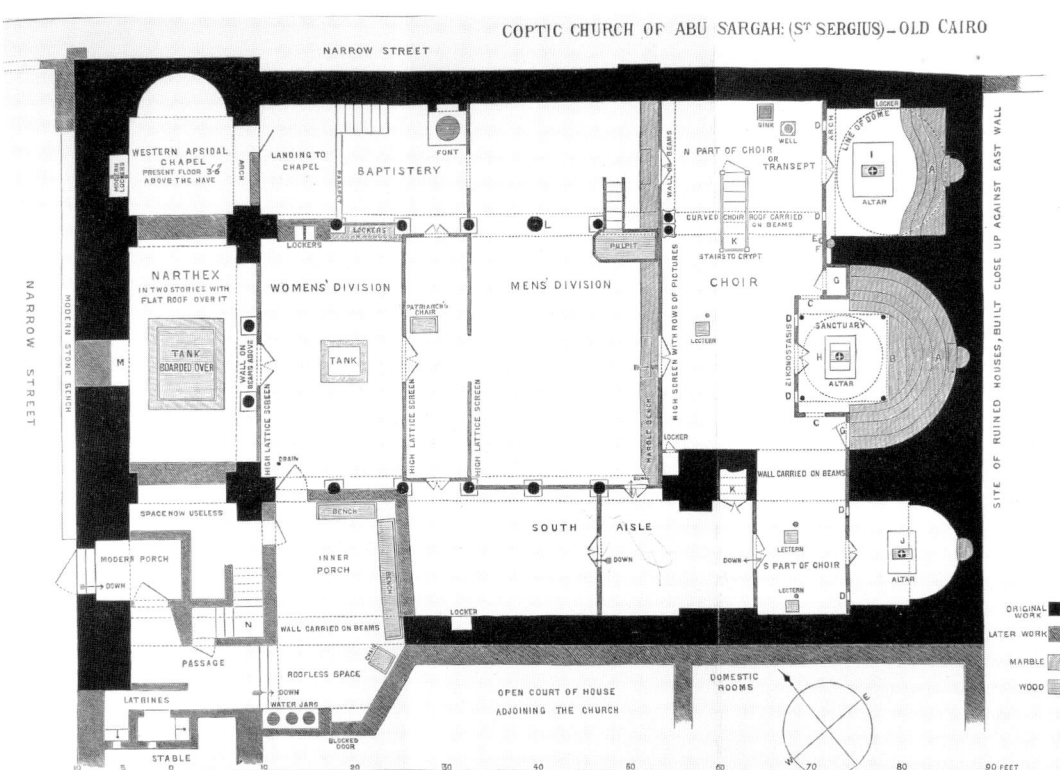

Fig. 59. Alfred Butler's 1884 plan of Abu Serga, showing many of the post-medieval elements of the church that were later removed by the Comité.

the southern part of the church. The continued presence of the Franciscans and their use of the crypt for Mass and baptism were probably behind the somewhat clumsy conversion into its present form of a small chapel with colonnaded arcades, sanctuary wall, and baptismal font.[132] Although the precise date of these changes remains uncertain, they were certainly in place before 1631, when Stochove saw *"une voute soutenue de trois arcades."*[133] Removal of the hard mortar beneath the Comité marble floor revealed that patches of the floor of this phase were preserved at the very edges of the crypt and other inaccessible places, such as between columns. Enough of the floor survived to suggest that parts of the central "sanctuary" were paved with marble and the rest with limestone.[134] Below the floor were thick makeup layers of first brick and then limestone rubble (fig. 58). Both these materials were used to fill in the gaps in the Roman stone that had formed the early medieval pavement of the "nave" of the crypt. Archaeological work showed that seven of the eight columns in the crypt were inserted at the same time as the later medieval limestone pavement, several of them being cut through both the limestone blocks of the Roman canal wall and the original medieval brick floor of the eastern end of the crypt (pl. 42). We are certain that these are the columns seen by Gemelli Careri in 1693, who describes the crypt as *"supportée par trois colonnes à la gauche et quatre à la droite, qui font trois petites séparations."*[135] The indifferent use of columns of different provenance and uneven length is indicative of the rather maladroit work of this phase. Since these marble columns were of different length and the skill or means to cut them was not available, the relatively softer and less brittle limestone floor of the crypt was cut to the various depths needed to accommodate each column. In two cases the columns were actually too short, so capitals were placed under them to produce the desired length. We know from comparing these travelers' accounts that the eighth column, the one nearest to the foot of the northern stairs, was added between 1693 and 1714, when Lucas noted *"huit colonnes de marbre, quatre de chaque côté."*[136] The purpose of this last column seems to have been to create a small narthex or entrance porch to the crypt at the foot of the northern stairs, and we also noted evidence for the position of a screen between this column and the wall which would have divided the narthex from the northern aisle. The date of this final modification is perhaps significant in linking it to other administrative or ecumenical developments made in the Church at the beginning of the eighteenth century. By 1714 Lucas informs us that the Greeks and Armenians had also been granted permission to say Mass once a year in the crypt, and by 1717 we learn for the first time that the European clergy now had to pay for the right to celebrate Mass in the crypt.[137]

In this same period, around the beginning of the eighteenth century, the medieval southern wall of Abu Serga, with the exception only of the domed apsidal eastern end of the sanctuary with its wall paintings, was taken down and rebuilt as part of the new domestic buildings and courtyard built for the priest of the church along its southern edge.

Fig. 60. Jullien's 1889 view of Old Cairo. Note the South Gate still in use and the palm gardens to the east of the fortress walls in the area now occupied by the Greek Catholic cemetery. Courtesy IFAO.

Fig. 61. Caetani's 1911 panoramic photograph of Old Cairo taken from the hill of al-Rasad to the southwest. By this time construction of the Greek Catholic cemetery was well under way, while a number of the elements shown in Jullien's view had been completely rebuilt.

One of the intended results of this work was that the whole sanctuary end of the church and the crypt became directly accessible from the house of the priest via two arched doorways (pl. 43). The post-medieval modifications were largely swept away by the restorations of the Comité in the years after 1915, but Butler's plan and description show that many of the nineteenth-century modifications to the southern part of the church were related to its domestic use by generations of its clergy (fig. 59).[138]

The revival of the eighteenth century was short-lived; archaeological evidence, travelers' descriptions, and early photographs and maps all reveal that by the end of the nineteenth century much of Old Cairo was neglected or in ruins and largely inhabited by poor families clustered around the various churches and the synagogue. Butler talks of "a huddled mass of haphazard buildings which show that the architect's idea was concealment of the interior rather than adornment."[139] However, the antiquarian researches in Old Cairo at the end of the late nineteenth century had created a new awareness of the ancient origins of the churches of Old Cairo and the remains of the Roman fortress. These buildings in turn attracted the attention of the newly formed Comité, which carried out an extensive survey in 1897 as a prelude to the registration of a number of churches as listed monuments. Increased public access to Old Cairo was facilitated by the construction of the Cairo–Helwan railway in the early 1880s, which turned a day's journey from the center of the city into one of less than an hour. Improved travel facilities created the image of Old Cairo as an attractive destination that combined antiquity and pilgrimage, and the subsequent story of Old Cairo has been that of the response to this image (figs. 60 and 61).

Chapter 6

The Re-Making of Old Cairo in the Image of Its Past

The principal office of history I take to be this: to prevent virtuous actions from being forgotten, and that evil words and deeds should fear an infamous reputation with posterity.
—Tacitus (c. AD 55–120)[1]

The Rediscovery of Old Cairo at the End of the Nineteenth Century

Archival photographs and increasingly detailed travelers' descriptions show that the eighteenth-century revival in Old Cairo was relatively short-lived. The general state of the area by the end of the nineteenth century is shown in a pair of panoramic photographs taken from the top of the northern round tower after the destruction of the Church of St. George by fire in 1904. The photographs show that at this point much of the interior of the fortress was occupied by low-quality or run-down buildings clustered around the churches and the synagogue. The recently whitewashed walls of the synagogue, completely rebuilt only a few years earlier, appear in sharp relief against the general decay. Other notable features visible in these photographs are the first tombs and the church of the Greek Catholic cemetery in what had been in 1884 a palm garden against the southeast corner of the fortress walls. Beyond these we can see the numerous windmills along the edge of the hill of al-Rasad, dominating the vast, and still empty, ruin fields of al-Fustat (fig. 62).

Some of the buildings of the eighteenth-century revival were already partly ruined by the late nineteenth century. Excavations for the new toilets of the Coptic Museum carried out in its garden in 2000 demonstrated that the fine stone façade of 'Atfat Abu Serga had been dismantled and rebuilt in rough brick masonry long before the buildings of this part of Old Cairo were filled in and buried by the creation of the new wing and the northern part of the museum garden in the 1940s.[2] This general condition of neglect continued well into the first half of the twentieth century, for the detailed 1:500 cadastral survey maps of the area first made in the 1930s indicate a considerable number of plots as *kharab* or "ruins" (fig. 63).

The atmosphere of Old Cairo at the beginning of the twentieth century is vividly described by Herbert Loewe in 1906, visiting the Ben Ezra Synagogue for the Jewish festival of Rosh Hodesh Iyar:

Once arrived at Old Cairo, progress was more difficult, owing to the dense crowds which filled the narrow alleys. Few of these lanes can be wider than 7 or 8 feet. Owing to the street being the recognised receptacle for all rubbish and offal from the houses on both sides, the height and smell of the pathway is always increasing.[3]

In 1905 Gottheil described the "miserable surroundings" of the synagogue and as late as 1915 the same rather disreputable air continued to strike visitors.[4] W.G. Kemp described the interest of the fortress but noted that "the only drawback to visiting this most interesting spot is the smell of putrid dogs, dead bodies, and sewage, which pervades the air."[5]

The coming of the railway to Old Cairo in 1889 had important and long-term effects on the topography of Old Cairo. At a stroke, the railway visually and physically dislocated the area of the fortress from the Nile, with which it had been inextricably associated since Roman times. The frequent maps of the area made from this period onward also reveal the rapid expansion of the Christian cemeteries all around the north and east of the site, a product of easier access and the renewed image of Old Cairo as an urban pilgrimage center (figs. 5 and 48).

To a large extent the power of this image derived from the rediscovery of the antique origins of the churches of Old Cairo and the remains of the Roman fortress by the researches of learned Victorian scholars, particularly the

Fig. 62. Panoramic photograph of part of Old Cairo taken from the top of the northern round tower after the disastrous fire of 1904 that destroyed the medieval Church of St. George. Note the whitewashed walls of the synagogue that had been rebuilt a few years earlier. Comité archive.

Englishman Alfred Butler, tutor to Prince Tawfiq, from the early 1880s. Butler's descriptions and the drawings contained in *The Ancient Coptic Churches of Egypt* (1884) provide a last glimpse of many of the changes to the buildings of Old Cairo that had occurred during the medieval period and which were subsequently removed during the restorations which have characterized the area from the 1880s until the present day. These restorations have left a substantial and sometimes indelible mark in the archaeological record, which we have encountered at almost every site and which has allowed us to amplify details of the scope and extent of the often sketchily documented works.

At the time of Butler's visit to the Hanging Church in 1880, restoration was already under way. He suspected that information related by the priest that the church had been falling down "seven years ago" was part of a stratagem to explain away the absence of the medieval carved cedar door leaves which he had (as Butler later found out) sold to a collector for £100 and which are now in the British Museum. Describing the restoration, Butler comments, "It is said that the shape and details of the former building have been entirely reproduced," although his skepticism on the point is clear. However, in a note to the text he adds, "I revisited the church early in 1884 and am bound to admit that as a whole . . . the restoration has been carried out with more care and truthfulness than seemed possible."[6]

The western porch with its arrangement of four doors to the church seemed to Butler a new arrangement forming part of this late-nineteenth-century restoration. Some of the modifications appear to have been related to changes in the liturgy of the Coptic Church at this time. All the transverse screens, for example, had been removed by the time of Butler's visit, one effect of which was to leave the church without a *khurus*.

Fig. 63. The Ottoman façade of 'Atfat Abu Serga revealed during the 2000 excavations in the garden of the Coptic Museum. Note the carved stone blocks that would have carried the corbels for a projecting upper storey. This façade was later dismantled. (Peter Sheehan)

Some of the background to the restoration of the Hanging Church is related by the English architect Somers Clarke in 1896. At this time he made a detailed description and photographic record of the destruction of the Roman walls and towers that had taken place in the course of the 1880s restoration and the subsequent work in and around the Hanging Church between 1892 and 1896:

> A considerable number of years ago a certain Coptic gentleman, Nakhle Bey, either at his own entire charges, or greatly assisting others, took in hand the venerable church of Al Muallakah. It has been thoroughly 'restored'. The wall surfaces seem to be all quite new, the marble pillars have been scoured, the wood screens moved and the whole place thoroughly rearranged. . . . We must not blame unsparingly either those who did it or him who, with so very much liberality, paid for it. Until the traveller has seen the condition of an untouched Coptic church he cannot realise the hopeless state of squalid neglect into which the buildings have been allowed to fall . . . these things impress upon the mind how indifferent the Coptic community has become. The reaction from so sad a state of neglect is likely to result in doing too much. . . . With the most unstinting liberality Nakhle Bey has gone far to destroy in three or four years a monument which has stood the brunt of centuries, and this he has done with the best of motives[7] (figs. 64 and 65).

The assessment of the Nakhle Bey restoration carried out by the Comité in 1897 concluded that it had indeed replaced much of the fabric of the church. The painted decoration of the walls, for example, dates from this period (fig. 66) The few areas untouched by the work appear to have included the roof and some fourteenth-century stucco work in the southern chapel (the baptistery over the eastern Roman tower).

Similarly dramatic changes were being made to the Greek Orthodox Church and monastery of St. George (Mari Girgis Church) at the very beginning of the twentieth century. However, these extracts from Butler's description reveal its appearance and condition at the end of the nineteenth century:

> The modern entrance is on the third story. The aperture of a Roman window has been enlarged, and a flight of stone steps built up to it from outside the tower against the fortress wall . . . after the first staircase they entered a broad short passage leading into an irregular room, the roof of which is partly upheld by some ancient columns . . . there are really eight columns though some are nearly buried in Arab walls . . . on these eight columns rests a circular wooden architrave. . . . In the middle of this central room is a so-called well; but the Arabs say the water is never used, being brackish. The shaft of the well pierces down the very centre of the tower.[8]

Fig. 64. Somers Clarke view of the South Gate of Babylon around 1892 with the western tower still intact. Comité archive.

Fig. 65. Somers Clarke view of the Hanging Church and the eastern flanking tower of the South Gate around 1896, showing in the background the house that replaced the southwest corner tower of the Roman fortress. Comité archive.

A briefer description in Greville Chester's earlier 1872 description confirms the arrangement in the center of the tower: "inside at the top of a flight of steps in a circle of ancient pillars with capitals around a well."⁹

It is clear from Butler's account that his "irregular room" was in fact the central space of the Roman tower, surrounded by the second-floor gallery. At second-floor level the arrangement he describes of walled-in columns and partition walls is shown on the plan and section drawn by the Comité de Conservation des Monuments de l'Art Arabe in 1897. At that time the gallery had been replaced by a floor over the central space of the tower, since Butler's subsequent description of his investigation of the lower part of the tower makes clear that the initial entry was at this second-floor level (fig. 67):

[S]teps mounting up to the convent. These steps leading upwards are part of the old Roman staircase . . . descending downwards for two stories, with this difference, that below all is in pitch darkness; it is a place of mystery and horror, said to be peopled by devils, and is unknown and unvisited—happily even by the white-washer.¹⁰

Following the stairway down, Butler found that a short passage from the stairway led:

124   The Re-Making of Old Cairo in the Image of Its Past

Fig. 66. Comité detail of the interior of the Hanging Church around 1897, showing the painted decoration added during the late nineteenth century restoration. Comité archive.

into the central chamber of the first floor . . . a third circular wall has been built, corresponding to the ring of columns on the story above. Embedded in it may still be seen two of the eight columns it was designed to replace; and these are joined by a wooden architrave exactly like that above. Possibly the remaining six columns are completely immured; but no trace of them remains, though there is still visible, flush with the Arab wall, part of a Roman doorway, with lintel of freestone ornamented with dentels. The interior of this Arab circle is piled so thick with dust and rubbish in two of the four chambers into which it is divided, that the level varies 7 or 8 ft. in places, and gives at first the impression of two stories. . . . Outside too, there are walls of Arab work joining the Arab circle to the inner Roman wall; one passes from room to room by a doorway just large enough for a man's body. No doubt all these cells were contrived for monastic uses. The compartments between the Roman circles are also divided by Arab walls, lightened generally by high pointed arches, but forming together a ring; so that altogether round the well-shaft are ranged in four concentric circles two Arab and two Roman walls.[11]

As no access to the ground floor was available from the stairway, the tireless Butler then visited the head of the monastery to request permission to approach the building from the outside. His description of the location for this meeting reveals the existence of the monastery buildings clustered on the roof of the tower: "The next move was to call on the chief priest, whom I found in a little room at an immense height, even above the convent."[12] These buildings appear in Smith's sketch of 1868 and in a photograph taken from the south of the church at some time between 1896 and 1904, that faintly shows a small cupola (figs. 6 and 68).

Among the buildings seen by Butler on the platform created over the Roman tower was the:

Greek church of St. George, now perched like an eagle's nest on the very top of the tower . . . in itself a most ancient and curious structure. The church is hung with ostrich eggs and lamps of silver, and on the walls are some magnificent examples of both Damascus and Rhodian tilework. . . . The church is further interesting as being the only sacred building within these ancient walls which the Melkites have succeeded in retaining.[13]

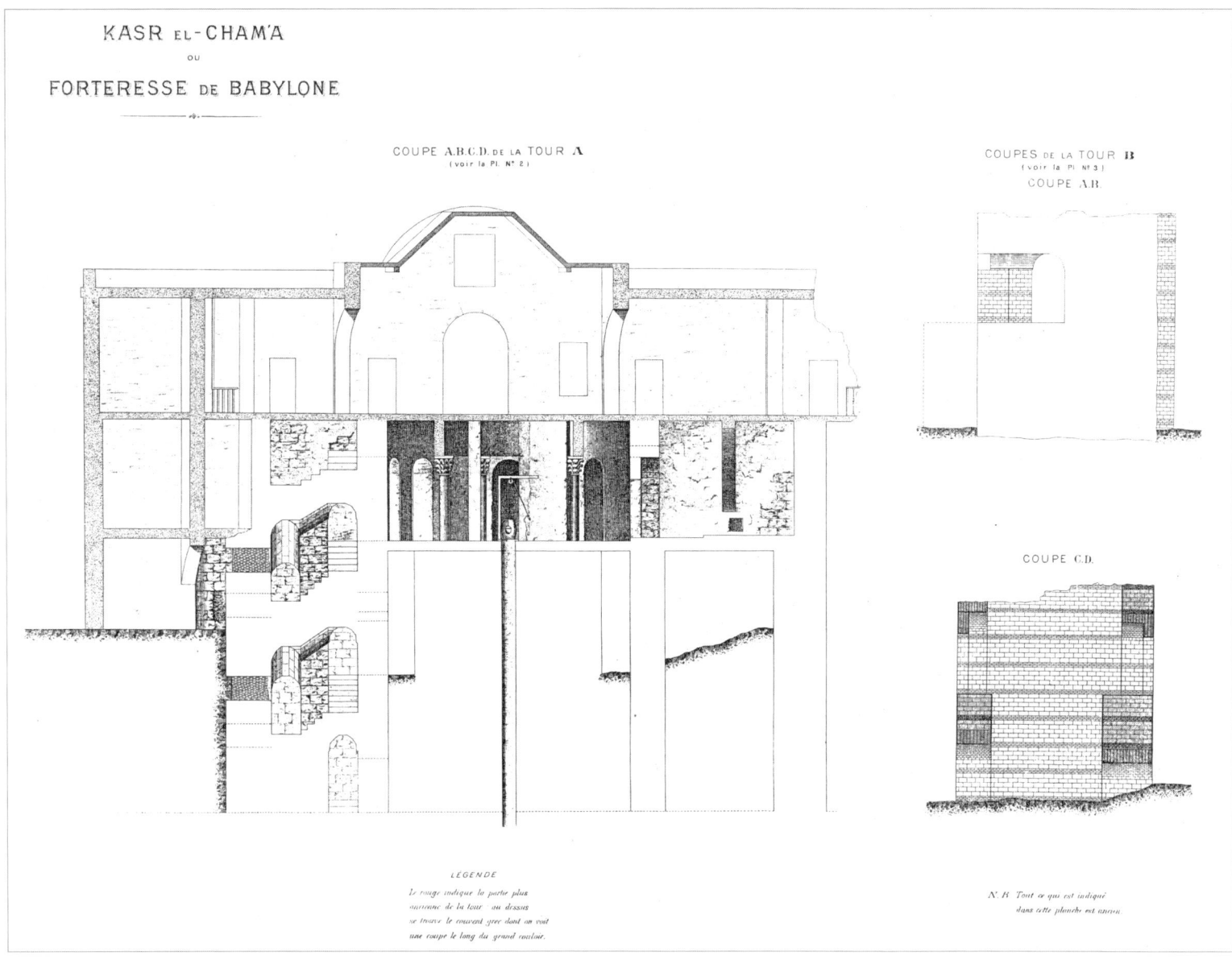

Fig. 67. Comité section through the northern round tower around 1897, showing the level of the fill inside and outside the tower by the end of the nineteenth century. Comité archive.

In 1872 Greville Chester also spoke of "the large and richly decorated church of St. George," but little is known of this church, which was subsequently destroyed by fire in 1904.[14] The church may have originally occupied the first and second stories of the tower and have been moved to the platform on top of the tower as the ground level inside and outside the tower rose. Part of the complex arrangement of rooms and later modifications inside the Roman tower described by Butler can be seen in the photographs taken from the tower after the disastrous fire of 1904. It is clear that both the church and the Roman tower below it were at this time barely discernible among the mass of other buildings covering and abutting the tower on every side. The French surveyors of the *Description* one hundred years previously appear to have not even been aware of the presence of the great round towers.

At ground floor level, Butler's search for the original entrance to the tower led him to its eastern side. Here he found an abandoned earlier medieval entrance to the tower through the Roman ground-floor windows. Butler mistakenly believed these windows to be the Roman entrance, which was actually located in the next chamber to the north and was still inaccessible at the time of his visit:

Close together—only 8 ft apart—were two similar doorways 4 ft 6 in in width. These both led into the same room or division between two radiating walls; one of these walls is pierced with a door, and the adjoining compartment has three additional doors—two for entrance from without, and one leading inwards into the central chamber. . . . It is not easy to see the need of the four original doorways, but they have their convenience now for the herd of swine, which are the sole tenants of the vacant chambers.[15]

The Jesuit scholar Père Jullien gives details of a similar candlelit adventure in the tower in the description of his visit in 1891. According to Jullien, a large building was constructed to the north of the tower in the late nineteenth century to serve as a hospice for people seeking a rest from the bustle of Cairo. It is likely that this is "the vast pile of buildings" described by Butler as being under construction in 1884.[16] These buildings survived the fire of 1904 and are shown in a photograph of 1931. They are also noted as a "hospice" on the 1935 Survey of Egypt plan.

Somers Clarke noted the work on and around the Greek church in his lament for the destruction being wrought on the fortress to the Society of Antiquaries of London in 1896:

> [T]wo immense towers. . . . That to the north is quite invisible from outside. On the top of it stands the Melkite Greek church, and this is surrounded by an agglomeration of buildings. Most of them have been built or renewed within the last few years, and present to the outside as commonplace an appearance as a rectangular, straight-fronted, three storied white box of a building can produce. The fact that the Greek church, a venerable building but very thoroughly 'done up' inside, stands on the great round tower, has preserved to us this part of the fortress. . . . Going southward from the great round tower on which the Greek church stands we come to a second tower like in plan and size to the first. . . . This tower is in a state far more dilapidated than many of its neighbours, and the curtain wall in the foreground is equally broken. Whether some of this damage is not very recent I doubt, for prodigious changes are in progress in this part of the fortress.[17]

These changes included the destruction of the corner tower at the junction of the western and southern fortress walls and the construction of a new ornamental gateway to the Hanging Church:

> [W]e were informed on the spot, but not by more than the gossip of the place, that the Bey (Nakhle Bey al-Barati) would complete the balance on either side of his grand gateway, by putting a wall and a drinking fountain. This will result in the destruction of the great circular tower.[18]

The last years of the nineteenth century saw "prodigious changes" too for the Ben Ezra Synagogue. The synagogue was completely rebuilt in 1892, removing almost all traces of the medieval structure. Some details of the post-medieval changes and the final form of the building prior to its demolition are preserved in visitors' accounts: In 1882, for example, the synagogue described by Butler still had an apse, while Chester in 1872 had remarked that "the eastern extremity of this edifice has evidently been reconstructed."[19]

In 1859 Jacob Saphir mentioned that the Jews of Cairo had "recently" decided on restoration work "to strengthen its walls and whitewash them, so that it may be more respectable and holy."[20] Jullien's account of 1889 shows that these works were either not carried out, or were not sufficient. He describes how the roof had collapsed and how the leaders of the community decided that it should be "rebuilt on the model of the old building, which was falling to pieces, and could not possibly be restored." Other sources from members of the Jewish community at that time confirm that the present 1892 building was conceived as a faithful copy of its predecessor.[21] Test pits carried out around the synagogue in 1989 confirmed that it was built to the same plan as the earlier building, as does the survival of the *mastaba*, the only element of the medieval synagogue remaining within the present building.[22] The *mastaba* is currently concealed behind the marble cladding added by a pious benefactor in 1911, but it was revealed and recorded during conservation work on the marble structure carried out in 1999 (fig. 55).

Fig. 68. A view around 1897 of the southern round tower showing in the background the small dome or cupola on the top of the Church of St George. Comité archive.

Herbert Loewe's 1906 description of the stone gives an interesting perspective on how the rebuilding of the synagogue carried out only fourteen years earlier had already come to be perceived by or described to visitors:

> It is called the synagogue of Moses. It has been built over a stone Mastaba, or slab. This is said to mark the spot where Moses stood when he delivered his message to Pharaoh. . . . The Mastaba is a solid stone block, shaped like a rectangular parallelopiped with a curved top. The spot is very holy, and the stone is covered with clothes and tapestry. The stone, till quite recently stood in the open, but the idea seemed irreverent; so they built a synagogue over it, thereby destroying the far more interesting remains of the older structure which used to stand close by.[23]

Butler provides more evidence for the decline of the churches of Old Cairo during the course of the nineteenth century and their consequent condition. At the time of his first visit to the Church of St. Barbara in 1880, part of the north aisle and all of the narthex at the west end of the church had been walled off to form a kind of reception and smoking area.[24] The same modernizing current he had seen at the Hanging Church was sweeping through the other churches of Cairo. He found St. Barbara "undergoing a mischievous restoration," in which the wooden screens dividing the church into various sections were removed. At gallery level the *triforia*, or women's galleries, had been rendered unnecessary by recent liturgical changes that allowed women to take their place in the main church. In consequence the *triforia* here, as at Abu Serga, had been converted to the domestic use of the poorly paid Coptic clergy. At St. Barbara the priest kindly sent word to his family to vacate the area, so that Butler might visit this upper section of the church. There he noted the remains of former chapels over the north transept, as well as paintings on the south wall of the southern *triforium*, which unfortunately had been stolen—an act he described darkly as "the work of an Englishman"—by the time of his second visit in 1884.

The southern part of the Church of Abu Serga had also been converted to the domestic use of generations of its clergy. At the time of Butler's visit, access to the church was through the southern door in the principal western façade and then via a complex arrangement of passages and porches (fig. 59). The southern part of the *triforium* had been walled in for use by the family of the priest and Butler was unable to confirm his theory that an altar existed on this level at the end of the southern aisle:

> The churlish priest of Abu Serga . . . angrily refused to let me look, and neither soft words nor hard, neither fiat of patriarch nor glitter of money, could conquer his stubborn resistance.

Although the paintings in the southern *haykal* were invisible at this time, Butler was the first to record the existence of the figured paintings on the columns of the nave.[25] Other paintings on the apse of the present baptistery at the western end of the north aisle led him to suggest that this had been a chapel originally accessed from the nave to the south (pl. 46).

The Work of the Comité in Old Cairo

> *In affectionate remembrance of the late*
> Alfred J. Butler Esq. L.L.D., F.S.A.
> Author of "The Ancient Coptic Churches of Egypt" . . . etc. The first of these books appeared in 1884 and was directly responsible for the action of the Author of this Guide in prevailing upon the Government to place the ancient churches under the control of the Comité de Conservation des Monuments de l'Art Arabe. They were thus saved from slow but certain decay. Not only this, but the subsequent foundation of the Coptic Museum derived its inspiration from the same source.[26]

Simaika Pasha's dedication of the Coptic Museum Guide in 1938 shows the extent to which the interest of antiquarians, and in particular that of Butler, had stimulated action by the newly formed Comité de Conservation des Monuments de l'Art Arabe. The Comité carried out an extensive survey of Old Cairo in 1896–97 as a prelude to the registration of a number of its churches as listed monuments. From the beginning of its work in Old Cairo, however, the approach of the Comité was to remove subsequent accretions and return these buildings to what was considered to be their "original" state. The intention and scope of this work is made clear by the bulletin of the Comité for the period from 1915–19:

> The extensive program of clearing and restoration of most of the Coptic monuments of Old Cairo which the Comité has been pursuing for many years being almost entirely completed in 1918 . . . .[27]

As we have seen, the Hanging Church had been the subject of a major restoration in the 1880s under the auspices of Nakhle Bey al-Barati, so the Comité concentrated their activities around the church from 1896 onward on excavating and exposing the façade of the South Gate of the Roman fortress beneath the church.

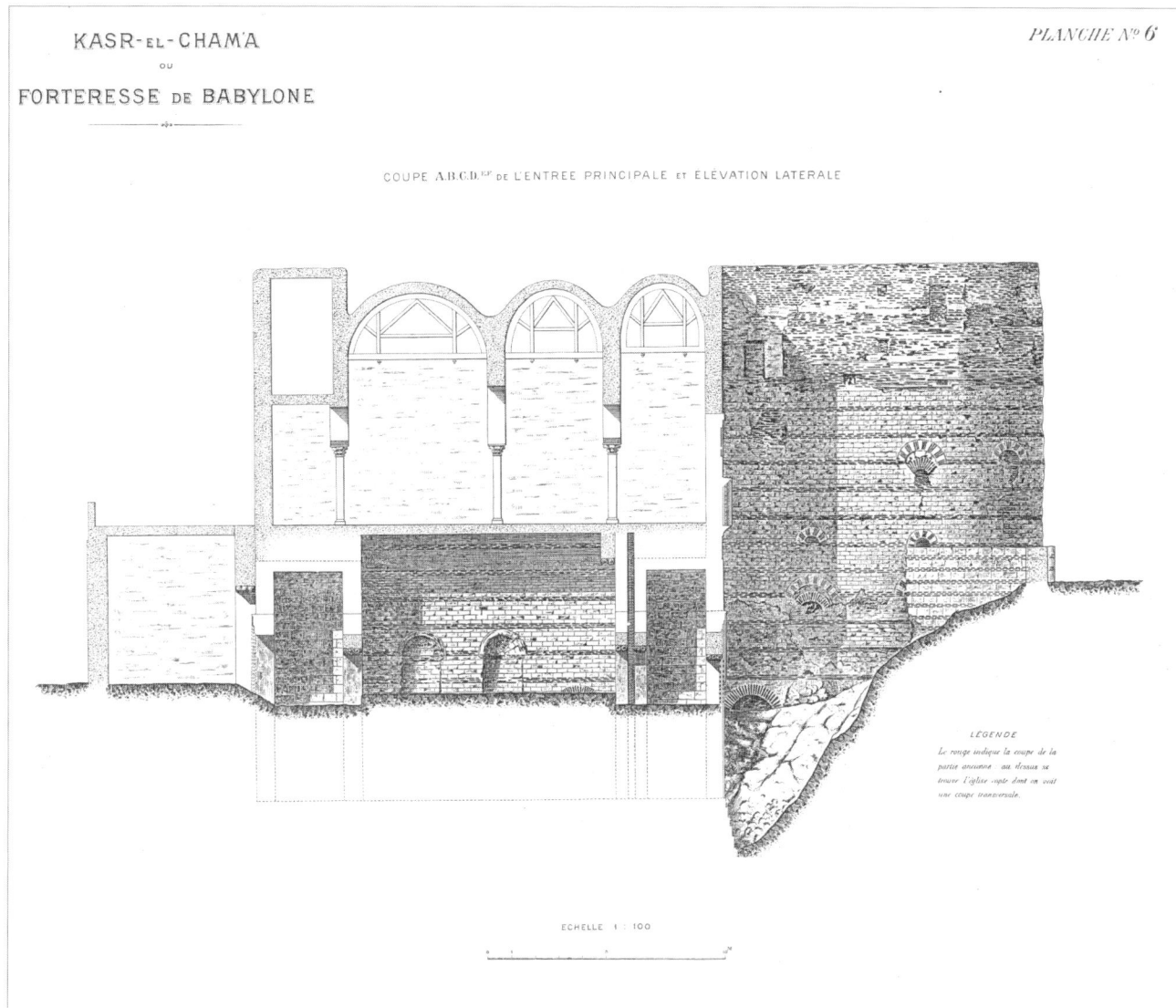

Fig. 69. Unpublished proof of a north–south cross section looking east through the South Gate and the Hanging Church, drawn by the Comité under the supervision of Max Herz around 1902 and showing the depth of fill outside the gate and within the gatehouse. Comité archive.

Initial work included dismantling the upper part of the western tower flanking the gate, as well as the construction of a retaining wall around the newly excavated gateway. At the same time a detailed survey of the Roman structure and its relationship to the church above was undertaken. The reports of the Comité from the Hanging Church show that minor modifications and *mises en état* continued to be made in the period 1915–19. Windows were inserted in the north wall of the church and the west wall of the chapel in the Roman tower to admit more light to the building, in the latter case so that the paintings there could be better appreciated. The ancient wooden lintel showing Christ's Entry into Jerusalem was taken down from the west wall of the church (where it had been installed during the Nakhle Bey restoration) and moved to the Coptic Museum, newly created in 1908. The roof of the church, which had been described as being in a poor state in reports of the Comité between 1915 and 1919, was finally restored in 1927.

Investigations and clearance in the Diocletianic gatehouse underneath the church began in 1915. The desire to reveal the features of the Roman gateway meant that some of the medieval structures that had been supporting the floor of the church were removed. In 1916 the records of the Comité show that the contractor Filippo Garozzo was paid the sum of LE100 to build the piers needed to replace these earlier supports.[28]

The southern round tower of the Roman fortress was another of the monuments to receive the early attention of the Comité. Some of the initial repairs can be traced in photographs of the exterior of the tower between 1896 and 1902. The extent of the clearance work in the southern half of the tower (carried out between 1901 and 1902) is shown

The Work of the Comité in Old Cairo 129

Fig. 70. A view of the southern round tower probably taken in the 1930s after some repairs had already been carried out by the Comité, showing the houses still in place on the northern half of the tower.

on a 1:5000 plan showing the work of the Comité between 1882 and 1910, and on the more detailed unpublished 1:100 plan of the Roman tower made during Max Herz's investigations of the fortress around 1902.[29] The 1:5000 plan shows that a retaining wall around the excavated southern portion of the tower was in place by this time.

In 1908 this southern part of the tower was incorporated into the garden of the Coptic Museum, founded in that year on *waqf* land belonging to the Coptic Church and incorporating "marble columns, fountains and mosaics, which were brought from the ruins of the ancient houses belonging to the Coptic Community."[30] The buildings still in place at this time over the northern part of the tower can be seen in a photograph probably taken during the 1930s, after the Comité had carried out repairs to the exterior of the part of the tower that lay within the grounds of the museum (fig. 70). Information on the ownership of these houses is preserved in plans of 1917 and 1924, which document the attempts of the Comité to gain control of these buildings. The northern part of the tower remained in private hands until the 1940s, when its acquisition was finally achieved after one of the buildings became unsafe and the Comité succeeded in persuading the authorities to prevent the owners from repairing it. The completion of the retaining wall around the tower, as well as the general state of the tower around 1951, are shown on a plan and photographs from that year. However, no conservation or restoration of the newly acquired part of the tower was to take place until the 1980s.

Work on the South Gate of the fortress had given the members of the Comité the belief that a similar gate existed between the two round towers, and the exploratory excavations made when the buildings over the Roman Tower were cleared away between 1946 and 1951 are illustrated in a series of photographs taken during the work (fig. 29). Following these excavations the Comité received a request in 1952 from the Ministry of Public Health to backfill the tower on account of the health risk posed by standing water in the tower during the forty-day period every year when the Nile was at its highest following the inundation.[31]

In the Church of Abu Serga, the involvement of the Comité began in 1897, although the initial phase consisted only of a detailed survey of the building, with a view to its subsequent registration as a monument. This survey included valuable photographs showing the condition of the church before the processes of change and modification that had produced this state were put into reverse (fig. 71). As late as 1912, access to the church continued to be through the annex situated at the southwest corner of the building described by Butler. Work carried out in that year revealed the existence of three doors in the medieval western façade, corresponding to the nave and aisles of the church. Max Herz Bey suggested to the Comité that the street level outside the church should be lowered to that of the threshold of these doors, but his idea was not acted upon, and the current arrangement of railing and steps was installed instead.

Pl. 31. The north wall of the church of Abu Serga showing how the ground level rises to the east as it crosses the line of the east wall of the Amnis Traianus. (Tim Loveless)

Pl. 32. The entrance to the crypt of Abu Serga from the north sanctuary of the church. In the center of the picture is the masonry of the east wall of the Amnis Traianus. (Tim Loveless)

Pl. 33. The entrance to the crypt of Abu Serga from the south sanctuary. (Tim Loveless)

Pl. 34. A variant of the Pagano map of 1549 showing the urban layout of Cairo by the mid-sixteenth century. The settlement along the bank of the river at Old Cairo is clearly visible, as is the course of the khalig and the later canal of al-Nasir Muhammad. Courtesy Jose Santos.

Pl. 35. Claude Sicard's view of old Cairo from 1715, showing that the district enclosure of Old Cairo was already in place by that date. The line of the khalig is still clearly visible running through the medieval city.

Pl. 36. The Convent of St George: The photograph shows how the stone foundations of the medieval qaʻa have blocked an earlier drain within the Fatimid-period brick building beneath the great wooden doors at the entrance to the majlis. (Peter Sheehan)

Pl. 37. The eighteenth-century painted wooden ciborium from Abu Serga. The painted wooden altar canopy is an example of the renaissance of Coptic Art carried out through individual or portable objects that is a feature of churches in this period. (Peter Sheehan)

Pl. 38. A 1984 view of the Ottoman house façade in 'Atfat Mari Girgis adjacent to the Wedding Hall of St. George. The carved stonework around the entrance was later stolen, probably at the same time as the foundation inscription in the sabil façade. The building at the end of the street with the distinctive bell tower was demolished in 2006 during the restoration of the Qasriyat al-Rihan complex. (Michael Mallinson). Courtesy Michael Mallinson.

Pl. 39. A 1984 view of the Ottoman house to the north of Abu Serga church that was demolished in 1989. Note the carved stone corbels that carried a projecting upper storey. The site is currently occupied by an extension to the Old Cairo bazaar. (Michael Mallinson). Courtesy Michael Mallinson.

Pl. 40. Mari Girgis. The central area of the northern round tower showing the Roman arcade columns and the medieval wall built above them. The piers on either side of the columns were inserted during the early twentieth century so that the columns could be displayed. (Tim Loveless)

Pl. 41. Another medieval feature of the Mari Girgis complex is this vaulted cistern with a central column to the east of the northern round tower. Comparison with other medieval cisterns in Cairo suggests it probably dates to the thirteenth or fourteenth century. (Tim Loveless)

Pl. 42. The columns of the crypt separating the 'nave' and the southern aisle, showing how in some areas the Roman stonework was cut to provide the required height for inserting columns of uneven length. Conversely the column on the left of the picture had an inverted capital placed beneath it to achieve the same effect. The capital would then have been buried beneath the brick makeup (some of which is shown around the column in the center of the picture) below the medieval floor of the crypt. (Tim Loveless)

Pl. 43. Two blocked doorways that once led to the southern sanctuary of Abu Serga from the priest's house, built adjoining the church during the eighteenth century. (Peter Sheehan)

Pl. 44. A view of the exterior of the central apse of Abu Serga probably added during the late twelfth or thirteenth century. This part of the church was revealed when a window in the southern *haykal* of the church was opened during conservation work on the paintings there in 2005. The beams above belong to later buildings added against the church which were then sealed in the space between the two apses when the Comité demolished these buildings and built a straight wall across the back of the church (shown on the right on the picture). (Peter Sheehan)

Pl. 45. Painted figures of saints on the columns of the south side of the nave in Abu Serga. (Peter Sheehan)

Pl. 46. The ornate interior of the Greek Orthodox Church of St. George. (Tim Loveless)

Fig. 71. An early photograph taken by the Comité of Abu Serga around 1897, showing the medieval roof structure. The later walls blocking the spaces between the columns of the first floor triforia were still in place at this time. Comité archive.

Between 1908 and 1913 a number of other modifications were carried out to "disengage" the church from its surroundings. The buildings against the east end of the church were demolished to allow the insertion of a window in the south wall that would bring light to the central sanctuary. During work in 2005 on the medieval wall paintings in the southern *haykal* of the church, beams of a wooden floor were revealed in the external angle of the medieval church formed by the curved apses of the central and southern sanctuaries (pl. 44). These beams represent the surviving part of the buildings that formerly abutted the apsidal exterior of the medieval church and were cut away to create the current straight external face of the eastern wall. The foundations of these nineteenth-century buildings were also noted and recorded during the excavation of Shaft 4 to the east of the church in 2000. Other "modern" constructions abutting the eastern part of the ground floor on the south side of the church were also cleared away by the Comité at this time. Inside the church, the floors at ground level and in the *triforium* (first floor gallery) were replaced, while the blockings between the columns of the latter were removed and a stairway to this first-floor gallery was constructed within the present bell tower against the southern façade.

Further works were carried out by the Comité in 1915–19, including extensive repairs to the damaged walls of the northern chapel. Within the sanctuary the *opus sectile* marble revetment of the tribune within the apse was restored, while the exterior cupola of the baldachin over the altar, as well as the bases and capitals supporting it, were replaced, as was the altar itself. The shifting of the altar from the position over the tribune shown on Butler's plan (as well as on the plan of the Comité from 1897) to its present position over the crypt dates to this period. The marble floor of the crypt encountered in our recent work and the repairs to the stairs almost certainly belong to the same phase. At the same time the nave was cleared of the screens that are shown in the earlier photographs, and windows and a door were opened in the north wall. The baptistery was restored to its former position in the apsidal former "chapel" at the western end of the northern aisle and a new basin was installed there (fig. 72).

After 1919, restoration work in the church appears to have been on a more modest scale, and the records made of this work even more so. General repairs are mentioned in the accounts of the Comité, as well as clearing to re-establish the original level of the courtyard to the south of the church. In 1950 repairs to the roof and the masonry supporting the roof timbers were carried out and in 1951 new stone tiles were laid on the roof and in the church, work that was followed in 1952 by the construction "in old brick" of the south parapet wall.[32]

The "mischievous restoration" of the 1880s described by Butler at the Church of St. Barbara included the addition of a dome, a construction that is clearly shown on the post-1904 photographs taken from the top of the northern round tower (fig. 62). This dome was a source of chagrin to the Comité for

The Work of the Comité in Old Cairo   131

Fig. 72. A photograph probably taken around 1919 in the crypt of Abu Serga after the work carried out by the Comité, including the insertion of a marble floor. Comité archive.

many years from the period of their first involvement in Old Cairo in the 1890s onward. The Comité carried out a detailed survey of the church in 1902 as a prelude to the planned restoration work, but only in 1918 could sufficient funds be allocated to carry out remedial work to restore the church to what they considered to be its original state.

Unlike much of the work carried out in Old Cairo in modern times, the major restoration of the church carried out by the Comité from 1918 to 1922 was extensively photographed and described, providing valuable archaeological information and allowing us to form a detailed picture of the nature and scale of the project, as well as some idea of the condition of the structure before this work was carried out.

Restoration began in 1918 with the demolition of the dome and the piers that had been inserted to support it. At the same time all the "modern" walls in the west of the church were removed. The ground surface was lowered to the original stone floor level and repairs were made to the western wall. These included the unblocking of the three original doors in the western façade and the discovery of the carved ancient wooden doors in the central one of these openings. These doors have been dated to between the fourth and sixth centuries and are now in the Coptic Museum. At the same time tombs, structures, and other debris against the exterior face of the eastern wall were removed to a depth of 4.5 m so that the windows in this wall could once again provide light and air to the church (figs. 73 and 74).

The work in the Church of St. Barbara appears to have continued for a number of years, for in 1927 we can still read in the *Bulletin* of the Comité of repairs and replacements being made to the ancient column bases in the nave of the church. The foundations of the northern arcade were revealed at this time, and the foundations under the southern altar were consolidated. Repairs to the women's gallery or *triforium* were also undertaken in the late 1920s.

A plan and section drawn by the Comité in 1906 provides an invaluable resource for the constructional history of the Convent of St. George and its condition before the changes of the twentieth century. These drawings show the building just before the construction of the present convent and the extensive changes to the layout and fabric carried out between 1906 and 1913.[33] One version of the 1906 plan also reflects the concerns of the Comité by distinguishing only between *anciens murs* and *constructions avoisinantes*; our recent archaeological work has revealed the constructional history of the building to be a much more subtle and complex affair (fig. 46).

One of the major differences shown by the 1906 plan of the convent is the entrance to the medieval *qaʿa* before the construction of the present arched passageway. Before 1906, access to the convent was via an alley leading from Harat Mari Girgis toward the southeast corner of the building. The end of this alley was marked by a doorway situated some three meters to the west of the present entrance,

Fig. 73. The façade of the Church of St. Barbara in a photograph taken before the Comité restoration with two of the three doorways still blocked. Note the remains of buildings from the Ottoman period facing the church that were then cleared away to create a more imposing view of the façade. Comité archive.

Fig. 74. The façade of the Church of St. Barbara viewed around the 1930s after the Comité restoration. Comité archive.

which is now at the foot of the stairs of the passage leading to the *qa'a* (fig. 75). It is quite likely that the actual door is the same and has been merely shifted eastward to its present location. Before 1906 this door led to another at the southeast corner of the medieval hall, in the area that now functions only as a *manwar* or light-well enclosed by walls on all four sides. In turn, this door gave onto an internal corridor that ran along the eastern wall and into the central hall, via a door (now blocked) to the east of the great doors. This corridor also contained a stairway to the first floor, lit by a *mashrabiya* window or gallery at first-floor level.

The 1906 plan and sectional elevation show that the central hall was accessed from the convent buildings to the east by a series of doors in the eastern wall. The main entrance from this side was in its present location in the middle of the eastern wall. The main door was linked by a corridor to the passage that wound through the convent, going through the area now occupied by the "old church" and then via a courtyard to the passage leading across 'Atfat Mari Girgis to the Church of St. George. This passage marked the continued survival of the east–west Roman via principalis, so it is interesting to note, even as late as 1906, the presence of two columns along the continuation of its southern edge. The positions of two of the other doors in the eastern wall of the central hall are marked now only by recessed niches, but the northernmost door survives, although it is currently kept closed. It is not clear from the 1906 plan which of these rooms should be seen as forming part of the medieval structure, for the arrangement of the rooms flanking the eastern side of the *qa'a* may already have been extensively modified. Parallels with similar Mamluk buildings suggest that the rooms to the east of the *qa'a* may have had domestic functions, an analogy here supported by the presence of the well and cistern in this area and the extensive remains of canalization, as well as the disposition and appearance of the rooms on the 1906 plan.

Inside the central hall, the 1906 plan shows a wooden screen separating the central *durqa'a* from the northern iwan, as well as a basin in the northeast corner of the

Fig. 75. A photograph taken around 1950 showing the façade of the modern part of the Convent of St. George, which was built sometime after 1906. Comité archive.

durqaʻa. Only the stairway in the southwest corner of the great hall survives of the three that are shown on the 1906 plan. The construction details of the surviving stairway and the pavement of the first-floor gallery suggest that most of the western rooms have not been greatly modified, although large parts of the external wall were rebuilt during the construction of the modern cells to the west of the *qaʻa*. The tradition within the convent is that these western cells formed the oldest part of the complex. The buildings here were, however, in ruins by modern times and the area was rebuilt in the 1980s.

Between 1906 and 1913 the eastern wall of the great hall was rebuilt to form the western wall of the main convent building. A later photograph from around 1950 (fig. 75) shows the façade and construction details of this building, recently revealed again below thick layers of modern cement plaster. At the same time the medieval stonework of the western wall of the hall was modified to create a symmetrical arrangement with the eastern wall, which was itself completely rebuilt between the northern *iwan* and the southern *majlis*. The inspiration for this modification appears to have been the desire to create a broad passage leading from the cells to the west of the *qaʻa* through the center of the great hall to what is now known as the "old church" of the convent. The 1906 plan shows that before the creation of this passage, no door existed between the *qaʻa* and the area of cells to the west. Instead the buildings that did exist in this area were accessed, as today, from the doorway that survives in the northwestern corner of the garden. At that time this door lay within a large building (the *tahuna* or mill room) abutting the southern exterior wall of the *qaʻa*. Although this building was demolished its north wall was retained, presumably to buttress and support the south wall of the medieval hall, a decision that created the curious-looking façade of the building visible today.

The other major architectural change that took place between 1906 and 1913 was the blocking of the entrance to the southeast corner of the *qaʻa* and its replacement by the current arched entrance passageway (fig. 53). As we have seen, the western wall of this passage now became the exterior wall of the new convent building. At ground-floor level this involved the complete removal of the network of passages and rooms shown on the 1906 plan. The arches of the new passage created a route from the garden that was perpendicular to that leading from the cells through the great hall to the church. Where these two routes met they were joined by a third through the door (now blocked by the mosaic of St. George) at the foot of the main stairs leading down to the church from the upper level of the new convent building. At the junction of these routes, three steps led to the door of the church, which opened into a narthex that was created by covering the cistern and converting it into a well.

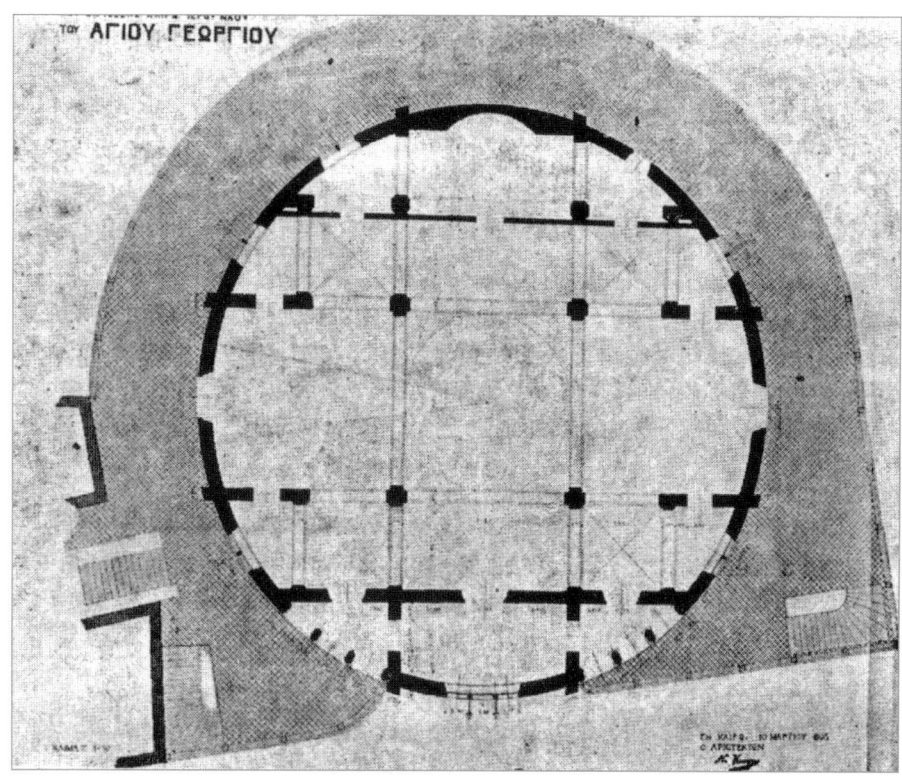

Fig. 76. Architectural drawing from 1909 showing a proposed design for the internal layout of the Greek Church of St. George that was not executed (from Michailidis 1935).

All these changes appear to be related to the creation of the "old church" of the convent. The piers dividing this church actually reflect the position of the Roman wall forming the southern edge of the via principalis, which was breached to form the northern aisle of the church. Even after the recent rehabilitation of the church, these piers are still 1.6 m wide, just like the Roman wall recently recorded running under the middle of the entrance passage. The southern aisle of this church thus lies in the northwest corner of a very large Roman building at the junction of the east–west via principalis and the north–south road through the western enclosure of the fortress. Before 1906 this area was accessible only from the northern iwan of the great hall and appears also to have formed part of the domestic rooms in the east of the qa'a. The northern part of the "old church" actually lies outside the area covered by the convent buildings before 1906 and thus now encloses part of the via principalis. Before 1906 this ancient route was still being used by the nuns, crossing 'Atfat Mari Girgis and passing through a vaulted passage to the Church of St. George, the principal medieval and post-medieval church of the convent located next to the tomb of its major benefactor, Ibrahim al-Gohari. All this changed with the disastrous fire which destroyed the Church of St. George at the end of the nineteenth century and ruptured the relationship between the church and the convent that had been laid out at least as early as the eighteenth century and probably during the medieval period. Although the Church of St. George was eventually rebuilt, the construction of the "old church" within the convent can be seen as a product of the changes to its liturgical life that had taken place in the wake of the fire.

In any event, the post-1906 architectural arrangement of passages leading to the convent church was rather short-lived. The 'old' cells (actually created between 1906 and 1913) to the west of the qa'a have now been demolished and replaced by a new concrete block. The passageway leading from these cells through the great hall has been blocked, as has the doorway at the foot of the stairs, which now contains a contemporary mosaic of St. George, triumphantly (if perhaps inadvertently) located over the center of the massive wall of one of the major buildings of the Roman fortress.

More major restoration work carried out by the Comité at the Convent of St. George occurred between 1950 and 1952, when written records and photographs indicate that the roof of the majlis was dismantled and surviving fragments of decorated medieval woodwork were incorporated into the restored ceiling or reset within a number of new doors in the hall. Much of the lower part of the walls, in both the medieval building and the 1906 additions, were replaced at this time with red bricks in a hard cement mortar, presumably as a consequence of rising damp created by the low elevation of the building relative to the surrounding ground level.

Changes to the Greek Orthodox Church and Monastery of St. George from 1904 to the 1950s

The destruction by fire of the Coptic Church of St. George at the end of the nineteenth century brought about profound changes in the topography of the northern part of the Roman fortress. No less profound consequences ensued from the unfortunate coincidence that on 4 August, 1904 the Greek Orthodox Church of St. George above the northern round tower was also destroyed by a disastrous fire. The aftermath of this fire is vividly shown in photographs of the tower taken from the west and from the top of the tower looking down into its interior. These photographs show how the fire acted as a kind of *deus ex machina* for the Roman tower beneath the church, for it propelled the Greek community into a rediscovery of the building, which was excavated and largely cleared of later accretions over the course of the next twenty years.

Some of the design issues raised by the project to construct a church that would replace the one destroyed in the fire are detailed in a letter to the patriarch written by the official architect of the Khedive's palaces, Fabricius Pacha; drawings of the architectural scheme as originally proposed in 1909 also survive (fig. 76). In the letter, Fabricius Pacha, who had fulfilled his promise to the patriarch that he would visit the site, advised that before the construction of the church could take place, the "consolidation of the basement" should be completed. Our recent work in the tower shows that this consolidation took the form of backfilling the bottom part of the tower with more than two meters of compacted *homra* (broken brick and limestone fragments cemented together to form an extremely durable and impermeable mass). This consolidation was clearly preceded by a major program to remove the many medieval and "Arab" walls described by Butler and others, which can still be traced as "ghosts" within the extensive refacing of the masonry inside the tower. The khedivial architect also advised against leaving the columns in the "underground church" (that is, the first- and second-floor structures), "leaning as they were found," arguing that it would be both "more aesthetic" and very easy to restore them. The arcades of the first and second floors inside the church were duly dismantled and rebuilt, and the Comité wrote to the patriarch to thank him for his efforts to return the building to its "original aspect."

From the structure of the present church we can see, however, that Fabricius was unable to dissuade the patriarch from having the interior of the new church built as a round structure. While diplomatically agreeing that the patriarch's idea was very beautiful, Fabricius Pacha raised the objection that its execution would create "material difficulties" that would be unable to be overcome. In the event, the patriarch got his wish and the interior of the church was built round (pl. 47).

The building campaign of the new church began in 1909 and involved the construction of the present rotunda on a concrete slab forming a platform over the Roman tower. The edge of this platform was marked by a colonnade around the inner rotunda of the tower. The colonnade built at this time around the church lasted until 1941, when it was dismantled and replaced with the present massive arcaded arrangement.[34] Structural problems shown by differential settlement in parts of the earlier colonnade appear to be the most likely explanation for this change. During our recent work we noted that the foundations of the piers of the 1940s arcade are not homogenous, for at its southwest corner the arcade is partly built over the huge ancient stone wall built between the two towers. To the east of this, the 1940s foundation level becomes much lower, showing that the foundations of the arcade wall and its predecessor were influenced by the structures encountered at different points during the excavations that preceded the construction of the church.

This change from colonnade to arcade at first-floor level was part of a huge program of excavation and rebuilding carried out between 1941 and 1945. In 1943 the former hospice immediately to the north of the tower was dismantled and the area beneath it excavated and laid out as an open-air museum. Unfinished elements, such as the carved capitals of the gallery overlooking the excavated area, indicate that this work was still in progress to the end of the 1940s, when much of the large Greek community of Egypt left its shores forever following the change in the status of foreigners and the unrest that led to the Free Officers' coup of 1952. These excavations and the display of sections of the fortress wall within the Greek cemetery to the north appear to have been largely the work of the archimandrite Agathangelos.[35] Many of the archaeological objects displayed around the first-floor arcade, in the church, and in the museum of the monastery were clearly found during these excavations. Over the same period the present massive monastery building was built to the north of the church, although we have little idea what buildings it replaced. Further repair work was carried out to the stonework of the Roman tower at this time. The records of the Comité show that discussions were held with the Greek authorities to ensure that the design of the arcades provided for a more sympathetic handling and view of the stonework of the Roman tower behind them than had been the case with the 1909 colonnade.

The Activities of the Jewish Community around the Ben Ezra Synagogue from 1892 to 1948

After the rebuilding of the synagogue in 1892, the early years of the twentieth century were spent on its gradual decoration and embellishment. This may have been a slow process, for Richard Gottheil observed in 1905: "There is nothing at all remarkable about the building except its extreme poverty."[36] Herbert Loewe's account of his visit in 1906 confirms that the area was still inhabited by the poorer sections of the Jewish community. Donations to support the synagogue and the poorer Jews living around it came from the wealthier members of the Jewish community of Cairo, who continued to use the synagogue for festivals and regular monthly services. From 1911 onward the land around the synagogue was increasingly used to provide accommodation for aged and needy members of the Jewish community, and this aspect increased under the administration of Ralph Green during the 1930s and 1940s.

Most of the Jewish population of Egypt emigrated in the period following the first Arab–Israeli conflict in 1948 and the 1956 and 1967 wars, and the synagogue endured a long period of neglect throughout the 1960s and 1970s. The community housing was demolished around the time of the 1967 war.

Old Cairo: The Present and the Future

Over the past twenty years Old Cairo has become the focus of attention for a number of groups with widely differing and at times conflicting agendas. Tourism and differing interpretations of heritage management have now been added to the traditional mix of business, religion, and politics as elements in the modern making of Old Cairo.

Since the early 1990s the Egyptian tourism industry has brought hugely increased numbers of foreign visitors to the area and its antiquities. The monuments of Old Cairo have been much vaunted as an architectural symbol of the interrelationships between Judaism, Christianity, and Islam throughout the history of Egypt and a model for peaceful coexistence in its future. The increase in tourism is perhaps surprising, given that the impressive remains of the Roman fortress have been largely inaccessible due to high levels of standing water, and that the available information about the fortress and the buildings within it is both scarce and largely inaccurate. More importantly, however, the organization of mass tourism has improved and Old Cairo has been identified and marketed as an ideal half-day "package," at once culturally more familiar to Western visitors and in an environment that is more controlled and predictable than the more "popular" and conservative quarters in which the architectural splendors of the medieval city are to be found.

Notwithstanding its role as the symbol of historical harmony between Egyptians of different faiths, the particular interest of Old Cairo for western Christian visitors continues to make it an important point of contact with the minority Coptic community of Egypt. At the same time, the increasing solidarity of the Coptic community from the early 1980s onward has seen a greater emphasis on the area's traditional role as a cultural and religious center for Egyptian Christians. Other historical centers of Coptic Christianity, such as the Red Sea monasteries of St. Paul and St. Antony, have become similar "engines" for spiritual renewal in the same period. Like them, Old Cairo shares the dynamic of renewal, funded and supported by the wider Coptic community, who also provide the consultants, engineers, and laborers needed to give this revival concrete form.

The higher profile brought by increased visitor numbers has contributed, not only to regular cycles of "restoration" on the monuments to which these visitors are drawn, but also to the formation of a restoration industry that is by now firmly established in and around Old Cairo. The engineering consultants who worked on Abu Serga in the 1980s are still engaged in rebuilding projects at the Church of the Virgin (Qasriyat al-Rihan) and the Monastery of St. Mercurius (Abu Sayfayn). Similarly, the same contractors who dismantled and rebuilt the Church of the Virgin at Babilun al-Darag immediately to the south of Old Cairo in the 1990s have been following the same approach at Qasriyat al-Rihan since 2000 and more recently the convent of St. George. The piecemeal and unplanned way in which much of the work has been carried out no doubt partly reflects its funding. It has also certainly contributed to the long-term presence of the same contractors and the long periods during which buildings have been "under repair" and at least partly inaccessible. An abundance of unskilled labor and a shortage of skilled artisans familiar with traditional building methods is a phenomenon not confined to the monuments of Old Cairo. In the absence of skilled artisans, the art of finishing has become such an elusive goal that it is now rarely attempted. Instead the continual presence of contractors has constantly stimulated the creation of new work, but rarely ensured the completion of the old. In the 1980s and early 1990s much of the restoration work in Old Cairo was carried out by the Egyptian Antiquities Organization (EAO), but the period subsequent to the earthquake of 1992 saw the entry of the private companies or *sharikat* into cultural heritage management in Egypt. These often consisted of large multi-departmental companies offering a turnkey solution to the conservation of historic monuments, supervised by the newly formed Supreme Council of Antiquities (SCA).

In contrast to these full-scale restoration projects, more limited conservation and maintenance of the buildings and monuments of Old Cairo has played a less active part in recent years. Only one project has actually been headed by a qualified conservation architect: the restoration of the Ben Ezra Synagogue, carried out by the Belgian architect Johan Bellaert on behalf of the Canadian Centre for Architecture in the early 1990s.[37] Foreign institutions with a conservation remit, such as the American Research Center in Egypt (ARCE) and the Programa de Patrimonio Cultural de la

Cooperacion Española, have been concerned more with the conservation of individual elements of artistic heritage, such as wall paintings and Coptic icons, within the churches rather than the buildings themselves.

Some idea of the scope of the restoration industry and its contribution to the remaking of Old Cairo can be afforded by a brief description of the restoration projects of the last twenty years.

Between 1982 and 1988 the eastern wall of the Hanging Church was entirely refaced and the chapel inside the Roman tower was extensively restored by the EAO. Paintings discovered during this work were cleaned and restored. In 1983–84 the northern half of the southern round tower exposed in the 1950s was finally restored. Unlike the early-twentieth-century work carried out by the Comité, this project made no visual distinction between restored and original areas but consisted merely of the refacing of the tower in brick and stone, using a hard cement mortar. Other work carried out at this time included gypsum repairs to the vaulting of the Roman stairway and a restoration of the upper blocks of this stairway chamber.

From 1987–92 the Church of Abu Serga underwent extensive restoration. Many of the walls on both the internal and external faces were reinforced by concrete "jacketing"—one meter deep or more—laid in trenches excavated for this purpose. Much of the wooden roof structure of the church was removed and replaced at this time. Rising groundwater levels in Old Cairo were already a serious problem, so perforated drain lines were laid in two parallel trenches running north–south across the church in front of the sanctuary and in the center of the nave, linked to another system laid around the external perimeter wall. No serious archaeological record was made during this work, although a fragment of inscribed stone from the reign of Ptolemy V was recovered, apparently from somewhere under the north wall of the church.[38] An attempt was also made to extend the perforated drain system around the crypt. However, this was postponed and then abandoned, so the trench dug for it in the southern sanctuary lay open until 2002, when it was actually backfilled ahead of the structural and archaeological review of the buildings of Old Cairo, carried out by the consultants Camp, Dresser & McKee (CDM), on behalf of USAID.

The peace treaty agreement between Egypt and Israel in 1979 generated the political will to initiate projects aimed at conserving monuments of Jewish culture in Egypt as a way of furthering dialogue between Muslims and Jews in Egypt. Preparations for the restoration of the Ben Ezra Synagogue had begun in 1981 at the instigation of the World Jewish Congress, but actual restoration work did not begin until 1988. A comprehensive program of restoration and conservation on the building and its internal fixtures and fittings was then carried out by the Canadian Centre for Architecture between 1988 and 1992.[39]

After initial survey and assessment of the conservation requirements, the restoration and conservation work carried out on the building concentrated on a number of key areas and issues, most of them concerned with problems caused by the high groundwater levels of Old Cairo. Rising damp had resulted in extensive damage to both exterior and interior wall surfaces. The EAO vetoed successive project proposals for a damp-proof course and aeration trenches inside the building. In the absence of a definitive solution to the problem of rising damp, the approach adopted involved a number of measures, including replacement of the damaged plinth masonry followed by the application of a sacrificial render. The basement and steps to the well were sealed so that their high relative humidity could be maintained and the damaging effects of the repeated cycle of wetting and drying avoided. Inside the building, the damp in the stone column bases and corrosion in the cast-iron columns were covered by new marble cladding.

Work at this time included restoration of the windows and doors of the synagogue and the stairway to the women's gallery, as well as reconstruction of the entire footbridge. The top of the "Well of Moses" was rebuilt and brought up to garden level and the wall of the stairway leading to the well passage was partly dismantled and rebuilt with the addition of a damp-proof course. Other work on the ancillary buildings of the synagogue was also carried out. The terrace structure along Harat Sitt Barbara was dismantled and rebuilt. Clearing of debris revealed severe problems at the boundary wall with the land of the Church of St. Barbara, where the structure was on the point of collapse and required elaborate shoring. New concrete foundations were followed by underpinning and restoration in new fair-faced brick masonry. At the request of the EAO a semicircular arch was constructed to exhibit one of the brickwork arches discovered in the course of reconstruction work on this wall.

Between 1992 and 1994 the EAO carried out restoration work at a number of locations within Old Cairo. The roof of the Church of St. Barbara was repaired and the replastering of the frontage, begun by the church in 1986, was finally completed in 1994. The part of the Roman fortress wall to the east of St. Barbara in the cemetery, and the surviving flanking tower of the East Gate, also received partial refacing with brick and stone in a hard cement mortar. In 1994 the tomb of al-Gohari was given new ceilings, and the EAO work in this area was extended to the Wedding Hall of the Church of St. George between 1997 and 1998, where the lower 2 m of the walls were rebuilt in red brick on a concrete foundation.

When the work of the EAO/SCA at the Wedding Hall was complete, the church itself was reconstructed by private contractors under the supervision of the SCA. In the main, nineteenth-century part of the church, west of the sanctuary, this work involved underpinning the existing walls and then demolishing and rebuilding them piecemeal. The Roman building revealed under the east end of the church and the fine medieval brickwork of which the eastern end of the church is composed were not demolished but were integrated into the rest of the work by the application of a thick cement render. This work coincided with the beginning of the ARCE/EAP archaeological monitoring project in Old Cairo, allowing us to make some record of the presence and nature of these ancient elements and the scope of the modern project.

A similar approach to restoration has characterized work at the nearby Church of the Virgin (Qasriyat al-Rihan), which began in 2000 with the demolition of the existing building. Unlike the Church of St. George, this was a registered monument that had been extensively damaged by fire in 1979. The composite nature of the building revealed by the fire damage showed a complex history of rebuilds, while its low ground level relative to the surroundings was a clear indication that parts of the structure may have dated back as early as the first references to the church at the beginning of the tenth century. The architect of the restoration project allowed the ARCE archaeological monitoring project to carry out photographic documentation during the demolition of the church, and later agreed to retain *in situ* two ancient granite columns revealed during demolition. The agreement to retain the columns was based on our suggestion to display them as an element within the rebuilt church, but this proved impossible within the construction parameters of the project, so they are now hidden from view.

From 1998 until 2005 extensive restoration and rehabilitation of the Hanging Church took place as part of a joint project covering the church and the Coptic Museum. The project was carried out for the SCA by a consortium. This work followed some damage to the part of the Coptic Museum adjoining the church sustained in the 1992 earthquake and included extensive concrete underpinning and grouting in the Roman Gate, as well as the installation of a perforated drain system. However, some limited archaeological recording was carried out by the ARCE project in the large area impacted by this project. Controversy surrounded the apparent destruction during this work of the wall paintings inside the baptistry of the church (inside the former Roman tower) that had been discovered during the 1982–84 work by the EAO.[40]

Between 2000 and 2006 construction activities in Old Cairo were greatly increased by the activities of Contract 102, the USAID-funded Cairo Wastewater Organization (CWO) project aimed at lowering the groundwater level in a number of selected locations: the Orthodox Church of St. George (Mari Girgis), the Roman tower in the garden of the Coptic Museum, the crypt of Abu Serga Church, the Ben Ezra Synagogue, the Wedding Hall of the Coptic Church of St. George, and the Convent of St. George.[41] One of the aims of Contract 102 was to provide access to the site "owners" to allow them to carry out repairs and maintenance, and following successful lowering of the groundwater, four of the targeted monuments (the Wedding Hall, the Roman tower, the crypt of Abu Serga, and the Convent of St. George) have received refurbishment to the norms of recent restoration in Old Cairo.

The Wedding Hall project consisted of extensive cement rendering of the interior and exterior of the building, followed by a thin coat of archaizing lime-based render, applied in deference to the accepted moratorium on the use of Portland cement on historic monuments that was confirmed during the UNESCO-sponsored conference held to debate the conservation work in Historic Cairo in 2002.

In the huge round Roman tower in the garden of the Coptic Museum, Contract 102 lowered the groundwater level and provided a new stone floor in 2001–02. In 2003, however, the Contract 102 project consultants CCJM and the ARCE archaeological monitoring project had to intervene to stop the wholesale refacing of the surviving Roman masonry in the tower. This work remained in abeyance until 2005, when work in the tower resumed in preparation for the reopening of the Coptic Museum, scheduled for early 2006. The brick repairs made by the Comité to distinguish ancient work from modern restoration were removed and replaced with alternating brick and stone, completing the refacing of the tower begun in 1983. To complete the cosmetic effect, the outer few centimeters of the cement pointing visible in previous work was then carefully chipped out and replaced with a lime and sand mortar.

At Abu Serga the Contract 102 groundwater lowering works in 2003–04 revealed the crypt and the sanctuary end of the church to be built over the massive stone wall that once formed the eastern bank of the Red Sea canal of the emperor Trajan. The religious and archaeological importance of the crypt made its conservation and preservation a major concern. A presentation design that involved display of the stone pavement by means of a security glass floor supported on a stainless-steel frame was proposed by the ARCE archaeological monitoring project in March 2004 and developed during the rest of that year.[42] In January 2005, however, the Contract 102 consultants, CCJM, decided to return to their original design requirement to lower the water at least 50 cm below the floor level and excavated additional trench lines in the two side aisles through the Roman stones forming the floor of the crypt. In consequence the ARCE archaeological monitoring project took no further part in the subsequent Contract 102 work in the crypt, which consisted of laying a new marble floor over a concrete substrate. The Roman stonework is now hidden, and although the crypt is dry, the high humidity levels and the higher rate of moisture intake through the walls partly resulting from this sealed floor have now effectively returned it to the same state, inaccessible for the general visitor, that existed before the project. Air conditioning and a video link to the church are currently being considered to facilitate access to one of the most holy Christian sites in Egypt.

At the Convent of St. George the prospects initially seemed better for a more sympathetic conservation following the successful implementation of the Contract 102 groundwater lowering works in 2005. In collaboration with the convent, the ARCE archaeological monitoring project supervised the removal of modern cement render and the preparation of lime plaster to treat the water-damaged lower parts of the walls. However, this initial direction foundered with the insistence of some of the nuns on using the roof of the *qa'a* to build new cells with toilets located directly over the painted medieval ceiling at the northern end of the *qa'a*. The first stage of this work was carried out despite the objections of the SCA and led to the water used for curing the concrete actually pouring through the wooden ceiling. Despite the assurances of the patriarch's representative that the work would be stopped, further applications of water to the concrete took place. In the face of such an untenable position regarding the conservation of the building, the archaeological monitoring project reluctantly withdrew from further involvement at the convent. Subsequently, in 2007 other contractors carried out extensive repairs to the walls using hard cement-based render as well as complete replacement with modern sawn timber of the palm logs that had been used throughout the original medieval construction.

A number of recurrent themes can be discerned even from this brief consideration of some of the recent restoration and conservation projects in Old Cairo. The first of these relates to the structure of conservation and the mechanisms by which the monuments have been defined and protected. Despite its clear boundaries, distinct identity, and unique combination of structures of widely different eras, no authority has successfully maintained or attempted to conserve Old Cairo as a single unified area. As a result, conservation problems, exacerbated since 1979 by rising groundwater levels, have produced widely different responses in the individual buildings, ranging from the 'model' conservation of the Ben Ezra Synagogue to the total demolition of the Church of the Virgin (Qasriyat al-Rihan). The masterplan project, developed by Mallinson Architects of London for ARCE in 1998, identified the need for coordination and indicated some ways in which the value and significance of the area might be presented and conserved. The absence of a long-term follow-up project to push this agenda, however, has meant that the proposed consensus has not been reached. In the wake of the structural studies of the historic buildings of Old Cairo commissioned from CDM by USAID in 2002, ARCE reviewed the prospects of possible future work in Old Cairo and came to the conclusion that "it would seem natural and desirable if the substantial effort of de-watering the monumental area of Old Cairo was followed by a project aiming at taking the full advantage of the benefits of the de-watering." However, ARCE also concluded that such a project was beyond its capacity and would require a new organizational framework.[43] Other area-wide projects have suffered from a similar lack of follow-up, such as the CDM structural review of the buildings of Old Cairo carried out on behalf of USAID in 2002.

The major administrative apparatus for the conservation and protection of the antiquities of Old Cairo remains the Old Cairo inspectorate of the Supreme Council of Antiquities, whose role is still largely confined to the protection of buildings defined as monuments by the Comité in the early years of the twentieth century. While the mechanism of registering the monuments has in general protected them from outright demolition, the Comité's strictures on returning the buildings to an idealized original state inevitably required extensive rebuilding. This in turn created an ethic of restoration that has continued to this day and has impacted heavily on the authenticity of the buildings. The SCA has also had little or no role to play in the conservation of the wider area during a period when the forces remaking Old Cairo have been largely concentrated on the unregistered buildings forming the mass of the urban fabric around the monuments.

One consequence of structural failures in heritage management is the alarming amount of destruction and demolition that has occurred to the structure of the built environment of Old Cairo. Destruction and demolition of its physical fabric is not a new theme in the making of Old Cairo. As we have seen, a number of authors lamented the destruction of parts of the fortress by the various communities at the end of the nineteenth century. Even those organizations concerned with the conservation of the area have contributed to this process of demolition. One of the first actions of the Comité in Old Cairo, for example, was the dismantling of the upper part of the western tower flanking the South Gate of the fortress.

Restoration projects on the monuments of Old Cairo over the past twenty years have been accompanied by extensive demolition and redevelopment of the urban fabric between and around these monuments. The Ottoman buildings to the north and west of the Church of Abu Serga were swept away at the end of the 1980s. Archaeological observations confirmed the survival of early medieval structures in this area, as well as the alleys and plot boundaries recorded on the Survey of Egypt plans from the 1930s. Following the demolition of the Ottoman buildings to the north of the church, this site lay empty for nearly fifteen years while building work on a tourist bazaar slowly proceeded. In 2008 the eighteenth-century arched entrance to the *hara* of Abu Serga was demolished to improve access between the different areas of the bazaar (fig. 78, compare with fig. 8). The ownership of the land taken up by the various parts of the bazaar remains unclear. Much of it comes under the jurisdiction of the *majlis al-milli*, or general council, established by Khedive Ismail in 1874 for Copts to supervise Coptic schools and religious endowments (*awqaf*).

As we have seen, even registered monuments like the Church of the Virgin have been demolished in the modern period, making the scale of the destruction of unregistered elements in the urban fabric perhaps less surprising. The eighteenth- and nineteenth-century tombs in the Muqauqas area in the southeast corner of the Roman fortress, archaeologically investigated in 1994 by a joint team from the German Archaeological Institute and the Canadian Centre for Architecture, had been removed after 1990 during works for the Coptic Museum project (fig. 77).[44] Other demolitions have occurred as a consequence of construction activity, such as that of the 1930s synagogue annex building in the summer of 2004. Fortunately the attempt to build its replacement on a 2-m-plus concrete foundation foundered over important archaeological structures and deposits immediately below ground level, and the building and its 2-m-plus foundation have been shifted to a location above ground to the east of the fortress wall in the area of the former Jewish community housing. During various restoration projects a number of substantial ancillary buildings have sprung up or been extended around the churches, a feature which is particularly true of the project to restore the Church of the Virgin, which has produced not only these buildings but even two churches where before there was only one.

Within the actual work of the restoration projects two parallel themes stand out: the decline of craftsmanship and traditional building skills, coupled with an increasing reliance on sometimes inappropriate engineering solutions. The value of structural, civil, and geotechnical engineering know-how in resolving particular problems in the historic buildings of Old Cairo cannot be doubted. At the same time, however, engineering interventions can be designed to minimize the impact to historic structures. This can only take place when engineers are prepared to understand ancient structures and be sympathetic to the fact that their very survival often demonstrates empirical qualities of strength and stability that are not necessarily commensurate with the engineering parameters in use today.

One of the aims of the Ben Ezra Synagogue restoration project was to encourage a local revival in traditional building

Fig. 77. Vaulted tombs of the former Catholic cemetery in the Muqauqas area to the east of the Coptic Museum that were demolished during the course of the Coptic Museum project. (Peter Sheehan)

Fig. 78. The arch leading to the *hara* of Abu Serga as rebuilt in 2008. Compare this with the view of the same entrance in 1984 shown in Fig 8. (Peter Sheehan)

skills and materials, and in particular the use of lime putty or 'fat' lime, slaked and matured on site. Despite the example of this project, however, hard Portland cement remains ubiquitous, while the state of traditional building skills has not advanced in the way the project hoped it would.

Sadly, the most common feature of many of the restoration projects of the last twenty years has been the almost complete absence of a meaningful archaeological component, either in terms of preliminary investigations or of recording during the progress of the work. Investigations have generally been confined to boreholes and test pits aimed only at gauging the depth of made ground, not its character. The lack of regard for archaeology has been rewarded with a failure to comprehend either the complexity of historic structures or the implications of proposed interventions.

Old Cairo displays a condition common to many of the archaeological sites and monuments of Egypt, faced with the conflicting agendas of tourism and restoration, as well as the wider context of the demographic and economic concerns facing the country at the beginning of the twenty-first century. However, despite the false steps and negative trends of recent times, there is still some room for hope as Old Cairo faces the fundamental issues of conservation and authenticity in the coming years.

One of the most positive signs is the growing awareness and appreciation of the material culture of Christian Egypt, both internationally and within the Coptic community. This gives hope that the regard for the material culture of Christian Egypt can be extended from its paintings and icons and integrated with a new appreciation of its buildings and archaeology. This process has already begun, first with the ARCE project in 2005 to conserve the wall paintings discovered during archaeological work in the Church of Abu Serga, and in a more general way with the reopening of the Coptic Museum in 2007.

An even more positive sign is the project to access the archaeology of Old Cairo currently being funded by ARCE. Although the groundwater control project technically achieved its aim to restore access to the ancient monuments flooded by rising groundwater, the results of this remain largely invisible because six out of the seven sites dealt with by the project are still not open to visitors. This new project, begun in December 2008, has already started to address this situation by a program of cleaning, conservation, and presentation that will allow the opening of one of these sites—the Roman tower in the Coptic Museum garden.[45]

Ultimately, the best chance for the conservation of Old Cairo rests with the information the archaeological monitoring project has gathered since 2000. We have seen throughout our work that in spite of truncation, removal, and restoration, ancient or modern, enough always seems to survive in the archaeological record below ground or in a forgotten corner to allow us to at least get near to the real story of the site and its buildings. It is a sincere hope that publication and presentation of this story will succeed in raising the profile of archaeology and making it a major consideration in future programs of presentation and conservation which would, and perhaps will, complete the making of Old Cairo.

Notes

Notes to Introduction

1. Abu-Lughod, "Cairo, an Islamic Metropolis," 19. For the dynamics governing the development of the modern city, see Sims, *Understanding Cairo*.
2. Lambert, *Fortifications and the Synagogue*, 55.
3. Warner, *True Description*, 161.
4. Six of these ancient buildings are churches, giving Old Cairo its distinctly Christian feel. Five of these are Coptic, the Church of the Virgin (known as the Hanging Church from its location suspended over the southern gate of the Roman fortress), the Church of SS. Sergius and Bacchus (known as Abu Serga), the Church of St. George, the Church of St. Barbara, and the Church of the Virgin (known as *Qasriyat al-Rihan* or the Pot of Basil), and one is Greek Orthodox, the Church of St. George, built over one of the great round towers of the fortress. Just to the north of the fortress is the Mosque of 'Amr (the oldest mosque in Africa, founded after the conquest of Egypt in AD 641) and, within the walls, the origins of the Ben Ezra Synagogue can be traced back to at least the ninth century.
5. El Messiri Nadim, "The Concept of the Hāra," 313–47.
6. For a discussion of the position of the eastern bank of the river at Old Cairo at various epochs and the suggestion that the line of the Metro represents the course of the Nile in Roman times, see Jones, "Archaeolgical Discoveries in Doqqi," 101–12.
7. Mean Sea Level (MSL) is expressed in meters above 0, as measured at Alexandria.
8. Sheehan, "Underwater Archaeology." For details of previous archaeological work in Old Cairo, see especially Lambert, *Fortifications and the Synagogue* and the two *Archäologischer Anzeiger* articles by Grossmann et al in 1994 and 1998.
9. Unpublished AMBRIC (American British Consultants) report on groundwater conditions, 1982.
10. Perring, "The Archaeology of Beirut," 196.
11. In this period restoration projects were carried out at the Hanging Church 1996–2005, Abu Serga Church 1984–90, the Ben Ezra Synagogue 1989–92, the Church of St. Barbara 2001–02, the Coptic Church of St. George 1998–2004, the Mosque of 'Amr 1999–2003.
12. This church is popularly known as *Qasriyat al-Rihan*. a name which first appears in a document of the end of the eighteenth century. The older name of the church used in Coptic sources is *Theotokos* (Mother of God), and the church is also sometimes additionally identified as being located at the Tetrapylon of Eusebius. Coquin, *Édifices chrétiens*, 140.
13. Spence, *Archaeological Site Manual*, 7.
14. Problems of subjective interpretation and recording of boreholes means that they are most reliable in the broader aim of distinguishing "made ground" from natural. However, the deep open excavation components of the project have offered the possibility of "ground truthing" by comparing samples from the boreholes with those from archaeologically recorded layers and deposits.
15. From a conservation viewpoint, the mitigation of groundworks was confined to reducing the impact of construction work only on the structures revealed in open trenches. Changing the location of shafts in response to archaeological features revealed by the groundworks would have required value judgments or an assessment of relative significance that was precluded by the lack of data at the design stage. Additionally, since most shaft excavation took place below groundwater level the conventional period-based visual conditions necessary for ascribing monumental significance to structures or deposits did not arise. The work was carried out in close collaboration with the Supreme Council of Antiquities (SCA) staff, who retained final responsibility for the response to archaeological material and structures encountered during the project.
16. This also provided an opportunity to attempt to quantify the degree of contamination and mixing of

17 vertically stratified deposits that might occur under these excavation conditions.

17 Although this material is in many ways rather one-dimensional, it does have the advantage that, unlike the shaft material, there is little risk of vertical contamination.

18 This became even more of a problem as excavation continued downward, since the lengths of the standard planks available meant that a further inner layer of sheeting was often sunk within the initial excavation, narrowing the trench still further.

19 After Contract 102 had achieved its aim of enabling access to the tower, restoration work on the tower, involving complete replacement of the early-twentieth-century Comité brick repairs and extensive re-facing and replacement of the weathered Roman masonry, was undertaken during 2005 by the Arab Contractors/ORASCOM Coptic Museum project.

20 Coquin, *Édifices chrétiens*, 71. It is interesting to note that the Orthodox Patriarchs of Alexandria and Africa are interred within the northern round tower of the Roman fortress to this day.

21 This is the reason why geophysical prospecting as a first phase of evaluation has become so popular, allowing a general picture to be gained and some "leads" to be established without the expense and other requirements of excavation. Urban locations like Old Cairo, however, with little open space and technical difficulties such as the high groundwater level and "background noise" (disturbed ground, scrap metal, and so on) present less ideal circumstances for geophysical prospecting. To date, a limited amount of rather inconclusive geophysical work has been carried out in Old Cairo.

22 Although the conditions were usually more akin to the watching brief usually specified in the UK only when the likelihood of encountering archaeological deposits is low.

23 Johannes, *Chronicle of John*.

24 Monneret de Villard, "Sul castrum romano," 176.

25 See Grossmann et al., "Zur Römischen Festung" and "Zweiter Bericht."

26 See, for example, Coquin, *Édifices chrétiens*, 94, for the various dates put forward for Abu Serga Church. In some cases the ascribing of structures to a single phase has had significant effects. In 2000 the Permanent Committee of the SCA allowed the demolition of the fire-damaged Church of the Virgin (Qasriyat al-Rihan). On the basis of historical records the church was considered to have been rebuilt in the eighteenth century: Coquin, *Édifices chrétiens*, 141. The low level of the church floor relative to the surrounding area was, however, an obvious archaeological indicator of a much greater antiquity. The photographic record made during demolition of the church showed that it was composed of a number of different phases, a feature shared by all the churches prior to their modern restoration.

Notes to Chapter 1

1 Miquel, "L'Egypte vue par un géographe arabe," 109; Sheehan "New Metropolis."

2 "Major segments of ancient Egyptian history may be unintelligible without recourse to an ecological perspective." Butzer, *Hydraulic Civilization in Egypt*, 56.

3 For a discussion of these land routes see Jones, "Roman Station at Abu Rawash." The cultural links established in prehistoric times between Nile Valley societies through these wadis to the northeast via Sinai into Palestine should be borne in mind as a factor encouraging settlement in the Cairo area.

4 Recent work by Judith Bunbury and David Jeffreys suggests, however, that the Delta head itself remained south of Memphis at least until the Middle Kingdom and may have been much farther south at the beginning of the Holocene (Judith Bunbury, personal communication).

5 For the taphonomic characteristics of alluvial systems, see Brown, *Alluvial Geoarchaeology*.

6 In Old Cairo, see Shafts 2/3 in Shari' Mari Girgis and Jones, "Archaeological Discoveries in Doqqi."

7 Note, for example, the usurpation of ancient ceremonies connected with the annual flood by the Fatimids as part of the legitimizing of their dynasty. See Sanders, *Ritual, Politics, and the City*, 43.

8 This state of affairs is shown by the map of the Geological Survey of Egypt, in which the area of Greater Cairo is an undifferentiated gray.

9 Hsu et al., "Late Miocene Dessication," 243.

10 One of the most striking illustrations of the sheer scale of landscape change is the evidence that this deep Miocene river valley, formed some 5–10 million BP, is larger than the Grand Canyon in the USA. Deep soundings in recent years have shown that the modern Nile Valley, and most human occupation within it, occupies only the very upper reaches of this enormous chasm. For this geology see Adamson et al., "Late Quarternary History of the Nile," and Said, *Geological Evolution*.

11 Said, *Geological Evolution*.

12 Herodotus, II.5.1.

13 Miquel, "L'Egypte vue par un géographe arabe," 129.

14 Sheehan, *Port of Babylon*, 104, Fig 12:3. A number of boreholes at this level show a variable but relatively

thin (1–6 m) layer of limestone overlying sand. Alternatively, some at least of this limestone "layer" at 6 m MSL may derive from dumping or leveling placed in the bottom of a natural channel.

15 Butzer, *Hydraulic Civilization*, 15. For the clay beds, see Bowden Smith, "Subsoil of Cairo," section EF.

16 Warner, *Monuments*, fig. 1, facing page 1.

17 Harvey and Grove, "A Prehistoric Source of the Nile."

18 North of Old Cairo the shift of the bedrock to the northeast had already created a lesser divergent stream that became the western arm of the Delta. See Butzer, *Early Hydraulic Civilization*, 16, for similar bedrock effects at Nag Hammadi, Dairut (the Bahr al-Yusuf), and Sohag, where, as at Old Cairo, a divergent western-edge channel is created immediately downstream of the bedrock spur. Between the major and minor channels huge natural flood basins would be formed.

19 Lutley and Bunbury, "Nile on the Move," 4.

20 Caution should be exercised in considering the borehole evidence for this early channel. The location of the boreholes was based on engineering requirements rather than landscape research, so for example the line of the section that was reconstructed from borehole profiles almost follows that of the channel itself rather than cutting across it.

21 Butzer, *Hydraulic Civilization*, indicates an average depth of 10–12 m for the Nile channel, 16.

22 This clay deposit was traced in places for a further 20 m downward.

23 Bowden Smith "Subsoil of Cairo," boreholes A1–2, C7–9, p. 241. Also inside the city: his Sections 5 at Sharia Guienet al-Gawaden and 20 at Sharia Beit al-Qadi. pl. II, p. 244.

24 Jeffreys and Tavares, "Historic Landscape," 154.

25 Jeffreys and Tavares, "Historic Landscape," 159.

26 The evidence of a single borehole to the north of the mosque suggests it may lie upstream of a shallow spur or island of bedrock.

27 Budge, *Dwellers*. Obviously there was a great deal of symbolism inherent in different aspects of the Nile, parts of which became incorporated in the nature and worship of the Nile god Hapi. Of particular relevance to our subject is the possible etymology of the name Babylon as deriving from "(the temple of) Hapi in On (Heliopolis)." For a similar idea equating the Nile with Osiris, see D. Delia, *JARCE* (1992).

28 Donald Bailey in *JEA* 85 (1999) on the provenance of ancient sherds found within the cultivation around the site of Antinoe.

29 For a summary of vertical accretion rates of the Nile, see Bunbury et al., "Stratigraphic Landscape Analysis," 356. For the level of the valley floor, Butzer, in *Hydraulic Civilization*, suggested a rise of 7 m since the beginning of the Dynastic period. Michael Jones has suggested the Roman ground level on the contemporary riverbank in the area of modern Dokki was around 15 m MSL. Jones, "Archaeological Discoveries." At Giza a wide area of Old Kingdom occupation is found between 12–14 m MSL. Jones, "Settlement Near Ausim." At Babylon, the top of the first-century AD harbor wall (next to the river and built to be above the highest possible flood waters) is around 17.4 m MSL.

30 Lane, *Description of Egypt*, chap. IV, "Physical Sketch of Egypt."

31 Pliny, *Natural History* V cap. 9. *Minores aquae non omnia rigant: ampliores detinent, tardius recedendo.*

32 Stanley, "Nile Flow Failure."

33 Bell, "Climate."

34 Lutley and Bunbury, "Nile on the Move." The mean value for many parts of the Nile Valley seems to be around 2 km per thousand years. Judith Bunbury (personal communication).

35 Bunbury et al., "Stratigraphic Landscape Analysis," 355.

36 Kubiak, *Al-Fustat*, 48.

37 Jeffreys and Tavares, "Historic Landscape."

38 Early Dynastic Memphis may alternatively have been a narrow extended settlement on the west side of the channel, which may explain pyramid distribution in this area. David Jeffreys, personal communication.

39 Jeffreys and Tavares, "Historic Landscape," for the Amnis Trajanis as the fourth-millennium channel. Supporting the general idea, if not the exact location, is the evidence especially of boreholes 1 and 9 in Bowden Smith, "Subsoil of Cairo."

40 Jones, "A New Old Kingdom Settlement," 96.

41 David Jeffreys, personal communication.

42 One indicator of the extent of the movement of the Nile to the east is the position of the Late Roman quay at Memphis and the low (below 20 m) elevation of the fields to the east of it. See Jeffreys and Tavares, "Historic Landscape," and Attia, *Deposits*.

43 Raue, *Heliopolis*, pl. I.

44 Jeffreys and Tavares, "Historic Landscape," 158.

45 Raue, *Heliopolis*, 28.

46 It is interesting, however, to note that statues of Merenptah have been found both at Old Cairo (Athar al-Nabi) and from Tell al-Maskhuta on the route of the canal in the Wadi Tumilat.

47 Bowden Smith, "Subsoil of Cairo," pl. I and 241–42.

48 In this it may have resembled the Bani Wa'il Canal which fed the seasonal "lake" of Birkat al-Habash (now

49 the densely occupied area of Dar al-Salam) in a similar bay to the south of Old Cairo.

49 Gebel Ahmar is the site of a purple quartzite quarry and a temple to Hathor mentioned on the stele of Rameses II found apparently *in situ* at Manshiet al-Sadr in 1907. A temple to Hathor of the reign of Rameses III was also discovered nearby at Almaza in 1938. Drioton, "Une statue prophylactique"; Raue, *Heliopolis*, 21.

50 Hamza, "The Statue of Meneptah," 50.

51 It is perhaps worth remarking that the number of inscribed fragments from the Late Period recovered in medieval Cairo exceeds that of the Old, Middle, and New Kingdoms combined. Porter and Moss, *Topographical Bibliography*.

52 Annales du Service des antiquité de l'Egypte 4, ASAE 23.

53 For the Early Dynastic tombs at Helwan/'Izbat al-Walda and their relation to Memphis/Heliopolis, see Wood, "Archaic Stone Tombs," and Mortensen, *Agypten und Levante*, 23. Also Debono and Mortensen, *Predynastic Cemetery*.

54 Raue, *Heliopolis*, 29.

55 Al-Sannusi and Jones, "Maadi Culture," 252.

56 At Heliopolis, Maadi, and Helwan, the wadis Iseimar, Digla, and Hof respectively.

57 Jeffreys and Tavares, "Historic Landscape," 43.

58 Wilkinson, "Early Dynastic Necropolis."

59 Kemp, *Ancient Egypt*, 88.

60 Raue, *Heliopolis*, 20.

61 Heiden, "Die Stele," 187.

62 Other architectural *spolia* found in the buildings of medieval Cairo or during excavations in al-Fustat have been given a broad Heliopolitan provenance. Despite al-Maqrizi's contention that the stone for the city walls was brought from Antinopolis, the scale of reuse in parts of the city wall of Saladin, as well as the size of some of the pieces, might plausibly show that they were quarried from the nearby funerary monuments of the southern part of the ancient city still standing in medieval times.

63 Hamza, "Statue of Meneptah," 235.

64 Gardiner, *Onomastica* II, 139.

65 Drioton, "Origines pharaoniques," 312.

66 In a Nineteenth Dynasty version of the *Book of the Dead* a serpent belonging to the river god Hapi is shown above the mountain of Kher-Aha. The same serpent appears on the bas-relief from the Temple of Philae, where the waters of the Nile waiting to flood are shown blocked at the "gate of the Nile" by the serpent's head. Following an invocation to the gods of the waters at Kher-Aha, the Assembly which governs the flood, the text describes in mythical terms how the flood waters were held behind a dike blocking the main irrigation canal, with the rise of the river being first measured and then at the right moment given free passage. The same mythical interpretation of the opening of the main canal during the Nile inundation, regulated by the Nilometer of Kher-Aha, appears in the Ptolemaic-period inscriptions of the Chamber of the Nile in the Temple of Edfu, although by this time the serpent has been replaced by a water deity and the iconography changed to reflect the supremacy of the Heliopolitan sun god Re. It is interesting to compare these rituals with those associated with the breaking of the Khalig dike in the medieval period. Drioton, "Les Origines Pharaoniques," 298.

67 A number of aspects of this mythological identification of the springs of Helwan as the manifestation of the river god Hapi have a strongly archaic character, which suggested to Drioton that the origins of the Nilometer at Per-Hapi/Helwan should be sought in the Predynastic period and the rule of Lower Egypt by the kings of Busiris.

68 Note Old Kingdom references to this on the Palermo Stone. Drioton suggested that chapter 149 of the New Kingdom *Book of the Dead* and the Ptolemaic texts from the Chamber of the Nile in the Temple of Edfu could be taken to indicate that one of the salient features of the landscape of Kher-Aha was the presence of a Nilometer. Drioton argues that the exact measuring of the Nile described in the texts as well as its announcement to "the Assembly" can only allude to the existence of a Nilometer. Drioton, "Origines pharaoniques," 314.

69 Note also textual reference to an eastern Memphis. Jones, "Settlement Near Ausim."

70 JE 39053: Kitchen, *Ramesside Inscriptions* II 193 ff 360. 10–15; Raue, *Heliopolis*, 406–407.

71 Bleeker, *Hathor and Thoth*; Pinch, *Votive Offerings*. In considering the location of the Mountain of Thoth we might remember the later astrological connection of al-Rasad in the Early Islamic period. For the stele see Gillian Pyke and Peter Sheehan, "A Stela from Old Cairo for *the Mistress of the Red Mountain*" (in preparation). We are grateful to Dietrich Raue for the suggestion that the stele text includes an actual depiction of the Red Mountain.

72 Hamza, "Statue of Meneptah I."

73 *Rec. de trav.* t. XI, 98–100.

74 Ibrahim Abdel-Rahman, personal communication.

75 Yoyotte, "Le 'Groupe Ankh-Psametik,'" discusses the Heliopolis sanctuaries in the Late Period, 115.

76 The modern name, "Belly of the Cow," is interesting given the connection of the mountain with Hathor and her link with a cow cult.

77 More reused fragments of Saite tombs were recovered during excavations around the Nilometer of Roda just to the west of Old Cairo. See Drioton, "Origines pharaoniques."
78 Boghdady, "Archaic Tomb," 158.
79 Drioton, "Origines pharaoniques," figs. 1 and 2.
80 A small amount of material from the tenth to mid-seventh century BC is found in both the eastern "limestone terrace" area and (mixed with later material) from the west of the fortress. However, the Late Period/Early Ptolemaic is quite conclusively present in stratified deposits from the eastern part of the fortress.
81 There are differences between specialists over the dating potential of these amphorae types.
82 Grace and Savvatianou-Petropoulakou, *Délos*, E3. Further evidence for a Ptolemaic presence at Old Cairo is the inscribed block from Abu Serga dating to the reign of Ptolemy V found during restoration works by the Egyptian Antiquities Organization in 1989. The blocks reused in the foundations of the western flanking tower of the South Gate of Babylon may be of a similar date (see Chapter 3).
83 Hamada, "Une troisieme tombe," 479. For the deposits in front of the South Gate, see Sheehan, *Port of Babylon*, 104, Fig 12:4.
84 More reused fragments of Saite tombs were recovered during excavations around the Nilometer of Roda just to the west of Old Cairo. See Drioton, "Origines pharaoniques."
85 Pyke, "Pre-Diocletianic Pottery," 5; Holladay, *Cities of the Delta*, 56.
86 Josephus, *Jewish Antiquities*, Book II cap. XV.
87 Toy, *Babylon*, 54. For Nebuchadnezzar's campaign against the Egyptian king Amasis in 568, see Roux, *Ancient Iraq*, 380.
88 Lambert, *Fortifications*, 55.
89 Diodorus Siculus, Book I, cap. 56.3. The king is Sesostris of the Middle Kingdom (Twelfth Dynasty), probably an anachronistic detail although Sesostris is much associated with building work in On (Heliopolis). He adds that Ctesias (a Greek historian of the fifth century BC) says that Babylon was founded by those who came to Egypt (from Babylon) with Queen Semiramis.
90 Strabo, *Geography*, Book XVII, cap.1, 30. Worth noting is the similarity of his description of the topography of the Roman camp to that of Golénischeff at Athar al-Nabi in 1889.
91 Herodotus Papyri refer to a quarter of Memphis still known as Syropersikon in 258 BC (PSI v.488)) and Polyaenus VII.3 refers to another area of the city called Karomemphitai after the Carian mercenaries brought in by Psammetichus 664–610 BC. CAH III, 36. Even medieval Arab sources preserve Greek toponyms for the area. See Casanova, "Les noms coptes," 193. For the Greek trading colonies, see James, "Naukratis Revisited."

Notes to Chapter 2

1 From Claudius Ptolemy's list of Egyptian nomes in *Geography*, IV, cap. 5.
2 Toy, "Babylon."
3 The course of the canal runs along the western edge of the Fatimid enclosure of Cairo. The southern part of the canal was backfilled in 1896 and is now Shari' Port Said.
4 Cooper, "Egypt's Nile-Red Sea Canals." I am grateful to John Cooper for discussions of the canal based on his earlier MA thesis *The Nile-Red Sea Canal in Antiquity: A Consideration of the Evidence for Its Existence, Duration and Route*.
5 Herodotus (*Historiae* II, 158), Aristotle (*Meteorologica* I, 14), Diodorus Siculus (*Bibliotheca* I, 33) Strabo (*Geographica* I, 38; XVII, 804), Pliny the Elder (*Naturalis Historia* VI, 165), Claudius Ptolemy (*Geographica* IV, 5, 54). A summary of the ancient sources is given by Toussoun, *Memoire*.
6 Lloyd, "Necho," 144.
7 Herodotus, *Histories* II, 158.
8 Posener, "Le Canal du Nil," 271. One of these stelae is now displayed in the museum at Ismailiya, another is in the Egyptian Museum.
9 Redmount, "On an Egyptian/Asiatic Frontier," 182.
10 Naville, *Store-city of Pithom*, 20–21.
11 Diodorus Siculus, *History* (I.33).
12 Redmount, "On an Egyptian/Asiatic Frontier," 177–88.
13 It may be that later Ptolemaic neglect of the canal was a consequence of these being ultimately unsuccessful. Lloyd, "Necho."
14 Brier, *Plutarch's Lives*: 229. Casson, *Periplus*, 51.
15 From Claudius Ptolemy's list of Egyptian nomes in *Geography*, IV, cap. 5.
16 Charles, *Chronicle of John* LXXII, 14, 55.
17 Charles, *Chronicle of John* LXXVII,1.
18 Papyri: *P. Oxy* 4070, II.5–9 (208AD); *SB*. 5.7676 (287 AD); *Ivi* II, 12–15 (297 AD); *P. Oxy* 12.1426 (332 AD); *PSI*. 87 (423 AD); *PSI*. 689 (423 AD).
19 Raue, *Heliopolis*, 28.
20 Bietak, *Tell el-Daba'a II*, 126.
21 Raue, *Heliopolis*, 28.
22 Miquel, "L'Egypte," 118. The location of Gebel Yashkur and the Ben Ezra Synagogue in Old Cairo on the edge of this early Nile channel is interesting given their legendary associations, respectively with Noah and later Moses's rescue from the bulrushes. For Noah,

see Gayer-Anderson, *Legends*, 33. For Moses see Lambert, *Fortifications*, 246. For Qal'at al-Kabsh, see Salmon, "Etudes."

23 Cooper, "Egypt's Nile-Red Sea Canals," 54.
24 A date as early as the fourth century has been traditionally ascribed to the Church of the Virgin. Seton-Williams, *Blue Guide*, 283.
25 In noting the presence of the stone walls in Old Cairo and the straight line of the canal and the *khalig*, it is worth noting the mention of similar massive 6-m-high stone walls noted in a borehole carried out during the 1920s in the Midan al-Zahir, which is located immediately to the east of the line of the *khalig*.
26 Miquel, "L'Egypte," 118. Kubiak, discussing the settlement of the central quarters of al-Fustat suggested that the original line had already gone out of use by the time of the Conquest and was allotted to and built over by the first settlers. Kubiak, *al Fustat*, 120.
27 Seton-Williams, *Blue Guide*, 347.
28 Since the vast necropolis of al-Fustat is located to the east of the city, the mosque may also follow the early Islamic tradition of building mosques over the house of the deceased. However, the practice of house burial was also known in Egypt in early Islamic times. See Williams, "The Cult of 'Alid Saints," 39.
29 The sinuous curve of the canal to the northwest between Mari Mina and Sayyida Zaynab postdates the foundation of these two buildings.
30 Although the date of the foundation of all these monasteries is not certain, a pre-Conquest date seems likely. Peter Grossmann dates the Church of St. Mercurius in the Monastery of Abu Sayfayn on architectural grounds to the sixth century AD. Grossmann, *Christliche Architektur*, 62. The position of the Mashhad of Zayn al-'Abidin may also be related to a Fatimid association with/usurpation of older and probably pre-Islamic shrines. It is interesting that most of the surviving Fatimid monuments of southern Cairo are located on pre-Islamic routes, either the canal or the land route from Babylon to the Citadel (see below).
31 Coquin, *Édifices chrétiens*, 6.
32 Miquel, "L'Egypte," 111.
33 Popper, *Cairo Nilometer*, 85.
34 Kubiak, *Al-Fustat*, 18.
35 Bennett, *Trajan*, 63.
36 Bennett, *Trajan*, 81. See also Sijpesteijn, "Trajan and Egypt," 109.
37 Lewis and Meyer, *Roman Civilization*, 61.
38 Tacitus, *Annals* III: liv. 6–8 (his paraphrase of Tiberius' letter to the Senate, AD 22).
39 Lewis and Meyer, *Roman Civilization*, 63–64.
40 Bennett, *Optimus Princeps*, 143; Lilli, "Il porto di Ancona."
41 Bennett, *Optimus Princeps*, 143.
42 Bennett, *Trajan*, 142. See Keay, *Rome, Portus and the Mediterranean*, and Keay, "Portus and the Alexandrian Grain Trade."
43 *Aelius Aristides* "To Rome" xi–xiii.
44 Bennett, *Trajan*, 184.
45 Butler, *Trajan's Road*, and Graf, "via Nova Traiana," 241.
46 CIL Vol. III, No. 14,149 (21–22) = Dessau 5, 834.
47 Lloyd, "Necho," 146.
48 However, some modern commentators have thought that this mention of the Red Sea is actually a mistake by Eutropius, and that the fleet would have been built in the Persian Gulf. Eutropius, 8.3.2.
49 Sijpestein, "Potamos Traianos," 82.
50 Sijpestein, "Potamos Traianos," 72.
51 Cooper, "Egypt's Nile-Red Sea Canals."
52 Bourdon, *Anciens canaux*, 109–10.
53 Sestini, "Nile Delta."
54 Cooper, "Egypt's Nile-Red Sea canals," 204.
55 Bennett, *Trajan*, 138.
56 http://www.livius.org/le.lh/legio/ii_traiana_fortis.html and http://www.livius.org/le.lh/legio/iii_diocletiana.html. Urloiu, "Legio II Traiana Fortis"; Urloiu, "Again on Legio II *Traiana Fortis*." Urloiu, however, believes that AD 123 is the earliest date for the arrival of Legio II *Traiana Fortis* in Egypt (*pers. comm.*).
57 Strabo, *Geog.* XVI. iv. 24; Pliny *Natural History* VI: xxvi. 100–106.
58 Strabo, *Geog.* XVI. iv. 24.
59 Young, *Rome's Eastern Trade*, 82.
60 Sidebotham, *Roman Economic Policy*, 68; Sidebotham, "Ports of the Red Sea," 488.
61 Scaife, "Origin of Some Pantheon Columns," 37.
62 Pliny, *Natural History* VI: xxvi. 100–106 from LCL.
63 For a general picture of Roman trade with India via the Red Sea, see Tomber, *Indo-Roman Trade* and Casson, *Periplus*.
64 Note the similar 40-m-wide canal leading from Trajan's hexagonal harbor at Portus to the Tiber, see Bennett *Optimus Princeps*, 140, and Meiggs, *Ostia*, 161–66.
65 Jones, "Archaeological Discoveries," 108.
66 The divers also reported encountering metal chains during the sinking of Shaft 2. In the Late Roman period the riverside may have received a colonnade, for part of a marble column base apparently standing *in situ* on the external face of the river wall was recovered by the divers. See also Kubiak, *Al-Fustat*, 117 and n. 49 for medieval references (Ibn Duqmaq and Maqrizi) to the

presence of a stepped quayside in the early medieval harbor of al-Fustat.
67　Casson, *Ships*, 370.
68　Along with reused blocks with relief carving possibly derived from other nearby ancient buildings (see below).
69　Lanciani, *Ancient Rome*, 248. These observations were made by the only archaeologist permitted to view the site made during the great changes carried out to the area during the nineteenth century by the Torlonia family.
70　The archaeological material recovered from the upper part of these deposits within the shaft contained only Late Roman material, another possible indication that the canal continued in use beyond the Early Roman period.
71　The position of the monastery of Abu Sayfayn provides another early topographical marker for the position of the river from at least the tenth century and probably as early as the sixth; Jones, "Archaeological Discoveries," 108.
72　Dio Cassius, *Roman History* LXXI, iii. I adapted from LCL.
73　Butler, *Arab Conquest*, 242, n.1.
74　Lane, *Description*, 95.
75　Miquel, "L'Égypte," 120; Fahmy, *Muslim Sea Power*.
76　See Loukianoff, "Forteresse Romaine"; regarding the Roman architect responsible for work at Old Cairo. Loukianoff felt happy to be able to "*restituer le nom d'Appollodore de Damas, tiré de l'oubli par les recherches de Grégoire Loukianoff,*" but the basis for this restitution remains sadly unknown.
77　Dio Cassius, *Roman History*, LXVIII. vi. I, xiii. I–XIV. 3 LCL.
78　Hassan, "Extreme Nile floods," 101ff.
79　Cooper, "Egypt's Nile-Red Sea Canals."
80　Sijpestein, "Potamos Traianos," 78.
81　Diodorus, *History* (I.33).
82　Casson, "Harbor and River Boats," 32.
83　Kubiak, *Al-Fustat*, 118.
84　Gayraud, "Istabl-'Antar (Fostat), 1987–89," 64.
85　Kubiak and Scanlon, "Fustat: Re-dating," 139.
86　Butler, *Ancient Coptic Churches*, 179.
87　Bowman, "Military Occupation."
88　Al-Muqaddasi writing in AH 375/ AD 985 writes of Egypt's cereals giving life to the Hijaz. See Miquel, "L'Egypte," 111.
89　Egypt was ruled for the emperor by a prefect and no Roman of senatorial or equestrian status was permitted even to enter the country without permission.
90　Strabo, *Geography*, XVII.1.12
91　Strabo, *Geography*, XVII.1.30.
92　Butler, *Babylon of Egypt*, 62.
93　Spiedel, "Augustus' Deployment." He estimates that 24,000 men were dealing with an estimated population of eight million.
94　Jones, "Archaeological Discoveries," 106.
95　Warner, *Monuments*, pl. 12.
96　Jones, "A Roman Station," 259.
97　D. Jeffreys, *The Survey of Memphis I*, 76, figs. 47, 48.
98　Jones, "Roman Station."
99　Ibn 'Abd al-Hakam, *Futuh*, 164–65.
100　Ibn 'Abd al-Hakam, *Futuh*, 162–63; Trombley, "'Amr b. al-'As's Refurbishment."
101　Bourdon, *Anciens canaux*, 6; al-Kindī's lost work *al-Jund al-Gharbī* is cited in al-Maqrīzī (*Khitat*: 3.474). Cooper, *The Nile-Red Sea Canal*, 54. Ibn Duqmaq/Vollers, *Description de L'Égypt*, 120.
102　The first use of this name for the canal appears in the ninth century; Kubiak, *Al-Fustat*, 118.
103　Ibn Duqmaq/Vollers, *Description de L'Égypt*, 120. Al-Maqrizi repeats the tradition that it was filled in 766 on the orders of the caliph al-Mansur.
104　Hassan, "Extreme Nile floods."
105　Miquel, "L'Egypte," 111.
106　Miquel, "L'Egypte," 118.
107　The same thing happened to the *khalig* west of the Fatimid city in modern times, when it was filled in and became the current Shari' Port Said.
108　For example, Carsten Niebuhr's plan of 1795.
109　'Ayn Shams, the ancient Heliopolis, is also mentioned as a city on the great route to Sham by al-Muqaddasi. Miquel, "L'Egypte," 120.
110　A new head of the canal was dug by the sultan Qalawun at the end of the thirteenth century, but by this time its use was largely in the yearly cleansing of the city, the replenishing of its water supply, and the irrigating of the agricultural areas of 'Ayn Shams/Matariya which followed the opening of the canal during the inundation.
111　The Shari' al-Khalifa is perhaps the successor of the ancient route between Kher-Aha and Heliopolis known as the Road of Sep. Hamza, "Statue of Meneptah," 240 and map, 235.

Notes to Chapter 3
1　Dio Cassius, *Roman History* LXXVI, xv 2.
2　Williams, *Diocletian*; Barnes, *New Empire*.
3　Grant, *Climax of Rome*, 19.
4　Lactantius, *Mortibus persecutorum* VII.
5　van Berchem, "L'occupation militaire;" El-Saghir et al., *Le camp romain*, 21.
6　Charles, *Chronicle of John LXXVII*, 1. It is interesting that Diocletian is described as an Egyptian here, although John does not mention him at all in the passage dealing with the Fortress of Babylon.
7　Zosimus, *Recent History* II, xxxii–xxxv.

8   Lander, *Roman Stone Fortifications* suggests the rounded interval towers at Qasr Qarun were modeled on those of Luxor during an AD 306 reconstruction, although the proximity to Babylon perhaps makes the latter a more likely inspiration. For an excellent plan of the fortresses of Roman Egypt, see Karelin, "Imaging." For Nag' al-Hagar, see Mustafa and Jaritz, "A Roman Fortress"; Mackensen, "The Tetrarchic Fort," and von Kienlin "Der Palast." For Luxor, see El-Saghir et al., *Le Camp romain*. The legionary fortress at Nicopolis is known only from nineteenth-century descriptions and a detailed map illustrating the second Battle of Alexandria in 1801. For Qasr-Qarun, see Schwartz, *Qasr-Qarun/Dionysias*. For Abu Sha'ar and the Red Sea *limes*, see Sidebotham, "Preliminary Report," and Power, *Red Sea*, 33.

9   Alston, *Soldier and Society*, 147. For the Legio III Diocletiana, see http://www.livius.org/le.lh/legio/iii_diocletiana.html. The *Notitia Dignitatum* 31.38 refers to at least part of III Diocletiania being stationed at Luxor.

10 The American Research Center in Egypt has now (2009) completed a conservation project dealing with these paintings and publication is proposed for 2011-2012. El-Saghir et al., *Le camp romain*, 20, 122. (Also note the controversy over supposedly similar paintings destroyed in the Roman tower inside the Mu'allaqa Church during recent restoration; *Al-Ahram Weekly*, 3–9 August 2000, 493, http://weekly.ahram.org.eg/2000/493/eg8.htm. For the chronology of Diocletian's visits, see the comments of Vandersleyen on the erection of Pompey's Pillar in 291; Vandersleyen, *CdE*, 1958. An inscription on the socle of the pillar indicates that Diocletian came to Egypt twice, first in 296–97 to quell the revolt of Domitius Domitianus and then in 302 to bring bread to Alexandria following disturbances over his fiscal reforms.

11 Southern, *Roman Empire*, 160; Potter, *Roman Empire*, 334.

12 Lewis and Reinhold, *Roman Civilization*.

13 Bonneau, *Fisc et Nil*.

14 Evelyn White and Oliver, *Temple of Hibis*, No. 4.

15 Oslo Papyrus No. 78 = *FIRA Fontes Iuris Romani Antejustiniani* 2nd ed. 3 vols. Florence: 1940–43, vol. I, no. 81.

16 Strabo, *Geography*, XVII. I. 48.

17 Monneret de Villard, "Ricerche" (*BSRGE* 13), 85.

18 Coquin, *Édifices chrétiens*, 158. Archaeological observations to verify this claim were not possible since the central "well" of the northern tower was filled with concrete in the early twentieth century, while in the southern tower our recent work only exposed the topmost 1 m of the inner concentric ring.

19 Davis, *Early Coptic Papacy*, 28.

20 Davis, *Early Coptic Papacy*, 29; *libelli* or certificates were required to show that these sacrifices had been carried out.

21 Barnes, *Constantine and Eusebius*, 20.

22 El-Saghir et al., *Le camp romain*, 21.

23 Eusebius of Caesarea, *HE* 8.2.4–5.

24 Lactantius, *De Mortibus persecutorum IX*.

25 Davis, *Early Coptic Papacy*, 41.

26 Van Den Berg-Onstwedder, "Diocletian."

27 Haas, *Alexandria*, 211.

28 A number of churches were also built inside the fortress that had been built by Diocletian at Luxor Temple, but these may have had a rather different significance given the nature of the site as a pagan temple. El-Saghir et al., *Le camp romain*, pl. I.

29 Woods, "Emperor Julian."

30 The earliest indication for the northern part of the fortress is Pococke's plan in 1736 and the latest the comments of the CCMAA in the 1940s regarding the need to preserve the remains of the Roman fortress north of Shari' Kitchener (which is now Shari' al-Imam). Possible fragments are also shown on Butler's plan of the fortress from 1884. Pococke *A Description of the East*; Ahmad, *La Mosque de 'Amr*, 3; Butler, *Ancient Coptic Churches*, plan facing page 155.

31 Grossmann et al., "Zur Römischen Festung," 279; Parker, *Limes Arabicus*; Lander, *Roman Stone Fortifications*, 223–26.

32 El-Saghir et al., *Le camp romain*, 20.

33 Possibly units of the Legio XIIIa Gemina. Monneret de Villard, "Sul castrum romano," 175 and http://www.livius.org/le-lh/legio/xiii_gemina.html.

34 Parássoglou *Archive, P. Sakaon*, 58.

35 Although large round buildings of a similar size that were built as mausolea for Diocletian and Galerius at this time survive in Split and Thessaloniki respectively. Both of them were later converted into churches.

36 Grossmann et al., "Zweiter Bericht," 178, 199. Stratigraphically they are later than the fortress wall but there seems no reason to see this as other than the schedule of construction, that is, the walls of the fortress were built first.

37 El-Saghir et al., *Le camp romain*, 23.

38 These excavations are shown in photographs preserved in the SCA Documentation Center.

39 Popper, *Nilometer*, 191.

40 Bourdon identified what he took to be a lock in the Roman structures at the Suez end of the canal. Bourdon, *Ancien canaux*, 143–44.

41 Sijpesteijn, Der ΠΟΤΑΜΟΣ ΤΡΑΙΑΝΟΣ, 74.
42 Sijpesteijn, Der ΠΟΤΑΜΟΣ ΤΡΑΙΑΝΟΣ, 77.
43 Toy, "Babylon," 70.
44 Sutherland, *Roman Imperial Coinage* VI RIC Rome 40a.
45 Wilkes, *Diocletian's Palace*.
46 Comité drawing dated March 31, 1946.
47 It is not clear how much the 1983 reconstruction by the Egyptian Antiquities Organization of the niche in the southern tower was based on archaeological evidence rather than simple analogy with the northern tower.
48 Bailey, "Honorific Columns," 161.
49 Toy, "Babylon," 62.
50 Grossmann et al., "Zweiter Bericht," 174.
51 El-Saghir et al., *Le camp romain*, pl. I.
52 Grossmann et al., "Zweiter Bericht," 189.
53 Strabo, *Geography*, XVII.1.30.
54 Archaeological evidence for such a structure may be adduced from the 1925 plan by Monneret de Villard showing (remains of?) a circular building on the line of the via praetoria in the area now occupied by buildings of the St. Barbara Club. Reggiori, F. "La fortezza romana," 32.
55 Coquin, *Édifices Chrétiens*, 133; 140.
56 Pococke, *Description*, pl. ix.
57 Butler, *Ancient Coptic Churches*, 155.
58 Although we use the term 'barracks,' the real function of these buildings may have been related to storage or another special function related to the canal and the riverside.
59 For the significance of this name and its relationship to the Melkite Patriarch Cyrus at the time of the Arab Conquest, see Butler, *Arab Conquest*, 508.
60 Loukianoff, "La Forteresse romaine," pl. iv.3 and pl. v.
61 Grossmann et al., "Zweiter Bericht," 200.
62 There is an Oxyrhyncus papyrus connecting Babylon with an otherwise unrecorded visit to Egypt by Constantine in 325. P.Oxy 1626, vol. xiv. For the history of the Early Egyptian papacy, see Davis, *Early Coptic Papacy*.
63 Nautin, "La conversion du temple de Philae"; Saradi-Mendelovici, "Christian Attitudes."
64 Davis, *Early Coptic Papacy*, 21.
65 Davis, *Early Coptic Papacy*, 43.
66 Davis, *Early Coptic Papacy*, 43; Butler, *Arab Conquest*, 168.

Notes to Chapter 4
1 For the extent to which Egyptians felt themselves part of this world we can note the frequent references to "Roman affairs" in documents relating to the struggle between the Egyptian and Byzantine churches, Davis, *Early Coptic Papacy*, 95.
2 Butler, *Arab Conquest*, 194; Kennedy, *Great Arab Conquests*, 139. See Power, *Red Sea*, 96.
3 Kuhrt, *Ancient Near East*, vol. II, 493ff.; Lloyd, "The Late Period," 369; Spalinger, "The Reign of King Chabbash," 142ff.
4 Butler, *Arab Conquest*, 69; Dignas and Winter, *Rome and Persia*.
5 Butler, *Arab Conquest*; Kennedy, *Great Arab Conquests*.
6 The popular etymology of the name al-Fustat was derived by medieval writers from the noun *fustat*, meaning tent, a reference to the tents of the army, and more particularly the tent of its commander, 'Amr ibn al-'As. More plausibly, Butler suggested that it derived from the Greek *fossaton*, "ditch," meaning a fortified camp, that is, one surrounded by a ditch. Butler, *Arab Conquest*, 340. It seems possible too that the ditch in question refers either to the Roman canal itself (and specifically its mouth) or to its re-excavation after the Conquest. See page 2, and for a wider discussion of local place names, see also Casanova, "Les noms coptes," 189.
7 Bloom, "Ceremonial," 99. For the administrative arrangements of the new government, see Sijpesteijn, "Landholding Patterns."
8 Kubiak, *Al-Fustat*, 34; Akbar, "Khatta."
9 Gayraud, "Fostat: Évolution d'une capitale arabe." The same use of mixed building material was observed in buildings excavated by the SCA in 1999 immediately to the west of the Fatimid-period tombs known as the Saba' Banaat and in the area of the National Museum of Egyptian Civilization west of the "lake" of 'Ayn al-Sira. Some of the earliest medieval buildings recorded in Old Cairo (for example, Shaft 4 and the trenches in front of the South Gate of the fortress in 2004) show similar use of mixed material.
10 Lambert, *Fortifications*, 204.
11 The first attempt to found a separate "royal" or administrative enclosure, a desire that became a regular and formative feature of the development of medieval Cairo, was that of Helwan 20 km to the *south* of al-Fustat by the Umayyad 'Abd al-'Aziz in 689–90; Kubiak, *Al-Fustat*, 128. As we have seen, Helwan, like Babylon, may already have had a Roman and ancient Egyptian identity as the location of the Memphis Nilometer. Drioton, "Origines Pharaoniques," 311.
12 Miquel, "L'Égypte," 118.
13 Miquel, "L'Égypte," 120.
14 Denoix, *Décrire le Caire*, 31ff.
15 Swanson, *Coptic Papacy*, 62. Parts of al-Fustat also may have been destroyed and abandoned during the Abbasid recapture of Egypt from the Tulunids in 905, just as a similar cycle of destruction and partial abandonment had occurred during the initial Abbasid conquest of al-Fustat in 750.

16 Denoix, *Décrire le Caire*, 54. Archaeological evidence shows that as well as ruins, buildings of the Fatimid necropolis still in use were also robbed. Gayraud, "Fostat: Évolution d'une capitale arabe."
17 Kubiak and Scanlon, "Fustat: Re-dating," 138.
18 Kubiak, "The Burning of Misr al-Fustat," 58, 63.
19 For the medieval references to individual buildings, see Coquin, *Édifices Chrétiens*.
20 Bahgat Bey and Gabriel, *Fouilles d'al Foustat*. See also Hawary, "Une maison."
21 Scanlon and Kubiak, "Fusṭāṭ Expedition"; Scanlon, "Fustat Expedition: Preliminary Report," (1964–78); Scanlon, "Fustat: Archaeological Reconsiderations."
22 Gayraud, "Istabl-'Antar (Fostat)"; "Fostat: Évolution d'une capitale arabe," 435ff.
23 Pococke, *Description*, pl. 7; Jomard, *Description, État Moderne* I, pl. 15.
24 Butler, *Ancient Coptic Churches*, 12.
25 Monneret de Villard, "Ricerche," 12 and 13; Goitein, *Mediterranean Society*; Goitein, *Mediterranean Society*; Reif, *A Jewish Archive*; Power, *Red Sea*, 212.
26 Seton-Williams and Stocks, *Blue Guide: Egypt*, 214.
27 Lambert, *Fortifications*, 226.
28 In al-Fustat the excavators considered this sequence to be "the norm for the site as a whole." Kubiak and Scanlon, "Fustat: Re-dating," 139. A similar sequence was noted in the French excavations at Istabl 'Antar, although the Fatimid phase here saw the transformation of the site into a cemetery, which clearly reflects wider changes in the urban landscape of al-Fustat. Gayraud, *AI 1985–1994*. Creswell identified parts of the fabric of the Mosque of 'Amr and the expansion to its present size as having taken place around 882. See Creswell and Allan, *Early Muslim Architecture*, 304–14.
29 Meri and Bacharach, *Medieval Islamic Civilization*, 173; Davis, *Early Coptic Papacy*, 121; Foss, "Egypt under Mu'āwiya."
30 Webster, *Fortress into City*.
31 Miquel, "L'Égypte." The Geniza archive was discovered during the rebuilding of the Ben Ezra Synagogue in the 1890s. For the circumstances of the discovery, see Lambert, *Fortifications*, 237.
32 Ibn 'Abd al-Hakam, *Futuh*, 164–65.
33 Just as the construction of the Ismailiya Canal (1867–79) parallel to the Khalig "opened a further gift of dry land between the built-up city and the newly stabilizing banks of the Nile." Abu-Lughod, "Cairo, an Islamic Metropolis," 19. The downtown area of modern Cairo was then built on this reclaimed land.
34 As with the Khalig west of the Fatimid city in modern times, which was filled in and became the current Shari' Port Said.

35 Gascoigne and Sheehan, "Babylon/Qasr ash-Sham." For earlier view, see Kubiak, *Al-Fustat*, 95–110. See Power, *Red Sea*, 218–19.
36 Williams, "The Cult of 'Alid Saints." The Shari' al-Khalifa is perhaps the successor of the ancient route between Kher Aha and Heliopolis known as the Road of Sep. Hamza, "Statue of Meneptah," 240.
37 Kubiak, *Al-Fustat*, n. 49 on 117.
38 The profligacy of modern construction and road-surfacing processes has increased this rate further. In Shari' Mari Girgis, the ground level has increased by around 2 m in the last fifty years.
39 Monneret de Villard, "Ricerche" (13) 84.
40 The antiquity of this street is also suggested by its alignment with the central door of the Church of St. Barbara, which may in turn derive from an earlier Roman street leading to the U-shaped tower east of the church.
41 Lambert, *Fortifications*, 93.
42 The fragment of a fine Ottoman façade revealed by this work was reburied and later destroyed in 2005 by Contract 102 preparations for an ancillary building for the church of Abu Serga. No work on this building has yet taken place.
43 Butler, *Arab Conquest*, 272.
44 Butler, *Arab Conquest*, 238.
45 Wilkes, *Diocletian's Palace*.
46 Kubiak, *Al-Fustat*, 96.
47 Kubiak, *Al-Fustat*, 103.
48 Kubiak, *Al-Fustat*, 55.
49 Grossmann, *Christliche Architektur*, 401; Swanson.
50 Grossmann, *Christliche Architektur*, 401, 528, 443, 441. He dates the original Church of St. Mercurius in the Monastery of Abu Sayfayn in Old Cairo to the sixth century on the basis of its very large apse: *Christliche Architektur*, 505.
51 Coquin, *Édifices chrétiens*, 117.
52 Fowden, *Barbarian Plain*; Woods, "Emperor Julian," 7, 335ff.
53 Lambert, *Fortifications*, 81; Fattal, *Le statut legal*, 180.
54 Miquel, "L'Égypte," 111.
55 Although at this point it is not clear to what extent (or even whether) the different groups had separate churches. See Haas, *Alexandria in Late Antiquity*.
56 Coquin, *Édifices chrétiens*, 87.
57 Woods, "Emperor Julian," 335ff.
58 Coquin, *Édifices chrétiens*, 91.
59 Swanson, *Coptic Papacy*, 2. Coquin, *Édifices chrétiens*, 69. Until the mid-eleventh century the patriarch was also consecrated at Alexandria and at the Church of Abu Makar in the Wadi Natrun. Swanson, *Coptic Papacy*, 10.
60 Coquin, *Édifices chrétiens*, 99.

61 Coquin, *Édifices chrétiens*, 93.
62 Coquin, *Édifices chrétiens*, 93.
63 Patricolo and Monneret de Villard, *La Chiesa di Santa Barbara*, 33.
64 Coquin, *Édifices chrétiens*, 128.
65 Butler, *Ancient Coptic Churches*, 235.
66 Patricolo and Monneret de Villard, *La Chiesa di Santa Barbara*, 39.
67 Kubiak and Scanlon, "Fustat: Re-dating," 140.
68 Goldziher, *Islamic Theology and Law*, 34. Swanson, *Coptic Papacy*, 34.
69 Abu Salih, *Churches and Monasteries of Egypt*, 117.
70 Den Heijer, "Religion, Ethnicity and Gender under Fatimid Rule," 47; Swanson, *Coptic Papacy*, 47–52.
71 Ambraseys et al., *The Seismicity of Egypt*. Sources from the twelfth century onward relate how the Coptic patriarch Michael (881–99) sold the church to the Jews in order to pay a 25,000 dinar tribute imposed on him by the ruler of Egypt, Ahmad Ibn Tulun. In some of the more modern versions of this account the building is described as a ruined former Melkite (Greek Orthodox) church that had come into the possession of the Coptic patriarchate. The sources upon which these nineteenth-century authors base this extra detail are not clear. Coquin, *Édifices chrétiens*, 173.
72 Monneret de Villard, "Ricerche" (12), 218.
73 Kubiak and Scanlon, "Fustat: Re-dating," 140.
74 Coquin, *Édifices chrétiens*, 99.
75 Monneret de Villard, "Ricerche" (12), 218.
76 That this occurred before 1072–73 is indicated by a reference in the document mentioning the Crusaders' siege of the northern Egyptian city of Damietta, which occurred in that year. Coquin, *Édifices Chrétiens*, 94, 120. Patricolo and Monneret de Villard, *La Chiesa di Santa Barbara*, 38.
77 Coquin, *Édifices Chrétiens*, 67. Seton-Williams and Stocks, *Blue Guide: Egypt*, 283.
78 Patricolo and Monneret de Villard, *Chiesa di Santa Barbara*.
79 Lambert, *Fortifications*, 81.
80 What appears to be the present back wall of the synagogue is actually part of the nineteenth-century expansion to enclose the passage to the well.
81 Ben-Sasson, "Medieval Period," 211.
82 Ben-Sasson, "Medieval Period," 212.

Notes to Chapter 5
1 Denoix, *Décrire Le Caire*, 125.
2 Monneret de Villard, "Ricerche" (12), 216.
3 Armanios, "Patriarchs, Archons," 61ff.
4 Monncret de Villard, "Riccrche" (12 and 13).
5 Ben-Sasson, "Medieval Period"; Hacker, "Mameluke and Ottoman Periods."
6 Meinecke-Berg, "Stadtansicht," 115; Warner, *True Description*.
7 Denoix, *Décrire Le Caire*, 54.
8 Kubiak, "The Burning of Misr al-Fustat," 540.
9 It was only reoccupied again when rural immigrants to Cairo started to settle on the abandoned ruin heaps during the 1980s, a demographic shift that largely signalled the beginning of the end of al-Fustat as an archaeological site. The apparently Fatimid *masbagha* or tannery that stands on the Museum of Egyptian Civilization site near the lake of 'Ayn al-Sira in the eastern part of al-Fustat shows that industrial activity may even have started earlier, perhaps on the parts of al-Fustat abandoned after the Abbasid conquest of Egypt in 750. There is still a substantial tannery industry located in the area of Fumm al-Khalig around the great Mamluk aqueduct immediately to the north of the area of *al-Gayara* (which takes its name from the *gir* or quicklime that used to be produced there). The area of post-medieval potteries known as the *fawakhir* survived in Old Cairo between the fortress and the Mosque of 'Amr until they were removed in 1998. Pottery and lime production continues in the area of Batn al-Baqara immediately to the east of the fortress.
10 Hampikian and Cyran, "Recent Discoveries."
11 Hampikian and Cyran, "Recent Discoveries."
12 Sanders, *Ritual, Politics, and the City*, 44, 60..
13 Bahgat and Gabriel, *Fouilles d'al-Foustat*, fig. 69, 133.
14 Haswell, "Cairo, Origins and Development," pl. II (map). Jones, "Archaeological Discoveries, 107.
15 Warner, *True Description*, 1.
16 Garcin "Outsiders in the City," 7ff.
17 Fischel, *Ibn Khaldun*.
18 Denoix, "A Mamluk Institution," 191ff.
19 Denoix, "A Mamluk Institution," 198–200. O'Kane, "Domestic and Religious Architecture," 151.
20 Fernandes, "Istibdal," 208.
21 Denoix, *Décrire la Ville*, 93. Apart from *waqf*s, investments were also financed for the Mamluk ruling group by the *iqta* or rural tax.
22 Fernandes, "Istibdal," 203. In many cases these developments were only possible by bringing land back into the market and modifying previous (and supposedly inalienable) *waqf* endowments through the sometimes controversial process of istibdal or exchange.
23 Rabbat, "*Khitat*," 21.
24 Rabbat, "*Khitat*." The *khitat* was a collection of anecdotes listing the particular character of a city and reflected national and local pride. Egypt had a special status in this genre, which we know was current from the Fatimid period onward although no pre-Mamluk examples are preserved.

25 Rabbat, "*Khitat*," 25.
26 Borsch, *Black Death*.
27 Hanna, *Urban History*; Kubiak, "The Nile."
28 Frederik Norden, *Plan de l'Isle de Rodda, avec ses Environs*, 1757. The northern part of the island is annotated "Partie de l'isle qui reste inondée." Warner, *Monuments*, fig. 6.
29 Warner, *True Description*.
30 Denoix, *Décrire le Caire*, 99. Note that sixteenth-century maps following Pagano show a water-lifting device in the area of the dike, which may represent further evidence of a deliberate attempt to modify the landscape. Warner, *True Description*.
31 Lane, *Description*, 95.
32 Carsten Niebuhr, *Urbis Kahira nec non oppidorum Bulak, Masr el Atik et Dsjise Ichnographia* (1774).
33 Gascoigne and Pyke, "The Roman Tower."
34 Thomas, "Arts of Christian Communities," 417; Swanson, "Monastery of St. Paul," 46.
35 Denoix, *Décrire Le Caire*, 125. The accounts of medieval writers such as Ibn Duqmaq and al-Maqrizi are probably most reliable for buildings founded fewer than two hundred years before their time, since they were often still standing and their written waqfs could still be consulted.
36 Swanson, "Monastery of St. Paul," 46.
37 Swanson, "Monastery of St. Paul," 47. The priest-monk who was later to become Patriarch Gabriel III (1268–71) tells us that he had lived in one of the brother's houses in Damascus and Cairo for ten years. Swanson, *Coptic Papacy*, 94, 97–98.
38 Bolman, *Monastic Visions*, 38; Bolman, "Medieval Paintings, Phase One," 163.
39 Swanson, "Monastery of St. Paul," 46.
40 Sucato, *Final Report*.
41 Bolman, "Report on the Paintings." They also show similarities with paintings from the Church of St. Mercurius in Old Cairo, within the monastery of the same name to the north of the Roman fortress; Jones "The Church of St. Antony," 21.
42 Sheehan, "New Archaeological Evidence," 114.
43 Abu Salih, *Churches*, 94. The "pillars of the apostles" refers to the figures of apostles painted on the columns, just like those preserved in Abu Serga. See also Butler, *Ancient Coptic Churches*, 187–88. Meinardus, in "Medieval Wall Paintings," appears to suggest this passage may actually refer to Abu Serga.
44 Patricolo and Monneret de Villard, *La Chiesa di Santa Barbara*. These medieval wooden ties can now be seen in the external face of the south wall revealed by the demolition of the synagogue annex building in 2005.
45 Coquin, *Edifices chrétiens*, 96. Sources earlier than the thirteenth century, like the *History of the Patriarchs of Alexandria* and Abu al-Makarim, mention the Hanging Church and Babylun al-Darag as places where the Holy Family stayed.
46 Coquin, *Édifices chrétiens*, 105. The earliest mention of the stairs to the crypt (1346) mentions nine steps, but by 1420 two sets of stairs are mentioned. In 1483 it is specified that each stair has twelve steps each and in 1485 ten steps, although in 1422 the number given is "about ten."
47 The relationship of the niche walls to the central apse and to the cruciform pier(s) over the crypt stairs appears to suggest that they form part of this medieval phase; at any rate it does not seem likely that the niches are a survival of the original arrangement of the crypt-church.
48 Bolman, "Theodore," 57.
49 Bolman, "Medieval Paintings, Phase Two," 181; Bolman and Lyster, "The Khurus Vault," 143.
50 O'Kane, "Domestic and Religious Architecture," 149.
51 Coquin, *Édifices chrétiens*, 147.
52 O'Kane, "Domestic and Religious Architecture," 150; Lézine, "Salles Nobles," 75.
53 O'Kane, "Domestic and Religious Architecture," 164.
54 Lézine, "Salles nobles," 77.
55 Hampikian and Cyran, "Recent Discoveries."
56 O'Kane, "Domestic and Religious Architecture," 151.
57 Karim, "Mosque of Ulmas"; O'Kane, "Domestic and Religious Architecture," 155.
58 O'Kane, "Domestic and Religious Architecture," 152, 157. There seems to have been a change in preference from vaulted to flat ceilings in religious architecture at the end of the thirteenth century, with the notable exception of the Mosque of Sultan Hasan.
59 Like the houses of al-Fustat, there was no doubt temporary roofing in the summer months. Bahgat and Gabriel, *Fouilles d'al Foustat*, 79. The *darabzin* or balustrade around the central *durqa'a* shown in the 1906 Comité drawing might have helped in temporary roofing arrangements.
60 Hunt, "al-Mu'allaqa Doors."
61 O'Kane, "Domestic and Religious Architecture," 155, n. 25; Lézine, "Salles nobles," 115.
62 The earliest definitive reference to this church is the silver gilt Gospel casket dedicated to the church in 1424 that is now in the Coptic Museum. Coquin, *Édifices Chrétiens*, 139; Simaika, *Guide*, 41.
63 Creswell, *Muslim Architecture of Egypt (I)*, 80 and pl. 28.
64 Patricolo and Monneret de Villard, *La Chiesa di Santa Barbara*, 38. Although the text of Patricolo and Monneret de Villard actually mentions the beginning of the

twelfth it seems likely from the context that thirteenth is meant.
65 Butler, *Coptic Churches*, 238; Patricolo and Monneret de Villard, *La Chiesa di Santa Barbara*, 39.
66 Creswell, *Early Muslim Architecture*, 304, n. 6.
67 Ben-Sasson, "Medieval Period," 220.
68 Le Quesne, "Legend and Tradition," 198. Sheehan, *BES Mastaba*.
69 Swanson, "Monastery of St. Paul," 49; Swanson, *Coptic Papacy*, 101–103.
70 Gril, "Émeute anti-chrétienne," 242; Swanson, *Coptic Papacy*, 102.
71 Gril, "Émeute anti-chrétienne," 266, 271. The shaykh involved in the disturbances, 'Abd al-Gaffar, ended his days at the Mosque of 'Amr in Old Cairo.
72 Little, "Coptic Conversion."
73 Monneret de Villard, "Ricerche" (12), 218. The first references to a Church of St. Sergius by Western travelers date from the seventeenth century. Coquin, *Édifices chrétiens*, 92.
74 Coquin, *Édifices chrétiens*, 67.
75 Coquin, *Édifices chrétiens*, 68; Swanson, "Monastery of St. Paul," 49.
76 Coquin, *Édifices chrétiens*, 68.
77 This column is mentioned by travelers until 1672, many of whom refer to the church "of the column." Others in the fourteenth and fifteenth centuries named the church after the stairway leading up it, which is variously described in 1350 as having thirty-six stone steps and in 1485 twenty-nine steps. Coquin, *Édifices chrétiens*, 74, 77.
78 Seton-Williams and Stocks, *Blue Guide: Egypt*, 283.
79 Hacker, "Mameluke and Ottoman Periods," 225; Ben-Sasson, "Medieval Period," 208.
80 Hacker, "Mameluke and Ottoman Periods," 225.
81 El-Leithy, "Coptic Culture"; Little, "Coptic Conversion."
82 Abd ar-Raziq, "Le Vizirat," 233.
83 Swanson, "Monastery of St. Paul," 49 n. 8; Swanson, *Coptic Papacy*, 115–17.
84 Monneret de Villard, "Ricerche" (12), 206.
85 Monneret de Villard, "Ricerche" (12), 207. The medieval walls in this area that were removed during the clearing of the Roman gateway are shown on an unpublished Comité plan.
86 No archaeological recording was carried out during any of the work undertaken to restore the Hanging Church and the Coptic Museum.
87 Ben-Sasson, "Medieval Period," 206.
88 Coquin, *Édifices chrétiens*, 68.
89 Hacker, "Mameluke and Ottoman Periods," 225.
90 Grossmann, "Neue Beobachtungen zur Sergioskirche," 18.
91 Coquin, *Édifices chrétiens*, 109.
92 Monneret de Villard, "Ricerche" (12), 216.
93 Monneret de Villard, "Ricerche sulla Topografia." Author's translation from the Latin.
94 A list of the sources relating to European pilgrims is given in Coquin, *Édifices Chrétiens*, 91.
95 Coquin, *Édifices chrétiens*, 105.
96 Coquin, *Édifices chrétiens*, 106.
97 Coquin, *Édifices chrétiens*, 106.
98 Coquin, *Édifices chrétiens*, 100. It has even been suggested that the church was donated to the Franciscans in 1698 by Venetian merchants who had acquired it. Jullien, *L'Égypte*, 228. In the eighteenth century, after the revival of the Coptic churches in Old Cairo, a number of references indicate that the Europeans had to pay for the rights to celebrate Mass in the crypt. Coquin, *Édifices chrétiens*, 101.
99 The Greek Catholic cemetery at the southeast corner of the fortress is a modern feature replacing the palm gardens described here by Butler in the 1880s. See view of Old Cairo from Jullien, *L'Égypte*, 223, reproduced in Coquin, *Édifices Chrétiens*, pl. II.
100 Hunt, "al-Mu'allaqa Doors."
101 Thomas, "The Arts of Christian Communities in the Medieval Near East," 420.
102 Hamilton, "Pilgrims," 76.
103 Hanna, *Urban History of Bulaq*.
104 Armanios, "Patriarchs."
105 Sheehan, "New Archaeological Evidence," 121.
106 Hanna, *Habiter au Caire*, 172ff.
107 Swanson, "Monastery of St. Paul," 56; Armanios, "Patriarchs," 65.
108 Fernandes, "*Istibdal*," 203ff.
109 Coquin, *Édifices chrétiens*, 157.
110 Coquin, *Édifices chrétiens*, 148.
111 Information received from the convent indicates that the *waqfiya* documents showing how much of Old Cairo was (and perhaps still is) the property of the Convent of St. George still exist.
112 Jomard, *Description*, II, vol I, pl. 15.
113 Warner, *Monuments*, 6, pl. 3.
114 For this church, see Coquin, *Édifices chrétiens*, 133–36. It was believed that nothing of the ancient church remains, although our recent archaeological observations show that the sanctuary end of the church actually survived the fire. Sheehan, "Wedding Hall," 54.
115 The arched entrance to the *hara* was demolished by the owner of the adjacent tourist bazaar in 2008.
116 The cistern itself is currently used as a septic tank for the current occupants of the *sabil*.

117 These stout doorways at the entrance to defined locales were a characteristic feature of the *hara*-based security arrangements of post-medieval Cairo. El Messiri Nadim, "Concept of the Hāra," 48.

118 The arched door was dismantled during work on the rebuilding of the Church of St. George and never rebuilt.

119 Monneret de Villard, "Ricerche" (12), 226.

120 Coquin, *Édifices Chrétiens*, 69.

121 Coquin, *Édifices Chrétiens*, 120.

122 Monneret de Villard, "Ricerche" (12), 227.

123 Patricolo and Monneret de Villard, *La Chiesa di Santa Barbara*, 39.

124 Grossmann, et.al, "Zweiter Bericht," 203.

125 Coquin, *Édifices chrétiens*, 171. *Survey of Egypt*, 1:1000 series, 1930.

126 Monneret de Villard, "Ricerche" (12), 215. Hacker, "Mameluke and Ottoman Periods," 226.

127 Coquin, *Édifices chrétiens*, 164. Translation by the author.

128 Coquin, *Édifices chrétiens*, 164. Translation by the author.

129 Monneret de Villard, "Ricerche" (12), 228.

130 Smith, *Collectanea*, 112, pl. XIV.

131 Butler, *Ancient Coptic Churches*, 161.

132 Coquin, *Édifices chrétiens*, 101.

133 Coquin, *Édifices chrétiens*, 106.

134 Butler, *Ancient Coptic Churches*, 201, fig. 12.

135 Coquin, *Édifices chrétiens*, 106.

136 Coquin, *Édifices chrétiens*, 106.

137 Coquin, *Édifices chrétiens*, 100–101.

138 Butler, *Ancient Coptic Churches*, plan opp. 182.

139 Butler, *Ancient Coptic Churches*, 12

Notes to Chapter 6

1 Tacitus, *Histories*, bk. 3, sct. 65.

2 This stone façade, seen and recorded, was then reburied. It was later demolished.

3 Lambert, *Fortifications*, 231.

4 Lambert, *Fortifications*, 232.

5 W.G. Kemp, "Babloon."

6 Butler, *Ancient Coptic Churches*, 209.

7 Somers Clarke, *Proceedings*, 64, 66.

8 Butler, *Ancient Coptic Churches*, 158, 159.

9 Chester, "Notes," 127.

10 Butler, *Ancient Coptic Churches*, 160.

11 Butler, *Ancient Coptic Churches*, 160–61.

12 Butler, *Ancient Coptic Churches*, 164.

13 Butler, *Ancient Coptic Churches*, 163.

14 Chester, "Notes," 127.

15 Butler, *Ancient Coptic Churches*, 164.

16 The church was pillaged by a mob in 1882 during demonstrations against the intervention of the foreign powers in Egypt, perhaps the cause of the rebuilding work noted by Butler in 1884. "Revisiting the scene in January, 1884, I found a vast pile of new buildings in course of construction actually against the tower." Butler, *Ancient Coptic Churches*, 158.

17 Clarke, *Proceedings*, 61.

18 Clarke, *Proceedings*, 65.

19 Butler, *Ancient Coptic Churches*, 170; Chester, *Ancient Christian Churches*, 126.

20 Lambert, *Fortifications*, Appendix, 244.

21 J. Mosseri, *A New Hoard of Jewish Manuscripts*, 39.

22 References to this *mastaba* appear from the fifteenth century onward.

23 Lambert, *Fortifications*, Appendix, 246.

24 Butler, *Ancient Coptic Churches*, 236.

25 These paintings were recently cleaned by a Spanish conservation team from the Programa de Patrimonio Cultural de la Cooperacion Española.

26 Simaika Pasha, *Guide*, iii.

27 *BCCMAA* 32, 1915–19.

28 Between 1951 and 1952 further work concentrated on repairs to the steps and corridors at the entrance to the church, as well as further work on the piers and arched supports supporting the floor of the church.

29 The 1:5000 plan was published by the Comité in 1914.

30 Simaika Pasha, *Guide*, ix.

31 The request was not acted on.

32 *BCCMAA* 40, 1946–53

33 The present building appears on the 1913 plan of Old Cairo made by the Survey of Egypt.

34 Columns of this first-phase arcade remain dotted around the present building.

35 Loukianoff, "La Forteresse romaine," 290.

36 Lambert, *Fortifications*, 231

37 Lambert, *Fortifications*, 135ff.

38 Gabra, "Ein Block Ptolemaios," 49.

39 Lambert, *Fortifications*, 21.

40 *Al-Ahram Weekly*, 3–9 August 2000, 493, http://weekly.ahram.org.eg/2000/493/eg8.htm.

41 Old Cairo Groundwater Lowering Project, Arabic/English brochure produced by USAID/CWO.

42 Memo from Chip Vincent of ARCE to Wafaa Faltaous of USAID, March 16, 2004.

43 Memo from Jaroslaw Dobrowolski to Robert Springborg, 5 September, 2002.

44 Grossmann et al.,"Zweiter Bericht," 183.

45 Sheehan, "Accessing the Archaeology."

References

Abbreviations

AARP	*Art and Archaeology Research Papers*
AI	*Annales Islamologiques*
ARCE	American Research Center in Egypt
ASAE	*Annales du Service des Antiquités de l'Égypte*
AUCP	American University in Cairo Press
BASP	*Bulletin of the American Society of Papyrologists*
BIE	*Bulletin de l'Institut d'Egypte*
BIFAO	*Bulletin de l'Institut français d'archéologie orientale*
BSRGE	*Bulletin de la Société Royale de Géographie d'Egypte*
CIL	*Corpus Inscriptionum Latinarum*
FIRA	*Fontes Iuris Romani Antejustiniani*
IFAO	l'Institut français d'archéologie orientale
JARCE	*Journal of the American Research Center in Egypt*
JE	*The Jewish Encyclopedia*
JEA	*Journal of Egyptian Archaeology*
JNES	*Journal of Near Eastern Studies*
JRS	*Journal of Roman Studies*
LCL	Loeb Classical Library
MDAIK	*Mitteilungen des Deutschen Archaölogischen Instituts Abteilung Kairo*
MIFAO	*Memoirs de l'Institut francais d'archéologie orientale*

Abd ar-Raziq, A. "Le Vizirat et les Viziers d'Égypte au Temps des Mamluks." *AI* 16 (1980): 183–239.

Abdel-Gawad, M. "The Gulf of Suez: A Brief Review of Stratigraphy and Structure." *Philosophical Transactions of the Royal Society of London. Series A, Mathematical and Physical Sciences* 267, no. 11 (1970): 41–48.

Abu-Lughod, J. *Cairo: 1001 Years of the City Victorious*. Princeton, NJ: Princeton University Press, 1971.

———. "Cairo, an Islamic Metropolis." In *Cairo, Revitalizing a Historic Metropolis*, edited by S. Bianca and P. Jodidio. Turin: Umberto Allemandi & C., 2004.

Abu Salih. *The Churches and Monasteries of Egypt and Some Neighbouring Countries attributed to Abu Salih, the Armenian*. Edited and translated by B.T. Evetts. Oxford: Clarendon Press, 1895.

Adam, R. *Ruins of the Palace of the Emperor Diocletian at Spalatro in Dalmatia*. London: Printed for the author, 1764.

Adamson, D.A., F. Gasse, F.A. Street, and M.A. Williams. "Late Quaternary History of the Nile." *Nature* 288 (1980): 50–55.

Ahmad, M. *La Mosque de 'Amr ibn al-As à Fustat*. Cairo: Ministry of Education, 1939.

Akbar, J. "Khatta and the Territorial Structure of Early Muslim Towns." *Muqarnas: An Annual on Islamic Art and Architecture* 6 (1990): 22–32.

Alston, R. *Soldier and Society in Roman Egypt: A Social History*. London: Routledge, 1995.

Ambraseys, N.N., C.P. Melville, and R.D. Adams. *The Seismicity of Egypt, Arabia and the Red Sea: A Historical Review*. Cambridge, UK: Cambridge University Press, 1995.

Antoniou, J., et al. *The Conservation of the Old City of Cairo*. London: UNESCO, 1980.

Armanios, F. "Patriarchs, Archons, and the Eighteenth-Century Resurgence of the Coptic Community." In Lyster, *Cave Church of Paul the Hermit*, 61–73.

Attia, M.I. *Deposits in the Nile Valley and the Delta*. Cairo: Geological Survey of Egypt, 1954.

Ayalon, D. "On the Eunuchs in Islam." *Jerusalem Studies on Arabic and Islam* 1 (1979).

Bahğat, 'A.B., and A. Gabriel. *Les fouilles d'al-Foustat et les origines de la maison arabe*. Paris: E. De Boccard, 1921.

Bailey, D. "Honorific Columns, Cranes, and the Tuna Epitaph." In *Archaeological Research in Roman Egypt: The Proceedings of the Seventeenth Classical Colloquium of the Department of Greek and Roman Antiquities, British Museum*, edited by D. Bailey, 155–68. Journal of Roman Archaeology supplementary series no. 19. Ann Arbor, MI: Journal of Roman Archaeology, 1996.

———. "Sebakh, Sherds and Survey." *JEA* 85 (1999): 211–18.

———, ed. *Archaeological Research in Roman Egypt: The Proceedings of the Seventeenth Classical Colloquium of the Department of Greek and Roman Antiquities, British Museum*. Ann Arbor, MI: Journal of Roman Archaeology, 1999.

Bareket, E. *Fustat on the Nile: The Jewish Elite in Medieval Egypt*. Leiden: Brill, 1999.

Barnes, T.D. *Constantine and Eusebius*. Cambridge, MA: Harvard University Press, 1981.

———. *The New Empire of Diocletian and Constantine*. Cambridge, MA: Harvard University Press, 1982.

Barrucand, M. *L'Égypte fatimide: Son art et son histoire*. Paris: Presses de la Sorbonne Nouvelle, 1999.

BCCMAA. *Bulletin du Comité de Conservation des Monuments de l'Art Arabe*, vols. 1–40, 1883–1961. Cairo. http://www.islamic-art.org/comitte/Comite.asp

Behrens-Abouseif, D. *Azbakiyya and its Environs from Azbak to Isma'il*. Cairo: IFAO, 1985.

———, ed. *The Cairo Heritage: Essays in Honor of Laila Ali Ibrahim*. Cairo and New York: AUCP, 2000.

Bell, B. "Climate and the History of Egypt: The Middle Kingdom." *American Journal of Archaeology* 79 (1975): 223–69.

Bellaert, J. "An Account of the Ben Ezra Synagogue Restoration Project, 1989–91." In Lambert, *Fortifications and the Synagogue*, 135–65.

Bennett, J. *Trajan: Optimus Princeps*. London and New York: Routledge, 2001.

Ben-Sasson, M. "The Medieval Period: The Tenth to Fourteenth Centuries." In Lambert, *Fortifications and the Synagogue*, 210–23.

Bietak, M. *Tell el-Daba'a II*. Vienna: Österreichische Akademie der Wissenschaften – Denkinschriften der Gesamtakademie IV, 1975.

Blachere, R. "L'agglomération du Caire vue par quatre voyageurs arabes du Moyen Âge." *AI* 8 (1969): 2–26.

Bleecker, C.J. *Hathor and Thoth: Two Key Figures of the Ancient Egyptian Religion*. Leiden: Brill, 1973

Bloom, J.M. "Ceremonial and Sacred Space in Fatimid Cairo." In *Cities in the Pre-Modern Islamic World: The Urban Impact of Religion, State and Society*, edited by A.K. Bennison and A. Gascoigne, 96–114. London: Routledge, 2007.

Boak, A.E.R., and H.C. Youtie, eds. *The Archive of Aurelius Isidorus*. Ann Arbor, MI: University of Michigan Press, 1960.

Boghdady, F. "An Archaic Tomb at Old Cairo." *ASAE* 32 (1932): 153–60.

Bolman, E.S. "The Medieval Paintings in the Cave Church, Phase One." In Lyster, *Cave Church of Paul the Hermit*, 163–77.

———. "The Medieval Paintings in the Cave Church, Phase Two." In Lyster, *Cave Church of Paul the Hermit*, 179–207.

———. "Report on the Newly Discovered Paintings in Abu Sarga, Babylon, Old Cairo: The *Logos* Made Visible." Unpublished report, ARCE, Cairo, 2006.

———. "Theodore, 'The Writer of Life,' and the Program of 1232/1233." In Bolman, *Monastic Visions*, 37–76.

———, ed. *Monastic Visions: Wall Paintings in the Monastery of St. Antony at the Red Sea*. New Haven and London: Yale University Press/ARCE, 2002.

Bolman, E.S., and W. Lyster. "The Khurus Vault, An Eastern Mediterranean Synthesis." In Bolman, *Monastic Visions*, 127–54.

Bonneau, D. *La crue du Nil: Divinite Égyptienne*. Paris: n.p., 1964.

———. *Le Fisc et le Nil*. Paris: Cujas, 1971.

Borsch, S.J. *The Black Death in Egypt and England: A Comparative Study*. Austin: University of Texas Press, 2005.

Bourdon, C. *Anciens canaux, anciens sites et ports de Suez*. Mémoires de la Société Royale de Géographie d'Égypte, 7. Cairo: IFAO, 1925.

Bowden Smith, E.C. "The Subsoil of Cairo." *Cairo Scientific Journal* 8 (1914): 230–50.

Bowman, A. *Egypt after the Pharaohs*. Oxford, UK: Oxford University Press, 1990.

———. "The Military Occupation of Upper Egypt in the Reign of Diocletian." *BASP* 15 (1978): 25–38.

Brown, A.G. *Alluvial Geoarchaeology: Floodplain Archaeology and Environmental Change*. Cambridge and New York: Cambridge University Press, 1997.

Bruyère, B. *Fouilles de Clysma-Qolzoum (Suez), 1930–1932*. Cairo: IFAO, 1966.

Budge, E.A.W. *The Dwellers on the Nile*. 1926. Reprint, New York: B. Blom, 1972.

Bunbury, J.M., A. Graham, and M.A. Hunter. "Stratigraphic Landscape Analysis: Charting the Holocene Movements of the Nile at Karnak through Ancient Egyptian Time." *Geoarchaeology: An International Journal* 23, no. 3 (2008): 351–73. Published online in Wiley Interscience (www.interscience.wiley.com). DOI:10.1002/gea.20219

Burckhardt, J.L. *Arabic Proverbs; or, The Manners and Customs of the Modern Egyptians*. London: J. Murray, 1830.

Butler, A.J. *The Ancient Coptic Churches of Egypt*, vol. 1. Oxford: Clarendon Press, 1884.

———. *The Arab Conquest of Egypt and the Last Thirty Years of the Roman Dominion*, edited by P.M. Fraser. Oxford: Clarendon Press, 1902. Revised 2nd edition, 1978.

———. *Babylon of Egypt, A Study in the History of Old Cairo*. London: Clarendon Press, 1914.

Butler, H.C. *Trajan's Road from Bosra to the Red Sea*. Publications of the Princeton University Archaeological Expeditions to Syria in 1904–5 and 1909, III.A.2, vii–xvi. Leiden, 1921.

Butzer, C. *Early Hydraulic Civilization in Egypt: A Study in Cultural Ecology*. Chicago: University of Chicago Press, 1976.

Caetani, L. *Annali dell'Islam,* vol. 4. Milan: U. Hoepli, 1911.

Calderini, A. "Richerche sul regime delle acque nell'Egitto greco-romano." *Aegyptus* 1 (1920): 37–62.

Casanova, P. "Essai de reconstitution topographique de la ville d'al Foustât au Misr." *Mémoires publiés par les membres de l'Institut français d'archéologie orientale du Caire*, no. 35. Cairo: IFAO, 1913–19.

———. "Les noms coptes du Caire et localités voisines." *BIFAO* 1 (1901): 139–224.

Casson, L. "Harbour and River Boats of Ancient Rome" *JRS* 55 (1965): 31–39.

———. *The Periplus Maris Erythraei. Text with Introduction, Translation and Commentary*. Princeton: Princeton University Press, 1989.

———. *Ships and Seamanship in the Ancient World*. Baltimore: Johns Hopkins University Press, 1995.

Cataudella, M.R. "Quante vie d'aqua fra il Mediterraneo e la Persia?" In *Stuttgarter Kolloquium zur historischen Geographie des Altertums 7, 1999. Zu Wasser und zu Land. Verkehrswege in der antiken Welt*, edited by E. Olshausen and H. Sonnabend, 48–59. Stuttgart: Franz Steiner Verlag, 2002.

Chester, G.J. "Notes on the Ancient Christian Churches of Musr el Ateekah, or Old Cairo, and Its Neighbourhood." *The Archaeological Journal* 29 (1872): 120–34.

CIL. *Corpus inscriptionum latinarum, consilio et auctoritate Academiae litterarum regiae borussicae editum*. Berlin 16 vols, 1862– .

Colliery Engineering Co. *A Treatise On Architecture And Building Construction Vol 2: Masonry. Carpentry. Joinery*. The Colliery Engineering Company, 1899.

Comité de Conservation des Monuments de l'Art Arabe. *Procès-Verbaux des séances et rapports de la section technique; Comptes rendus*. 1897–1953.

Cooper, J.P. "Egypt's Nile–Red Sea Canals: Chronology, Location, Seasonality and Function." In *Connected Hinterlands: Proceedings of Red Sea Project IV, Held at the Centre for Maritime Archaeology, University of Southampton, 25th–26th September 2008*, edited by L.K. Blue, J.P. Cooper, R. Thomas, and J. Whitewright, 195–209. Society for Arabian Studies Monograhs 8, British Archaeological Reports, S2052. Oxford: Archaeopress, 2009.

———. "The Nile–Red Sea Canal in Antiquity: A Consideration of the Evidence for Its Existence, Duration and Route." Unpublished master's thesis, University of Southampton, 2005.

Coquin, C. *Les Édifices Chrétiens du Vieux Caire*, vol. 1, *Bibliographie et Topographie historiques*. Cairo: IFAO, 1974.

Creswell, K.A.C. *The Muslim Architecture of Egypt*. 2 vols. Oxford: Clarendon Press, 1952–59.

———. *A Short Account of Early Muslim Architecture*. Revised and supplemented by J.W. Allan. Aldershot: Scolar Press, 1989.

Davis, S. *The Early Coptic Papacy: The Egyptian Church and Its Leadership in Late Antiquity*. Vol. 1 of *The Popes of Egypt: A History of the Coptic Church and Its Patriarchs from Saint Mark to Pope Shenouda III*, edited by S.J Davis and G. Gabra. Cairo and New York: AUCP, 2004.

Debono, F., and B. Mortensen. *The Predynastic Cemetery at Heliopolis. Season March–September 1950*. Mainz: Philipp von Zabern, 1988.

Delia, D. "The Refreshing Water of Osiris." *JARCE* 29 (1992): 181–90.

Den Heijer, J. "Religion, Ethnicity and Gender under Fatimid Rule. Three Recent Publications and Their Wider Research Context." *Bibliotheca Orientalis* 65, nos. 1–2 (January–April 2008): 38–72.

Denoix, S. *Décrire Le Caire: Fustat Misr d'après Ibn Duqmaq et Maqrizi*. Cairo: IFAO, 1992.

———. "A Mamluk Institution for Urbanization: The *Waqf*." In Behrens-Abouseif, *Cairo Heritage*, 191–202.

Dessau, H. *Inscriptiones Latinae Selectae*. 3 vols. Berlin: Berolini apud Weidmannos, 1892–1916.

Dignas, B., and E. Winter. *Rome and Persia in Late Antiquity: Neighbours and Rivals*. Cambridge: Cambridge University Press, 2007.

Dio Cassius. *Roman History*, with an English translation by E. Cary, Ph.D., on the basis of the version of H.B. Foster, Ph.D. 9 vols. Harvard: LCL, 1914–27.

Diodorus Siculus. *Diodorus of Sicily, with an English translation by C.H. Oldfather*. Loeb Classical Library Series. London: W. Heinemann, 1933–67.

Drioton, É. "Les Origines Pharaoniques du Nilométre de Rodah." *BIE* (1953): 291–316.

———. "Une Statue Prophylactique de Ramses III." *ASAE* 39 (1939): 57–89 and pl. ii–vi.

Duncan Jones, R. "Pay and Numbers in Diocletian's Army." *Chiron* 7 (1978): 541–60.

Eusebius of Caesarea. *Historia Ecclesiastica (Church History)*. Translated by G.A. Williamson. New York: Penguin, 1965.

Eutropius. *Abridgement of Roman History*. The Rev. J.S. Watson. London: Henry G. Bohn, York Street, Covent Garden, 1853.

Evelyn-White, H.G., and J.H. Oliver. *The Temple of Hibis in El-Khargeh Oasis, Part II, Greek Inscriptions*. New York: Metropolitan Museum of Art, 1938.

Fahmy, A.M. *Muslim Sea Power in the Eastern Mediterranean from the Seventh to the Tenth Century A.D.* Cairo: Tipografia Don Bosco, 1950.

Fairholt, F.W. "Babylon in Egypt." In Smith, *Collectanea Antiqua*, 110–16.

Faostino da Toscolano. *Itinerario di Terra Santa*. Edited by W. Bianchini. Spoleto: Centro Italiano di Studi Sull'Alto Medioevo, 1992.

Fattal, A. *Le statut legal des non-musulmans en pays d'Islam*. Beirut: Imprimerie Catholique, 1958.

Fedden, R. "Two Notes on Christian Cairo in the Turkish Period." *Bulletin de la Société d'Archéologie Copte* 10 (1944): 33.

Fernandes, L. "*Istibdal*: The Game of Exchange and Its Impact on the Urbanization of Mamluk Cairo." In Behrens-Abouseif, *Cairo Heritage*, 203–22.

Fischel, W.J. *Ibn Khaldun in Egypt: His Public Function and His Historical Research (1382–1406); A Study in Islamic Historiography*. Berkeley and Los Angeles: University of California Press, 1967.

Foss, C. "Egypt under Muʿāwiya, Part I: Flavius Papas and Upper Egypt." *Bulletin of the School of Oriental and African Studies* 72, no. 1 (2007): 1–24.

Fowden, E.K. *The Barbarian Plain: Saint Sergius between Rome and Iran*. Berkeley: University of California Press, 1999.

———. "Sergius of Rusafa: Sacred Defense in Late Antique Syria-Mesopotamia." Unpublished PhD diss., Princeton University (UMI no. 9611553), 1995.

Gabra, G. "Ein Block Ptolemaios' V. Epiphanes aus Babylon." *Hildesheimer Ägyptologische Beiträge, Festschrift Jürgen von Beckerath, Zum 70*, 30 (1990): 49–51 and pl. 2.

Galtier, M.E. "La Legende de Saint-George." *BIFAO* 4 (1905): 153–70.

Garcin, J.-C. "Outsiders in the City." In Behrens-Abouseif, *Cairo Heritage*, 7–15.

———. "Toponymie et Topographie Urbaines Medievales a Fustat et au Caire." *Journal of the Economic and Social History of the Orient*, vol. 27, part 2 (1984): 113–55.

Gardiner, A. *Ancient Egyptian Onomastica* II. Oxford, UK: Oxford University Press, 1947.

Gardner Wilkinson, J. *Modern Egypt and Thebes, Being a Description of Egypt*. New edition. London: J. Murray, 1847.

Garín, A., ed. *Abu Sirga: La iglesia copta de San Sergio y San Baco del Viejo Cairo*. Madrid: Fundacion Carolina, Ediciones El Viso, 2004.

Gascoigne, A. "Pottery from the ARCE/EAP Contract 102 Old Cairo Groundwater Lowering Project: Fabrics and Wares." Unpublished report, ARCE, Cairo, 2005.

Gascoigne, A., and G. Pyke. "Pottery from the ARCE/EAP Contract 102 Old Cairo Groundwater Lowering Project: The Roman Tower." Unpublished report, ARCE, Cairo, 2002.

Gascoigne A., and Sheehan P. "Babylon/Qasr al-Shamʿ: Continuity and Change at the Heart of the New City 641–969." Proceedings of the Conference: *Fustat et le controle des territoires*, IFAO, 9–11 April 2013. In press.

Gayraud, R.-P. "Fostat: Évolution d'une capitale arabe du VIIe au XIIe siècle d'après les fouilles de'Istabl ʿAntar." In *Colloque International d'Archéologie Islamique*, edited by R.-P. Gayraud, 435–60. Cairo: IFAO, 1998.

———. "Istabl-Antar (Fostat), 1987–89, 1990, 1994. Rapport de fouilles." *AI* 25, 27, 29.

Gil, M. *Documents of the Jewish Pious Foundations from the Cairo Genizah*. Edited with translations, annotations, and general introduction by M. Gil. Leiden: Brill, 1976.

———. "Maintenance, Building Operations, and Repairs in the Houses of the Qodesh in Fustat: A Geniza Study." *Journal of the Economic and Social History of the Orient* 14, no. 2 (August 1971): 136–95.

Goitein, S.D. *A Mediterranean Society: The Jewish Communities of the Arab World as Portrayed in the Documents of the Cairo Geniza*. Berkeley: University of California Press, 1967–88.

Goldziher, I. *Introduction to Islamic Theology and Law*. Princeton, NJ: Princeton University Press, 1981.

Golénischeff. "Lettre à M. G. Maspero sur trois petites trouvailles égyptologiques." *Receuils de Travaux* 9 (1889): 98–100.

Goodfriend, G.A., and D.J. Stanley. "Rapid Strand-plain Accretion in the Northeastern Nile Delta in the 9th Century A.D. and the Demise of the Port of Pelusium." *Geology* 27, no. 2 (February 1999): 147–50.

Grabar, O. "The Meaning of History in Cairo." In *Architectural Transformations in the Islamic World*, Aga Khan Award Architecture, 1–24. Singapore: Concept Media for the Aga Khan Award for Architecture, 1985.

Grace, V.R., and M. Savvatianou-Petropoulakou. "Les Timbres Amphoriques Grecs." In *Exploration Archéologiques de Délos faite par l'École Francaişe d'Athènes 27: L'Îlot de la Maison des Comédiens*. Paris: E. De Broccard, 1970.

Graf, D. "The Via Nova Traiana in Arabia Petraea." In *Roman and Byzantine Near East: Archaeological Research*, edited by J.H. Humphrey, 241–67. Journal of Roman Archaeology supplementary series no. 14. Ann Arbor, MI: Journal of Roman Archaeology, 1995.

Grant, M. *The Climax of Rome*. London: Weidenfeld & Nicholson, 1968.

Grenfell, B.P., and A.S. Hunt. *The Oxyrhynchus Papyri*. London: Egypt Exploration Fund, 1898– .

Greville J.C. "Notes on the Ancient Christian Churches of Musr el Ateekah, or Old Cairo, and its Neighbourhood." *Archaeological Journal* 29 (1872): 120–34.

Gril, D. "Une émeute anti-chrétienne à Qus au début du VIIIe-XIVe siècle." *AI* 16 (1980): 241–74.

Grossmann, P. *Christliche Architektur in Ägypten*. Leiden: Brill, 2002.

———. "Neue Beobachtungen zur Sergioskirche von Alt-Kairo." *Bulletin de la société d'archéologie copte* 45 (2006): 7–24.

Grossmann, P., M. Jones, C. Le Quesne, H.-C. Noeske, and P. Sheehan. "Zweiter Bericht über die Britisch-Deutschen Grabungen in der Römischen Festung von Babylon, Alt-Kairo." *Archäologischer Anzeiger* 1 (1998): 173–207.

Grossmann, P., C. Le Quesne, and P. Sheehan. "Zur Römischen Festung von Babylon-Alt-Kairo." *Archäologischer Anzeiger* 2 (1994): 271–87.

Grover, J.W. "Suez Canals from the Most Ancient Times to the Present." *Journal of the British Archaeological Association* 33 (1877): 447–55.

Guest, R. "The Foundation of Fustat and the Khittahs of That Town." *Journal of the Royal Asiatic Society (*1907): 49–83.

Haas, C. *Alexandria in Late Antiquity: Topography and Social Conflict*. Baltimore: Johns Hopkins University Press, 1997.

Hacker, J.R. "The Mameluke and Ottoman Periods: The Fifteenth to Eighteenth Centuries." In Lambert, *Fortifications and the Synagogue*, 224–27.

Hamada, A. "The Clearance of a Tomb Found at al-Fostat, 1936." *ASAE* 37 (1936): 58–70.

———. "Tomb of Pawen-Hatef at al-Fostat," *ASAE* 37: 135–42.

———. "Une Troisieme Tombe a el-Foustat." *ASAE* 38: 479–92.

Hamilton, A. "Pilgrims, Missionaries and Scholars. Western Descriptions of the Monastery of St. Paul from the Late Fourteenth Century to the Early Twentieth Century." In Lyster, *Cave Church of Paul the Hermit*, 75–93.

Hampikian, N., and M. Cyran. "Recent Discoveries Concerning the Fatimid Palaces Uncovered during the Conservation Works on Parts of the al-Salihiyya Complex." In Barrucand, *L'Égypte fatimide*, 649–57.

Hamza, M. "The Statue of Meneptah I Found at Athar en-Nabi and the Route of Pi'ankhi from Memphis to Heliopolis." *ASAE* 37 (1937): 233.

Hanna, N. *Habiter au Caire, la maison moyenne et ses habitants aux XVIIe et XVIIIe siècles*. Cairo: IFAO, 1991.

———. *An Urban History of Bulaq in the Mamluk and Ottoman Periods*. Cairo: IFAO, 1983.

Harvey, C.P.D., and A.T. Grove. "A Prehistoric Source of the Nile." *Geographical Journal* 148, no. 3 (1982): 327–36.

Hassan, F.A. "Extreme Nile Floods and Famines in Medieval Egypt (AD 930–1500) and Their Climatic Implications." *Quaternary International* 173–74 (2007): 101–12.

Haswell, C.J.R. "Cairo: Origin and Development. Some Notes on the Influence of the River Nile and Its Changes." *BSRGE* 11 (1922).

Hawary, H. "Une maison de l'époque toulounide." *BIE* 15 (1932–33): 79–87.

Hay, R. *Illustrations of Cairo*. London: Tilt and Bogue, 1840.

Heiden, D. "Die Stele des P'–dj-Pp." *Studien zur Altägyptischen Kultur* 30 (2002): 187–201.

Herodotus. *The Histories of Herodotus of Halicarnassus*. Translated and introduced by H. Carter. London: Oxford University Press, 1962.

Herz, M. "Babylon und Qasr esh-Sham." *Der Islam* 8 (1918): 1–14.

Holladay, J.S. *Cities of the Delta III. Tell el-Maskhuta*. ARCE Reports 6. Malibu: Undena Publications, 1982.

Hourani, A. *A History of the Arab Peoples*. London: Faber & Faber, 2005.

Hsu, K.J., W.B.F. Ryan, and M.B. Cita. "Late Miocene Dessication of the Mediterranean." *Nature* 242 (23 March 1973): 240–44.

Hunt, L.-A. *Byzantium, Eastern Christendom and Islam: Art at the Crossroads of the Medieval Mediterranean*. 2 vols. London: Pindar Press, 1998.

———. "The al-Mu'allaqa Doors Reconstructed: An Early Fourteenth Century Sanctuary Screen from Old Cairo." *Gesta* 28, no. 1 (1989): 61–77.

Ibn 'Abd al-Hakam. *The History of the Conquest of Egypt, North Africa and Spain, known as the Futuh Misr of Ibn Abd al-Hakam, edited from the manuscripts in London, Paris and Leyden, by Charles C. Torrey*. New Haven, CT: Yale University Press, 1922.

Ibn Duqmaq. *Kitab al-Intisar li Wasitat 'Aqd al-Amsar*. Edited by K. Vollers. *Description de L'Égypt par Ibn Doukmak*. Cairo: Imprimiere Nationale, 1893.

Ibn Khaldun. *The Muqaddimah: An Introduction to History*. Translated by Franz Rosenthal. 3 vols. Bollingen Series 43. Princeton, NJ: Princeton University Press, 1967.

International Charter for the Conservation and Restoration of Monuments and Sites. Venice: IInd International Congress of Architects and Technicians of Historic Monuments, 1964.

James, P. "Naukratis Revisited." *Hyperboreus: Studia Classica* 9, no. 2 (2003): 235–64.

Jeffreys, D. "Joseph Hekekyan at Heliopolis." In *Studies on Ancient Egypt in Honour of H S Smith*, edited by M.A. Leahy and W.J. Tait, 157–68. London: Egypt Exploration Society 1999.

———. *Survey of Memphis 1*. London: Egypt Exploration Society, Occasional Publications 3, 1985.

Jeffreys, D., and A. Tavares. "The Historic Landscape of Early Dynastic Memphis." *MDAIK* 50 (1994): 154.

Johannes, Bishop of Nikiou. *The Chronicle of John, Bishop of Nikiu, translated from Zotenberg's Ethiopic Text by R.H. Charles, ed*. London: Published for the Text and Translation Society by William & Norgate, 1916.

———. *Chronique de Jean, Éveque de Nikiou. Text Etheopien publie et traduit par H. Zotenberg*. Paris: Imprimerie Nationale, 1883.

Johnson, S. *Late Roman Fortifications*. London: B.T. Batsford, 1983.

Jomard, E.F., ed. *Description de l'Égypte, ou receuil des observations et des recherches qui ont été faites en Égypte pendant l'expédition de l'armée française*. Paris: Imprimerie de C.L.F. Panckoucke, 1820–30.

Jones, M. "Archaeological Discoveries in Doqqi and the Course of the Nile at Cairo during the Roman Period." *MDAIK* 53 (1997): 101–12.

———. "The Church of St. Antony." In Bolman, *Monastic Visions*, 21–30.

———. "The Conservation and Management of the Coptic Christian Cultural Heritage in Egypt." In *British-Egyptian Relations from Suez to the Present Day*, edited by N. Brehony and A. El-Desouky, 234–46. London: SOAS Middle East Issues, 2008.

———. "A New Old Kingdom Settlement Near Ausim: Report of the Archaeological Discoveries Made in the Barakat Drain Improvements Scheme." *MDAIK* (1995): 85–98.

———. "A Roman Station at Abu Rawash" *MDAIK* 52 (1996): 251–62.

Josephus. *Jewish Antiquities, Books I–IV*. Translated by H. St. John Thackeray. Cambridge MA: Loeb, 1967.

Jullien, M. *L'Égypte, souvenirs bibliques et chrétiens*. Lille: Société Saint-Augustin, 1889.

———. "Une visite au Vieux Caire, souvenirs de la Sainte Famille." *Les missions catholiques* 19:536–38, 544–46, 557–60, 570–72, 584–86.

Karelin, D. "Imaging of the Late Roman Castrum: Hypothetical Computer Reconstruction of Nag el-Hagar Fortress in Egypt." *Architecture And Modern Information Technologies* 2, no. 15 (2011). http://www.marhi.ru/AMIT/2011/2kvart11/karelin/abstract.php

Karim, C.F. "The Mosque of Ulmas al-Hajib." In Behrens-Abouseif, *Cairo Heritage*, 123–47.

Keay, S. "Portus and the Alexandrian Grain Trade Revisited." In *XVII Conference of the Associazione Internazionale di Archeologia Classica* (Rome 2008), edited by L. Fentress et al., 11–22. *Bolletino di Archeologia* online 1 (2010). [In special issue: B/B7/3].

———, ed. *Rome, Portus and the Mediterranean: Archaeological Monographs of the British School at Rome 21*. London: British School at Rome, 2012.

Kemp, B.J. *Ancient Egypt: Anatomy of a Civilization*. London: Routledge, 1989.

———. "The Palace of Apries at Memphis." *MDAIK* 33 (1977): 101–108.

Kemp, W.G. "Babloon." *Egyptian Illustration, a Miscellaneous Record of Local History, Etc* no. 5, 1 (May 1915).

Kennedy, H. *The Great Arab Conquests: How the Spread of Islam Changed the World We Live In*. London: Phoenix, 2008.

Kent, R.G. *Old Persian: Grammar, Texts, Lexicon*. New Haven: American Oriental Society, 1950.

al-Kindi. *The Governors and Judges of Egypt*. Edited by R. Guest. Leiden: E.J. Brill, 1912.

Krautheimer, R. *Three Christian Capitals: Topography and Politics*. Berkeley: University of California Press, 1983.

al-Kretli, S., R.G. Gayer-Anderson, A. Abdu, and N. Warner. *Legends of the House of the Cretan Woman*. Cairo and New York: AUCP, 2001

Krijgsman, W., F.J. Hilgen, and I. Raffi, et al. "Chronology, causes and progression of the Messinian salinity crisis." *Nature* 400 (12 August 1999): 652–55.

Kubiak, W. "The Burning of Misr al-Fustat in 1168. A Reconsideration of Historical Evidence." *Africana Bulletin* 25 (1976): 51–64.

———. *Al-Fustat, Its Foundation and Early Urban Development*. Cairo and New York: AUCP, 1987.

———. "The Nile in the Urban Region of Cairo." *Africana Bulletin* 46 (1998): 23–40.

Kubiak, W., and G. Scanlon. "Fusṭāṭ Expedition: Preliminary Report, 1971: Part II." *JARCE* 17 (1980): 77–96.

———. "Fustat: Re-dating Bahgat's Houses and the Aqueduct." *AARP* December 1973:138–48.

Kuhrt, A. *The Ancient Near East. c|. 3000–330 BC II*. London and New York: Routledge, 1995.

Lactantius. *De Mortibus Persecutorum*. Edited and translated by J.L. Creed. Oxford: Clarendon Press, 1984.

Lambert, P., ed. *Fortifications and the Synagogue: The Fortress of Babylon and the Ben Ezra Synagogue, Cairo*. London: Weidenfeld and Nicholson, 1994.

———. "Towards an Interfaith Centre." In Lambert, *Fortifications and the Synagogue*, 19–37.

Lanciani R. *Ancient Rome in the Light of Recent Discoveries*. 12th print edition. Boston and New York: Houghton, Mifflin and Company, 1888.

Lander, J. *Roman Stone Fortifications: Variation and Change from the First Century A.D. to the Fourth*. British Archaeological Reports International Series 206. Oxford: British Archaeological Reports, 1984.

Lane, E. *Cairo, Fifty Years Ago*. London: J. Murray, 1896.

———. *Description of Egypt*. Cairo and New York: AUCP, 2000.

El-Leithy, T. "Coptic Culture and Conversion in Medieval Cairo, 1293–1524 AD." Unpublished Ph.D. diss., Princeton University, 2005.

Le Quesne, C.H.L. "Legend and Tradition at the Ben Ezra Synagogue." In Lambert, *Fortifications and the Synagogue*, 197–99

———. "The Modern Period." In Lambert, *Fortifications and the Synagogue*, 229–35.

———. "The Synagogue." In Lambert, *Fortifications and the Synagogue*, 79–97.

Lewis, N., and M. Reinhold. *Roman Civilization: Sourcebook 1–The Republic, Sourcebook 2–The Empire*. New York: Harper Torchbooks, 1966.

———. *Roman Civilization: Volume 2, The Roman Empire*. New York: Columbia University Press, 1990.

Lézine, A. "Les salles nobles des palais mamelouks." *AI* 10 (1972): 63–148.

Lilli, M. "Il porto di Ancona in età romana: documentazione archeologica e dati di archivio." *Journal of Ancient Topography* 7 (1997).

Linant de Bellefonds, M.A. *Mémoires sur les principaux travaux d'utilité publiques executés en Égypte depuis la plus haute antiquité jusqu'a nos jours*. Paris: Arthus Bertrand, 1872.

Little, D.P. "Coptic Conversion to Islam Under the Bahri Mamluks, 692–755/1293–1354." *Bulletin of the School of Oriental and African Studies* 39 (1976): 552–69.

Livius: Articles on Ancient History. http://www.livius.org

Lloyd, A. "The Late Period." In *The Oxford History of Ancient Egypt*, edited by I. Shaw, 369–94. Oxford and New York: Oxford University Press, 2003.

———. "Necho and the Red Sea." *JEA* 63 (1973): 142–55.

Loukianoff, E. "La Forteresse Romaine du Vieux Caire." *BIE* 33 (1950–51): 285–94.

Lucas, A. "The Level of the Subsoil Water in Cairo." *Cairo Scientific Journal* 4 (1910): 95–98.

———. "The Level of the Underground Water in Cairo." *Cairo Scientific Journal* 3 (1909): 4–6.

Lutley, K., and J. Bunbury. "The Nile on the Move." *Egyptian Archaeology* 32 (2008): 3–5.

Lyster, W., ed. *The Cave Church of Paul the Hermit at the Monastery of St. Paul, Egypt*. New Haven: Yale University Press/ARCE, 2008.

Mackensen, M. "The Tetrarchic Fort at Nag el-Hagar in the Province of Thebaïs: Preliminary Report (2005–08)." *Journal of Roman Archaeology* 22 (2009): 286–312.

Maclaren, C. "Account of the Ancient Canal from the Nile to the Red Sea." *Edinburgh Philosophical Journal* 13 (1825): 274–91.

Al-Maqrizi. *Description Topographique det Historique de l'Égypte*. Translated by U. Bouriant. "Mémoires de la Mission archéologique française en Égypte 17, 1900" pts i–ii; and P. Casanova, "Mémoires du Institut français d'archéologie orientale" pts. iii–iv. Paris, 1906–20.

Maxfield, V.A., and D.P.S. Peacock. *Survey and Excavations at Mons Claudianus*, vol. 2. *Excavations*. Cairo: BIFAO, 2001.

McCann, A. *The Roman Port and Fishery of Cosa*. Rome: American Academy in Rome, 2002.

Meiggs, R. *Roman Ostia*. 2nd edition. Oxford, UK: Clarendon Press, 1973.

Meinardus, O. *Christian Egypt, Ancient and Modern*. Cairo: Cahiers d'histoire égyptienne, 1965.

———. "The Mediaeval Wall-paintings in the Coptic Churches of Old Cairo." *BSAC* 20 (1971): 119–42.

Meinecke-Berg, V. "Eine Stadtansicht des mamlukischen Kairo aus dem 16. Jahrhundert." *MDAIK* 32 (1976): 113–32.

Meri, J.W., and J.L. Bacharach. *Medieval Islamic Civilization: An Encyclopedia*. New York: Routledge, 2005.

al-Messiri Nadim, N. "The Concept of the Hāra: A Historical and Sociological Study of al-Sukkariyya." *AI* 15 (1979): 313–47.

Michailidis, E. *ΕΙΚΟΝΟΓΡΑΦΗ ΜΕΝΟΝ ΑΕΥΚΨΜΑ*. Alexandria, 1959.

———. "ΜΟΝΗ ΤΟΥ ΑΓΙΟΥ ΓΕΩΡΓΙΟΥ ΕΝ ΠΑΛΑΙΩ ΚΑΙΡΩ." *ΕΚΚΛΗΣΙΑΣΤΙΚΟΣ ΦΑΡΟΣ (1908–1934)*. Alexandria, 1935.

Middleton, J.H. "The Copts of Egypt and Their Churches." *The Academy*, Sept. 30, 1882—No. 543; Oct. 7, 1882—No. 544; Oct. 18, 1882—No. 545; Oct. 28, 1882—No. 547.

Miquel, A. "L'Egypte vue par un géographe arabe du iv/x siecle." *AI* 11 (1972): 109–39.

Monneret de Villard, U. "Ricerche sulla Topografia di Qasr esh-Sham." *BSRGE* 12 (February 1924): 205–32 and 13 (May 1924): 73–94.

———. "Sul Castrum Romano di Babilonia d'Egitto." *Aegyptus* 5 (1924): 174.

Mortensen B. "Change in the Settlement Pattern and Population in the Beginning of the Historical Period." *Ägypten und Levante* 2 (1991): 11–37.

Mosseri, Jack. "A New Hoard of Jewish Manuscripts." *The Jewish Review* 4 (1913): 39.

———. " Le Synagogues of Egypt: Past and Present." *The Jewish Review* 5 (1914): 31–44.

Al-Muqaddasi. *The Best Divisions for Knowledge of the Regions*. Translated by B.A. Collins. Reading, UK: Ithaca Press, 2001.

Mustafa, M., and H. Jaritz. "A Roman Fortress at Nag' el-Hagar: First Preliminary Report." *ASAE* 70 (1984–85): 21–32.

Nautin, P. "La conversion du temple de Philae en église chrétienne." *Cahiers Archéologiques* 17 (1967): 1–43.

Naville, E. *The Store-city of Pithom and the Route of the Exodus*. London: Trübner & Co., 1903.

O'Kane, B. "Domestic and Religious Architecture in Cairo: Mutual Influences." In Behrens-Abouseif, *Cairo Heritage*, 149–82.

Oleson J., and A. Raban. *The Harbours of Caesarea Maritima: Results of the Caesarea Ancient Excavation Project, 1980–1985*. Oxford UK: B.A.R., 1989.

Paice, P. "The Punt Relief, the Pithom Stele, and the Periplus of the Erythraean Sea." In *Contacts between Cultures West Asia and North Africa*, vol. 1, edited by A. Harrak, 227–35. Lewiston, NY: Edwin Mellen Press, 1992.

Parker, G.R. *The Making of Roman India*. Cambridge, NY: Cambridge University Press, 2008.

Parker, T. "Limes Arabicus Project 1980–85." *British Archaeological Reports* Int. Ser. 340 (1987).

Patricolo, A., and U. Monneret de Villard. *La Chiesa di Santa Barbara al Vecchio Cairo*. Florence: Fratelli Alinari, 1922.

Peacock, D.P.S., and V.A. Maxfield. *Survey and Excavation at Mons Claudianus,* vol. 1 *Topography and Quarries*. Cairo: IFAO, 1997.

Perring, D. "The Archaeology of Beirut: A Report on Work in the *Insula* of the House of the Fountains." *Antiquaries Journal* 83 (2003): 196.

Petrie, W.M. Flinders. "The Palace of Apries (Memphis II)." *BSAE* 17 (1909). London: School of Archaeology in Egypt, University College and Bernard Quaritch.

Pinch, G. *Votive Offerings to Hathor*. Oxford: Griffiths Institute, 1993.

Pliny the Younger. *Natural History*. 10 vols. Translated by H. Rackham, W.H.S Jones, and D.E. Eichholz. Cambridge, MA: LCL, 1938–62.

———. *Panegyric* 51:2–5. In R.A.B. Mynors, *XII Panegyrici Latini*. Oxford: Clarendon Press, 1964.

Plutarch. *Plutarch's Lives of Caesar, Brutus and Antony*. Edited by M. Brier. New York: Macmillan Company, 1909.

Pococke, R. *A Description of the East and Some Other Countries*. London: Printed for the author, 1743–45.

Polybius. *The Histories*, vol. 3. Translated by W.R. Paton. Cambridge, MA: LCL/Harvard University Press, 1923.

Popper, W. *The Cairo Nilometer: Studies in Ibn Taghri Birdi's Chronicles of Egypt, I*. Berkley and Los Angeles: University of California Press, 1951.

Porter, B., and R. Moss. *Topographical Bibliography of Ancient Egyptian Hieroglyphic Texts, Reliefs and Paintings IV, Lower and Middle Egypt*. Oxford UK: Clarendon Press, 1934.

Posener, G. " Le Canal du Nil à la Mer Rouge avant les Ptolémées." *CdÉ* 13, nos. 25–26 (1938): 258–73.

Potter, D.S. *The Roman Empire at Bay: AD 180–395*. New York: Routledge, 2005.

Power, T.C. *The Red Sea from Byzantium to the Caliphate AD 500–1000*. Cairo: AUCP, 2012.

Power, T.C., and P. D. Sheehan. "Babylon–Fustat.' *Encyclopedia of Ancient History*. Wiley-Blackwell. http://www.encyclopediaanciethistory.com/

Ptolemy, C. *Geography of Claudius Ptolemy*. Translated and edited by Edward Luther Stevenson. New York: New York Public Library, 1932.

Pyke, G. "The Pre-Diocletianic Pottery from the ARCE/EAP Contract 102 Old Cairo Groundwater Lowering Project." Unpublished report, ARCE, Cairo, 2002.

Rabbat, N. "Al-Maqrizi's Khitat, an Egyptian *lieu de memoire*." In Behrens-Abouseif, *Cairo Heritage*, 17–30.

Raue, D. *Heliopolis und das Haus des Re: Eine Prosopographie und ein Toponym im Neuen Reich*. Abhandlungen des Deutschen Archäologischen Instituts Kairo, Ägytpologische Reihe Band 16. Berlin: Achet-Verlag, 1999.

Ravaisse, P. *Essai sur la topographie du Caire d'après Maqrizi*. Mémoires publiés par les membres de la Mission archéologique française au Caire 1 no. 3; 3 no. 4. Paris: n.p., 1887–90.

Redmount, C. "On an Egyptian/Asiatic Frontier: An Archaeological History of the Wadi Tumilat." Unpublished PhD diss., University of Chicago, 1989.

———. "The Wadi Tumilat and the 'Canal of the Pharaohs.'" *JNES* 54, no. 2 (April 1995): 127–35.

Reggiori, F. "La fortezza romana al Vecchio Cairo." *L'illustrazione italiana* 52, no. 2 (1925): 32–36.

Reif, S.C. *A Jewish Archive from Old Cairo*. Richmond, Surrey: Curzon, 2000.

Rodenbeck, M. *Cairo. The City Victorious*. Cairo: AUCP, 1999.

Roux, G. *Ancient Iraq*. London: Penguin, 1992.

El-Saghir, M., J-C. Golvin, M. Reddé, E. Hegazy, and G. Wagner. *Le Camp romain de Louqsor*. Cairo: IFAO, 1986.

Said, R. The *Geological Evolution of the River Nile*. New York: Springer-Verlag, 1981.

———. *The River Nile: Geology, Hydrology and Utilization*. Oxford: Pergamon Press, 1993.

———. "Subsurface Geology of Cairo Area." *Memoires de l'Institut d'Egypte* 60. Cairo: Egyptian Company for Printing and Publishing, 1975.

———, ed. *The Geology of Egypt*. Rotterdam: Balkema, 1990.

Salmon, G. *Études sur la topographie du Caire: La Kal'at al-kabch et la Birkat al-fil*. MIFAO 7. Cairo: IFAO, 1902.

Sanders, P. *Ritual, Politics, and the City in Fatimid Cairo*. SUNY Series in Medieval Middle East History. Albany: SUNY Press, 1994.

Al-Sannusi, A., and M. Jones. "A Site of the Maadi Culture near the Giza Pyramids." *MDAIK* 53 (1997): 241–53.

Saradi-Mendelovici, H. "Christian Attitudes toward Pagan Monuments in Late Antiquity and Their Legacy in Later Byzantine Centuries." *Dumbarton Oaks Papers* 44 (1990): 47–61.

Sasel, J. "Trajan's Canal at the Iron Gate." *JRS* (1973): 80–85.

Sawirus ibn al-Muqaffa. *History of the Patriarchs of the Coptic Church of Alexandria*. Translated by Basil Evetts. Paris: Firmin-Didot, 1904.

Sawyer, E.H. "Babylon of Egypt." *Antiquity* 4 (1930): 483–86.

Sayed, A.M.A.H. "On the Non-existence of the Nile–Red Sea Canal (so called Canal of Sesostris) during the Pharaonic Times." In *The Red Sea in Antiquity. A Collection of Papers Published in the Arabic and European Periodicals*, edited by A.M.A.H. Sayed, 127–47. Alexandria: Dar al-Ma'rifa al-Gami'iya, 1993.

Sayyid, A.F. "La Capitale de l'Égypte jusqu'à l'Époque Fatimide: al Qahira et al-Fustat. Essai de reconstruction topographique." Beiruter Texte und Studien 48. Beirut: In Kommission bei Franz Steiner Verlag Stuttgart, 1998.

Scaife, C.H.O. "The Origins of Some Pantheon Columns" *JRS* 43 (1953): 37 and pl. V.

Scanlon, G.T. "Ancillary Dating Materials from Fustat." *Ars Orientalis* 7 (1968): 1–17.

———. "Fustat: Archaeological Reconsiderations." In *Colloque international sur l'histoire du Caire, 27 mars–5 avril 1969*, 415–28. Cairo: Ministry of Culture of the Arab Republic of Egypt, 1972.

———. "Fusṭāṭ Expedition: Preliminary Report 1965: Part I." *JARCE* 5 (1966): 83–112.

———. "Fusṭāṭ Expedition: Preliminary Report 1965: Part II." *JARCE* 6 (1967): 65–86, I–X.

———. "Fusṭāṭ Expedition: Preliminary Report 1968: Part I." *JARCE* 11 (1974): 81–91.

———. "Fusṭāṭ Expedition: Preliminary Report 1968. Part II." *JARCE* 13 (1976): 69–89.

———. "Fusṭāṭ Expedition: Preliminary Report, 1972 Part I." *JARCE* 18 (1981): 57–84.

———. "Fusṭāṭ Expedition: Preliminary Report, 1972 Part II." *JARCE* 19 (1982): 119–29.

———. "Fusṭāṭ Expedition: Preliminary Report, 1978." *JARCE* 21 (1984): 1–38.

———. "The Pits of Fusṭāṭ: Problems of Chronology." *JEA* 60 (1974): 60–78.

———. "Preliminary Report: Excavations at Fustat, 1964." *JARCE* 4 (1965): 6–30.

Scheil, V. "Inscriptions de Darius a Suez." *Revue d'Assyriologie* 27 (1930): 93–97.

Schwartz J. *Qasr-Qarun/Dionysias, 1950*. Cairo: IFAO, 1969.

Sestini, G. "Nile Delta: A Review of Depositional Environments and Geological History." *Geological Society of London, Special Publications* 41, no. 1 (1989): 99–127.

Seton-Williams, V., and P. Stocks. *Blue Guide: Egypt*. 2nd edition. London: A. & C. Black, 1988.

Sheehan, P. "Accessing the Archaeology of Old Cairo." *Bulletin of the American Research Center in Egypt* 200 (Spring 2012): 34–39.

———. "Archaeological Investigations around the Ben Ezra Synagogue, Old Cairo, 2001 & 2005." Unpublished report, ARCE, Cairo, May 2007.

———. "Archaeological Investigations around the Church of Abu Sayfayn, Old Cairo, 2000–2003." Unpublished report, ARCE, Cairo, May 2007.

———. "Archaeological Investigations at Abu Serga Church, Old Cairo, 2003–2004 & 2005." Unpublished report, ARCE, Cairo, June 2006.

———. "Archaeological Investigations in the Area of the Wedding Hall of the Coptic Church of St. George, Old Cairo, 2002." Unpublished report, ARCE, Cairo, November 2006.

———. "Conservation of the BES *mastaba*: An Archaeological Watching Brief for The Canadian Centre for Architecture." Unpublished report, August 1999, Montreal.

———. "New Archaeological Evidence for the Architectural Development of the Cave Church." In Lyster, *Cave Church of Paul the Hermit*, 109–125.

———. "The New Metropolis: Cultural Transitions in a Shared Landscape." In *One God: Abraham's Legacy on the Nile*, edited by C. Fluck and E. O'Connell. London: British Museum Press, in press.

———. "Old Cairo, The Two Towers: Archaeological Investigations in 'the Roman Tower' in the Garden of the Coptic Museum and the Round Tower beneath the Holy Orthodox Church of St. George, Old Cairo, 2001–2002." Unpublished report, ARCE, Cairo, January 2007.

———. "The Port of Babylon in Egypt." In *Navigated Spaces, Connected Places. Proceedings of Red Sea Project V held at the University of Exeter, 16–19 September 2010*, edited by D.A. Agius, J.P. Cooper, A. Trakadas, and C. Zazzaro. Oxford: Archaeopress, 2012.

———. "The Roman Fortress." In Lambert, *Fortifications and the Synagogue*, 49–63.

———. "The Roman Fortress of Babylon in Old Cairo." In *Archaeological Research in Roman Egypt: The Proceedings of the Seventeenth Classical Colloquium of the Department of Greek and Roman Antiquities, British Museum*, edited by D. Bailey. Ann Arbor, MI: Journal of Roman Archaeology, 1999.

———. "Sailing to Babylon." *Egyptian Archaeology* 24 (2009): 3–6.

———. "Underwater Archaeology in Old Cairo." In *Preserving Egypt's Cultural Heritage: The Conservation Work of the American Research Center in Egypt 1995–2005*, edited by R. Danforth, 101–110. Cairo: ARCE, 2010.

Sidebotham, S. "Ports of the Red Sea and the Arabia–India Trade. In *Rome and India: The Ancient Sea Trade*, edited by V. Begley and R.V. De Puma, 12–38. Madison: University of Wisconsin Press, 1991.

———. "Preliminary Report on the 1990–1991 Seasons of Fieldwork at 'Abu Sha'ar (Red Sea Coast)." *JARCE* 31 (1994): 159–68.

———. *Roman Economic Policy in the Erythra Thalassa, 30 BC–AD 217*. Mnemosyne, Supplements 91. Leiden: Brill 1986.

Sijpesteijn, P.J. "Der ΠΟΤΑΜΟΣ ΤΡΑΙΑΝΟΣ." *Aegyptus* 43 (1963): 70–83.

———. "Trajan and Egypt." *Papyrologica Lugduno-Batava Papyri Selectae* 13 (1965): 106–13.

Sijpesteijn, P.M. "Landholding Patterns in Early Islamic Egypt." *Journal of Agrarian Change* 9, no. 1 (January 2009): 120–33.

Simaika Pasha, M. *A Brief Guide to the Coptic Museum and to the Principal Ancient Coptic Churches of Cairo*. Cairo: Government Press of Egypt (Bulaq), 1938.

Sims, D. *Understanding Cairo: The Logic of a City Out of Control*. Cairo: AUCP, 2010.

Smith, C.R. *Collectanea Antiqua, Etchings and Notices of Ancient Remains, illustrative of the Habits, Customs and History of Past Ages VI*. London: Printed for subscribers only and not published, 1868.

Solomonides, A. *The Holy Monastery of St. George in Old Cairo* (in Greek), 3 vols. 1945.

Somers Clarke. *Proceedings of the Society of Antiquaries of Scotland* 16 (1895–97): 58–68.

Southern, P. *The Roman Empire from Severus to Constantine*. New York: Routledge, 2001.

Spalinger, A. "The Reign of King Chabbash: an Interpretation." *Zeitschrift für Ägyptische Sprache und Altertumskunde* 105 (1978): 142–54.

Speidel, M.P. "Augustus' Deployment of the Legions in Egypt." *CdE* 57 (1982): 120–24.

Speiser, P. "Die Geschichte der Erhaltung arabischer Baudenkmäler in Ägypten." ADAIK Islamische Reihe 8. Heidelberg: Heidelberger Orientverlag, 2001

Spence, C., ed. *Archaeological Site Manual*. 3rd edition. London: Department of Urban Archaeology, Museum of London, 1994.

Stambaugh, J.E. *The Ancient Roman City*. Baltimore: Johns Hopkins University Press, 1988.

Stanley, J.-D., M.D. Krom, R.A. Cliff, and J.C. Woodward. "Nile Flow Failure at the End of the Old Kingdom, Egypt: Strontium Isotopic and Petrologic Evidence." *Geoarchaeology* 18, no. 3 (2003): 395–402.

Stewart, J. "The Ben Ezra Synagogue and the Ethics of Restoration and Conservation." In Lambert, *Fortifications and the Synagogue*, 101–11.

Strabo. *The Geography of Strabo with an English Translation by Horace Leonard Jones, Based in Part Upon the Unfinished Version of J. R. Sitlington*. Loeb Classical Library Series. London: W. Heinemann, 1931.

Sucato, A. "Church of Saint Sergius (Abu Serga) in Old Cairo: Restoration of Wall Paintings in the Apse of the Southern Sanctuary (*Haikal*)." Unpublished final report, ARCE, Cairo, 2005.

Sutherland, C.H.V., and R.A.G. Carson. *The Roman Imperial Coinage (RIC) Vol VI, From Diocletian's Reform AD 294 to the Death of Maximinus AD 313*. London: Spink and Son Ltd., 1967.

Swanson, M.N. *The Coptic Papacy in Islamic Egypt 641–1517*. Vol. 2 of *The Popes of Egypt: A History of the Coptic Church and Its Patriarchs from Saint Mark to Pope Shenouda III*, edited by S.J Davis and G. Gabra. Cairo: AUCP, 2010.

———. "The Monastery of St. Paul in Historical Context." In Lyster, *Cave Church of Paul the Hermit*, 43–59.

Tacitus. *Annals*, bk 3 sct 65. Translated by A.J. Church and W.J. Brodribb. London: Macmillan, 1864–77. http://www.sacred-texts.com/cla/tac/

Thomas, T. "The Arts of Christian Communities in the Medieval Near East." In *Byzantium, Faith and Power (1261–1557)*, edited by H.C. Evans, 415–26. New York: Metropolitan Museum of Art; New Haven: Yale University Press, 2004.

Tomber, R. *Indo-Roman Trade: From Pots to Pepper*. London: Duckworth, 2008.

Toussoun, O. *Memoire sur les anciennes branches du Nil*. Cairo: IFAO, 1923.

Toy, S. "Babylon of Egypt." *Journal of the British Archaeological Association*, 3rd ser., I: 52 (1937).

Trombley, F.R. "'Amr b. al-'As's Refurbishment of Trajan's Canal: Red Sea Contacts in the Aphrodito and Apollōnas Anō Papyri." In *Connected Hinterlands: Proceedings of Red Sea Project IV, Held at the Centre for Maritime Archaeology, University of Southampton, 25th–26th September 2008*, edited by L.K. Blue, J.P. Cooper, R. Thomas, and J.Whitewright, 99–109. Society for Arabian Studies Monographs 8, British Archaeological Reports, S2052. Oxford: Archaeopress, 2009.

Tuplin, C. "Darius' Suez Canal and Persian Imperialism." In *Achaemenid History VI Asia Minor and Egypt: Old Cultures in a New Empire. Proceedings of the Groningen 1988 Achaemenid History Workshop*, edited by H. Sancisi-Weerdenburg and A. Kuhrt, 237–83. Leiden: Nederlands Instituut voor Het Nabije Oosten, 1991.

Tvedt, T. *The Nile: An Annotated Bibliography*. London: I.B.Tauris, 2004.

Urloiu, R. "Again on Legio II *Traiana Fortis*." N.d. https://www.academia.edu/5063209/AGAIN_ON_LEGIO_II_TRAIANA_FORTIS

———. "Legio II Traiana Fortis and Judaea under Hadrian's reign." *Cogito* 2, no. 4 (December 2010).

Van Berchem, D. *L'armée de Dioclétien et la réforme constantinienne*. Paris: Imprimerie Nationale et P. Geuthner, 1952.

Van Den Berg-Onstwedder, G. "Diocletian in the Coptic tradition." *Bulletin de la Societe d'archeologie copte* 29 (1990): 87–122.

———. "L'occupation militaire de la haute Égypte sous Dioclétien." In *Studien zu den Militärgrenzen Roms. Vorträge des 6. Internationalen Limeskongresses in Süddeutschland*, 123–27. Cologne and Graz: Böhlau Verlag, 1967.

Vandersleyen, C., "Title Missing." *Chronique d'Égypte* 33 (1958): 113–34.

Vansleb, J.-M. *Nouvelle Relation en forme de journal, d'un voyage fait en Égypte par le P. Vansleb, R.D. en 1672 & 1673*. Paris: Chez E. Michallet, 1677.

von Kienlin, A. "Der Palast im spätrömischen Kastell von Nag el-Hagar." In *Bericht über die 44. Tagung für Ausgrabungswissenschaft und Bauforschung vom 24. bis 28. Mai 2006 in Wroclaw/Breslau*. Bonn: Rudolf Habelt, 2008.

Warner, N. *The Monuments of Historic Cairo: A Map and Descriptive Catalogue*. Cairo and New York: AUCP/ARCE, 2005.

———. *The True Description of Cairo, A Sixteenth-Century Venetian View*. 3 vols. Oxford, UK: Arcadian Library in association with Oxford University Press, 2006.

Webster, G. *From Fortress into City: The Consolidation of Roman Britain in the First Century*. London: Batsford, 1988.

Wilkes, J.J. *Diocletian's Palace, Split: Residence of a Retired Roman Emperor*. Occasional Publications 2. Sheffield: Dept. of Ancient History and Classical Archaeology University of Sheffield, 1986.

Wilkinson, T. "A Re-examination of the Early Dynastic Necropolis at Helwan." *MDAIK* 52 (1996): 337–54.

Williams, C. "The Cult of 'Alid Saints in the Fatimid Monuments of Cairo, Part II: The Mausolea." *Muqarnas* 3 (1986): 40–60.

Williams, S. *Diocletian and the Roman Recovery*. London: B.T. Batsford, 1985.

Wikipedia, s.v. "Trajan's Bridge." http://en.wikipedia.org/wiki/Trajan%27s_Bridge

Wood, W. "The Archaic Stone Tombs at Helwan." *JEA* 73 (1987): 59–70.

Woods, D. "The Emperor Julian and the Passion of Sergius and Bacchus." *Journal of Early Christian Studies* 5 (1997): 335–67.

Worman, E.J. "Notes on the Jews in Fustāt from Cambridge Genizah Documents." *Jewish Quarterly Review* 18, no. 1 (October 1905): 1–39.

Young, G.K. *Rome's Eastern Trade International Commerce and Imperial Policy, 31 BC–AD 305*. London: Routledge, 2001.

Yoyotte, J. "Le 'Groupe Ankh-Psametik.' La decadence d'Heliopolis et la montée de Babylone." *BIFAO* (1954): 111–15.

Zosimus. *Historia Nova*. Translated by F. Paschoud Zozime. Histoire Nouvelle II xxxii–xxxv. Paris, 1971.

Web-only resources:

On John, bishop of Nikiu: http://www.tertullian.org/fathers/nikiu2_chronicle.htm#98
On the coinage of the Roman Tetrarchs: http://tetrarchy.com/coppermine/thumbnails.php?album=20
On the history of the Legio XIII Gemina: http://www.livius.org/le-lh/legio/xiii_gemina.html
On Roman military and fortification terms: http://www.Roman-Britain.org

Glossary

aghani (Arabic; 'singers' galleries') Mashrabiya-screened galleries overlooking the main reception hall of a dwelling.

archon (Arabic, arkhun, pl. arakhina, via Greek, archon, 'a high magistrate') Title of respect given to influential Coptic notables in Muslim Egypt.

Arianism The doctrines of Arius, denying that Jesus was of the same substance as God and holding instead that he was only the highest of created beings, viewed as heretical by most Christian churches.

atfa (Arabic) Alley or small lane.

bey (Turkish; 'lord') In the Ottoman administrative and military system, a rank between 'pasha' and 'effendi.' In Ottoman Egypt, one of a group of grandees that governed the country's major subprovinces or held important positions.

bima/bema Raised platform or pulpit in a synagogue, from the Greek bema 'step.'

birka (Arabic) Lake.

burg (Arabic) Tower of a fortress or city walls. The Burgi Mamluks were so called because they were based in the Cairo citadel in contrast to the earlier Bahri Mamluks who had been based on the island of Roda (from the Arabic bahr 'river').*

cardo decumanus (Latin) Dorsal axis of a Roman fort. The longer of the two principal axes on which a fort was laid out, crossed at right angles in the center of the camp by the cardo maximus, and providing the line of both the via praetoria at the front and the via decumana at the rear of the camp.

cardo maximus (Latin) Lateral axis of a Roman fort. The shorter of the two principal axes of a Roman fort which provided the line of the via principalis.

Council of Chalcedon The fourth of the first seven Ecumenical Councils. The Council adopted the position of dyophysitism which stated that Christ is one person in two natures although emphasizing that these are "without separation." The council resulted in a major schism between the Western and Eastern Orthodox churches and the monophysite/miaphysite Oriental Orthodox churches that refused to accept this doctrine.

dakka (Arabic) A compacted surface.

darabzin (Arabized Persian) Balustrade.

dayr (Arabic) Monastery.

Dodecaschene The southernmost frontier border area of Egypt during the Roman occupation.

durqa'a (Arabic) The central, sometimes covered, area between two or more iwans.

gebel/jebel (Arabic) Mountain.

geniza Storeroom or depository of a synagogue. The Cairo Geniza refers to the hoard of medieval documents found in the Ben Ezra Synagogue in Old Cairo.

hara (Arabic) A neighborhood or quarter.

haykal (Arabic) Sanctuary in a Coptic church.

homra (Arabic) A compacted broken-brick layer often used in the foundations of buildings.

iqta' (Arabic) Land granted to a military official for a limited period of time in lieu of a regular salary. Established in the ninth century as a grant of appropriation to a Muslim officer entitling him to collect the kharāj or property tax from a non-Muslim landowner. In Ayyubid and Mamluk Egypt the iqta', primarily agricultural land, was leased for a limited time for a contracted sum of money.

istibdal (Arabic; 'exchange') The process whereby properties originally forming part of the inalienable endowment of a religious building could be sold and redeveloped if it could be proved that they were neglected and not generating adequate income.

iwan (Arabic) Vaulted open hall with a rectangular or arched façade.*

khalig (Arabic) Canal.

khurus (Greek; 'choir') A transitional room in Coptic churches, located between the nave and sanctuary (haykal), which is reserved for priests.

kufi/kufic The oldest calligraphic form of the Arabic script, originating from Kufa in Iraq, utilizing straight lines and angles and frequently elongated verticals and horizontals. This was the script in use at the time of the emergence of Islam.

latera praetorii (Latin) 'Beside the praetorium.' This was the central range of the camp, separated from the praetentura at the front of the fort by the via principalis. The main buildings of the camp were built in the latera praetorii; the principia or headquarters building was almost always located at the physical center of the fort in this area, surrounded to the rear and sides by the praetorium (commanding officer's house) and other administrative and storage buildings.

made ground Made, or artificial, ground that may consist of various kinds of materials, such as refuse earth and other materials derived from excavations or from manufacturing activities. A treatise by the Colliery Engineer Company sums it up in saying, "It should not be built on, if the structure is of importance, without investigating the nature of the subsoil, though for minor edifices a suitable foundation may often be obtained on good made ground."

majlis (Arabic) A reception hall generally overlooking a courtyard. In the Mamluk period it meant a room that was closed to differentiate it from an iwan.*

malqaf (Arabic) Windcatcher located to receive the cool prevailing north wind and to create air circulation in a building.

Mamluk (Arabic; 'possessed') Military slave, ultimately manumitted and often entrusted with great authority.

manwar (Arabic) Light shaft.

maqsura (Arabic) An enclosed section of a mosque originally set aside for the sultan during communal prayer.

mashhad (Arabic) Shrine or sanctuary.*

mashrabiya (Arabic) Projecting window enclosed with complex wooden screens to provide privacy and ventilation, most commonly found on the street side of buildings.

mastaba	Arabic for bench, often used to describe oblong tombs.		Incarnate, of two essences, divine and human.
maydan	(Arabic) Originally used to denote a polo ground, but now refers to a city square or open space.*	**pasha**	(Turkish) The highest non-royal military-administrative rank in the Ottoman empire granted to provincial governors and other important officials.
mazaar	(Arabic) Literally a 'visiting place' but also used in reference to a holy site or a mausoleum or burial place.*	**praetentura**	(Latin; 'forward extent') This was the front part of the camp, between the via principalis and the porta praetoria, and bisected by the via praetoria. This area was generally filled with the barrack-blocks of the garrison, the first cohort of a legion being always housed here.
miaphysitism	Christological position that in the one person of Jesus Christ, Divinity and Humanity are united in one "nature" (physis). Coptic and Syrian Christians profess this doctrine.		
minbar	(Arabic) A pulpit-like structure in a mosque placed to the right of the mihrab from where the imam usually gives the sermon. A minbar usually consists of a staircase with a landing or seat at the top, so the imam can be seen and heard by the congregation.	**praetorium**	(Latin) Commander's house. In permanent Roman camps the praetorium of the unit commander was displaced from the center of the camp and located in the latera praetorii, adjacent to the administrative offices of the garrison which were retained at the center of the fort in the principia.
monophysitism	From the Greek monos meaning 'one, alone' and physis meaning 'nature.' Position that Christ has only one nature (divine).	**principia**	(Latin) Headquarters building. The administrative and religious center of the later Roman forts, situated in the center of the latera praetorii. The building was visible as soon as one entered the main gate of the fort.
mu'allim	(Arabic; 'teacher' or 'elder') Polite title often bestowed on leading Christians and Jews in Muslim Egypt.		
muqarnas	(Arabic) A type of corbel used as a decorative device in traditional Islamic and Persian architecture from the mid-tenth century; often applied to domes, pendentives, and the undersides of vaults.*	**qa'a**	(Arabic) A hall usually composed of two (or more) elevated iwans and a central durqa'a.
		qasaba	(Arabic) Central avenue of a town or citadel. It usually comprises the main axial area.*
musalima	(Arabic) Term used in the medieval period to refer to Christians and Jews who converted to Islam.	**sabil**	(Arabic) Charitably endowed public water fountain.
		tahuna	(Arabic) A mill room.
naos	(Greek; 'temple') In Egypt the term is applied to small boxlike shrines.	**tell**	(Arabic) Mound.
nashki	(Arabic) Rounded, cursive form of Arabic script.	**tetrapylon**	Roman monument with a gate on each of its four sides, usually set at a crossroads.
Nestorianism	The doctrine that Christ exists as two individuals (hypostases), the man Jesus and the divine Son of God, or logos, rather than as one individual (hypostasis), God the Word	**triforia**	(sing. triforium) Screened-in galleries overlooking the main seating area of the church; often referred to as "women's galleries" in Coptic churches until liturgical

changes allowed women into the main area of the church.

via praetoria (Latin; 'the praetorian way') This road branched off at right angles from the center of the via principalis immediately before the entrance to the principia, and bisected the praetentura along the line of the cardo decumanus. The point at which this road pierced the fort's defenses generally marked the main entrance to the camp, named the porta praetoria. The via praetoria was so named because in the legionary marching camp it led from the tent of the legionary commander to the front gateway; the commander of a Roman legion being an ex-praetor in rank.

via principalis (Latin; 'the principal way') This street lay across the cardo maximus, the shorter axis of the camp, and passed in front of the principia in the center of the fort. The via principalis generally continued through the defenses where gateways were maintained, the porta principalis sinistra and porta principalis dextra, to left and right of the principia.

via sagularis (Latin; 'way of the cloak') This road is sometimes called the 'intervallum road' as it lay in the space between the rampart and the buildings in the interior of the fort, the intervallum. The via sagularis thus ran around the entire perimeter of the camp within the rampart, encircling the interior buildings. The etymology of its name seems to derive from the sagulum or small military cloak worn by the soldiers when on guard duty. The road may be so named because it 'encloaks' the interior of the camp in the same manner the sagulum encircles the shoulders, or possibly, because the soldiers were required to wear the sagulum when on patrol in the interior of the camp along this road.

waqf/waqfiya (Arabic) A system by which income generated from allotted plots of land were used to endow the upkeep and functioning of a specially founded religious building or complex. The waqfiya was the "endowment deed" that meticulously described the building(s) and their function, and designated an administrator of the waqf, among other things.

*Definition from the Islamic Art Network Technical Glossary

Roman fortification terms derived from http://www.Roman-Britain.org

Index

Abbasid dynasty/era, 20, 80, 82, 83, 92, 97, 100, 151n15
'Abd al-Aziz (Umayyad), 151n11
'Abd al-Aziz ibn Marwan, 89
Abu al-Makarim, 92
Abu Ghurab, 30
Abu Mina monastery, *See* Monastery/monasteries
Abu Mina, shrine of, 88
Abu Qir (martyr), 88, 89
Abu Rawash, 28, 30, 51
Abu Sayfayn Monastery, *See* Monastery/monasteries
Abu Serga church, *See* Churches
Abu Sha'r, 56
Abusir, 30
adventus domini paintings, 56, 65, 150n10
Aelius, Aristides, on Roman maritime trade, 40–41
Agathangelos, 136
aghani (singer's gallery), 108
ahl al-dhimma, 88
Ahl al-Raya, 85
Ahmad al-Higazi, 116
Ahmad Ibn Tulun, 39, 80, 153n71
Akkadian Empire, 27
Alexandria, 2, 17, 20, 79, 85
'Ali (caliph), 53, 86
Almaza, 146n49
amal asfal/amal fawq, 79, 80
Amasis II, 31
American Research Center in Egypt (ARCE), 1, 137
Amnis Trajanus (canal), 3, 17, 19, 20, 27, 28, 29, 35, 37, 38, 36, 39, 40–42, 43 (fig. 19), 50–53, 55, 59, 63, 66, 79, 84 (fig. 39), 86, 103, 113, 145n39
    archaeological evidence for, 42, 44–45, 48–51, 83
amphorae, 32
'Amr ibn al-'As, 80
al-Amshati family, 112
Ancona, harbor of, 40
al-Andalus, 112
annona/cura annona, 40
Antinopolis, 146n62
aqueduct(s), 39, 79, 80 (fig. 37), 82, 100

Aphrodito (village), 50
Arab Conquest, 1, 2, 3, 20, 50–51, 75, 79, 82, 112
arakhina (notables), 115
ARCE *See* American Research Center in Egypt (ARCE)
ARCE Archaeological Monitoring Project, 139, 140, 142
ARCE/Egyptian Antiquities Project, 11, 14
architectural *spolia,* 146n62
architectural symbolism, Roman, 65
'Atfat Abu Serga, 87
'Atfat Mari Girgis, 9, 52, 86, 87, 121, 123 (fig. 63)
Aristius Optatus, 56
Aristotle, 36, 37
al-Ashmunayn, basilica at, 88
al-'Askar, 80, 81 (fig. 38), 151n11
Aswan, 56
Aswan High Dam, 12, 27
Athar al-Nabi, 29, 30, 31, 33, 145n46
Atum, 31
Augustus (Caesar), 37, 40, 55
Ausim, 28
Avaris (royal capital), 41
Awlad al-'Assal, 106
awqaf (religious endowments), 141
Aydagmash (amir), 113
'Ayn al-Sira, 31, 151n9, 153n9
'Ayn Shams, 149n109, 149n110
Ayyubid dynasty/era, 2, 82, 105
al-'Aziz bi-llah, 92

Bab al-Bahr (River Gate), 102
Bab al-Barqiya, 30
Bab Zuwayla, 53, 86, 102
Babylon (of Egypt), 1–2, 16, 20, 33, 38, 50, 75, 79, 88
    Arab siege of, 49, 87
    and development of medieval Cairo, 79–82
    between Diocletian and Arab Conquest, 74–75
    name of, 33, 38
    Roman, 39, 56
Badr al-Gamali (vizier), 82, 99
Baghdad, 80, 112

Bahgat Bey, plan by, 81 (fig. 38), 100 (fig. 47)
Bahr al-Libeini (canal), 27, 28
Bahri Mamluks, 19, 97, 100
Bani Wa'il Canal, 31, 145n48
al-Barati house, 48
Barbara (saint), 95, 117
Barquq (Mamluk ruler), 102
Barsbay, 102
Basra, 79
al-Bassatin, 80
Batn al-Baqara
    pottery and lime production in, 153n9
    tombs, 31, 33
Battle of Actium, 37
Battle of the Pyramids, 106 (fig. 51)
Baybars (sultan), 112
Bayn al-Qasrayn, 99
bedrock, 26, 145n18
benben (primeval mound), 30
Ben Ezra Synagogue, 2, 9, 10, 12, 16, 18, 74, 87, 95–96, 98, 113, 121, 122 (fig. 62), 127, 136–37, 147n22, 152n31
    annex building, 141
    community housing by, 137
    groundwater level lowering in, 139
    Holy Ark in, 112
    medieval mastaba in, 112 (fig. 55), 127, 128, 156n22
    visitors' accounts of, 127
    restoration of, 137, 138, 140
    Well of Moses, 87, 138
Berenice, 41
beys, 97, 115
Biggeh (island), 30
Bilbeis, 28
Birkat *See* lakes
bishop, of al-Fustat–Misr, 89
Black Death, 102
Blemmyes, 56
Book of the Dead, 30, 31, 146n66, 146n68
Bourdon, C., plan of canals, Cairo to Suez, 36 (fig. 17)
bridge(s), Roman, 49–50, 70, 99, 103
British Museum, 110, 122
Bubastis, 36
Bulaq, 3, 28, 83, 103, 115
Burg al-Saqya, 103
Burgi sultans/mamluks, 102, 115
Butler, Alfred, 73, 111, 122, 123, 124
    Ancient Coptic Churches of Egypt, 122
    dedication of *Coptic Museum Guide* to, 128
    descent into northern round tower, 118
    plan of Old Cairo, 18 (fig. 13), 116
Buto, 33
Byzantine Period rule, 39, 50, 79, 89

Cairo, 102, 115
    ancient, 23–33, 83
    downtown area of, 152n33
    elite Christian and Jewish communities shift to, 113
    Fatimid, 39, 99
    maps/plans of, 84 (fig. 39), 97, 98 (fig. 45), 105 (fig. 50)
    medieval, 1, 2, 23, 97
    "Roman landscape" of, 51
    topography of, 3, 8–18, 102

Cairo–Helwan Light Railway, 10, 100, 120
Cairo Wastewater Organization (CWO), 139
Cambyses (Persian king), 31
Camp, Dresser and McKee (CDM), 138, 140
Canadian Centre for Architecture, 137, 138, 141
Canal of Trajan *See* Amnis Traianus; and, Sweet Water Canal
Canal of Nasir Muhammad, 103
canal(s), conversion to road(s), 36 (fig. 17)
caravan route(s), 29, 41, 53
castrum (at Luxor), 71
Catholic hospice, 117
cemeteries, 10, 17, 23, 28, 29, 30, 31, 59, 71, 83, 121
    Greek Catholic, 121, 136
    Saba' Banaat tombs, 151n9
ceremonies, related to Nile flooding, 40, 144n7
Chalcedonian (Melkite) church, 89
Chester, Greville, 124, 126, 127
Christian(s)/Christianity, 53, 55, 74, 85, 86, 92, 112
    in administration, 112
    in army, 3, 58
    holy places of Egypt, 115
    persecution/riots against, 16, 55, 58, 74
    a "subject" group, 112
    sumptuary laws imposed on, 112
    tensions between Muslims and, 83
Church of Abu Serga (Church of SS. Sergius and Bacchus), 3, 10, 11, 17, 19, 20, 35, 39, 42, 52, 53, 58, 82, 83, 85, 88, 89, 92, 93, 94, 95, 98, 106, 107 (fig. 52), 180, 113–14, 137, 144n26
    altar of, 131
    axonometric view of, 91 (fig. 41)
    baptistry of, 131
    Butler's plan of, 119 (fig. 59), 120, 131
    clergy of, 128
    and Comité, 130–31
    crosses, 114 (fig. 56, fig. 57)
    crypt/crypt-church of, 12, 17, 20, 40, 42, 49, 66, 89, 92, 93, 94, 107, 108, 111, 114–15, 118 (fig. 58), 119, 130, 132 (fig. 72), 138, 139, 154n46, 154n47
        drainage trenches beneath, 42, 138
        façade of, 53, 112
        groundwater level in, 139
        and Holy Family, 107, 108, 114
        inscribed stone (Ptolemy V period), 138
        paintings in, 128, 156n25
        photographs of, 130, 131 (fig. 71)
        pillars of the apostles, 107
        Trajanic canal walls beneath, 38, 39, 42, 44, 66, 140
        wall paintings in, 106, 107, 131, 142
    cult of Sergius and Bacchus, 89
    disengagement from its surroundings, 131
    roof, structure of, 131 (fig. 71), 138
    travelers' accounts of, 114–15
Church of Mari Mina (Coptic), 39, 40
Church of St. Barbara, 10, 53, 58, 74, 87, 88, 89, 90, 92, 95, 107, 111, 117, 128, 131, 138, 151n54, 154n44
    carved doors of, 132
    dome of, 131–32
    façade of, 133 (figs. 73–74)
    link with Hanging Church, 111
    reception/smoking area, 128
    restoration by the Comité, 95, 131–32
    social club of, 116

tombs, 132
triforia (womens' gallery), 128
Church of St. George (Coptic), 9, 17, 58, 87, 88, 89, 116, 126, 133, 155n114
    brickwork, medieval, 139
    destruction by fire, 121, 135, 136
    kiln beneath, 105
    reconstruction of, 139
    Roman buildings beneath, 87, 90, 126, 139
Church of St. George (Mari Girgis), (Greek Orthodox), 3, 8 (fig. 5), 9 (fig. 6), 10, 12, 16, 17, 20, 35, 40, 42, 58, 65, 68 (fig. 32), 73, 87, 88, 99, 118, 123, 125, 136, 156n16
    columns of, 123
    groundwater levels of, 139
    layout of, 68 (fig. 31), 135 (fig. 76)
    open air museum of, 136
    rebuilding of, 136
    stone walls beneath, 38, 39, 42, 45, 52, 67
    tilework in, 125
Church of St. Menas, 58
Church of St. Mercurius (Red Sea), 92, 116, 148n30, 152n50
Church of the Assumption, 116
Church of the Holy Virgin (al-'Adra), 9, 12, 16, 19, 49, 53, 73, 110–11, 137, 141, 143n12
    demolition of, 15, 98, 111, 139, 140, 141, 144n26
    photographic documentation of, 139
    granite columns of, 139
    restoration projects on, 143n11
Church of the Virgin *See* Hanging Church
Church of the Virgin (Babilun al-Darag), 137
Church of the Virgin (Haret Zuwayla), 113
church(es), 1, 3, 12, 17, 19, 20, 39, 83, 85, 88–90, 121, 143n4, 143n11
    ancillary buildings, 141
    ban/restrictions on construction of, 92, 143n11
    closed 1301 and 1320–23, 113, 114
    cultural and building revival, 115–16
    decline of, 128
    dedicated to martyrs, 88
    demolished/destroyed, 113, 141
    ecumenical initiatives of, 115
    Egyptian, 55, 58, 74, 89
    general form and plan of, 85
    patronage, 114
    registered as Listed Monuments, 120, 128
    repairs to, 113
    restoration of, 97
cisterns, 15, 79, 110
Citadel, of Cairo, 2, 3, 39, 73, 82, 100
    of Roda, 84, 97, 100, 103
civil law, Roman, 74
Civitavecchia, harbor of, 40
Clarke, Somers, 123, 124, 127
Claudius Ptolemy, 38
clay beds, 35
Cleopatra, 37
Clysma (city), 37, 38, 50
Comité de Conservation des Monuments de l'Art Arabe, 8, 9, 18, 67, 120, 124
    registration of listed monuments by, 128
    restoration of monuments by, 107, 128
    Survey of Old Cairo (1896–97), 128

    work in Old Cairo, 128–36, 140
Constans II (emperor), 74
Constantine (emperor), 74, 151n62
Contract 102 *See* Groundwater Lowering Project
Convent of St. George, 2, 3, 9, 12, 17, 58, 65, 73, 82, 83, 87, 92, 95, 108, 110, 116, 117, 118, 132–35
    ceiling (medieval painted), 140
    cells of, 134
    cement render removed, 140
    doors, carved, 90, 110, 122
    drain(s), 110
    durqa'a, 133–34
    entrance to, 86, 132
    façade of, 134 (fig. 75)
    groundwater level lowering in, 139
    inscriptions in, 110
    majlis roof, 135
    manwar (light well), 133
    medieval house in, 95, 98, 99
    mosaic of St. George, 134, 135
    nuns of, 140
    "old church" of, 135
    plan of, 98 (fig. 46), 110, 118, 133
    qa'a of, 83, 94, 99, 108, 109 (fig. 53), 110, 132, 140
    refurbishments to, 139
    restoration work on, 132–35
    stairway(s), 134
    wall, Roman, 135
    waqfiya documents of, 155n111
Coptic Church, 17, 55, 85, 89
    agitation and measures against, 112
    clergy, 128
    liturgy of, 122
    patriarch(s) of, 89, 152n59
Coptic Museum, 10, 16, 48, 49, 87, 117, 121, 141, 142
    damage from 1992 earthquake, 129
    guide to, 128
    lintel showing Christ's Entry into Jerusalem, 129
    tower in garden of, 16, 130, 142, 144n19
Coptic Revival period, 8, 20, 84, 97, 105–106
Copts, 39, 40, 88, 89, 97, 113
    in administrative and financial affairs, 105, 115
    compulsory conversion of, 113, 137, 141
    notables, 115
Coptus, 42
Council of Chalcedon (AD 451), 74, 75
Council of Ferrara-Florence (AD 1440), 115
Council of Ephesus (AD 431), 50
Corniche, monuments along, 50
crosses
    at Abu Serga church, 114 (figs. 56–57)
    bronze, 15 (fig. 12), 17, 94
crusades/crusaders, 112, 115
    Crusade, Fifth, 82, 103
cult of Sergius and Bacchus, 89
Cyrus (Melkite patriarch), 151n59

Damietta, siege of, 115, 153n76
Danube River, Trajanic bridge over, 49–50
Dar al-Salam (Cairo district), 145n48
Darb al-Hamra, 29
Darb al-Tuwara, 29

al-Dardir, *qa'a* of, 110
Darius I (Persian king), 36–37, 38
Dayr al-Banat *See* Convent of St. George
Decius (emperor), 58
    persecution under, 74
decorative arts, Coptic, 106
Dendera, basilica at, 88
Description de l'Egypte (Napoleonic), 14, 97–98, 103
Diocletian (emperor), 1, 2, 3, 15, 20, 33, 38, 40, 42, 50, 55–56, 57, 65, 73, 149n6, 150n10, 150n35
    building campaign of 55–59
    persecution of Christians under, 55, 56, 58, 74, 113
Diodorus Siculus, 1–2, 33, 37
Dioscorus (patriarch), 74–75
Dodecaschene settlements, 56
Domitius Domitianus, 56, 150n10
drain(s)/drainage systems, 13, 15, 16, 19, 33, 42, 110, 113

earthquake(s), 82, 92, 99, 113, 137

Edfu Temple, 30, 146n66, 146n68
Egypt, 79
    Arab conquest of, 1, 2, 3, 20, 50–51, 75, 79, 82, 112
    Assyrian conquest of, 79
    Christian, material culture of, 142
    civil and intellectual society of, 55
    dynastic capital(s), 30
    religious history of, 113
    Egyptian Antiquities Organization (EAO), 137
Egyptian Museum (Cairo), 12
Elephantine, 57
Eusebius, of Caesarea, 58
Eutropius, 41, 148n48
Eutychius (Greek Orthodox patriarch), 89
    Annales of, 89, 90

Fabricius Pacha, 136
Farag ibn Barquq (sultan), 102
Fatimid dynasty/era, 2, 39, 49, 50, 53, 73, 80, 85, 92, 100, 144n7
    monuments of, 148n30
    necropolis of, 152n16
fawakhir (potters), 10, 15, 153n9
Fayyum, 56
fortifications, Roman, 51
Fortress of Babylon, 1, 2, 3, 8, 10, 12, 14, 16, 18, 28, 33, 35, 49, 50, 51, 52, 55–75, 82, 83, 86–88, 97, 98, 121
    barracks in, 65, 71 (fig. 36), 73, 74, 151n58
    buildings in, 88, 95, 99
    cemetery in, 117, 138
    churches within, 58, 59
    convent in, 118
    destruction of parts of, 140
    as fortified imperial palace, 65, 88
    gates, 65, 67, 71, 73, 85, 87, 128, 130, 140
    internal layout of, 71, 73–74, 86
    kiln in, 103, 105
    and Luxor fortress, 63
    mosques in area of, 113
    northern part of, 73, 83, 95, 150n30
    plan of, 18 (fig. 13), 43 (fig. 19), 61 (fig. 26), 71 (fig. 35), 117, 150n30
    praetorium of, 73
    principia of, 65
    rebuilding program of, 110
    siege of, 79
    towers of, 67–70, 86, 103, 116, 127, 130, 136, 138, 140
    walls of, 86, 87, 150n36
Francis (saint), 115
Franciscans, 115, 119, 155n98
Fumm al-Khalig, 39, 153n9
al-Fustat (Arab city), 1, 2, 3, 20, 39, 40, 50, 52, 81 (fig. 38), 82, 83, 85, 88, 92, 96, 100, 146n62, 151n15
    abandonment of, 82, 83, 97, 99
    Babylon as nucleus of, 79–82
    etymology of name, 151n6
    maps/plans of, 83, 100 (fig. 47)
    residences in, 88
    ruin fields of, 82, 83, 121, 153n9
    topographical influences on, 85–86
al-Fustat/Misr, 97
Futuh Misr, 51

Gabriel III (patriarch), 154n37
Galerius, 56, 58, 74, 150n33
Garozzo, Filippo (contractor), 129
gate(s), 65, 66
    East, 62 (fig. 28), 71, 72, 116
    South, 17, 44 (fig. 20), 45, 48, 65 (fig. 30), 67, 71, 85, 87, 113, 124 (fig. 64), 128, 129 (fig. 69), 130, 139
    West, 50, 71
gateway (Roman), 129
al-Gayara, 153n9
Gayraud, Roland, 83
Gebel Ahmar, 29, 30, 146n49
Gebel al-Nahya, 28
Gebel Yashkur, 27, 39, 51, 80, 147n22
Geniza archive, 83, 84, 85, 89, 96, 97, 112, 152n31
George (saint), 58, 88, 108
German Archaeological Institute, 141
Ghandar al-Afram (amir), 103
al-Ghuri (sultan), 39, 102, 103
Gisr al-Afram, 103
Giza, fortified "suburb" of, 88
Giza Plateau, 12, 28
Golenischeff, W., 31
Gottheil, Richard, 121, 136
Great Road to Sham, 53, 86
Greek community, 4, 8, 16, 136
Green, Ralph, 137
Groundwater Lowering Project (Contract 102), 11–12, 13 (fig. 10), 15, 17, 52, 74, 98, 139, 144n19
    borehole(s), 18, 42, 65, 142
        from 1920s (Midan al-Zahir), 148n25
        records (logs) of, 14, 24, 26, 42, 144n14, 144n20
    manholes, 15, 16
    micro-tunnels/tunneling, 42, 44, 45, 48, 49, 66
    national grid coordinates, 13
    pipe trenches, 15–16
    shaft(s), 14 (fig. 11), 15, 16, 32, 98
        collector and conveyance, 14, 15
        excavation material from, 13, 24
        locations plan, 13 (fig. 10)
        Shaft 2, 44, 65, 67, 148n66
        Shaft 3, 44, 66, 70
        Shaft 4A, 70

　　　　Shaft 5, 74
　　　　Shaft 11, 14 (fig. 11)
　　　　Shaft HC1, 29, 31, 33, 62, 66
　　　　Shaft HC2, 32
　　　　Shaft HC3, 44, 45 (fig. 23), 65, 66
　　　tunnels, 1, 14, 42, 74
Gulf of Suez, 41

Hadrian, 57
Hamra, 85
Hanging Church (al-Mu'allaqa), 8, 17, 20, 39, 87, 95, 113, 116, 124 (fig. 65), 129 (fig. 69)
　　　baptismal chapel of, 110, 115, 138
　　　Byzantine influences in, 115
　　　carved cedar door of, 122
　　　and Church of St. Barbara, 117
　　　closed and pillaged, 113
　　　Comité work on, 128
　　　decoration, painted, 124 (fig. 65)
　　　gateway to, 127
　　　haykal screen in, 115
　　　interior of, 125 (fig. 66)
　　　khurus of, 122
　　　lintel (wooden) of, 129
　　　marble column of, 113, 155n77
　　　paintings, 129, 138, 139
　　　　　destroyed in, 150n10
　　　patriarch enthroned at, 89, 94
　　　as patriarchal residence, 113
　　　porch, 122
　　　quayside below, 66
　　　restoration(s) of, 117, 122–23, 138, 139
　　　　　by Nakhle Bey, 123, 128, 129
　　　roof of, 129
　　　stairway to, 48, 138, 155n77
　　　windows of, 129
Hapi (Nile-god), 2, 30, 33, 145n27, 146n67
Hara-based security arrangements, 117, 156n117
Harat *See* streets
harbor, Trajanic 2, 19, 38–42, 43 (fig. 19), 44–45, 48–50, 55, 56, 57, 59, 62, 66,
　　　axonometric of, 46–47
　　　gate/gatehouse of, 48, 129
　　　relationship to Fortress, 45
　　　stepped quayside of, 65, 86
　　　wall, 44–45, 86
Hathor, temple to, 30, 31, 146n49
Heliopolis, 28, 29–30, 31, 38, 50
Helwan, 30, 151n11
　　　Memphis Nilometer at, 151n11
　　　springs of, 146n67
Heraclius (Byzantine emperor), 79, 85
　　　coins issue of, 74
Herodotus, 24, 33, 36
Herz, Max (bey), 19, 129 (fig. 69), 130
hippodrome, 51, 73
Holy Family in Egypt, 2, 17, 39, 89, 92, 93, 94, 108, 114, 154n45
Holy Land, pilgrims to, 114

Ibn 'Abd al-Hakam, 51, 52, 85
Ibn 'Abd al-Zahir, khatat of, 102
Ibn Duqmaq, 52, 57, 81, 83, 97, 105, 112, 113, 154n35

Ibn Khaldun, 102
Ibrahim al-Gohari, 8, 116, 117, 135, 138
icons, 115, 116, 138, 142
IFAO, 83
immigration
　　　from Baghdad, 37
　　　from Magreb countries, 80
imperial cult, 58
incense trade, 36
India, 41, 42
industries, noxious, 89
inscriptions, 11, 29, 63, 108, 146n51
iqta (rural tax), 153n21
Iraq, 79
Isaac (Coptic patriarch), 89
Ismail (khedive), 141
Ismailiya Canal, 28, 152n33
Istabl 'Antar (fort), 27, 31, 99, 152n28
　　　aqueduct at, 79 (fig. 37)
istibdal ("exchange"), 116
Italians, 114
'Izbat al-Walda, 30
'Izbat Abu Qarn, 10, 15

Jaqmaq (sultan), 113
Jerusalem, 102
Jewish community, 4, 8, 16, 17, 20, 38, 80, 92, 93, 112, 117, 136–37
　　　housing of poor, 137, 141
Jewish Museum (New York), 112
John (bishop of Nikiu), 19, 33, 38, 56, 57
John XVI (patriarch), 117
Josephus, 33
Jtj Canal, 29, 38, 53
Julian (the Apostate), 58
Jullien (père), 127
al-Jund al-Gharbi (al-Kindi), 52, 149n101

Kafr Hamza, 41
al-Kamil (sultan), 105, 115
Kemp, W. G., 121
al-Khalig al-Misri, 3, 20, 35, 39, 42, 53, 64, 86, 102, 152n34
al-Khalig Amir al-Mu'minin, 52
Khalil Salah al-Din al-Ashraf, 113
Kharafa al-Kubra, 31
Kher-Aha ("the battlefield"), 30, 31, 149n111
khitat, 102, 153n24
Khittat Ahl al-Raya, 88
kiln(s), 83, 103
King's Highway, 41
Kom Ghurab, 27, 85
Kubiak, Wladyslaw, 83
Kufic (script), 110
Kujuk, tomb of, 110
Lactantius, 55, 56, 58
lakes, 26, 103
　　　of 'Ayn al-Sira, 31, 151n9, 153n9
　　　Birkat al-Fil, 26, 39
　　　Birkat al-Habash, 29, 31, 79, 80, 145n48
　　　Birkat al-Hagg, 29, 53
　　　Birkat Baghala, 39
　　　Bitter Lakes, 35, 36, 37
　　　of Isthmus of Suez, 41

Lake Timsah, 35, 36, 37
land, 17, 27, 84, 103
    agricultural, taxes on, 102
    cadastral valuation of, 56
    routes, 23, 53
landscape
    ancient, 3, 20, 23, 144n10
    medieval, 82
laws, sumptuary, 112
legions, Roman, 41, 51, 56, 65
    Legio II Traina Fortis, 41, 56
    Legio III Cyrenaica, 41, 56
    Legio III Diocletiana, 56, 63, 150n9
    Legio XIII Gemina, 150n33
Loewe, Herbert, 121, 128, 137
Louis IX (French king), 103
Lower Egypt, land route to, 65–66
Lucuas (king), 38
Luxor/Luxor Temple, 59
    Avenue of the Sphinxes, 63
    "Chapel of the Ensigns," 56, 150n10
    fort at, 56, 63, 150n28
    tetrapylons at, 73

Maadi-Buto culture, 29
Maadi settlement, 30
al-Ma'ali family, 112
al-ma'aridj (embankment), 86
madrasa(s), 97, 102, 105, 110, 112
    of al-Kamiliya, 111
    al-Madrasa al-Kharubiya, 103
Maghreb countries, 80, 112
majlis al-hiri bi kummayn, 108
majlis al-milli (general council), 141
majlis-iwan, 108
al-Malik al-Kamil, 113
Mallinson Architects (London), 140
malqafs (windcatchers), 108
Mamluk rule, 83, 97, 102, 112, 113
Manicheans, 58
Manshiet al-Sadr, 31, 146n49
al-Mansur (caliph), 52, 149n103
al-Maqrizi, 57, 81, 83, 113, 117, 120, 153n35
Mari Girgis *See* Church of St. George (Greek) under "Churches"
Mark Antony, 57
martyria, 74
martyrs/martyrdom, 2, 3, 58, 88
    cult of, 74, 88
    relics of, 94
    "voluntary", 113
    mashhad (shrine), 39
    of Zayn al-'Abidin, 148n30
mashrabiya, 108
Maximinus Daia, 58
maydans, 103
mazaar (visiting place), 108
Melkites, 125
Memphis, 23, 28, 29, 30, 33, 38, 51, 145n38, 145n42
merchants, 57, 103, 114
Merenptah, statues of, 29, 31
Michael (Coptic patriarch), 153n71
military architecture, Roman, 19, 59
Ministry of Public Health, 130

Misr al-qadima See Old Cairo
missionaries, Catholic, 115
Moesia (Bulgaria), 59
monastery/monasteries, 17, 28, 74, 83, 88, 97, 106, 115, 148n30
    Abu Mina Monastery, 28
    Abu Sayfayn Monastery (Monastery of St. George), 17, 18, 28, 92, 134, 137, 148n30, 149n71, 152n50
    Monastery of Dayr al-Malak, 31
    Monastery of St. Anthony, 106, 108, 115, 118, 137
    Monastery of St. Catherine, 114
    Monastery of St. Mercurius, 58
    Monastery of St. Paul, 106, 118, 137
    Monastery of Wadi Natrun, 108
    of Red Sea area, 108, 115, 137
    White Monastery (Sohag), 88
monasticism, 55, 125
Monneret de Villard, Ugo, 19, 92, 111, 151n54
Mons Porphyrites, 42
monuments, listed/registered, 128, 139, 140
mooring post, lion-headed, 44, 45
Moses, 147n22
Moses Maimonides, 112
Mosque, 83
    Gami' al-Qubba, 113
    of Abu Su'ud, 53, 83, 86
    of 'Amr ibn al-'As, 2, 10, 12, 13 (fig. 11), 53, 73, 80, 83, 86, 100, 112, 152n28
    of Aqsunqur, 110
    of Ibn Tulun, 39, 51, 52, 53, 80, 83, 86
    of Muhammed al-Saghir, 103
    of Sayyida Zaynab, 39, 40
    of Sultan Hassan, 154n58
    of al-Suwaydi, 103
    of Ulmas al-Hajib, 110
    of Zayn al-'Abidin, 27
al-Mu'allaqa *See* Hanging Church
al-Mu'ayyad Shaykh, 102
Muhammad al-Ga'fari, 86
al-Muqaddasi, 39, 49, 50, 53, 80–81, 89
muqarnas vault, 113
Muqattam, 12, 23, 24, 25, 31
al-Muqauqas, 73, 117, 141, 151n59
musalima, 113
museum(s), 151n9
    Coptic Museum, 10, 16, 48, 49, 87, 117
    Museum of Egyptian Civilization, 151n9, 153n9
al-Mustansir (caliph), 82, 99
Musturud, 39
al-Mutawakkil, 92
Myos Hormos (Quseir al-Qadim), 41, 42

Nabatea, 41
Nag' al-Hagar, 56
Nakhle Bey al-Barati, 123, 127
Napoleonic expedition (1798–1801), 14, 18
Narmer Palette, 30
al-Nasir Muhammad ibn Qalawun (sultan), 102, 103, 115
naskhi (script), 110
Naville, Edouard, 37
Near Eastern trade, 36
Nebuchadnezzar, 33, 38
Necho II, 36
New Kingdom, 28, 30

Nicopolis (Alexandria), 56
Nile River, 3, 10, 12, 20, 23–24, 28, 42, 44, 48, 51, 82, 88, 144n10, 145n27
    accretion rate of, 27, 145n29
    alluvial environment of, 23–24, 79
    annual flooding of, 24, 25, 25 (fig. 14), 27, 35, 50, 52, 57, 85, 144n7
    at Cairo, 25–31, 50
    Pelusiac branch of, 29, 36, 41
    relationship of settlement to, 28–29, 82
    westward movement of, 39, 50, 82, 103
Nilometer(s), 51, 56, 57, 151n11
Noah, 147n22
North Sakkara, 30
nuns, 2, 108, 117, 118

Obadiah, of Bertinoro, 113
Old Cairo, 1–3, 12, 20, 57, 75, 82, 83, 85, 88, 118, 120, 121
    alleys of, 141
    antiquarian accounts of, 8, 19–20, 120
    archaeology of, 8–20, 32–33, 82, 95, 97, 98, 138
    as architectural symbol of inter-religious relationships, 137
    buildings of, 82, 84, 85, 92, 97, 140, 141
    canal in, 86
    churches of See Church(es)
    Comité work in, 128–36, 140
    Description de l'Egypte plan (1821), 13, 116
    documentary material, 87
    eighteenth century revival in, 121
    entrance to, 9 (fig. 7)
    evidence for the "making" of, 82–84
    fires in, 99
    al-Fustat, parallels with, 84, 97
    geological background of, 24–25
    harbor of, 40–42, 44, 83
    historic structures of, 13, 140
    industrial activity in, 83
    landscape (ancient) of, 24, 32–33
    maps of, 18, 83, 97
    medieval history/phases of, 85, 92, 97, 99, 100
    monuments of, 4 (fig. 3), 5–6 (fig. 4), 11
    "Ottoman revival" in, 116
    panoramic photograph of, 120 (fig. 61), 122 (fig. 62)
    patriarchate in, 17
    Persian/Sassanian rule of, 38, 75
    as pilgrimage center, 4, 11
    plans of, 4 (fig. 3), 11 (fig. 9), 18 (fig. 13), 60 (fig. 25), 141
    plot boundaries, 141
    poverty in, 115
    property boundaries in, 116
    restorations/rebuilding in, 11, 84, 92–96, 137, 138, 140, 141
    settlement(s), 3, 38
    strategic importance to Roman rule, 97, 100
    themes in making of, 82–83
    topography and archaeology of, 3–4, 20, 24, 83, 97, 99–100, 102–103, 105, 117
    tourism in, 137
    tourist bazaar in, 141
    travelers' accounts of, 8, 27, 83, 114
    view(s) of, 120 (figs. 60–61)
    water supply and drainage of, 82–83
    written sources on, 97
Omar (caliph), 52, 85
'Omari (Helwan), 29
On (ancient city), 2, 30
"Opening of the Canal" ceremony, 40
"Ornamental Master", 108
Ostia, harbor at, 82
Ottoman Empire era, 4, 82, 83, 97, 98, 115
    buildings from, 11, 83
    Coptic notables during, 84
Oxyrhyncus, papyrus of, 65

P'a-di-Pep, tomb of, 30
paganism, 56, 74
paintings, 56, 65, 106, 108, 142, 149n10, 154n41
    See also wall paintings
palace(s), 80, 99, 100, 136
Palestine, 36
palm gardens, 121, 155n99
Pantheon, portico of, 42
parade ground, 73, 112
Parthians, 41, 57
patriarchs of Alexandria and Africa, 17, 74, 75, 94, 144n20
Patricolo, A., 92, 111
patronage, Coptic, 97, 106, 108
Pax Romana, 55
peace treaty agreement (Egypt/Israel), 138
Per-Hapi, 30
Per-Rameses, 38
persecution, 55, 74, 85, 97
Persian period occupation(s), 18, 29, 32, 36, 38, 75, 79
Peter of Alexandria (patriarch), 58
Philae temple, 146n66
Piankhi (Piye) stele, 31
Pietro de Pennis, 113
pilgrim medals, 117
pilgrimage center(s), 2, 8, 12
pilgrims
    burial of, 117
    writings of, 89, 92, 97
pipes, ceramic, 110
Pipinus de Bononia, Franciscus, 94, 114
Pithom Stone, 37
plague, 27, 82, 102
Pliny, the Younger, 37, 40, 41
Pococke, Richard. *A Roman Castrum at Old Cairo*, 73
    maps by, 84 (fig. 39)
Pompey's Pillar, 150n10
porphyry, 42
port(s), 3, 42, 50, 83
Portus, harbor at, 40, 48, 49, 148n64
Posener, G., 37 (fig. 18)
Potamos Babylonos, 41
Potamos Ptolemaios, 37
Potamos Traianos, 65
pottery/potteries, 11, 33, 83, 87, 99, 103, 153n9
prefect (Roman), 51, 149n89
pre-Roman finds, 15, 32
processional cross, 12 (fig. 12)
Programa de Patrimonio Cultural de la Cooperacion Española, 137
Ptolemaic level, 19, 147n82

Ptolemy II, 37
Punt, 36

qa'a, of Convent of St. George, 83, 94, 99, 108, 109 (fig. 53), 110
al-Qahira, 39, 80, 81, 82
al-Qahira al-Mahrusa, 82, 100
Qal'at al-Kabsh (Fort of the Ram), 27, 39, 51
Qalawun (sultan), 53, 108
Qaramaydan, 73
Qa'at al-Irsan *See* Wedding Hall
Qasaba, 53
Qasr al-Sham, 84 (fig. 39)
    Melkite church, 113
Qasr Qarun (Fayyum), 56, 150n8
Qasriyat al-Rihan ("the pot of basil") *See* Church of the Holy Virgin (al-'Adra)
al-Qata'i', 80, 81 (fig. 38)
Qaytbay, 102
quarries, 42
quays/quayside, 32, 45, 50, 64, 65, 66, 145n42, 148n66
Qus, riot at, 112

railway, 84, 121
Ramses II, 31, 146n49
Ramesside period, 28
al-Rasad, 27, 51
Red Mountain, 31, 146n71
Red Sea, 29, 41, 42
Red Sea Canal, 1, 2, 3, 14, 18, 19, 25, 33, 35, 38, 41, 52, 58, 65, 85, 139
refugees, Muslim, 112
Re-Horus, 31
religious literature (Coptic) in Arabic, 106
restoration cycles/works, 3, 8, 12, 84, 122, 137, 141
    lack of archaeological component in, 142
    on churches, 113, 143n11
riots, anti-Christian, 17
riverside settlement(s), 28, 66
Road of Sep, 53, 81, 149n111, 152n36
Road to Sham (the Great), 53
roads, Roman, 9, 41, 71, 73, 86, 87
Roda (island), 3, 10, 70, 83, 103
    citadel on, 84, 103, 110
    plan of, 104 (fig. 49)
Roman Catholic(s), 115
Roman Empire, 56
Roman occupation, 37, 51, 55
Roman structures, 15, 16, 62
Rosh Hodesh Iyar (festival), 121
Rumayla, 51, 53, 73, 112

Saba' Banaat tombs, 151n9
sabil, 9, 117
sacrifice, to Roman gods, 58, 150n20
Saite period tombs, 29, 147n84
al-Sakkawi, 113
Salah al-Din, 2, 100
al-Salih Najm al-Din al-Ayyub (sultan), 100, 102, 110
Santa Maria de Cova, 113
Saphir, Jacob, 127
Saqqara, 28
Sassanian Persians, 55, 57, 79, 85
Sayyida 'Atiqa, 86

Sayyida Ruqayya, 86
Sayyida Zaynab Square, 52
Scanlon, George, 83
Schechter, Solomon, 112
scholars, Victorian, 121–22
sebakhin, 83
Semeonis, Symon, 113
Semiramis (queen), 147n89
Sergius and Bacchus, cult of, 89
Sesostris (king), 36, 147n89
Seth, 30
Shi'a rule, 100, 105
shipbuilding, 37
silver gilt Gospel casket, 154n62
silver signet ring, 17, 94
Simaika Pasha, 128
Sinai, 36, 42
Society of Antiquaries of London, 122
Sokrates II (potter), 32
Split (Croatia), 65, 88, 150n35
stelae, of Darius (Persian), 36–37 (fig. 18)
Strabo, 31, 33, 37, 38, 41–42, 51, 57, 73, 147n90
street(s), 10, 13, 102
    'Atfat Abu Serga, 87
    'Atfat Mari Girgis, 8, 86, 116, 117
    Harat Abu Serga, 10 (fig. 8)
    arched entrance to, 141, 142 (fig. 78)
    Harat Dayr Mari Girgis, 8, 9, 86, 87
    Harat Mari Girgis, 9, 112
    Harat Sitt Barbara, 9, 10, 86, 87
    Harat Zuwayla, 39, 95, 113
    Qasaba, 53, 86
    Roman, 17, 86, 87, 110
    Shari' al-Imam, 59, 150n30
    Shari' al-Khalifa, 53, 86, 149n111, 152n36
    Shari' al-Khiyamiya (Street of the Tent Makers), 53, 86
    Shari' al-Surugiya (Street of the Saddlers), 53, 86
    Shari' Fustat, 15
    Shari' Ibn Tulun, 53
    Shari' Kitchener, *See above* Shari' al-Imam
    Shari' Mari Girgis, 8, 10, 15, 31, 42, 48, 49, 65, 86, 152n38
    Shari' Port Said, 41, 147n3, 149n107, 152n34
    See also at *via*
Sudd basin (Sudan), 26
Suez, 2, 30, 35, 37
"Sultan of the Copts", 8, 116
Supreme Council of Antiquities (SCA), 31, 137, 143n15
    Old Cairo inspectorate, 140
    Survey of Egypt (1935), 127, 141
al-Suyuti, 102
swallow-tailed cramp(s), 62, 65
Sweet Water Canal, 41
synagogue(s), 1, 12, 83
    Synagogue of Moses, 128
    Synagogue of the Babylonions, 118
        See also Ben Ezra Synagogue
Syria, 36, 79

Takla Haymanot (saint), 115
Tamerlane, 102
Tanis (royal capital), 41
tanneries, 83

tax system/taxes, 3, 41, 55, 56, 57
Tell al-Maskhuta, 33, 37
Tell al-Yahudiya, 28, 29, 38
"Temple of the Ennead", 31
Tetrapylon of Eusebius, 73
Tetrarchy/Tetrarchs (Roman), 65, 71
Tewfiq (prince), 122
Tewfikiyya Canal, 29
Thutmoses III, 15, 29
    Saite tombs, 147n84
    stele of, 31, 63
Tiberius Julius Alexander, edict of, 56–57
Tilul Zaynhum (rubbish mound), 53
tomb(s), 83
    of 'Ayn al-Sira, 31, 51
    of Coptic Catholic cemetery, 117
    Fatimid period, 53, 86, 151n9
    of Ibrahim al-Gohari, 8
    in the Muqauqas, 141, 141 (fig. 72)
    royal, 28
    Saba' Banaat, 151n9
    shaft, 31, 33
    vaulted, 17
tower(s) Roman, 8, 9, 11, 15, 18, 42, 52, 61, 70, 116, 124
    in garden of Coptic Museum, 16, 139, 142, 144n19
    Nilometer in, 47
    as Nilometers, 70
    northern (round), 17, 48, 69 (fig. 33), 70, 87, 118, 122 (fig. 62), 126 (fig. 67), 130, 144n20, 150n18
        monastery buildings on, 125
        plan and section of, 124
    round, 59, 67–70, 85, 126, 127, 139
        plan, 68 (fig. 31)
        section through, 68 (fig. 32)
    southern (round), 16, 33, 42, 52, 64 (fig. 29), 67, 70 (fig. 34), 88, 127 (fig. 68), 129, 130 (fig. 70), 150n18, 151n47
    U-shaped, 57, 71, 87, 116, 129, 140
trade/trade routes, 19, 32, 36, 51
Trajan (emperor), 1, 2, 3, 19, 33–35, 38, 40, 41, 55, 57, 103
Trajan's canal *See* Amnis Traianus
travelers' accounts, 8, 27, 83, 85, 97, 98, 99, 114, 117, 119, 121
Tulunid dynasty/era, 80, 151n15
Turah, 29

Umm an-Nar civilization (Arabia), 27
Ummayad period, 52, 80, 82
UNESCO Conference on Conservation Work (2002), 139
USAID (United States Agency for International Development), 1, 11, 139

Vansleb, Johann-Michael, 114, 116, 117, 118
vaulted structures, 17, 73, 74, 108, 110, 114
Via Appia, 41
Via Nova Traiana, 42
via praetoria, 9, 51, 53, 74, 85, 86
via principalis, 133
via Quintana, 86
via sagularis (perimeter road), 71, 74, 86, 87
Virgin Mary, 113

wadi(s), 21 30, 51, 144n3
    Wadi Digla, 26, 29, 30, 146n56
    Wadi Hof, 26, 146n56
    Wadi Iseimar, 146n56
    Wadi Natrun, 108
    Wadi Tumilat, 28, 35, 36, 37, 41
wall paintings, 17, 108
wall(s), 74, 82, 100
    circuit, 38
    city, 97
    defensive, 100, 102
    embankment, 20
    filter, 52
    "ghost," 136
    northern, 39, 88, 116
    paintings, 17, 108, 138, 142
    Roman, 49, 123, 135
    stone, 1, 16, 18, 38, 52
waqf endowments, 102, 116, 153n22, 154n35
    land belonging to Coptic Church, 131
Wasit, 79
watchtowers, 67
water
    drainage, 17, 82–83, 85, 95
    supply systems, 12, 17, 18, 35, 82–83, 85, 95
    tower, 39
Wedding Hall/Qa'at al-'Irsan (Coptic Church of St. George), 3, 9, 12, 17, 19, 52, 83, 92, 99, 110, 117, 138, 139
    Comité plan of, 111 (fig. 54)
    refurbishment of, 139
well(s), 12, 26, 123, 125
    of Moses, 87, 138
wharves, 64, 66
White Monastery (Sohag), 88
windmills, 121
World Jewish Congress, 138

Yuhanna (martyr), 88

Zosimus, 56